Acting Chinese

Acting Chinese is a year-long course that, together with the companion website, integrates language learning with the acquisition of cultural knowledge, and treats culture as an integral part of human behavior and communication.

Using modern day examples of Chinese discourse and behavioral culture, it trains students to perform in culturally appropriate fashion, whilst developing a systematic awareness and knowledge about Chinese philosophy, values and belief systems that will prepare them for further advanced study of Chinese language and culture. Each lesson contains simulated real-life communication scenarios that aim to provide a concrete opportunity to see how native speakers generally communicate or behave in social situations.

An essential guide for intermediate to advanced level second language learners, *Acting Chinese* provides a unique and modern approach to the acquisition of both cultural knowledge and language proficiency.

Yanfang Tang is Emeritus Chancellor Professor of Chinese Studies at the College of William and Mary. She has taught courses in Chinese literature, culture, film, cross-cultural communication, and language acquisition at various levels. Her research interests span several interdisciplinary fields including literature, language, philosophy, and communications, with the analysis of the underlying cultural and philosophical interconnections as a unifying theme. She has published widely on poetry and philosophy, culture and text, language and thought, and language and communication, as well as the integration of culture with foreign language education. She founded the Chinese minor and major programs at W&M and served as the Director of the Chinese Studies Program for most of her tenure at W&M. Tang was awarded the Phi Beta Kappa Faculty Award for Excellence in Teaching in 2013 and promoted to Chancellor Professor of Chinese Studies in 2016.

Kun-Shan Carolyn Lee is a professor of the Practice of Chinese and the Director of the Chinese Program at Duke University. She has also served as the general director of the Duke Study in China program since 2001. Before joining Duke in 1995, Lee was a lecturer in the Chinese Department at Middlebury College, Vermont, from 1993 to 1995, and an instructor for the intensive Summer Chinese School at Middlebury College from 1993 to 1996. She has taught Chinese courses at all levels. Her current research interests are language use and intercultural communicative competence, community-based language learning, articulation of foreign language programming, task- and content-based instruction, and needs analysis on language curriculum design. Lee has given lectures in several teacher training workshops including StarTalk. She was a co-principal investigator of a federal grant from ProjetGo in the Asian Pacific Studies Institute at Duke from 2015 to 2018.

Li Xu is a lecturer at Duke Kunshan University, Kunshan, China. Before working at this job, she served as a Chinese lecturer at Princeton University from 2007 to 2011 and as the Language Director at the Alliance for Global Education from 2011 to 2014. Li Xu has also taught at various other prestigious programs such as the Princeton in Beijing Intensive Language Program (2006, 2007, and 2010), the Middlebury College Chinese School (2008), and the Critical Language Scholarship Program (2011 and 2012).

Jin Zhang is a visiting assistant teaching professor at the University of Notre Dame. She served as Academic Director of the Chinese Flagship Overseas Center in Beijing, China, from 2016 to 2019. She taught Chinese language classes at all levels at the Massachusetts Institute of Technology from 2000 to 2016. Prior to joining the M.I.T. Chinese Program, she was a lecturer at Princeton University. In addition to teaching in a regular university setting, she has also taught at various intensive summer programs such as Princeton in Beijing (1998–1999) and the Middlebury College Chinese School (2000–2017), where she was the lead teacher for level II and Level IV from 2006 to 2013 and from 2014 to 2017 respectively.

Peng Yu is a lecturer II of Chinese at the University of New Mexico (UNM), where he is also serving as the faculty advisor to the Chinese Language and Culture Club on the UNM campus. In 2018 Yu founded the Chinese Language Teachers Association of New Mexico and has been serving as the President since then. Prior to joining UNM, Yu was a lecturer in Chinese Studies at the College of William and Mary from 2011 to 2016, where he also served as the faculty advisor to the Chinese Language House, the website editor of the Chinese Studies Program, and the faculty advisor to the Chinese Language Partner Program. Before beginning his college teaching career, Yu was a full-time instructor in the comprehensive online Chinese courses offered by Virtual Virginia (VVa) affiliated with the Virginia Department of Education. At VVa he taught Chinese language courses to Virginia public school students (grades 7–12) from Level I up to AP Chinese. He also developed the online learning modules for the VVa AP Chinese Language and Culture course and taught the course for three years.

Acting Chinese 行为汉语

An Intermediate-Advanced Course in Discourse and Behavioral Culture

Yanfang Tang, Kun-Shan Carolyn Lee, Li Xu, Jin Zhang, and Peng Yu

LONDON AND NEW YORK

First published 2021
by Routledge
2 Park Square, Milton Park, Abingdon, Oxon OX14 4RN

and by Routledge
52 Vanderbilt Avenue, New York, NY 10017

Routledge is an imprint of the Taylor & Francis Group, an informa business

British Library Cataloguing-in-Publication Data
A catalogue record for this book is available from the British Library

Library of Congress Cataloging-in-Publication Data
Names: Tang, Yanfang, author. | Lee, Kun-shan Carolyn, author. | Xu, Li, author. | Zhang, Jin, author. | Yu, Peng, author.
Title: Acting Chinese : an intermediate-advanced course in discourse and behavioral culture 《行为汉语》 / Yanfang Tang, Kun-shan Carolyn Lee, Li Xu, Jin Zhang, Peng Yu.
Description: New York : Routledge, 2020. | Includes index.
Identifiers: LCCN 2019052954 (print) | LCCN 2019052955 (ebook) | ISBN 9781138064577 (hardback) | ISBN 9781138064621 (paperback) | ISBN 9781315160313 (ebook)
Subjects: LCSH: Chinese language—Textbooks for foreign speakers—English. | Chinese language—Grammar. | Chinese language—Spoken Chinese.
Classification: LCC PL1129.E5 T349 2020 (print) | LCC PL1129.E5 (ebook) | DDC 495.18/0071—dc23
LC record available at https://lccn.loc.gov/2019052954
LC ebook record available at https://lccn.loc.gov/2019052955

ISBN: 978-1-138-06457-7 (hbk)
ISBN: 978-1-138-06462-1 (pbk)
ISBN: 978-1-315-16031-3 (ebk)

Typeset in Times New Roman
by Apex CoVantage, LLC

Visit the companion website: www.routledge.com/cw/tang

Contents

Preface

This textbook is composed of domain-specific teaching materials devoted to the study of Chinese behavioral culture in the settings of teaching and learning Chinese as a foreign/second language (CFL or CSL). It targets learners at the intermediate-to-advanced level, i.e., learners who have completed four semesters of Chinese language study in a typical Chinese program at an American, Canadian, or British undergraduate school. It is also suitable for the Chinese programs where the target language is used to help students to learn Chinese culture or Chinese communication behavior in both native and cross-cultural settings. Furthermore, this textbook could be effectively used in a study- or work-abroad environment. The learner can apply the training on site in their real-life communications with Chinese people and thereby achieve the optimal results intended by this textbook.

The goal of learning a foreign language is to communicate with the people using that language. As communication is, in G. Philipson's words, "a deeply cultured process" (*Speaking Culturally: Explorations in Social Communication*, SUNY Press, 1992), mere linguistic competence is not adequate to ensure proper and effective exchange of ideas. Learners must know what to say and, most importantly, how to say what is to be said in ways that are culturally correct and appropriate. However, despite the copious study of the importance of culture in foreign language acquisition, integrating cultural instruction with language training has largely remained an unsolved problem.

Considered as the most relevant for foreign language study, the teaching of the "little-c" or behavioral culture particularly baffles foreign language education in general or the CFL field in particular. One big obstacle lies in the absence of appropriate teaching materials, and this gap in turn results from the difficulty of compiling such course materials due to the nature of the subject that defies such an attempt. It goes without saying that human behaviors are intangible, multifarious, and intricately context-bound. While speeches can be, and have been, analyzed and codified in the forms of word formations, sentence patterns, and pronunciation rules, speech acts are illusive, multifaceted, and too context-driven to render themselves for easy analysis and codification. Teaching human behaviors across different cultures adds, undoubtedly, further challenge to this task.

Knowing the difficulty of carrying out such a task, this team of authors decided to press forward and engage themselves with scholarly research, empirical analysis, and on-site observations that have eventually culminated in this "first-of-its-kind" textbook that represents many years of concerted efforts and classroom tryouts. This textbook is intended to fill a widely-felt gap in CFL education, albeit temporarily. The authors are keenly aware of their own limitations, and we offer this set of materials only as a "jade-attracting" or "jade-turning" brick, as the common Chinese idiom 抛砖引玉 goes, in the hope that more and better such textbooks will become available in the future. It is the consensus of foreign language teaching professionals that cultural learning must go hand-in-hand with language training, and this team of authors wish to pave the way for adoption of this fully integrated approach to foreign language education in the CFL curriculum.

Much thought has gone into the designing of this textbook which operates on two fronts, one to train students in language acquisition and the other in cultural competence Through the inclusion of abundant goal-specific training materials, this textbook aims to achieve the following among many other pedagogical objectives:

1. To derive the most common behavioral and discourse patterns from Chinese interpersonal communications and organize them into proper categories for clear and focused study.

   Fourteen lessons represent the opportunities to study 14 major Chinese behavioral patterns in conversations, some personal, some professional, and some social. This focus by no means captures the multifaceted and complex picture of Chinese communications, given the unlimited variables in the backgrounds of the individuals participating in conversations.

   Moreover, culture undergoes constant transformations, particularly in the case of mainland China where decades of economic developments have brought about rapid changes in people's attitudes, social practices and even interpersonal relationships. Despite the rapid change, however, certain core values and philosophical attitudes that constitute a culture's identity take time to evolve. This is especially true in China, where much pride and reverence is attached to its cultural traditions and their conservation, so much so that both the government and the masses still look to the past for wisdom and moral guidance even as they embrace modernity in most if not all of their social practices and personal lifeways. Underneath the seemingly fast changes of the social and technological landscape of China are the steady, slowly evolving constancies of the time-honored Chinese cultural traditions. This textbook introduces students to the major behavioral tendencies still highly characteristic of ordinary Chinese people as they engage in social and interpersonal communications in present.
2. To integrate the study of "cultural practices" (behavioral patterns) and that of "cultural perspectives" (philosophical ideas) so that students can make informed sense of Chinese interpersonal communication in the larger context of Chinese philosophy, values, and social institutions.

   Fourteen behavioral patterns are explained from the angles of six major cultural perspectives that represent important Chinese philosophies and folk beliefs that serve either as the openly advocated moral guidelines or as the quietly observed unwritten rules in the everyday lives of the Chinese people.

   This rather neat arrangement of Chinese cultural practices with cultural perspectives undoubtedly contain some arbitrariness, for among other things one cultural practice could also be explained through the lens of another or even several inherently related philosophical perspectives. Arbitrariness of this nature is unavoidable due to, as stated previously, the sprawling and inherently integral nature of the subject. As much as this presentation reflects the authors' insights obtained from their long-term scholarly research, it was formulated in this textbook primarily for pedagogical purposes.
3. To integrate the study of culture and language, not only by explaining how the Chinese communicate but also by demonstrating what they actually say and do as they interact with one another in everyday life.

The scenario dialogues that follow the main texts in each lesson function as concrete examples for the discussion in the text. They were also created as platforms for the student to learn and master the words and expressions that are needed for communicating with the Chinese in similar situations.

In designing these dialogues, we were guided by the theoretical position that in foreign language education, culture should not only be taught as a body of describable knowledge, a common characteristic of traditional textbooks. Rather, because the ways in which humans communicate are essentially coded in "cultural scripts" in their minds, students would be best served if they were required to learn and memorize those cultural scripts by actually enacting them.

4. To provide both formal (written) and informal) conversational) discourse materials.

   This textbook intends to develop students' linguistic competence in both written and conversational styles. We believe is very important for students of the intermediate-to-advanced and even advanced levels. Whereas we agree that intermediate-to-advanced students should begin to be trained in formal written language, they should continue to be given ample opportunities to develop and consolidate their conversational skills as well. For this reason, the language of the 14 main texts becomes increasingly formal in discourse as the lessons progress, but the dialogues remain casual and intentionally idiomatic, with the level of difficulty increasing gradually along with the texts.

This team of authors is composed of five members teaching in five different Chinese programs in America and China. We have worked closely as a team, sharing ideas and assisting in proofreading of each other's work throughout the entire project. However, we have divided the tasks among us as follows:

- **Yanfang Tang**: Masterminded the compilation of the entire textbook. She designed the basic framework of the project, provided general guidance as it was developed, and drafted some of the earliest versions of the materials. She is also the author of the main texts in the 14 lessons.
- **Kun-Shan Carolyn Lee**: Served as the project manager supervising the progress of the entire project as it was developed, completed and published. She composed the exercises in the Cross-cultural Communication section in every lesson, assisted in the writing of the scenario dialogues, and was responsible for completing the discourse behavior explanations that follow them.
- **Li Xu**: Wrote the scenario dialogues in each of the 14 lessons and composed the initial drafts of the discourse behavior explanations. She also wrote the critical incidents under the heading of "Situation analysis" in the Cross-cultural Communication section in every lesson.
- **Jin Zhang**: Assumed primary responsibility for the language-training component of this two-leg-walking textbook. She co-authored the sections on vocabulary, word usage explanation, and the language acquisition exercise of the 14 lessons.
- **Peng Yu**: Co-authored the sections on vocabulary, word usage and explanations, and the language acquisition exercises for the 14 lessons. Most notably, he is the technology support of this project; He worked with the technology team of the publisher to design the web companion and to provide ongoing maintenance.

Finally, a word of acknowledgement is in order. We would like to extend our sincere thanks and appreciation to the following individuals: first, we would like to thank the anonymous readers who reviewed the proposal and the sample lessons of this textbook. We kept in mind some of their highly insightful comments, which served as guidance as we developed this textbook. To Professor Xizhen Qin of the University of South Florida, we offer our sincere thanks for her participation in the early discussions of this project. Her contribution of ideas that helped shape this textbook is deeply appreciated. To Professor Yuhui Lü of Beijing Normal University, we would like to note our special appreciation for piloting this course material in her class and particularly for her careful reading and critiquing many of the draft lessons. In addition, we are deeply grateful for Professor Liwei Jiao of Brown University for his generosity in providing us resources and feedback whenever we ran into questions or disagreement on some of the linguistic issues. We are also very thankful to Professor Xiuqin Lin of Beijing Capital Normal University for her kind assistance in locating three talented individuals Shanshan Li, Yilang Liu-Jia, and Haoyi Zhu-Sheng for recording the scenario dialogues of this project. Last but not least, we would like to thank the colleagues at the College of William and Mary, Duke University, Chinese Flagship Overseas Program in Beijing, University of New Mexico, and Duke Kunshan University for their trial use of this textbook in their respective courses. Their discoveries during the process and their suggestions for the revision of this textbook are greatly appreciated.

Chief Editor: Yanfang Tang

Teacher's guide 教材使用指南

《行为汉语》是专门为培养汉语为第二语言学习者的跨文化交际能力而精心策划编写的中高年级-高年级综合汉语教程。本书参照中国交际文化研究热点与《ACTFL语文能力大纲》的中级高等（intermediate-high）和高级（advanced）标准，通过六个文化视角（cultural perspective）、十四种常见的文化行为（cultural behavior）模式，系统地介绍了中国人的日常行为文化（the "little-c" culture）与其背后的价值观和思想体系。在横向结构上，全书的话题以循序渐进的方式介绍了中国人典型的行为方式、价值体系以及语言表达背后的文化涵义。在纵向结构上，每一课的内容则由三大板块组成，各板块相辅相成，以螺旋渐进的方式，逐步带领学习者探究这十四种行为文化模式与中文母语者思维方式之间的关系。

本书有配套的教材支持网站，为使用者提供了一个多元的教学与学习平台。鉴于网络已逐渐成为学生们自主学习的方式，课本里的课文、情境对话（scenario dialogues）和误解分析（situation analysis）也都放在了网上，以便学生能随时随地上网学习这几个部分的内容、使用网上点击词典自学生词、听录音、做语言练习等等。教师也可以善加利用网站上的补充材料做为备课或出试卷的参考资料。

《行为汉语》的作者群在多年编写的过程中，曾多次在个人任教的学校或当时服务的单位试用本教材，其中包括美国的公立大学、私立大学、留华项目、在华的私立大学等。试用的对象包含对外汉语课的三年级（多数学生没有华裔背景）、高年级口语课、高年级商业汉语课、华裔班的二年级等。本书既适合做为跨文化交际课程的主要教材，也适合跟其它主题式教材搭配使用。教师甚至可根据特定的课型需要，灵活使用三个板块。以下将进一步说明教材中三大板块的设计理念与教学目标，并根据作者群试用教材的经验跟读者分享一些教学建议。

第一板块： 课文、生词表、词语与句型（Text, new words, expressions and sentence patterns）

第一个板块具备了一般语言教材都有的基本元素，亦即课文、生词表、词语与句型介绍。虽然这几个部分只占每一课篇幅的三分之一，但却是学习全课主题和语言内容的基础。受篇幅所限，我们慎重挑选了六个基本文化视角，用六个单元十四篇课文介绍群体意识、礼的观念、贵和思想、面子心理、人情法则、差序格局等概念。每一篇课文除了宏观地讲述某个行为模式的特征、背后的核心价值观及其形成的原因以外，也经常用新闻事件或生活中的小故事，深入浅出地举例说明主题内容。全书课文的篇幅随着主题的拓展而逐渐加长。文体以书面语为主，包含了许多正式的词汇，有助于培养学生连句成段的口语表达能力和阅读学术文章（亦即学术汉语 academic Chinese）的能力。

本书为课文内容编写了详细的生词表、词语和句型介绍，力求帮助学生理解语言形式的意义、结构和功能。在教学支持网站上，每一课都配有丰富的语言练习，以便学生课下继续熟悉和巩固所学的语言知识。他们可以随时查看课文，回忆教师在课堂上的讲解，思考如何解答问题等。语言练习有一部分习题在网上完成后会自动提示答案。这种题型设计不但对学生具有鼓励的作用，也节省教师一部分修改作业的时间。

第一板块的教学目标：

- 学生能了解中国人的基本日常行为，并能说明这些行为背后的世界观或价值观及其形成的历史和社会原因。
- 学生能用比较正式的词语成段地表述中国行为文化与自身母语行为文化的一些基本特点，并比较二者之间的异同。
- 学生能用中文阅读相关话题的文章，并创作短篇论述性的文章。

教学建议：

- 以50分钟一个课时为标准，我们建议教师根据学生的语言程度，用2–3个课时完成第一板块里的内容。课前可要求学生针对要学的内容，每人至少准备一个问题，上课时提出来讨论。
- 在介绍新课文以前，要求学生留意每个单元标题、课文标题和行为聚焦的意思，联想它们之间的意义关系。也可让学生课前上网用英文阅读跟单元标题有关的文章，建立背景知识。此外，也可用第二板块中的情境对话做为热身活动。比方说，让学生学习一两个对话，通过情境、言语行为例说来猜测课文要介绍的重点，引起学生的好奇感。
- 语言练习里每个部分的题目基本是按照课文段落顺序编写的。教师可以根据学习课文的进度，指定学生每天完成一部分的练习，以逐步吸收语言知识。
- 教师除了可以按照课本中板块的顺序安排进度以外，也可根据不同的课型需要，调整使用板块的顺序。具体安排方式请参考教学支持网站上的范例。

第二板块：交际情景 (Communication scenarios)

第二个板块包括三个对话、四个"言语行为例说"（Notes on discourse behavior）和体演情景的练习。所有的对话内容都跟本课的主题相呼应，既是课文叙说的具体范例，也是汉语为母语者之间交流方式的演示。语言风格以日常交谈语体为主，并特别注意了语言的自然性和真实性。每一个对话之前都有英文导言，提醒学生们在学习该对话时需要留意的某种行为文化倾向。对话之后有"思考与讨论"问题，检查学生的理解情况，并让他们特别注意母语者之间沟通或解决问题的方式。所有的对话都经过多位母语者的检测，以力求内容及语言的典型和真实性。"言语行为例说"则用英文介绍在对话中出现的一些与主题相关而又带有文化内涵的成语俗话、词语结构及其英文中对应的说法。每一个例说之后又再以两个迷你对话做为例子，展示该词语在不同情境中的用法。

全书的情景对话主要围绕王大伟一家在生活和工作中发生的事展开，学生可以通过学习对话，观察、体会中国人在生活中和在职场环境里与人打交道的方式。因为考虑到每个学生的汉语学习背景和词汇量不同，这一板块里可能是生词的词语在网站上用橘红色标示，以提醒学生通过语境猜测该词的意思，或使用网上点击词典自学生词。对话的录音采用广播剧的概念录制，旨在留给学生们更多想象的空间，让他们在听录音时，除了把注意力放在理解内容上，同时也揣摩对话中人物的表情、态度和肢体语言。最后通过"体演情景"的练习，在熟记对话文本之后，将自己投入角色，把对话在课堂中表演出来，跟同学们一起分享学习的经验和成果。

第二板块的教学目标：

- 学生能理解中国的行为文化跟人们思维方式的关系，以及它们对日常交际的影响。
- 学生能运用从课文中所学的知识，分析交际情形和策略，并提出个人的见解，以及探讨在相同或相似的交际情形下解决问题的方法。
- 学生能学习自然而地道的中文口语，以有效提升自身的口语交际能力。

教学建议：

- 可用一堂课的时间带领学生讨论交际情景的对话和行为例说；体演情景的练习可根据进度酌情安排。
- 如前所述，这部分除了可以做学习课文之后的延伸活动，也可以做介绍课文以前的热身活动。
- 要求学生课前必须上教学支持网站听录音，自学生词，把对话熟记下来。鼓励他们尽量模仿录音演员的发音、语气和语调。
- 提醒学生在学习对话时，注意对话发生的场合、人物的年龄和职业、人物之间的家庭和社会关系等，因为这些都可能与对话中的用词有关系。

第三板块：跨文化交际（Cross-cultural communication）

第三板块包括误解分析、口语交际练习、写作练习，以及特别为留学项目所设计的任务型教学活动等。"误解分析"的设计概念乃受到美国跨文化交际领域里公认最有效的培训方法之一——cultural assimilator——的启发。这个部分通过四个不同的关键事件（critical incident），描述外国人在目标语环境中，因为文化差异而跟中文母语者之间产生的误解、矛盾或冲突。每一个事件的叙述之后都有2–3个"思考与讨论"问题，引导学生们进行观察，并反思自身族群和文化与目标语文化的族群有什么相似或不同的地方。"误解分析"旨在加强学生对汉语文化行为的敏感度和换位思考的能力，很适合做为课下阅读、课上讨论以及角色扮演的材料。

为了扩大学生探究每个话题的学习空间，口语交际练习的第二道题以访谈、观赏视频或电影、辩论、社会调查等各式各样的活动进行，并且进一步提供相关的真实材料或实例，创造跟母语者直接交流的机会。例如，学生们在学了第六课"礼之用，和为贵"之后，先要上网搜索浏览跟中国政府在2004年提出的"和谐社会"理念有关的海报，然后挑选2–3张自己觉得最有意思的海报跟母语者讨论指定的问题。双方都能借着这个活动，以观察、比较、验证的精神，思考所学的行为文化与传统价值观对当代中国社会的影响。口语交际活动之后的写作练习也为学生提供一个总结、探究、反思甚至评判的学习机会。对于在目标语国家留学的学生，"文化探索"的活动则要求他们实地调查所学的行为文化如何反映在人们的日常生活中。这个活动鼓励学生以客观和开放的态度与当地人互动，多了解当地人的社会生活和价值取向，以提高他们对目标语环境的观察能力，同时增加运用语言的机会。

第三板块的教学目标：

- 学生能意识到文化差异的重要性，进而培养自身对文化差异的敏感度及判断和思辨的能力。
- 学生能了解由于不同的文化观念而产生的误解，改变既有的刻板印象，减少偏见。
- 学生能运用从课文中所学的知识，分析相关事件，并能举一反三，提高换位思考的能力
- 学生能增强对目的语社会及汉语母语者价值取向的理解，有效地跟母语者进行交流。

教学建议：

- 用一堂课做跨文化交际活动。比方说，前半堂课进行"误解分析"部分的讨论和角色扮演，后半堂课进行口语交际练习第二个活动的课上讨论或口头报告。
- 将学生分组，并让各组自选一题"误解分析"，将其内容编写成剧本。上课时做角色扮演或者拍成视频做为口语作业。
- 将写作练习与口语交际练习的第二题结合起来，不但能使学生对整个活动进行反思与评估，也让他们体验从口语转换到书面语的过程，注意不同的场合要用不同的语体表达方式。教师上课时也可带领学生做词汇和句型的对比分析，提升他们用正式语体的口头表述能力。

在编写和试用教材的过程中，我们体会到，作为教师首先必须提高自身的文化及跨文化素养。我们既不主张摒弃自身的价值观，也反对用A文化视角审视批判B文化的观念和行为。我们的目标是帮助学生在二元或多元文化之间，加深对不同文化的了解，并培养学生同中求异、异中求同的同情同理心。如前言所说，作者群本着抛砖引玉的态度，在试图将理想付诸于实践，亦即将跨文化教育融入对外汉语教学的同时，也希望《行为汉语》能填补目前汉语言文化教材发展的一点空白，更好地为以中文为第二语言的学习者将来进入全球化的工作或生活环境做准备。

由于作者群的知识和工作经验有限，本教材难免有疏漏或不足之处，敬请同行或读者不吝指正。

主编 李坤珊

Abbreviations and symbols

adj	adjective
adv	adverb
bf	bound form [used as part of a compound]
conj	conjunction
m	measure
n	noun
NP	noun phrase
phr	phrase
prep	preposition
pron	pronoun
S	subject
v	verb
VP	verb phrase
()	encloses words for collocation
[]	encloses information for clarification on usage
/	separates alternate forms

词汇、句型部分的参考文献

汉典，www.zdic.net

现代汉语词典（第七版），商务印书馆，2016年，北京。

现代汉语八百词（修订版），商务印书馆，1999年，北京。

ABC汉英大词典，汉语大词典出版社，2003年，上海。

Chinese Grammar Wiki, *AllSet Learning*. https://resources.allsetlearning.com/chinese/grammar

Mandarin-English Dictionary & Thesaurus, *Yellowbridge*. www.yellowbridge.com/chinese/ dictionary.php

Ross, Claudia, and Ma, Jing-heng Sheng. *Modern Mandarin Chinese Grammar–A Practical Guide*. New York: Routledge, 2006.

Yip, Po-Ching, and Rimmington, Don. *Chinese–A Comprehensive Grammar*, 2nd ed. London: Routledge, 2016.

情境对话主要人物表
Characters in communication scenarios

王为民：他在一家公司工作多年，是部门经理。他的妻子叫李爱华，儿子叫王大伟。

Wang Weimin: He has worked many years at a company as a branch manager. His wife's name is Li Aihua, and his son's name is Wang Dawei.

李爱华：她是一位大学老师。她贤惠细心，努力照顾家人，也热情好客，喜欢交友。

Li Aihua: She is a college professor. She is kind and attentive. She works hard to take care of her family. She enjoys having guests and making friends.

王大伟：是王伟民和李爱华的儿子，今年上大学四年级。他性格外向开朗，爱帮助朋友。王大伟除了上学也在一家公司里实习。

Wang Dawei: He is Wang Weimin and Li Aihua's son. He is a college senior. He has an extroverted, optimistic personality and enjoys helping his friends. Besides attending school, Dawei is interning at a company.

王爷爷和王奶奶：王为民的爸爸和妈妈，跟王为民一家住在一起。

Grandfather Wang and Grandmother Wang: Wang Weimin's father and mother. They live with Wang Weimin and his family.

艾杰森：美国大学生，目前在中国留学。他非常喜欢学中文，也对中国文化很有兴趣。

Jason Adams: He is an American college student who is currently studying in China. He really enjoys studying Chinese language and is very interested in Chinese culture.

张莉莉：王大伟的同学、朋友。她性格随和，学习好又很谦虚。

Zhang Lili: Wang Dawei's classmate and friend. She has a very amiable personality. She is an excellent student and is very modest about her accomplishments.

周强：王大伟的同学、朋友。他的个性活泼，爱运动，偶尔也会给父母惹麻烦。

Zhou Qiang: Wang Dawei's classmate and friend. He is very lively, enjoys sports, but occasionally gives his parents cause for worry.

赵学东和刘少红：赵学东是王为民的同事，他的妻子刘少红跟李爱华也是好朋友。

Zhao Xuedong and Liu Shaohong: Zhao Xuedong is Wang Weimin's colleague. His wife, Liu Shaohong, is best friends with Li Aihua.

赵静：赵学东、刘少红的女儿，王大伟的朋友。她在读高中，性格安静懂事。

Zhao Jing: The daughter of Zhao Xuedong and Liu Shaohong. Wang Dawei's friend. She is currently in high school. She has a calm and sensible personality.

第一单元 **Unit one**

文化视角：群体意识

Cultural perspective: group mentality

第一课 一起吃饭是缘分

行为聚焦：爱凑热闹
Behavior highlighted: love to be part of the fun

课文 *Text*

厦门大学易中天教授在他的《闲话中国人》一书中，详细地介绍了他多年来对中国文化的思考。他认为，中国文化最根本的特点就是“群体意识”；与之相反，西方文化最根本的特点是“个体意识”。易教授以吃饭为例来说明他这个观点。他说，中国人吃饭，所有的筷子都伸向同一个菜盘，所有的勺子都伸向同一个汤碗，不管什么菜，大家都一起吃。而在西方国家，人们各点各的菜，各吃各的饭。在中国人看来，一起吃饭是“缘分”，也是为了享受在一起的感觉。如果大家还是各点各的，各吃各的，那又何必聚餐呢？

易教授还讲了一个笑话：一次，一个中国人请他的几个朋友和两位“老外”一起到餐馆吃饭。出于礼貌，主人请每个人都点一道菜。两位外国朋友一个点了芙蓉鸡片，另一个在犹豫，不知点什么菜好。主人发现还少了一个汤，就建议他点一个榨菜肉丝汤，反正大家一起吃饭嘛。服务员上的第一道菜就是芙蓉鸡片。点这个菜的“老外”得知这是自己要的菜以后，就接过盘子放到自己的面前。过了一会儿，榨菜肉丝汤也上来了，点这个汤的外国朋友也把汤碗接过来放在自己的面前。菜上齐了以后，大家就开始吃了起来。两位“老外”自己吃自己点的菜，完全没有要跟别人分享的意思。几个中国人只好“主随客便”，按照西方人的习惯各吃各的菜。当然，点汤的那位外国朋友那顿饭也只喝下了一大碗榨菜肉丝汤。

易教授用这个有趣的故事说明中国人的群体意识和西方人的个体意识。简单地说，群体意识就是认为每个人都是群体中的一员，群体的利益就是个人的利益，群体的利益比个体的利益更重要。而西方人重视个人的独立和自由，你是你，我是我，他是他。每个人都有选择的自由，每个人的行为，他人也都不能干涉，除非是危害了公众的利益。很多西方人喜欢独自活动，他们常常一个人散步，一个人锻炼身体；年轻人一个人背着个大包在国外旅游也很常见。中国人一般爱凑热闹，喜欢大家一起活动。比方说打麻将、下象棋、坐在一起拉家常等等，这些都是中国人喜欢的群体活动。现在中国人有钱了，出去旅游的人也多了，也经常是大家约好报个旅游团一起去。

生词 New words

简体	繁體	拼音	词性	英文翻译
1. 行为	行為	xíngwéi	n	behavior, conduct, action
2. 聚焦		jùjiāo	v	focalize, focus
3. 凑	湊	còu	v	gather together, pool, collect [凑热闹còu rè.nao: join in the fun]
4. 缘分	緣分	yuán.fèn	n	predestined affinity or relationship, fateful coincidence
5. 详细	詳細	xiángxì	adj	detailed, in detail
6. 思考		sīkǎo	n/v	reflection; reflect on, ponder over
7. 根本		gēnběn	adj	fundamental, basic
8. 特点	特點	tèdiǎn	n	characteristic
9. 群体	群體	qúntǐ	n	group
10. 意识	意識	yì.shí	n	consciousness [群体意识: group-oriented consciousness]
11. 与	與	yǔ	conj	and [more formal than 和 and 跟]
12. 之		zhī	pron	[only in object position; formal] it, him, her, this
13. 相反		xiāngfǎn	adj	contrary, opposite
14. 个体	個體	gètǐ	n	individual (person or entity) [个体意识: individual-oriented consciousness]
15. 例		lì	n	example [as in 以……为例, 例子, etc.]
16. 说明	說明	shuōmíng	v/n	illustrate, show, explain; explanation
17. 观点	觀點	guāndiǎn	n	point of view, viewpoint
18. 伸		shēn	v	extend, stretch
19. 向		xiàng	prep	to, towards
20. 勺子		sháozi	n	spoon
21. 享受		xiǎngshòu	v	enjoy
22. 感觉	感覺	gǎnjué	n/v	feeling; feel
23. 何必		hébì	adv	why should, there is no need [何: what; 必: must]
24. 聚餐		jù//cān	v	get together and have a meal together
25. 笑话	笑話	xiàohua	n/v	joke; laugh at
26. 出于	出於	chūyú	v	(do sth.) out of (politeness, curiosity, compassion, etc.), due to
27. 礼貌	禮貌	lǐmào	n/adj	courtesy, politeness, manners; polite
28. 犹豫	猶豫	yóuyù	adj	hesitant

简体	繁體	拼音	词性	英文翻译
29. 发现	發現	fāxiàn	v/n	discover, find; discovery, findings
30. 建议	建議	jiànyì	v/n	suggest, advise; suggestion, advice
31. 反正		fǎn.zhèng	adv	anyway, anyhow, in any case, under whatever circumstances
32. 得知		dézhī	v	learn of
33. 接		jiē	v	take over (something handed to oneself)
34. 齐	齊	qí	adj	complete, all present
35. 分享		fēnxiǎng	v	share (food, happiness, rights, etc.)
36. 按照		ànzhào	prep	according to, in accordance with
37. 主随客便	主隨客便	zhǔ suí kè biàn	phr	As a host, one does as the guest thinks fit. [主随客便 is a spinoff of the idiom 客随主便 (As a guest, one should do as the host thinks fit.)]
38. 有趣		yǒuqù	adj	intriguing
39. 故事		gù.shi	n	story
40. 员	員	yuán	bf	member [as in 一员, a member]
41. 利益		lìyì	n	benefit, (someone's) interest
42. 个人	個人	gèrén	n	individual [person]
43. 重视	重視	zhòngshì	v	attach importance to, take . . . seriously
44. 独立	獨立	dúlì	n/adj	independence; independent
45. 自由		zìyóu	n/adj	freedom, liberty; free, unrestrained
46. 选择	選擇	xuǎnzé	n/v	choice, option; choose, select
47. 他人		tārén	pron	other people [more formal than 别人]
48. 干涉		gānshè	v	interfere
49. 除非		chúfēi	conj	unless
50. 危害		wēihài	v	jeopardize, harm, endanger
51. 公众	公眾	gōngzhòng	n	the public
52. 独自	獨自	dúzì	adv	by oneself
53. 活动	活動	huódòng	v/n	engage in various activities; activity
54. 散步		sàn//bù	v	take a walk, go for a stroll
55. 锻炼	鍛鍊	duànliàn	v	do physical exercise, work out
56. 背		bēi	v	carry on one's back or shoulder(s)
57. 打麻将	打麻將	dǎ májiàng	phr	play *mahjong*
58. 下象棋		xià xiàngqí	phr	play Chinese chess
59. 拉家常		lā jiācháng	phr	chat about domestic trivia

简体	繁體	拼音	词性	英文翻译
60. 约	約	yuē	v	make an appointment (with someone)
61. 报	報	bào	v	sign up [as in 报名]
62. 团	團	tuán	n	team, group [as in 报(旅游)团]

专有名词 Proper nouns

简体	繁體	拼音	英文翻译
1. 厦门	廈門	Xiàmén	sub-provincial city in Fujian, a.k.a. Amoy
2. 易中天		Yì Zhōngtiān	Chinese historian, scholar and TV personality, author of 《闲话中国人》 [闲话 xiánhuà: talk casually about]
3. 芙蓉鸡片	芙蓉雞片	fúróng jī piàn	chicken egg *foo young* [芙蓉: hibiscus]
4. 榨菜肉丝汤	榨菜肉絲湯	zhàcài ròusī tāng	pickled mustard tuber and shredded pork soup

词语与句型 Expressions and sentence patterns

1. 与之相反 — on the contrary; to be the opposite of it

课文例句：中国文化最根本的特点就是“群体意识”；与之相反，西方文化最根本的特点是“个体意识”。

❖ A……，与之相反，B……
❖ A……，B 与之相反，……

- 现在中国年轻人自己旅游的越来越多了。与之相反，很多中老年人还是喜欢报团去旅游。
- 法文是从左往右写，阿拉伯 (Ālābó: Arab) 文与之相反，是从右往左写。

2. 以…… 为例 — use ... as an example; take ... as an example

课文例句：易教授以吃饭为例来说明他这个观点。

“以…… 为例” serves as an adverbial, which is a sentence element that functions like an adverb in modifying a verb or adjective. It can precede a verb phrase (example 1), or it can form a standalone clause when followed by another clause that serves as discussion or explanation (example 2).

❖ S以…… 为例VP
❖ Sentence 1。以……为例，sentence 2

- 李小文以美国人对学习的看法为例说明了中美家长的一些不同。
- 中美教育孩子的方式有一些不同。以运动为例，美国家长一般都比较重视，而中国家长很多都觉得不那么重要。

3. 不管……（S）都 VP — No matter ..., S (always/still) VP.

课文例句：中国人吃饭，所有的筷子都伸向同一个菜盘，所有的勺子都伸向同一个汤碗，不管什么菜，大家都一起吃。

A clause containing 不管 is normally used at the beginning of a sentence and must be in the form of a question, such as in a "wh-question" (example 1), an "A不A" question (example 2), or an alternative question (example 3). However, it is ungrammatical to use a "statement + 吗" question right after 不管.

都 is used in the second part of the sentence to stress that the results or conclusions will not change under any conditions. The subject of the 都 clause must precede 都 if it differs from that of the 不管clause.

- 中国人聚餐的时候，不管是谁点的菜，一般都会一起分享。
- 这门课不管最后的考试难不难我都会选，因为我很喜欢开课的教授。
- 在美国，不管是在大城市还是小地方，现在都吃得到中国菜。

不管 and 无论(wúlùn) are interchangeable, except that the latter is more formal.

4. 而 ①：……，而……　　　　..., and/but/yet ...

课文例句：中国人吃饭，所有的筷子都伸向同一个菜盘，所有的勺子都伸向同一个汤碗，不管什么菜，大家都一起吃。而在西方国家，人们各点各的菜，各吃各的饭。

而 can act as the conjunction "and" or "but" when it connects two stand-alone clauses. Context determines whether the conjunction is "and," linking the two clauses together (example 1 below), or "but," to indicate a contrast (see the example from the text, also examples 2 and 3 below). When 而 means "but," the adverb 却(què) can be added to the second clause to emphasize the contrast.

- 长江是中国第一长河，而黄河是中国的第二长河。
- 一般来说，中国人更重视群体的利益，而西方人更重视个体的利益。
- 中国和加拿大都很大，但中国有十几亿(yì: 100 million)人，而加拿大却只有三千多万人。

5. S何必VP呢？　　　　why must ...; why bother ...

课文例句：在中国人看来，一起吃饭是"缘分"，也是为了享受在一起的感觉。如果大家还是各点各的，各吃各的，那又何必聚餐呢？

何必 is used to form a rhetorical question in the form of "S 何必 VP呢?" It indicates that in the speaker's opinion there is no need to do something (as represented by the verb phrase). When the context is clear, the verb phrase can be omitted (example 2).

- 王大文的室友："大文，在网上买书便宜得多，你何必去书店买呢？"
- 你对经济不感兴趣，但是选了两门经济课，何必呢？

6. 出于NP　　　　out of NP; due to NP

课文例句：一次，一个中国人请他的几个朋友和两位"老外"一起到餐馆吃饭。出于礼貌，主人请每个人都点一道菜。

- ❖ 出于NP，S VP。
- ❖ S出于NP + VP。
- ❖ S VP 是出于 NP。

- 出于兴趣，王大文这个学期选了一门西班牙语课。
- 王大文这个学期出于兴趣选了一门西班牙语课。
- 李教授每天都给父母打一次电话，拉拉家常。她这么做是出于对父母的关心和爱。

7. 反正　　anyway; in any case; under whatever circumstances

课文例句：主人发现还少了一个汤，就建议他点一个榨菜肉丝汤，反正大家一起吃饭嘛。

The conjunctive adverb 反正 can be used to state a resolution or decision (example 1), or to state a condition or a reason (example 2).

- 这件衬衫挺便宜，但是颜色不太适合我，反正我不会买的。
- 你现在反正也没有什么事儿，跟我出去散散步吧。

8. S只好VP　　S has no alternative but to VP.

课文例句：两位“老外”自己吃自己点的菜，完全没有要跟别人分享的意思。几个中国人只好“主随客便”，按照西方人的习惯各吃各的菜。

- 王大文想给小东打电话，但是手机没电了，只好用电脑给他发了封电子邮件。
- 昨天晚上我回到学校的时候，食堂已经关门了，我只好去外面吃了点儿东西。

9. 除非　　unless

课文例句：西方人重视个人的独立和自由……每个人的选择和行为，他人都不能干涉，除非是危害了公共的利益。

The conjunction 除非 introduces a prerequisite, e.g. a condition that must be fulfilled. When the 除非 clause begins a sentence, the second clause may start with 要不然 or the more formal 否则 (fǒuzé: otherwise) to express what may happen when the condition in the 除非 clause is not fulfilled.

❖ ……，除非(是)……　　..., unless ...
❖ 除非(是)……，(要不然/否则)……　　Unless ... (or/otherwise) ...

- 他一定不会选择那所大学，除非大学给他特别高的奖学金。
- 除非是吃西餐，要不然中国人聚餐一般都是大家一起点菜一起吃。
- 对刚开始学中文的外国学生来说，汉字除非经常练习，否则很容易忘记。

语言练习 To practice and reinforce what you have learned from the Text, New Words, and the section “Expressions and sentence patterns” in this lesson, please visit the companion website to download a PDF version of the exercises.

交际情景 Communication scenarios

Study the following conversations between native speakers on the textbook companion website. Use the plug-in feature to find the definitions of the new words highlighted in orange. Try to visualize the scene as you read and listen to each dialogue. Discuss your reactions to these scenario dialogues with a classmate.

1. An internship brought high school classmates Wang Dawei (王大伟), Zhang Lili (张莉莉) and Zhou Qiang (周强) together. Wang Dawei offers to treat Zhang Lili and Zhou Qiang

to lunch. Observe closely what the host and the guests say when they order dishes together, and guess what they might have in mind when they decide which dishes to order.

王大伟：今天我请客，大家想吃什么，随便点。
张莉莉和周强：你请客，就你来点菜吧，客随主便嘛。
王大伟：那你们有什么不吃的吗？
张莉莉和周强：没有，吃什么都行。
王大伟：那我点个芙蓉鸡片吧。再来个麻婆豆腐，这个有点儿辣，你们能吃辣的吗？
张莉莉和周强：好啊，没事儿。
王大伟：再要个青菜吧。
张莉莉：醋溜白菜怎么样？
王大伟：行啊。再来个汤吧。榨菜肉丝汤还是酸辣汤？
周　强：都行，你说吧。
王大伟：那就榨菜肉丝汤，主食要什么呢？
张莉莉和周强：米饭就行啦。
王大伟：再来一份饺子吧。
张莉莉和周强：好，好。

思考与讨论：

1） 在这段对话中，从什么地方可以看出张莉莉和周强"客随主便"的做法？请最少举两个例子。
2） 菜上来后，你觉得他们三个人会一起吃，还是自己吃自己点的菜？为什么？
3） 如果你跟朋友一起出去吃饭，点菜时你也会问朋友的意见吗？为什么？

2. Wang Dawei, Zhang Lili and Zhou Qiang want to hang out and catch up after lunch by visiting a park. In the taxi, one sits in the front and two in the back. Pay attention to the nuance in the conversation that leads to an agreement among the three friends about who is to pay the taxi fare.

王大伟：高中毕业以后我们都好几年没见面了，没想到现在能在同一家公司实习，我们真是有缘分。
张莉莉：是呀，我也没想到我们又能聚到一起了。
出租车师傅：公园到了，一共是五十二块。
王大伟（坐前座）：好。师傅，我用支付宝吧。
张莉莉和周强（坐后座）：我来，我来。
王大伟：我坐前面，就我来给吧，方便。
张莉莉和周强：那行，等一下回去的时候我们来。
王大伟：没关系，都是老同学，不用分得那么清楚。

思考与讨论：

1） 你觉得"我来"在这段对话中的意思是什么？为什么三位乘客都这么说？
2） 王大伟坐在什么地方？为什么他不跟别人商量一下就付钱？
3） 最后王大伟说"都是老同学，不用分得那么清楚"，他为什么这样说？你同意这样的想法吗？

3. Li Aihua (李爱华) is inviting her friend Liu Shaohong (刘少红) to go on a trip organized by her son. Observe how the conversation evolves from initially having a family trip to later organizing a group tour that also includes other friends.

李爱华：我儿子昨天说要给他爸和我报个团去旅游。你和你老公要不要也一块儿来，我们做个伴儿？

刘少红：好啊。前些年我们也是跟几个朋友报团去了日本，玩儿得挺好的。你们要去哪儿？
李爱华：还没定。现在流行去北美。别人都说在美国买名牌更便宜，我想去买几个名牌包。
刘少红：太好了，咱们办公室钱老师的女儿在美国念书，她可能也会有兴趣。
李爱华：那好啊，人越多越热闹，那你问问她吧。

思考与讨论：

1） 你觉得李爱华为什么要找朋友参加她们夫妻的旅行？
2） 你觉得刘少红会不会跟李爱华一家一起报团旅行？为什么？
3） 他们为什么很有可能去北美旅行？请说出两个原因。

言语行为例说 Notes on discourse behavior

1. 对话例句：王大伟：今天我请客，大家想吃什么，随便点。
   张莉莉和周强：你请客，就你来点菜吧，客随主便嘛。

   客随主便, meaning "as a guest, one should do as the host thinks fit," is a polite social etiquette that is widely followed in Chinese culture. Guests will respond to questions from the host with this expression to show their unwillingness to impose.

   - 甲：我们家没有可乐也没有咖啡了，你要不要喝一点儿我新买的绿茶？
     乙：客随主便，喝什么都可以，别太麻烦你。
   - 甲：欢迎你们来访问，明天早上我们参观一下公司，中午就在餐厅吃饭，下午两点跟我们经理见面。你们觉得这样安排可以吗？
     乙：谢谢，谢谢。客随主便，这样安排没问题。

2. 对话例句1：王大伟：那你们有什么不吃的吗?
   张莉莉和周强：没有，吃什么都行。
   对话例句2：王大伟：…… 再来个汤吧。榨菜肉丝汤还是酸辣汤？
   周 强：都行，你说吧。
   对话例句3：王大伟：我坐前面，就我来给吧，方便。
   张莉莉和周强：那行，等一下回去的时候我们来。

   都行, 都可以, 行, or 随便 is used when expressing agreement with other people. However, as a communicative behavior, such agreement should not always be taken at face value, because it is very possible that the speaker may have expressed agreement only out of consideration for others.

   - 甲：这次我们去北京，你想坐飞机还是火车？
     乙：都行，我没意见。
   - 甲：今天我们不去公园了，天气不好。下个星期去，你说怎么样？
     乙：都可以，随便。

3. 对话例句：张莉莉和周强：那行，等一下回去的时候我们来。
   王大伟：没关系，都是老同学，不用分得那么清楚。

   不用分得那么清楚 is used as a response to a person who wants to repay a favor that the speaker did for him or her before. It literally means "no need to be so clear in dividing up responsibility," and the speaker would like to refuse repayment. Normally, the speaker will first acknowledge the close relationship between the two parties and then follow it by saying 不用分得那么清楚, or its equivalent saying, 不用那么客气.

- 甲：今天你请客，下次我们请客啊。
  乙：都是同学，不用分得那么清楚。
- 甲：你今天帮了我一个大忙，太谢谢你了。晚上我一定要请你吃饭。
  乙：都是朋友，不用那么客气。

4. 对话例句：李爱华：我儿子昨天说要给他爸和我报个团去旅游。你和你老公要不要也一块儿来，我们做个伴儿？
   刘少红：好啊。前些年我们也是跟几个朋友报团去了日本，玩儿得挺好的。

做伴(儿), 有伴(儿), or "给/跟sb做伴(儿)" means to keep company with somebody. As a common conversational phrase, it reflects the Chinese people's general preference for doing things together or as a group. Not only is having company important and adds to the fun in the eyes of many people, but offering or being willing to keep someone company is also considered a polite and thoughtful act.

- 甲：周六你要去上海啊，我跟你一起去吧，我也要去看个朋友。
  乙：行啊，这样路上也有个伴儿。
- 甲：晚上陪我去公司吧，我不想一个人去加班。
  乙：好吧，我也没有什么事儿，去给你做个伴儿。

体演情景 Perform the scenario

Select a dialogue from this section and listen to its recording several times. Imitate the speakers in pronunciation, intonation and discourse behavior in terms of both the words they use and the ways in which they carry themselves. Memorize the dialogue for performance in class.

跨文化交际 Cross-cultural communication

一、误解分析 Situation analysis

Break into groups and discuss the misunderstanding in each of the cross-cultural communication incidents below. For each incident, the group should generate an answer that best explains the cultural assumptions behind the ways in which the individuals say and do things. In addition, discuss possible strategies to avoid these misunderstandings in similar situations.

（一）Jason正在中国留学，他跟两位刚刚认识的中国朋友王大伟和周强一起去吃饭。在餐馆里坐下以后，王大伟说："今天我请客。"周强说："好啊，那我不客气了。下次我再来请"。然后他们开始点菜。王大伟要了一个铁板牛肉，周强要了一个红烧肉，两个人问 Jason 想点什么菜。 Jason说，他要一杯可乐，再要一个宫保鸡丁。王大伟看了一下周强后说："那我不要铁板牛肉了，改成醋溜白菜吧。"

思考与讨论：

1) 为什么王大伟知道Jason要点宫保鸡丁以后，决定把铁板牛肉改成醋溜白菜了呢？
2) 如果你是 Jason，在这样的情况下你应该怎么点菜？

（二）Samantha和中国同学王大伟、张莉莉、周强打算用暑假的时间去香港旅行。出发前几个星期，大家聚在一起讨论行程。王大伟兴奋地说："听说香港有一家特别好的美术馆，最后一天我想去看看。"可是其他几个人都说想用最后一天的时间去逛街。王大伟听了以后想了想说："那我还是不去美术馆了。" Samantha 说："那多可惜啊，你去美术馆，我们几个人去逛街就好了。"大伟说："没事没事，我们大家一起玩儿。" Samantha 还是没有明白为什么大伟改变了主意。

思考与讨论：

1) 王大伟真的不想去美术馆了吗？为什么听了大家的话以后，他改变了主意？
2) 如果你是王大伟，这时候你会怎么选择？

（三）为了庆祝王大伟的生日，周强和其他几个好朋友打算一起去KTV唱歌。他们也请了Jason一起去。Jason第一次去KTV，他觉得很兴奋。但是到了那儿以后Jason发现KTV太吵了，本来他的中文就不好，在那么吵的地方就更没有办法跟同学们聊天儿了。待了一会儿他就觉得没有意思了，所以就跟大家说："我还有事，我先回去了。"Jason一说要走，大家都纷纷说"别走了，我们一起玩儿多热闹啊""再待一会儿吧""我们才来你就要走，太没意思了"。可是不管大家说什么，Jason还是坚持要走。王大伟本来想找Jason一起玩儿，让他多认识些朋友，没想到这个人这么不合群，真扫兴。

思考与讨论：

1) 为什么王大伟觉得Jason不合群？
2) 如果你是 Jason，碰到这种情形时，你会怎么做？

（四） Tom暑假在成都实习。为了学习中国文化，他到了那里几天以后就开始早上起来到公园去跟中国人学打太极拳。一个星期天的早上，打完太极拳以后，几个一起打拳的人跟他拉起了家常。他们问他有女朋友了没有，爸爸妈妈都是做什么的，家里有几口人，等等。Tom想，这几个人怎么这么没有礼貌，他们才刚认识，就问他这么多有关个人和家庭的问题。他决定以后不再去那个公园跟那几个人一起打拳了。他想，换一个公园就不会有人问他那么多个人和家庭的问题了。

思考与讨论：

1) 你认为Tom的这个想法和决定会有用吗？为什么？
2) 如果你是Tom, 碰到这种情形时，你可以怎么回答？

二、口语交际练习 Oral communication exercises

1. 角色扮演 Role play

Pair up with a peer and refer to one of the critical incidents in *Situation analysis* to create a five-minute skit with a similar storyline. Use new vocabulary and speech patterns that you have learned from this lesson in your skit. Perform the dialogue in class and discuss whether each skit properly reflects typical Chinese discourse behavior.

2. 访谈与比较 Interview and comparison

跟一位中国朋友讨论下面几个问题，并一起思考中国的群体意识跟西方的个体意识有什么不同。请做笔记。在谈话中请考虑到这位中国人的年龄(niánlíng)、职业(zhíyè)和教育背景 (bèijǐng) 等因素(yīnsù)对他的思考方式可能会有什么影响。With a native speaker, discuss the questions below on the differences between Chinese collectivism and Western individualism. During your conversation, consider how factors such as a person's age, occupation, and educational background may influence his or her way of thinking. Take note of what was said.

1）"每个人都是群体中的一员，群体的利益就是个人的利益，群体的利益比个体的利益更重要。"你的中国朋友对这句话有什么看法？在日常生活中有哪些行为反映出中国人受群体意识的影响？
2）"西方人重视个人的独立和自由，你是你，我是我，他是他。每个人都有选择的自由，每个人的行为，他人都不能干涉，除非是危害了公共的利益。"你们对这句话有什么看法？在日常生活中有哪些行为反映出西方人受个体意识的影响？
3）你认为自己比较受个体意识还是群体意识的影响？ 为什么？
4）从小到大，家庭和学校的教育对你个体意识或者群体意识的产生有什么样的影响？请你跟中国朋友根据自己的经验，各自举三个例子说明。

群体意识	*个体意识*
•	•
•	•
•	•
•	•

(Add rows as needed.)
向全班同学报告你访谈的结果。

三、写作 Composition

1. 作文 （两题选一题）

题目1：点菜
提示(tíshì: prompt)：

- 如果你跟朋友一起去饭馆吃饭，你会自己点自己想吃的菜呢，还是会跟朋友一起点菜，然后跟大家分享？
- 你觉得你的做法和想法跟个体意识或群体意识有没有关系？为什么？
- 请用2–3段 (duàn: paragraph) 话谈谈你对点菜的看法。

题目2：You are a writer for the bilingual blog 行为文化笔记/Notes on Behavioral Culture, that chronicles critical incidents that have happened to learners of Chinese as a second language in intercultural communication. You seek to promote understanding between cultures. Using the pen name求知 (qiúzhī: seeker of knowledge), you respond to letters about cross-cultural issues related to Chinese-speaking communities. Here is a letter from a reader:

> Dear 求知，
>
> I just arrived in Shanghai to participate in a study abroad program. Last night, I hung out with a new friend named Xiao Zhang (小张). When I mentioned that I wanted to see downtown Shanghai, he immediately volunteered to take me there to experience the nightlife. At the subway station, he offered to pay for my ticket. I thought it was very nice of him and thanked him. We then took a taxi to a market, and when we got there, Xiao Zhang paid the fare too. When we stopped at a restaurant later, I wanted to buy him a drink to thank him, but he refused to accept it.
>
> I was touched by Xiao Zhang's generosity and had a great time hanging out with him. However, a few days later, I heard from my 语伴 (language partner) that Xiao Zhang usually works long hours and rarely hangs out with friends. Why didn't Xiao Zhang let me know he was busy, and why didn't he let me pay for anything? How can I repay his generosity, and what should I do if I'm in a similar situation next time?
>
> Thanks,
> 一个老外

- Write an editorial in Chinese in response to this letter. First, acknowledge the letter writer's feeling of awkwardness, and then explain the cultural logic that most likely dictates Xiao Zhang's behavior. In the conclusion, suggest what the letter writer should do the next time he/she hangs out with a Chinese friend.
- Your response should include at least five of the following phrases: 缘分 / 不用分得那么清楚 / 除非 / 与之相反 / 反正 / 而.

2. 文化探索Cultural exploration: For learners who are currently studying or working in the target culture.

Visit a nearby park once, either in the morning, later in the afternoon, or evening. While walking, observe what Chinese people are doing. Take note of how many activities are done in groups, what people do in these activities, and the average age and gender of the participants. Find an opportunity to chat with some of those people to learn: (1) how frequently they meet in the park, (2) the benefits of participating in the activity, (3) the duration of the activity, (4) what job they have or if they are retired. Record what you observe and hear in your notebook. Make a copy of the table in Appendix 1: cultural exploration of this book and fill it, in Chinese, with the information from your notes. Also, include a paragraph of your own reflection on the data collected. Submit your table and reflections to your teacher after completion.

第二课 人多力量大

行为聚焦：从众行为

Behavior highlighted: follow the pack

课文 *Text*

中国文化的特点是群体意识，这可能是因为在中国人看来，先有群体，然后才有个体。个体是群体的一员，个体不能离开群体而单独地存在。最近几年，汉语里又出现了一个新的词语“从众”，用来描述中国人爱跟风的现象。什么是“从众”？“从”字里有两个“人”字，表示一个人跟着另外一个人。“众”字表示三人站立，“三”代表很多，所以“三人”也就是很多人或者群体。“从众”指的就是个人跟着群体，别人做什么，自己也做什么，表示个人追求大家的认同，希望得到大家的认可。

“从众消费”一词指的是跟着别人买一样的东西；“从众行为”这个词说的是别人怎么做，我也怎么做。听说过“中国式过马路”吗？这曾经是微博上一个流行的说法，说的是现在仍然经常可以见到的中国人过马路的方式。在中国，不少人认为是不是路口，甚至是不是绿灯都无所谓，只要聚起了一些人就可以一起过马路了。这个说法一在网上发表就引起很多网民的共鸣，一天之内被转发了近10万次。许多网友评论说，这描述得太形象了！我们这里就是这样！不少网友还表示，自己也经常是“闯灯大军”中的一员。

重庆的一名网友说，“中国式过马路”反映了中国人的从众行为，同时也反映了中国人特有的一种心理，即“法不责众”。国家是有法律的，但是很多中国人认为，如果某种行为具有一定的群体性，即使不合法，也不一定会受到法律的惩罚。有人批评说，“中国式过马路”反映了中国人的规则意识淡薄，但也有人认为，这种现象的产生有它的社会原因。中国人多、车多，为了不造成交通堵塞，红绿灯给车辆通过的时间有两三分钟，而给行人过马路的时间只有几十甚至十几秒，有时行人过马路得小跑才来得及。

现在很多中国人喜欢跳的“广场舞”是另外一种引起许多争议的从众行为。中老年人，其中大多数是退了休的妇女，出来和邻居们一起跳跳舞、锻炼锻炼身体是一件好事，可是她们大声播放的音乐却影响了周围居民的休息。广场、街道、公园等是公共空间，“大妈”们跳广场舞的时候，同时也影响了他人享受这些公共的空间。有的居民也抱怨，可是拿跳舞的人没办法，因为她们是“群体”，人多力量大啊！

生词 New words

简体	繁體	拼音	词性	英文翻译
1. 力量		lì.liàng	n	power, force, physical strength [人多力量大 (*proverb*): There is strength in numbers.]
2. 从众	從眾	cóngzhòng	v	follow the crowd, conform
3. 单独	單獨	dāndú	adv	individually, on one's own
4. 存在		cúnzài	v/n	exist; existence
5. 出现	出現	chūxiàn	v	appear, emerge
6. 描述		miáoshù	v	describe
7. 跟风	跟風	gēnfēng	v	follow the trend
8. 表示		biǎoshì	v	indicate, show, express
9. 代表		dàibiǎo	v/n	represent; representative, representation
10. 指		zhǐ	v	refer to, point at; finger
11. 追求		zhuīqiú	v	pursue, seek after
12. 认同	認同	rèntóng	v	identify oneself with
13. 认可	認可	rènkě	v	approve of
14. 消费	消費	xiāofèi	v	consume
15. 曾经	曾經	céngjīng	adv	once, ever
16. 微博		wēibó	n	micro-blog, micro-blog post [usu. refers to the Sina (新浪: Xīnlàng) micro-blog platform, www.weibo.com]
17. 仍然		réngrán	adv	still, yet
18. 方式		fāngshì	n	way, style, pattern
19. 甚至		shènzhì	conj	even
20. 无所谓	無所謂	wúsuǒwèi	v	not to matter, be indifferent
21. 发表	發表	fābiǎo	v	publish (article, opinion, viewpoint, etc.)
22. 引起		yǐnqǐ	v	give rise to, lead to
23. 网民	網民	wǎngmín	n	netizen, Internet users [网友: Internet user, cyber acquaintance]
24. 共鸣	共鳴	gòngmíng	n	resonance, sympathetic response
25. 转发	轉發	zhuǎnfā	v	forward (mail, SMS, etc.), repost (tweet, online post, etc.)
26. 许多	許多	xǔduō	adj	many, a lot of
27. 评论	評論	pínglùn	v/n	comment on; comments
28. 形象		xíngxiàng	adj/n	(description or portrayal) true to life; image

简体	繁體	拼音	词性	英文翻译
29. 闯	闖	chuǎng	v	rush, dash [闯红灯: run a red light]
30. 军	軍	jūn	n	troops, armed forces
31. 名		míng	m	[used with multisyllabic nouns for people, such as 网友, 学生; more formal than 个]
32. 反映		fǎnyìng	v	reflect
33. 特有		tèyǒu	adj	specific to, characteristic of
34. 心理		xīnlǐ	n	mentality, psychology
35. 即		jí	v/adv	be the same as, be precisely [more formal than 就是]; namely
36. 法不责众	法不責眾	fǎbùzézhòng	idiom	The law does not punish numerous offenders./The law fails where violators are legion.
37. 法律		fǎlǜ	n	law
38. 某		mǒu	pron	some (kind of)
39. 具有		jùyǒu	v	possess (characteristics, functionalities, etc.)
40. 一定		yídìng	adj/adv	a certain (extent), given; definitely, surely
41. 性		xìng	bf	nature, property, attribute [can be used as a suffix, corresponding to -ness or -ity to form a noun, as in 合法性, 准确性, etc.]
42. 合法		héfǎ	adj	lawful, legitimate, rightful
43. 惩罚	懲罰	chéngfá	n/v	punishment; punish
44. 批评	批評	pīpíng	v	criticize
45. 规则	規則	guīzé	n	rule, regulation
46. 淡薄		dànbó	adj	weak (sense of . . .), thin, light
47. 现象	現象	xiànxiàng	n	phenomenon
48. 产生	產生	chǎnshēng	v	arise, come in being
49. 社会	社會	shèhuì	n	society
50. 造成		zàochéng	v	bring about, cause
51. 交通		jiāotōng	n	traffic
52. 堵塞		dǔsè	n/v	(traffic) jam, congestion; jam, congest
53. 车辆	車輛	chēliàng	n	[collective] vehicles, cars
54. 通过	通過	tōngguò	v/prep	pass through, get through; by means of, through
55. 行人		xíngrén	n	pedestrian

简体	繁體	拼音	词性	英文翻译
56. 秒		miǎo	n	second
57. 来得及	來得及	lái.dejí	v	able to do sth. in time [来不及: unable to do sth. in time]
58. 广场	廣場	guǎngchǎng	n	public square, plaza [广场舞: square dancing, plaza dancing]
59. 争议	爭議	zhēngyì	n/v	controversy; dispute
60. 大多数	大多數	dàduōshù	n	the majority
61. 退休		tuìxiū	v	retire
62. 播放		bōfàng	v	broadcast, transmit
63. 周围	周圍	zhōuwéi	n	vicinity, surroundings
64. 居民		jūmín	n	resident, inhabitant
65. 空间	空間	kōngjiān	n	space, room
66. 抱怨		bào.yuàn	v	complain, grumble

专有名词 Proper nouns

简体	繁體	拼音	英文翻译
1. 重庆	重慶	Chóngqìng	Chongqing or Chungking, a direct-controlled municipality under China's central government

词语与句型 Expressions and sentence patterns

1. 用来 VP (people) use (it) to VP; be used to VP

课文例句：最近几年，汉语里又出现了一个新的词语“从众”，用来描述中国人爱跟风的现象。

- 图书馆的这几台电脑是让人们用来查资料的，不是用来上网买东西的。
- 易中天教授举了中国人一起点菜一起吃的例子，用来说明中国人的群体意识。

2. A 指的是 B What A refers to is B.
A 说的是 B What A means is B.

课文例句1：“从众”指的就是个人跟着群体，别人做什么，自己也做什么，表示个人追求大家的认同，希望得到大家的认可。

课文例句2：“从众消费”一词指的是跟着别人买一样的东西；“从众行为”这个词说的是别人怎么做，我也怎么做。

Both patterns are commonly used to provide explanation or clarification.

- “大苹果”指的是纽约市，“风城”指的是芝加哥(Zhījiāgē: Chicago)。
- “自助游”说的是自己旅游，不跟团。

3. (在) time period 之内 within a time period

课文例句：这个说法一在网上发表就引起很多网民的共鸣，一天之内被转发了近10万次。

- 这本书我需要在一周之内读完 。
- 我弟弟现在也在学中文，他希望两年之内能到中国旅行一段时间。

4. 同时 at the same time; meanwhile

课文例句1：重庆的一名网友说，"中国式过马路"反映了中国人的从众行为，同时也反映了中国人特有的一种心理，即"法不责众"。
课文例句2：广场、街道、公园等是公共空间，"大妈"们跳广场舞的时候，同时也影响了他人享受这些公共的空间。

❖ S VP1，同时 (也/还) VP2
❖ S1 VP，同时S2也VP

- 上个学期小王选了中文课，同时还选了法文课，学习法语。
- "中国式过马路"反映了不少中国人"法不责众"的心理，同时也说明中国的一些路口留给行人过马路的时间太短了。
- 在这个路口，车特别多，同时很多行人也要过马路，一定要小心。

5. 即 namely; that is; *i.e.*

课文例句：重庆的一名网友说，"中国式过马路"反映了中国人的从众行为，同时也反映了中国人特有的一种心理，即"法不责众"。

即 is a formal verb that translates to 就是. What follows 即 provides an explanation or description of the matter being discussed.

- "从众消费"即跟着他人买一样的东西。
- 中国人常说的"北上广"，即北京、上海、广州(Guǎngzhōu: Canton)，是中国消费最高的几个城市。

6. 即使……，（S）也 …… even if ..., (S) ...

课文例句：国家是有法律的，但是很多中国人认为，如果某种行为具有一定的群体性，即使不合法，也不一定会受到法律的惩罚。

- 中国人口多，即使是小城市，一般也有一二百万人。
- 我最近很忙，没时间去旅游。即使有时间，我也不会报团出去玩儿。

7. 却 but, yet, however

课文例句：中老年人，其中大多数是退了休的妇女，出来和邻居们一起跳跳舞、锻炼锻炼身体是一件好事，可是她们大声播放的音乐却影响了周围居民的休息。

The adverb 却 indicates that a situation is contrary to expectations (examples 1 and 2), or that there is a sharp contrast between the situations expressed in the two clauses (example 3).

The two clauses form a converse relationship. When understood, the subject of the "却 clause" can be omitted. If there is a subject, however, 却 must follow it.

❖ S……，(但是/可是) 却…… S ..., but ...
❖ S1……，(而/但是/可是) S2 却…… S1 ..., S2, however,...

- 小高考试以前没有时间好好复习，但是却考得不错。
- 小李在网上订了一件中号的大衣，可是他们却给他寄了一件大号的。
- 西方人重视个体，而中国人却重视群体。

语言练习 To practice and reinforce what you have learned from the Text, New Words, and the section "Expressions and sentence patterns" in this lesson, please visit the companion website to download a PDF version of the exercises.

交际情景 Communication scenarios

Study the following conversations between native speakers on the textbook companion website. Use the plug-in feature to find the definitions of the new words highlighted in orange. Try to visualize the scene as you read and listen to each dialogue. Discuss your reactions to these scenario dialogues with a classmate.

1. The next-generation iPhone is coming out. Listen closely as to why Zhou Qiang wants to buy a new cell phone even though he has a decent one, and how his friends respond to him.

张莉莉：你们听说苹果下个月又要出新一代的iPhone了吗？
周　强：当然听说了。我都吃了三个月的方便面了，就是为了等它一出来就换新的。
王大伟：你原来的手机不是还挺新的吗？
周　强：新倒是挺新的，可是我们宿舍的同学都换了苹果手机了，我也想换。听说新出的样式和颜色都挺时髦的，我一定要买一个。
张莉莉：就是嘛，不然三个月的方便面就白吃了。
王大伟：说的也是。哎呀，你们说得我都动心了！

思考与讨论：

1）周强为什么想换个新手机？请最少说两个原因。
2）你会因为别人都换了新手机而动心吗？

2. Wang Dawei runs into a neighbor's daughter Zhao Xiaoming (赵小明) in the hallway of their apartment building. Knowing that Xiaoming, who is a middle school student, will study abroad soon, Dawei chats with the girl about where things stand. Pay attention to how the study abroad plan was made in terms of the destination and Xiaoming's attitude towards it.

王大伟：小明，你去加拿大留学什么时候走啊？
小　明：我爸本来说要送我去加拿大的，可是他听说他两个同事的孩子都要去美国留学，所以想让我也跟着他们一起去美国，这样也有个伴儿。
王大伟：你自己想去哪儿呢？
小　明：我觉得加拿大挺好的，我特别喜欢看他们的冰球比赛。不过好像现在都流行去美国留学，那我就随大溜，去美国吧。
王大伟：别人去哪儿你就去哪儿吧，大家都这么选，肯定不会错的。

思考与讨论：

1） 小明的爸爸为什么想让她去美国留学？小明自己的看法呢？
2） 为什么王大伟说“别人去哪儿你就去哪儿吧”？
3） 如果你决定出国留学，你会随大溜吗？

3. Wang Dawei and Zhou Qiang, who are in a hurry, are waiting for a green light to cross the street. Observe their exchanges closely with respect to what factors are considered before the two people decide to go through the red light.

周　强：这个红灯怎么这么长时间啊，我们都快来不及了。
王大伟：是啊，马路还这么宽，我们得小跑过去才来得及。
周　强：（指着左边的几个人）你看，他们已经开始过了，灯还没绿呢。
王大伟：我们也过吧，要不然就真的来不及了。
周　强：好，我们走吧。

思考与讨论：

1） 对话中哪里表现出了“法不责众”的心理？
2） 在你的国家，红灯时如果有人过马路，其他人也会跟着过吗？“法不责众”的心理在你的国家普遍吗？为什么？

言语行为例说 Notes on discourse behavior

1. 对话例句：王大伟：你原来的手机不是还挺新的吗？
周　强：……听说新出的样式和颜色都挺时髦的，我一定要买一个。
张莉莉：就是嘛，不然三个月的方便面就白吃了。
王大伟：说的也是。哎呀，你们说得我都动心了！

时髦 means fashionable, stylish, or in vogue. 赶时髦 means “to keep up with the trends,” which is a common human mentality. To demonstrate involvement in a conversation, such as the one shown in Dialogue 1, the party listening can say 就是嘛, equivalent to of “that’s right,” “that’s true,” “exactly,” or “absolutely.” Alternately, the person listening can respond with说的也是, meaning “what you said makes sense,” to agree with what the speaker just said.

- 甲：姐，我又想买条新裙子，今年流行这个颜色。
乙：你的柜子里有那么多裙子，你还买？你就知道赶时髦。
甲：说的也是，那我先不买了。
- 甲：我不太喜欢在网上买衣服。买衣服还是得穿上试一试才知道合适不合适。
乙：就是嘛，不然还要换来换去的，多麻烦。

2. 对话例句：王大伟：你自己想去哪儿呢？
小　明：我觉得加拿大挺好的，我特别喜欢看他们的冰球比赛。不过好像现在都流行去美国留学，那我就随大溜，去美国吧。

“现在 (都) 流行……” means that a condition, a practice, or an object has become popular. The expression often occurs in a conversation in which the speaker is deciding on things to do or on goods to buy, or alternately, offering advice to someone else on what should be done or things to be purchased. The Chinese love to follow others when doing or buying something, hence the frequency of this saying in Chinese conversations.

- 甲：儿子，你去帮我买一份今天的报纸，我要看看新闻。
  乙：爸，现在都流行用手机 app 看新闻，谁还在报纸上看啊？！
- 甲：什么？你姐要买车，现在她的工资那么低，买什么车啊？
  乙：妈，现在出去玩的时候都流行"自驾游"，我也想买呢。没事儿，可以贷款。

3. 对话例句：王大伟：你自己想去哪儿呢？
   小　明：我觉得加拿大挺好的，我特别喜欢看他们的冰球比赛。不过好像现在都流行去美国留学，那我就<u>随大溜</u>，去美国吧。

随大溜(suí dàliù) or 随大流(suí dàliú) means "talking or acting according to what the majority is doing." It implies that a person is doing whatever others are doing regardless of their own preferences or opinions.

- 甲：你这一票投给谁啊？
  乙：我就随大溜，大家都投谁我就投谁。
- 甲：明天你要去参观那个博物馆？我记得你对历史没有什么兴趣啊。
  乙：几个朋友一起去，我就是随大流。

4. 对话例句：小　明：…… 好像现在都流行去美国留学，那我就随大溜，去美国吧。
   王大伟：<u>别人去哪儿你就去哪儿吧</u>，大家都这么选，肯定不会错的。

"Sb1 does sth, sb2 就 does sth" means that sb2 copies whatever sb1's actions. This saying reflects the Chinese stereotype of the "herd mentality" (从众行为, literally "to follow the pack"). In Dialogue 2, Wang Dawei assures Xiao Ming that Ming's father's advice to follow where others go, "别人去哪儿你就去哪儿吧" when selecting a study abroad destination is a good idea. Wang Dawei endorses this plan by saying "肯定不会错的" (literally, "you can't go wrong with this") to stress the wisdom of such an action.

- 甲：你要喝点儿什么？我去点。
  乙：你喝什么？你喝什么我就喝什么。
- 甲：老师，"入乡随俗"是什么意思？
  乙：意思是如果你到了一个地方，那儿的人怎么做你就应该怎么做。英文里也有意思差不多的说法：When in Rome, do as the Romans do.

体演情景 Perform the scenario

Select a dialogue from this section and listen to its recording several times. Imitate the speakers in pronunciation, intonation and discourse behavior in terms of both the words they use and the ways in which they carry themselves. Memorize the dialogue for performance in class.

跨文化交际 Cross-cultural communication

一、误解分析 Situation analysis

Break into groups and discuss the misunderstanding in each of the cross-cultural communication incidents below. For each incident, the group should generate an answer that best explains the cultural assumptions behind the ways in which the individuals say and do things. In addition, discuss possible strategies to avoid these misunderstandings in similar situations.

（一）Ivy在上海的一家中国公司工作，她觉得中国同事陈欢欢这几天好像有什么心事。昨天吃了午饭以后Ivy就问陈欢欢最近怎么了。欢欢回答说："我要跟男朋友结婚了，可我心里还没准备好呢。"Ivy好奇地问："你没准备好，为什么要结婚？"欢欢为难地说："我的同学和朋友差不多都结婚了，我爸妈觉得我也该跟他们一样，就经常给我压力。我爸妈常说最近某个邻居或者某个同事的孩子结婚了，然后就逼我快结。我实在受不了，就同意结婚了。"Ivy听了以后心想，结婚是自己的事，为什么要按照朋友们结婚的时间来决定呢？

思考与讨论：

1) 是什么原因让陈欢欢同意结婚了？
2) 如果你是Ivy，明白陈欢欢的想法后，你会给她什么建议？为什么？

（二）正在北京工作的George平时上班很忙，周末的时候他想放松放松。听了一个朋友的建议以后，他周末坐出租车去几个景点玩儿了两天。George玩儿得很高兴。可是有一件事情让George不理解，那就是他知道中国的交通规则明明要求司机和乘客都系安全带，可是好几次坐出租车他都发现司机师傅不系安全带。他想，如果被警察抓到了，一定要罚不少钱。可是司机师傅们总是说"这么多车，大家都不系安全带，警察怎么可能每个人都抓呢？"George有点儿担心不安全，可是他不知道该不该劝司机系上安全带。

思考与讨论：

1) 为什么司机师傅不按照交通规则系上安全带，也不担心被警察抓？
2) 如果你在中国坐出租车时，看见司机不系安全带，你会劝说他系上安全带吗？

（三）Andrew作为国际交换生在上海一所大学读书。他和寄宿家庭的儿子—高三学生张明成为了好朋友。一天吃午饭时，他们俩聊起了张明上大学选专业的问题。Andrew问张明："马上就要高考了，你考虑过要选什么专业吗？"张明回答说："我想过了，虽然我对文学感兴趣，但我妈说念中文系不好找工作，还是经济管理专业比较好。"Andrew说："那你要听你妈妈的吗？"张明回答说："经管是热门专业，人人都想学。我有好几个同学都要念经管。还是听我妈的，随大流吧。"Andrew听了很不理解，心想，学自己不感兴趣的东西，不会觉得很无聊吗？

思考与讨论：

1) 是什么原因让张明决定选经济管理专业？
2) 如果你是Andrew，了解张明的想法后，你会跟他说什么？

（四）上个周末Jason和他的同学去曲阜旅行。曲阜是孔子的故乡，在山东省的西南部。到了那儿以后，他们看到一棵千年古树，上面挂了一个牌子，请游客不要摸。可是中国导游鼓励Jason和同学们都去摸一摸，因为这样可以带来福气。Jason指着牌子问导游："那个牌子不是说不能摸古树吗？"导游跟他们说："你们看，不是有那么多人都在摸吗？没关系的。"Jason很不理解，牌子上说得很清楚，导游为什么完全不在乎呢？

思考与讨论：

1) 导游为什么不在乎牌子上的要求？
2) 如果你是 Jason，你会跟导游说什么吗？你会摸古树吗？

二、口语交际练习 Oral communication exercises

1. 角色扮演 Role play

Pair up with a peer and refer to one of the critical incidents in *Situation analysis* to create a five-minute skit with a similar storyline. Use new vocabulary and speech patterns that you have learned from this lesson in your skit. Perform the dialogue in class and discuss whether each skit properly reflects typical Chinese discourse behavior.

2. 思考与访谈 Reflection and interview

中国有句老话说："羊随大群不挨(ái:suffer)打，人随大流不挨罚。"请你先用中文解释这句话是什么意思，然后把它翻译成英文，跟2–3位不同年龄、不同性别(xìngbié: sex)的中文母语者讨论下面几个问题。Use Chinese to write a short explanation on the meaning of "羊随大群不挨打，人随大流不挨罚", then translate the saying into English. Discuss the questions below with two or three Chinese native speakers of different ages and genders.

(1) 中国朋友对这句话有什么看法？
(2) 他们觉得这句老话反映出什么观念？
(3) 在西方有没有这样的说法？请举例说明。
(4) 这种情况 (qíngkuàng: situation) 在你的国家有什么一样或不一样的地方？
(5) 你认为很多中国人都有"随大流"和"从众"的观念吗？为什么？

把你对这句老话的中文解释和英文翻译交给老师，并向全班报告你访谈的结果。

三、写作 Composition

1. 作文题目：谈“跟风”

- 请根据下面两张图片，用三段 (duàn: paragraph) 话编写一个故事。

  第一段：谈谈图片的内容跟“跟风”有什么关系？
  第二段：这种情况在中国社会是怎么产生的？
  第三段：你对跟风的看法。

- 多用这一课的句型：指的是/用来/“sb1 does sth, sb2 就 does sth” /同时/即 / 即使……也…… / 却 / 无所谓。

中小学生出国留学

2. 文化探索 Cultural exploration: For learners who are currently studying or working in the target culture.

中国式过马路 (Chinese-style road crossing) is said to reflect the phenomenon of 法不责众 in Chinese society. Take a walk on the streets and observe whether the phenomenon of 中国式过马路 has changed in the place where you live. If the situation is different from what you have heard about 中国式过马路, find out what has caused it to change.

Suggested methodology: Search through videos, blogs, or articles with the phrase 中国式过马路. Review three to five hits and note when they had been posted. Then, on your walk, observe pedestrian behavior in real-time. Do pedestrians cross the street against the red light? If so, how do they cross and how many do it? How do drivers respond? Compare your observations with what you read online, then chat with at least two native speakers from different social groups about your questions. Write a paragraph on your findings and submit it to your teacher.

第三课　人人都是一个"角色"

行为聚焦：关系本位
Behavior highlighted: relation-based conduct

课文 *Text*

在中国人的意识中，人不是一个个独立的个体，而是通过各种家庭关系和社会关系联系在一起的。中国人在称呼他人的时候，首先要确定自己和那个人之间的相互关系。中国人的家庭关系很明确，除了父母和兄弟姐妹以外，对亲戚的称呼也分得清清楚楚。在社会上也是一样，除了称呼要加职业或职位（如张老师、王校长、李局长等等），对邻居、同事和朋友，大一辈的一般要叫大伯、大妈、叔叔、阿姨，同辈但年长一点的要叫大哥、大姐。对同辈但比自己年少的人，称呼对方小弟或小妹也很常见。总之，我不是"我"，你也不是"你"，大家都是人际关系里的一个"角色"。

社会关系的家庭化反映了中国文化中的"家本位"思想，而这种思想又是跟中国传统社会的特点分不开的。中国古代的农业生活决定了社会是由家庭组成的，不像古希腊的商业社会，是由单独的、具有独立思想的个人组成的。有人说，中国的社会就像一个大家庭，里面套着无数的小家庭。汉语中的"国家"这个词，说明了中国人的"家国"观念，即"家"就是"国"，"国"就是"家"。电影演员成龙唱过一首名叫《国家》的歌，里面有一句歌词就是："家是最小国，国是千万家"。在这样的社会里，完全独立的"我"是不存在的，或者说有一个"小我"，上面还有一个或几个"大我"。如果离开了"大我"，"小我"就无法实现自己的价值。

由于受到家本位思想的影响，中国人有着自己独特的人际关系和交往方式。大多数中国人的社交生活，都是由无数个"圈子"组成的。这从目前中国人普遍使用的微信就可以看出。一个人的朋友圈或微信群里，有家人圈、邻居圈、同学圈、同事圈、战友圈，等等。每个圈子里又可分出更多的小圈子，比如同学圈又可分成小学同学圈、中学同学圈等。微信能在很短的时间内成为中国人网络社交的主要工具，就是因为它在手机上成功地搭起了中国人熟悉的人际交往圈子。

有些学者认为，中国文化的根本特点不是群体意识，而是"关系本位"。其实，关系本位也是群体意识的一种表现，只是中国人意识中的群体不一定总是一个大的整体，而是经常表现为小群。有人问过这样一个问题：中国人崇尚集体主义，可是有的时候合作意识却不强，那应该怎样解释这个现象呢？这个问题的答案也许就在中国人的"小群意识"中吧。

生词 New words

简体	繁體	拼音	词性	英文翻译
1. 角色		juésè	n	role, part
2. 本位		běnwèi	n	one's own position (seen as being central) [关系本位: relation-based; 家本位: family-based, family-oriented]
3. 称呼	稱呼	chēng.hu	v/n	address, call; form of address, appellation
4. 首先		shǒuxiān	adv/pron	first; first of all, in the first place
5. 确定	確定	quèdìng	v/adj	determine, decide firmly; definite
6. 相互		xiānghù	adj/adv	mutual; mutually, reciprocally
7. 明确	明確	míngquè	adj/v	unequivocal, clear-cut; make definite
8. 亲戚		qīn.qi	n	relatives
9. 职业	職業	zhíyè	n	profession, occupation, vocation
10. 职位	職位	zhíwèi	n	position, post
11. 长	長	zhǎng	bf	chief, head [校长: headmaster, (university) president; 局长júzhǎng: bureau chief]
12. 辈	輩	bèi	n	generation, lifetime [同辈: the same generation; 大一辈: one generation older]
13. 大伯		dàbó	n	[address for father's eldest brother] [polite address for an elderly man]
14. 年长	年長	niánzhǎng	adj	senior, elderly, older in age
15. 年少		niánshào	adj	young of age
16. 对方	對方	duìfāng	n	the other party (of two)
17. 总之	總之	zǒngzhī	conj	in a word; in short
18. 人际	人際	rénjì	adj	interpersonal [人际关系: interpersonal relationship]
19. 化		huà	bf	-ize, -ify [added to a noun or an adjective to form a verb, as in 家庭化: familize, 现代化: modernize, etc.]
20. 思想		sīxiǎng	n	thought, thinking, idea, ideology
21. 传统	傳統	chuántǒng	adj/n	traditional; tradition
22. 古代		gǔdài	n	ancient times, antiquity
23. 农业	農業	nóngyè	n	agriculture, farming
24. 由		yóu	prep	by, from
25. 组成	組成	zǔchéng	v	form, make up, constitute
26. 商业	商業	shāngyè	n	commerce, trade, business
27. 套		tào	v/n/m	encase; cover, sheath; set (of . . .)
28. 无数	無數	wúshù	adj	innumerable, countless
29. 观念	觀念	guānniàn	n	sense, conception, notion, idea
30. 演员	演員	yǎnyuán	n	actor

简体	繁體	拼音	词性	英文翻译
31. 存在		cúnzài	v/n	exist, be; existence
32. 无法	無法	wúfǎ	v	unable to, cannot
33. 实现	實現	shíxiàn	v	realize, achieve, (dream) come true
34. 价值	價值	jiàzhí	n	value, worth
35. 由于	由於	yóuyú	conj/prep	due to, thanks to, owing to, as a result of
36. 独特	獨特	dútè	adj	unique, distinctive
37. 交往		jiāowǎng	v	associate (with), have dealings (with)
38. 社交		shèjiāo	n	social contact/interaction
39. 圈子		quān.zi	n	circle
40. 目前		mùqián	n	at present
41. 普遍		pǔbiàn	adj	universal, prevalent, common, widespread
42. 使用		shǐyòng	v	use (something to serve a purpose)
43. 战友	戰友	zhànyǒu	n	comrade-in-arms
44. 主要		zhǔyào	adj	main, principal, chief, major
45. 工具		gōngjù	n	tool, instrument
46. 搭		dā	v	put up, construct (platform, shed, rack, etc.)
47. 熟悉		shú.xi	v	know ... well, familiarize
48. 学者	學者	xuézhě	n	scholar, learned person
49. 表现	表現	biǎoxiàn	n/v	display, manifestation; show, display
50. 整体	整體	zhěngtǐ	n	entirety, whole entity, synthesis
51. 崇尚		chóngshàng	v	hold up (as a model), hold in esteem
52. 主义	主義	zhǔyì	n	-ism [as in 集体主义: collectivism; 个人主义: individualism; 社会主义: socialism]
53. 合作		hézuò	n/v	collaboration; collaborate, cooperate
54. 强	強	qiáng	adj	strong, powerful, vigorous
55. 解释	解釋	jiěshì	v	explain

专有名词 Proper nouns

简体	繁體	拼音	英文翻译
1. 希腊	希臘	Xīlà	Greece
2. 成龙	成龍	Chéng Lóng	Jackie Chan (1954–), Hong Kong martial artist, actor, film director, producer, stuntman, and singer
3. 微信		Wēixìn	WeChat, Chinese multi-purpose messaging, social media and mobile payment APP developed and first released in 2011 by Tencent [腾讯: Téngxùn] [www.wechat.com] [微信群: WeChat group]
4. 朋友圈		Péng.yǒuquān	Moments [WeChat's brand name for its social feed of friends' updates]

词语与句型 Expressions and sentence patterns

1. 不是……，而是……　　not ..., but ...

   课文例句：在中国人的意识中，人不是一个个独立的个体，而是通过各种家庭关系和社会关系联系在一起的。

   - 古代中国不是商业社会，而是农业社会。
   - 我没有选择那份工作不是因为工资低，而是因为它不能让我实现自己的价值。

2. ……。总之，……　　in a word; in short

   课文例句：中国人的家庭关系很明确，除了父母和兄弟姐妹以外，对亲戚的称呼也分得清清楚楚。在社会上也是一样，除了称呼要加职业或职位（如张老师、王校长、李局长等等），对邻居、同事和朋友，大一辈的一般要叫大伯、大妈、叔叔、阿姨，同辈但年长一点的要叫大哥、大姐。对同辈但比自己年少的人，称呼对方小弟或小妹也很常见。总之，我不是"我"，你也不是"你"，大家都是人际关系里的一个"角色"。

   - 在北京，可以看到很多高楼，汽车也很多。总之，北京已经很现代化了。
   - 现在的手机可以上网、看电影和电视、跟朋友聊天等等，总之，手机已经不再只是打电话的工具了。

3. 而②：……，而……　　and

   课文例句：社会关系的家庭化反映了中国文化中的"家本位"思想，而这种思想又是跟中国古代农业社会的特点分不开的。

   Lesson one defined 而 as a conjunction that can be used to express contrast. Lesson three adds a new usage for 而 to show the development of an idea between the first and second clauses. In this usage, the first clause makes a point, and the second clause expands further upon the point or illustrates it with an example.

   - 很多运动都可以帮助我们锻炼身体，而跑步是最方便、最简单的方式之一。
   - 在中国的大学里，计算机、法学、经济学、中文、外语等专业近年来一直很受欢迎，而经济学可以说是最受欢迎的。

4. 是……的

   课文例句：社会关系的家庭化反映了中国文化中的"家本位"思想，而这种思想又是跟中国传统社会的特点分不开的。

   The "是……的" construction here is used to emphasize or draw attention to the idea being expressed in the predicate.

   - 学外语不经常练习是很难学好的。
   - 中国人一般都是很重视家人的。

5. 由NP组成　　consist of NP; be composed of NP

   课文例句：中国古代的农业生活决定了社会是由家庭组成的，不像古希腊的商业社会，是由单独的、具有独立思想的个人组成的。

   - 美国主要是由50个州组成的。
   - 一般一支篮球队由12到15个运动员组成。

6. 由于 due to, thanks to, owing to, as a result of

课文例句：由于受到家本位思想的影响，中国人有着自己特有的人际关系和交往方式。

由于 introduces an explanation or a reason. 由于 and 因为 are often interchangeable, with the main differences being:

1) the cause can be placed after the "effect" clause when 因为 introduces it, whereas a 由于 clause containing the cause must be always used before the clause containing the effect;
2) 由于 is more formal than 因为, and由于 is usually used in conjunction with 因此 or 因而, whereas 因为 is usually used together with 所以.

- 现在，人们的生活方式由于受到网络的影响，有了很大的改变。
- 由于社会传统不同，(因此)现代中国文化与西方文化之间也存在着许多不同。

> **语言练习** To practice and reinforce what you have learned from the Text, New Words, and the section "Expressions and sentence patterns" in this lesson, please visit the companion website to download a PDF version of the exercises.

交际情景 Communication scenarios

Study the following conversations between native speakers on the textbook companion website. Use the plug-in feature to find the definitions of the new words highlighted in orange. Try to visualize the scene as you read and listen to each dialogue. Discuss your reactions to these scenario dialogues with a classmate.

1. Upon his arrival at home, Wang Dawei meets three guests who are visiting and playing *mahjong* with his grandfather in the living room. Pay attention to how Wang Dawei addresses the guests, keeping in mind the importance of family and its influence on interpersonal relationships in Chinese society.

刘少红：哟，大伟回来啦！我们闲着没事儿，来和你爷爷打一会儿麻将。
王大伟：刘阿姨好！
王大伟：（看见刘少红的先生赵学东，对他说）赵叔叔好!
爷　爷：（看了一下坐在他旁边的一位老先生)老孙，你以前没见过我这个孙子吧？（老孙摇摇头）
爷　爷：大伟，这位是爷爷以前的老同事，快叫孙爷爷。
王大伟：(看着老孙，很有礼貌地点了一下头）孙爷爷好！
爷　爷：孙奶奶在阳台跟你奶奶聊天儿呢，快去问个好。
王大伟：哦，好。

思考与讨论：

1）你觉得刘少红赵学东夫妇跟王家的人熟吗？从哪些地方可以看出来？
2）王大伟怎么称呼刘少红和她的先生？他怎么称呼爷爷的老同事呢？为什么？
3）在中国社会里称呼跟人际交往有什么关系？在你的国家也是这样吗？

2. Zhao Xuedong almost forgets that his daughter Zhao Jing (赵静)'s fifteenth birthday is tomorrow. The celebration that his wife Liu Shaohong has planned would conflict with his work schedule. Observe how he prioritizes the business of his "work unit (工作单位)" over his personal life and the similar mentality behind his daughter's comment.

   刘少红：明天是咱们女儿的生日。
   赵学东：真是的！明天是她十五岁的生日，我差点儿忘了！
   刘少红：那我们明天带她一起出去庆祝一下，好吗？
   赵学东：这……明天我有一个重要的会要参加。没办法，我这次不能陪你们出去玩儿了。
   刘少红：你去年就是因为工作没跟我们一起庆祝她的生日，今年又是这样！
   赵　静：（听到了父母的对话，走过来说）生日每年都可以过，但是爸爸的工作最重要。爸爸，明天不用陪我了，您就去开会吧！
   赵学东：我的女儿真的长大了，真懂事!

   思考与讨论：

   1） 为什么赵学东总是把工作看得最重要？他怎么看待自己和单位的关系？
   2） 为什么赵学东夸女儿真懂事？"懂事"是什么意思？
   3） 在你的国家，一般人们是怎么看待家庭跟工作的关系的？

3. Zhou Qiang plays on his school's basketball team. In a game today he made a three pointer at the buzzer that turned defeat into victory. Observe how he takes compliments from his teammate.

   队友：诶，你今天打得真不错啊！
   周强：没有没有，这都是教练教得好。今天能赢都得归功于教练平时对我们要求严, 还有大家的配合。
   队友：你就别客气了，还是你的球技高，换了别人，那个球不一定能进呢。
   周强：这也不是我一个人的功劳，今天咱们大家谁没拼命打啊？晚上一起出去庆祝庆祝吧。

   思考与讨论：

   1） 队友一直夸周强时，周强怎么回答？ 请举两个例子。
   2） "归功"是什么意思？周强说最后应该归功于谁？他为什么这样说？
   3） 在你的国家，个人成功后，也归功于家庭或者工作单位的支持吗？

言语行为例说 Notes on discourse behavior

1. 对话例句：刘少红：哟，大伟回来啦！我们闲着没事儿，来和你爷爷打一会儿麻将。
   　　　　　王大伟：刘阿姨好！

   When Chinese people meet people with whom they are acquainted, they often greet each other by naming the person and then saying or asking something that seems self-evident. In Dialogue 1, Liu Shaohong loudly makes the observation, "大伟回来啦！" upon seeing Wang Dawei enter the house. This type of greeting is meant to show that the speaker cares about the other person. When the greeting is in question form, such as "出去啊?" "吃饭呢?", or "去运动啊?", etc., the speaker does not expect a detailed answer, and the other party only needs to give a straightforward response. 你好 as a greeting is more well-known, but it is used when meeting somebody for the first time or in more formal social situations.

- 甲：（在办公室门口看到王老师）王老师，出去啊？
  乙：嗯，有点事儿，出去一趟。
- 甲：（在办公室）张姐，吃饭呢？
  乙：要不要一块儿坐下吃点儿？我包的饺子。
  甲：谢谢啊，我刚吃过了。

2. 对话例句：爷　爷：大伟，这位是爷爷以前的老同事，快叫孙爷爷。
   王大伟：（看着老孙，很有礼貌地点了一下头）孙爷爷好！

It is relatively uncommon to address someone by name when an age gap exists between two parties, or when they are not of the same social status. In addition to professional titles, kinship terms are often used to address acquaintances who are not related by blood in order to show respect or to express affection. Therefore, people will often try to ascertain each other's age when meeting the first time in order to determine the proper form of address. As an alternative, the speaker may try to avoid impoliteness by asking "不知道怎么称呼您?" (What should I call you?), allowing the other party to suggest the proper title by saying "就叫我……吧" (Just call me ...).

When meeting the friend of an elder, as seen in the example above, that elder will often suggest the correct appellation by saying "快叫……" (Call him/her ...). Younger people will often bow slightly when greeting an elder as well.

- 甲：小文，这是妈妈的朋友，快叫李阿姨。
  乙：李阿姨好。
  丙：你好，小文真懂事。
- 甲：我是这个月刚来公司的，不知道怎么称呼您合适？
  乙：我比大家都大几岁，他们都叫我王大姐。你也跟他们一样，就叫我王大姐吧。

3. 对话例句：爷　爷：孙奶奶在阳台跟你奶奶聊天儿呢，快去问个好。
   王大伟：哦，好。

People can gain a great deal of face when their child(ren) displays polite behavior in front of acquaintances. In addition to urging their children to 叫人 (to address someone by a respectful title), elders will often urge them to greet parties that they haven't talked to yet by telling them "快去问（个）好," as seen in Dialogue 1. Young people may also distinguish themselves by sending greetings to absent family members, such as a parent or spouse; this is done by saying "（请您）代我向……问（个）好" (Please give my best regards to ...).

- 甲：小云，你舅舅来了，在客厅，快去问个好。
  乙：好，这就去。
- 甲：杨老师，您回去以后代我向您先生问个好。
  乙：一定带到。

4. 对话例句：赵　静：……爸爸的工作最重要。爸爸，明天不用陪我了，您就去开会吧！
   赵学东：我的女儿真的长大了，真懂事!

懂事 is used to describe a person, usually a young person who is helpful and accommodating, and who can speak or act appropriately in keeping with Chinese etiquette. In conversation, it is often used as a compliment for the other party. Its negative form, 不懂事, is used to criticize improper behavior.

- 甲：妈，最近家里需要花钱的地方太多。我想先不买新电脑了，原来的还能用。
  乙：我女儿真懂事！
- 甲：张经理开完会以后怎么有点儿不高兴啊？
  乙：你这个年轻人，有点不懂事啊。你在大家面前说不同意张经理的看法，他当然 不高兴了。

5. 对话例句1：队友：诶，你今天打得真不错啊！
   周强：没有没有，这都是教练教得好。
   对话例句2：队友：诶，你今天打得真不错啊！
   周强：……今天能赢都得归功于教练平时对我们要求严还有大家的配合。

Nowadays, people often respond to compliments by saying "没有没有", "哪有, 真的吗" or "是吗". Like "哪里哪里" which is used a lot traditionally, people use these expressions in order to appear modest or humble. Alternately, a person may attribute individual success to the efforts of someone else or that of a collective. In such situations, most commonly used expressions include "这都是……" or "归功于……", as illustrated in Zhou Qiang's response in Dialogue 3.

However, due to western influence, young people may simply respond with "谢谢".

- 甲：张教授，你们的研究太了不起了。
  乙：哪里哪里，这应该归功于我们研究小组所有人的努力，我只是他们中的一员。
- 甲：小王，这个月的销售成绩非常好，你真是这方面的人才。
  乙：没有没有，这都是因为张经理您领导得好，我没做什么。

体演情景 Perform the scenario

Select a dialogue from this section and listen to its recording several times. Imitate the speakers in pronunciation, intonation and discourse behavior in terms of both the words they use and the ways in which they carry themselves. Memorize the dialogue for performance in class.

跨文化交际 Cross-cultural communication

一、误解分析 Situation analysis

Break into groups and discuss the misunderstanding in each of the cross-cultural communication incidents below. For each incident, the group should generate an answer that best explains the cultural assumptions behind the ways in which the individuals say and do things. In addition, discuss possible strategies to avoid these misunderstandings in similar situations.

（一）王婷婷最近心情不好，她的室友Joan问她发生了什么事。王婷婷说："明年我弟弟就要结婚了，他女朋友的父母想让男方买房。北京的房子那么贵，我弟弟没有那么多钱，想让我帮他的忙，借点钱给他。" Joan听了以后觉得很奇怪，她问婷婷："你弟弟买房，跟你有什么关系呢？"婷婷说："就是因为他是我弟弟，我没钱也得帮他的忙啊。" Joan不明白为什么王婷婷自己也没有什么钱，却还要给弟弟钱买房。

思考与讨论：

1) 为什么王婷婷觉得她应该出钱帮弟弟买房？为什么Joan不理解她？
2） 如果你是 Joan, 知道王婷婷的困难后，你会跟她说什么？

（二）李伟是Chris在中国留学时认识的语伴。大学毕业一年以后，因为Chris的公司派他去上海出差，所以两个人又见面了。Chris问李伟毕业后都做了什么。李伟说他在一家广告公司工作了两个月，但是那个公司离家很远，每天都要很早起床，而且一个月才挣 3000 块钱，所以就辞职不干了。李伟接着说，他反正跟爸妈住在一起，而且父母每个月还给他一些生活费，他就不急着找工作了。Chris心想，你已经大学毕业了却不工作，怎么还能心安理得地花父母的钱呢？

思考与讨论：

1） 李伟为什么不急着找新的工作？为什么他用父母的钱还很心安理得呢？
2） 如果你碰到像李伟这样的中国朋友，你会劝他不要用父母的钱吗？为什么？

（三）周强邀请留学生Jason去他家吃年夜饭。到了周强家，Jason惊讶地发现周强的爸爸竟然在除夕夜还在单位加班。周强解释说："我爸的单位每到过年的时候就特别忙，要加班，每年除夕都很晚才能回家。" Jason说："那就影响你们一家吃团圆饭了，不难过吗？"周强妈妈说："单位需要他就得去啊。中国有句话叫'舍小家，为大家'。" Jason不太明白这句话的意思。他知道春节是中国家庭最重要的节日，而中国人又是最重视家庭的，他不懂周强一家人为什么接受了这个情况，好像这是他们应该做的一样。

思考与讨论：

1） 周强一家为什么可以接受除夕加班这件事？
2） 如果你是Jason，你会对这件事感到惊讶吗？

（四）刘影和Emily都在苏州一家公司工作，而且是同一个小组的同事，平时关系不错。中秋节快到了，公司为员工准备了月饼作为礼物，并且发了电子邮件告诉大家领月饼的最后时间，过了这个时间就不能再领了。刘影和几个中国同事在忙一个新项目，把这件事忘得干干净净，等她们想起来的时候已经太晚了。刘影发现Emily领了月饼，但既没有提醒她们，也没有帮她们领回来。刘影这时就有些不高兴了，她对大家说："你们看别的小组，只要有一个人去领就帮组里所有人把月饼领回来了。再看看我们小组……" Emily 这时候觉得很尴尬，她不明白刘影为什么生气了。她心想，我也不知道你们没有领月饼啊，你们自己没领怎么是我的错呢？

思考与讨论：

1)　刘影为什么生气？她为什么觉得Emily有责任帮大家把月饼领回来？
2）如果你是Emily，领月饼的时候，你会帮大家都领回来吗？

二、口语交际练习 Oral communication exercises

1. 角色扮演 Role play

   Pair up with a peer and refer to one of the critical incidents in *Situation analysis* to create a five-minute skit with a similar storyline. Use new vocabulary and speech patterns that you have learned from this lesson in your skit. Perform the dialogue in class and discuss whether each skit properly reflects typical Chinese discourse behavior.

2. 观察与访谈 Observation and interview

   请上 YouTube 或优酷 (Youku) 网站搜索 (sōusuǒ) 成龙唱《国家》这首歌的音乐视频 (shìpín) 和这首歌的歌词。看了几遍视频后，请进行下面的活动。Search for Jackie Chan singing the song "Nation" on a video sharing service such as Youtube or Youku. Look also for the song lyrics online. Watch the video several times before doing the following activities.

   - 把这几句歌词翻译成英文："一心装满(zhuāngmǎn: fill up)国，一手撑起(chēngqǐ: hold up) 家。家是最小国，国是千万家。在世界的国，在天地的家，有了强的国，才有富的家。"
   - 跟2–3位不同年龄、不同性别的中文母语者讨论下列问题：

     （1）讨论你翻译的那几句歌词，谈谈你们对歌词中说的"国"和"家"的关系有什么看法。
     （2）你们怎么理解(lǐjiě: understand) "小我"和"大我"之间的关系？请每个人都举例说明。
     （3）你的国家有没有类似(lèisì: similar)的流行歌曲？跟《国家》有什么一样或不一样的地方？

   向全班同学报告你访谈的结果。

三、写作 Composition

1. 作文题目："小我与大我"

   提示 (tíshì: prompt)

- 小我与大我的观念是什么？它们跟“家本位”思想又有什么关系？
- 你国家的文化里有没有这种观念？如果有，有什么一样或不一样的地方？
- 你觉得这种观念对中国民众、社会和国家有什么样好或不好的影响？
- 最少写三段话。写作时请尽量用以下几个句型：不是……，而是……/由于/总之/而/是……的 (indicating emphasis)/……，（但是）S却……

2. 文化探索 Cultural exploration: For learners who are currently studying or working in the target culture

Create a WeChat account and develop an online virtual community with your Chinese friends. Explore WeChat functions, specifically those that control how your friends can be grouped. Chat with at least two Chinese native speakers about the following questions: (1) how they use WeChat to socialize with people, both personally and professionally; (2) how many friend groups they have; (3) how they manage group contacts for privacy. Record your observations in your notebook and write two paragraphs to reflect on the information that you collect. In your reflections, comment on how WeChat fits the Chinese mindset with regard to socializing and maintaining friendships. You can also include ideas on how you can use WeChat to help Chinese people classify you in their groups. Submit your reflections to your teacher after completion

第二单元 **Unit two**

文化视角：礼的观念

Cultural perspective: the concept of *li*

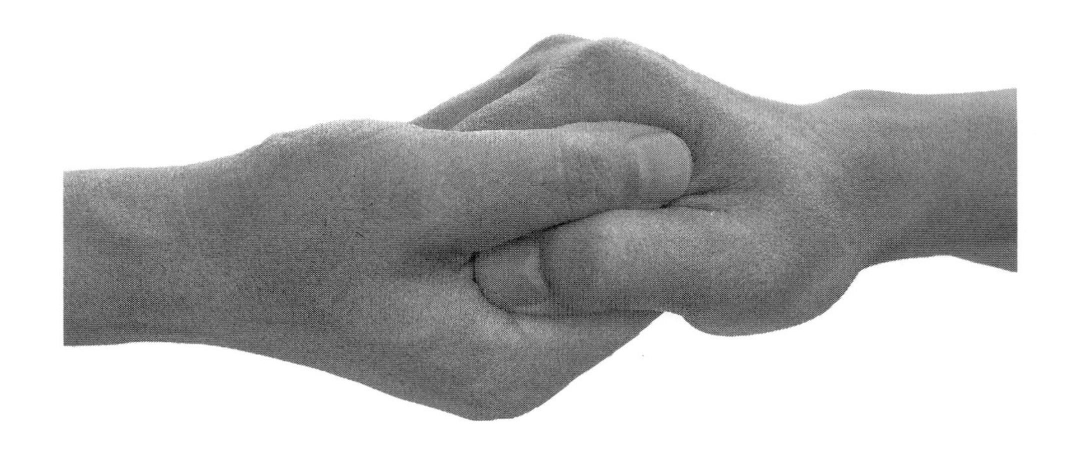

第四课　礼多人不怪

行为聚焦：礼俗客套
Behavior highlighted: *li*-based civilities

课文 *Text*

在西方社会，人与人、个体与群体之间遵循的主要是一种契约关系，维护这样的关系靠的是法律。而在中国文化里，由于家本位思想的影响，人与人、个体与群体的关系常常被视为先天的或天然的，维护这些关系主要不是靠法律，而是靠在今天仍然有着广泛影响的儒家思想和道德观念。

历史上儒家思想统治中国社会长达两千多年。儒家思想的核心是“礼”。“礼”也可叫作“礼仪”或“礼节”。中国人常把自己的国家称为“礼仪之邦”，其礼仪传统可追溯到古代的西周社会（公元前1046年—公元前771年）。到了春秋战国时期（公元前770年－公元前221年），孔子提倡“礼治”，把恢复周礼当做提高个人修养和治理国家的重要方法。孔子说：“不学礼，无以立”。可见，礼对中国人和中国社会是多么重要。

随着中国社会的长期发展，礼的内容发生了很大的变化。但是，当代的中国人在人际交往中仍然“好礼”，讲究客气。“客气”一词英文常常翻译成 polite，但它与“礼貌”（也英译为 polite）并不完全一样。“客气”主要的意思是“懂礼”，指的是按照约定俗成的礼节说话做事。“礼”的基本内容是对他人的尊敬和体贴，所以客气在行为上往往表现为“礼让”或“辞让”。以两个人一起去餐馆吃饭为例，从进门到坐下，从吃饭到离开，我们常常可以看到礼让式的客气。首先是“让门”：两个人同进一个门，出于客气，一个人常常停下来让另一个人先进；其次是“让座”：双方都要把好的座位让给对方，不这样做，就会被认为不客气；最后吃饭时，两人也要“让菜”：对于好吃的菜，自己少吃一点，让对方多吃一点，要不然就显得不够体贴。

有外国朋友说，在中国人家里做客，吃点什么或喝点什么，主人一定要让几次，客人也一定要推辞几次，这样你让我辞，大家看起来才有礼貌。其实，这是中国人典型的客气行为，是与中国人礼的文化传统分不开的。此外，这种礼让或辞让式的客气也表现在中国人日常生活的许多其它方面，比如赠送礼物、接受礼物、夸奖别人以及接受别人的夸奖等等。当然，在非常熟悉的朋友之间，特别是在现在的年轻人之间，情况会有些不同。中国人有句俗话说，“礼多人不怪”，意思是说，一个人越懂礼、越按照礼节做事，别人就越喜欢他。如果一个人不懂礼，他就不知道怎样“做人”，而在中国文化里没有人愿意跟一个不知道怎样做人的人交朋友。

生词 New words

简体	繁體	拼音	词性	英文翻译
1. 礼多人不怪	禮多人不怪	lǐ duō rén bú guài	idiom	One won't be blamed for being extra-polite. [怪: blame]
2. 礼俗	禮俗	lǐsú	n	etiquette and custom
3. 客套		kètào	n	civilities, polite formula
4. 遵循		zūnxún	v	follow, abide by, comply with
5. 契约	契約	qìyuē	n	contract, deed
6. 维护	維護	wéihù	v	safeguard, defend, uphold
7. 先天		xiāntiān	adj/n	inborn, innate; being inborn, innateness
8. 天然		tiānrán	adj	Natural
9. 广泛	廣泛	guǎngfàn	adj	wide-ranging, widespread
10. 道德		dàodé	n	morals, morality
11. 统治	統治	tǒngzhì	v	rule (a country), govern
12. 长达	長達	chángdá	phr	lengthen out to, extend as long as [长达两千年: extend as long as 2000 years]
13. 核心		héxīn	n	core, the heart of the matter
14. 礼仪	禮儀	lǐyí	n	rite, etiquette and ritual [礼仪之邦: state of ceremonies, state exemplary in observation of etiquette and rituals; 邦 bāng (bf): state] [礼节: etiquette]
15. 称	稱	chēng	v	address, call
16. 其		qí	pron	its, their, his, her [more formal than 他的, 她的,它的, 他们的]
17. 追溯		zhuīsù	v	be traced back to, date back to
18. 公元前		gōngyuán qián	n	B.C. [公元: A.D.]
19. 时期	時期	shíqī	n	period, phase
20. 提倡		tíchàng	v	advocate, promote
21. 治		zhì	v	rule, govern [礼治: rule of the rites; 法治: rule of law; 治理: govern, administer]
22. 恢复	恢復	huīfù	v	restore, recover
23. 周礼	周禮	zhōulǐ	n	the rites of Western Zhou Dynasty
24. 当做	當做	dàngzuò	v	treat as, regard as, look upon as
25. 修养	修養	xiūyǎng	n	self-cultivation

简体	繁體	拼音	词性	英文翻译
26. 方法		fāngfǎ	n	method, way, means
27. 不学礼，无以立	不學禮，無以立	bù xué lǐ, wú yǐ lì		If you do not learn the rules of Propriety, your character cannot be established. [from *The Analects* of Confucius; trans. by James Legge]
28. 随着	隨著	suí.zhe	prep	along with, in pace with, following
29. 内容	內容	nèiróng	n	content
30. 当代	當代	dāngdài	n	the present day, contemporary
31. 好		hào	v	like, be fond of [好礼: be fond of the rites and etiquettes]
32. 讲究	講究	jiǎng.jiu	v/adj	be particular about, pay special attention to; exquisite, tasteful
33. 约定俗成	約定俗成	yuēdìng-súchéng	idiom	established by popular usage, customary convention
34. 尊敬		zūnjìng	n/v	respect; respect, revere
35. 体贴	體貼	tǐtiē	n/v	showing consideration; be considerate
36. 辞让	辭讓	círàng	v	decline and yield [辞: decline, resign, dismiss; 让: yield]
37. 其次		qícì	conj	secondly, next
38. 双方	雙方	shuāngfāng	n	both sides, the two parties [对方: other side, opposite side, counterpart]
39. 对于	對於	duìyú	prep	regarding, with regards to
40. 显得	顯得	xiǎn.de	v	seem, look, appear
41. 做客		zuò//kè	v	be a guest
42. 推辞	推辭	tuīcí	v	decline (an offer, invitation, etc.)
43. 典型		diǎnxíng	adj/n	typical, representative; typical case
44. 日常		rìcháng	adj	day-to-day, everyday
45. 赠送	贈送	zèngsòng	v	present as a gift
46. 接受		jiēshòu	v	accept, receive
47. 夸奖	誇獎	kuājiǎng	v/n	praise; compliment
48. 以及		yǐjí	conj	as well as, and [more formal than 还有]
49. 俗话	俗話	súhuà	n	common saying, proverb
50. 做人		zuòrén	v	conduct oneself (according to *li*), behave with integrity

专有名词 Proper nouns

简体	繁體	拼音	英文翻译
1. 儒家		Rújiā	Confucian Philosophical School, initiated by Confucius (551–479 BC) and developed by Mencius (c. 372—c. 289 BC)
2. 西周		Xī Zhōu	Western Zhou Dynasty (1046–771 BC)
3. 春秋		Chūnqiū	Spring and Autumn Period (771–476 BC)
4. 战国	戰國	Zhànguó	Warring States Period (475–221 BC)
5. 孔子		Kǒngzǐ	Confucius, Chinese social philosopher and educator

词语与句型 Expressions and sentence patterns

1. S 把 A 称为 B　　S calls A "B"

课文例句：中国人常把自己的国家称为"礼仪之邦"。

称为 is the more formal equivalent of 叫做.

- 人们把跟着别人买一样东西的行为称为从众消费。
- 中国南方人一般把母亲的父母称为外公、外婆(wàipó)，而北方人把他们称为姥爷(lǎoye)、姥姥。

2. 可见　　it can be seen (that)

课文例句：孔子说："不学礼，无以立"。可见，礼对中国人和中国社会是多么重要。

可见 can be followed by a noun phrase (example 1) or an independent clause (example 2). A comma may not be used when 可见 is followed by a noun phase (example 1), but it can be used between 可见 and an independent clause (example 2).

- 中国人常说"有关系好办事"，可见"关系"对中国人的重要性。
- 如今，美国和中国大城市之间的直飞航班多了，可见，在中美之间往返的人比以前多了。

3. 并　　(not) at all

课文例句："客气"一词英文常常翻译成polite，但它与"礼貌"（也英译为polite）并不完全一样。

The adverb 并 is used before 不 or 没(有) to add emphasis. The construction calls attention to the fact that the state of things is the opposite of what people would expect.

- 小张是公司的领导，但是与其他同事比，他的经验并不多。
- Lisa中文说得特别好，很多人以为她在中国生活过很长时间，其实她并没有去过中国。

4. 在……上　　with respect to... ; when it comes to...

课文例句："礼"的基本内容是对他人的尊敬和体贴，所以客气在行为上往往表现为"礼让"或"辞让"。

- 两辈人之间在思想上有些不同是很自然的。
- 虽然中美两国在政治上有很大不同，但双方都应努力维护友好的关系。

5. 往往 more often than not; usually

课文例句：“礼”的基本内容是对他人的尊敬和体贴，所以客气在行为上往往表现为“礼让”或“辞让”。

往往indicates that things occur on a regular basis or according to some pattern. In contrast, 常常 indicates that things happen frequently without any expectation of regularity or pattern. 往往 can be used for events in the past or present, but it cannot be used for future, conditional, or hypothetical events like 常常. The negative of 往往 is 往往不 or 往往没, whereas the negative of 常常 is 不常.

- 外国学生刚到中国留学时，往往不知道中国人夸自己时应该说些什么。
- 虽然你常常练习，但是第一次参加比赛的人往往会觉得紧张，所以对你来说，现在最重要的就是放松。

6. 首先……，其次……，最后…… first and foremost..., secondly..., and lastly...

课文例句：以两个人一起去餐馆吃饭为例，从进门到坐下，从吃饭到离开，我们常常可以看到礼让式的客气。首先是“让门”：两个人同进一个门，出于客气，一个人常常停下来让另一个人先进；其次是“让座”：双方都要把好的座位让给对方，不这样做，就会被认为不客气；最后吃饭时，两人也要“让菜”：对于好吃的菜，自己少吃一点，让对方多吃一点，要不然就显得不够体贴。

- 我们大学的学生最关心的三种体育比赛首先是美式足球，其次是棒球，最后是篮球。
- 小李认为，在选择专业时，首先应该考虑自己的兴趣和爱好，其次要考虑以后找工作容不容易，最后得听听父母、老师和朋友的意见。

7. 对于…… regarding; with regard to ...

课文例句：最后吃饭时，两人也要“让菜”：对于好吃的菜，自己少吃一点，让对方多吃一点，要不然就显得不够体贴。

对于 and 对 are interchangeable when they are used as prepositions to mean “regarding” or “with regard to.” However, while 对 can be used after a modal verb or an adverb, the same is not true for 对于.

❖ S对于NP + VP
❖ 对于NP，S + VP

- 很多网友对于“中国式过马路”这个说法很认同，都说自己也是“闯灯大军”里的一员。
- 小东快大四了，对于毕业以后做什么样的工作，他已经有计划了。
- 大海的父母希望他能对自己的学习更重视一些。(Ungrammatical to use 对于)
- 我们都对这个问题很感兴趣。 (Ungrammatical to use 对于)

8. ……。此外，…… ... In addition, ...

课文例句：其实，这是中国人典型的客气行为，是与中国人礼的文化传统分不开的。此外，这种礼让或辞让式的客气也表现在中国人日常生活的许多其它方面，比如赠送礼物、接受礼物、夸奖别人以及接受别人的夸奖等等。

- 从众行为在日常生活中有很多表现，很多人报团去某个地方旅游就是个好例子。此外，“中国式过马路”也是一种从众行为。
- 老师让我们做一个关于环境保护的报告。我们得在网上找资料，还要跟小组里的其他同学讨论。此外，我们还要问三名中国学生他们对于这个问题的看法。

> **语言练习** To practice and reinforce what you have learned from the Text, New Words, and the section “Expressions and sentence patterns” in this lesson, please visit the companion website to download a PDF version of the exercises.

交际情景 Communication scenarios

Study the following conversations between native speakers on the textbook companion website. Use the plug-in feature to find the definitions of the new words highlighted in orange. Try to visualize the scene as you read and listen to each dialogue. Discuss your reactions to these scenario dialogues with a classmate.

1. Jason Adams (艾杰森 Ài Jiésēn) is an international exchange student living with Wang Dawei’s family. His birthday is coming up. Dawei and his father Wang Weimin (王为民) are hosting a birthday celebration for Jason at a Chinese restaurant. They have invited Dawei’s paternal grandparents as well as Jason’s classmates Zhang Lili et al. Pay attention to how seating is arranged in a formal dining situation like the one in the following scenario.

   王为民：大伟，你快请爷爷奶奶坐上座。杰森是今天的“主角”，让他坐到爷爷奶奶旁边。同学们也都请里面坐。
   张莉莉：王叔叔，您不用招呼我们，我们几个晚辈坐在门口这边就好了。
   王大伟：今天你们都是我请来的客人。来，你们坐里边吧。
   张莉莉：大伟，你跟我们客气什么？我们喜欢坐在外边，这样出去方便。

   思考与讨论：

   1）请用中文解释“上座”“晚辈”是什么意思。
   2）如果是一张圆桌，“上座”在什么位置？一般谁坐那个位子？
   3）张莉莉说他们喜欢坐在外边是因为出去方便，这是真实的原因吗？
   4）在你的国家请客吃饭时，对座位有要求吗？如果有，跟中国的有什么一样或不一样的地方？

2. Li Aihua came back from an overseas trip recently. On Saturday, she paid a visit to her friend Liu Shaohong and brought some gifts. Pay attention to how they take turns in conversation and what words they use as a gesture of “kèqi” (客气).

   刘少红：李姐，您怎么来了！快请进！好久不见了。
   李爱华：是啊，少红。我刚从美国旅游回来，这一趟走了两个礼拜呢。
   刘少红：以前您还说让我们跟你们一起去呢。可惜我老公太忙了。
   李爱华：下次一起去吧，美国可好玩儿了，买名牌也便宜。这不，我给你带了一点儿营养品。
   刘少红：您看您，来就来吧，还带什么礼物啊？
   李爱华：哎呀，也不是什么特别值钱的东西，你就收下吧。
   刘少红：真是不好意思，让您破费了。

思考与讨论：

1） 李爱华给刘少红带了什么礼物？她为什么说她送的礼物不值钱？
2） 刘少红表示感谢了吗？怎么表示的？
3） 在你的国家，人们之间送礼物的时候，送礼物的人会怎么介绍自己的礼物？接受礼物的人会怎么表示感谢？

3. A college freshman took a taxi from the railway station and just arrived at the university. Wang Dawei is at the school gate greeting the freshmen. Note how he offers to help and the freshman accepts the favor.

王大伟：你好，你是新生吧？欢迎你！
新　生：你是学长吗？你好！谢谢你来接我们。
王大伟：来，我来帮你拿行李。
新　生：不用了，不用了。我自己能拿。
王大伟：你看你的行李这么多、这么重，还是我来帮你吧。
新　生：没事儿的，这里离学生宿舍不远了，我自己能行。
王大伟：还有好几百米呢！来吧，给我吧。
新　生：那太麻烦学长了，谢谢，谢谢！

思考与讨论：

1） 请你查查"学长""学姐""学弟""学妹"这些词是什么意思。
2） 开始的时候，这个新生为什么拒绝王大伟帮她的忙？她真的不希望他帮她的忙吗？
3） 王大伟怎么表示他是真的愿意帮忙的？
4） 如果你想帮一个人忙，那个人告诉你："不用了，我自己能行"，根据你的国家的文化，这时你一般会怎么做？为什么？

言语行为例说 Notes on discourse behavior

1. 对话例句：王为民：大伟，你快请爷爷奶奶坐上座。杰森是今天的"主角"，让他坐到爷爷奶奶旁边。同学们也都请里面坐。
张莉莉：王叔叔，您不用招呼我们，我们几个晚辈坐在门口这边就好了。

Seating arrangement is an important part of Chinese dining etiquette. At a formal dinner, the seat of honor (上座) is customarily reserved for the person who is the oldest or with the highest social status in order to show respect. When seated at a round table, the seat of honor generally faces the entrance. Guests with high status, including the host, usually sit adjacent to the seat of honor. Guests who are younger or with lower social status usually sit closer to the door. As seen in Dialogue 1, Chinese individuals often say 请您(坐)上座 or 请里边坐 to express their respect for important guests, or 我坐门口 or 我坐外边 to show their humility.

- 甲：张经理，请您坐上座，王经理，来来来，也请里边坐。
  乙：李经理，还是请您坐上座吧。
  甲：不不不，今天您是客人，请您坐上座。

- 甲：高校长，请您上座，各位老师，也请里边坐。
  乙：李老师，您坐里边吧。
  甲：不用不用，我就坐门口吧。

2. 对话例句：李爱华：……我给你带了一点儿营养品。
   刘少红：您看您，来就来吧，还带什么礼物啊？
   李爱华：哎呀，也不是什么特别值钱的东西，你就收下吧。
   刘少红：真是不好意思，让您破费了。

   Chinese people often bring a gift when visiting someone at his or her home. Common gifts include fruits, snacks, tea, or health supplements of various kinds. As seen in Dialogue 2, the guest would say "我给你/您带了一点……" and the host would respond: "来就来吧，还带什么礼物啊？" Please note that such cliché response from the host does not indicate a lack of pleasure with the gift on her part; on the contrary she is expressing her gratitude or 客气 in a way as if she were scolding the guest for taking the trouble to get her a gift. On formal occasions, the guest may further respond, self-deprecatingly, with "小小礼物，不成敬意" (This is a trifling token that does not fully express my respect for you.), or under casual circumstances, "不是什么特别值钱的东西" (This is not a particularly valuable item.). To end the conversation, the host would again show her gratitude by saying "让你破费了" (I am sorry to have made you spend so much money.) or "下次来什么都不要买" (Do not buy anything next time you visit.). Generally speaking, the guest would still bring a gift on his/her next visit, because it would look impolite to show up at someone's home empty-handed.

   - 甲：张奶奶，我来看您了，给您带了您最爱吃的点心。
     乙：你看，来就来吧，还买什么东西啊？
     甲：张奶奶，这些都是您爱吃的，再说也不贵，不是什么特别值钱的东西。
     乙：下次可不要再买东西了啊。只要你能来，奶奶就高兴了。

   - 甲：李总，这次我去杭州，给您带了两盒绿茶，请您尝尝。
     乙：哎呀，你来就来吧，还带什么礼物啊？
     甲：小小礼物，不成敬意。请您收下吧。
     乙：让你破费了啊。谢谢，谢谢。

3. 对话例句：王大伟：来，我来帮你拿行李。
   新　生：不用了，不用了，我自己能拿。
   王大伟：你看你的行李这么多、这么重，还是我来帮你吧。
   新　生：没事儿的，这里离学生宿舍不远了，我自己能行。

   When someone offers to help or return a favor, the recipient generally turns it down at first. This is to show that the person does not want to impose on others. If the other party offers a second time, then the person may either decline or accept, depending on the situation and/or the closeness of their relationship. The person would usually accept the favor if help were offered a third time, as seen in Dialogue 3.

   - 甲：小李，你自行车坏了，骑我的吧。
     乙：不用不用，我可以走过去。
     甲：这么远，你还是骑我的车吧。
     乙：没事儿，走路也是运动嘛。

甲：你骑吧，今天晚上反正我也不用车。
乙：那好，谢谢你，我一回来就还给你。

- 甲：小王，你的快递还没拿吧？我去帮你拿吧。
  乙：太麻烦了，我自己去拿吧。
  甲：没事儿，不麻烦。
  乙：还是我自己去吧，你也挺忙的。
  甲：我正好也要去拿快递，顺便帮你带回来。
  乙：那麻烦你了。

4. 对话例句：王大伟：还有好几百米呢！来吧，给我吧。
   新　生：那太麻烦学长了，谢谢，谢谢！

麻烦 is a useful expression to learn. As discussed above, Chinese etiquette dictates that a person should not trouble people with whom s/he is not very well acquainted. However, when accepting help or a favor from someone, as seen in Dialogue 3, one may say "(那)麻烦你了" to indicate one's acceptance of help and to express one's gratitude. One may also say "这样会不会太麻烦你了？" to confirm that the other party is willing to help, or "可以麻烦你 do sth. 吗？" in a situation when one definitely needs help.

- 甲：这个周末你要去买菜吗？我开车带你去吧。
  乙：这样会不会太麻烦你了？
  甲：不麻烦，我也要买菜。
  乙：那就麻烦你了。周六我去你家找你。

- 甲：可以麻烦你帮我打一个电话吗？我手机没电了。
  乙：可以啊，什么号码？
  甲：13636357248，谢谢，麻烦你了。

体演情景 Perform the scenario

Select a dialogue from this section and listen to its recording several times. Imitate the speakers in pronunciation, intonation and discourse behavior in terms of both the words they use and the ways in which they carry themselves. Memorize the dialogue for performance in class.

跨文化交际 Cross-cultural communication

一、误解分析 Situation analysis

Break into groups and discuss the misunderstanding in each of the cross-cultural communication incidents below. For each incident, the group should generate an answer that best explains the cultural assumptions behind the ways in which the individuals say and do things. In addition, discuss possible strategies to avoid these misunderstandings in similar situations.

（一）第一次到中国留学的艾杰森被中国朋友张莉莉请到家里做客。张莉莉的妈妈准备了一大桌子菜。吃饭的时候，张莉莉的妈妈不停地给客人们夹菜。艾杰森虽然不习惯别人给他夹菜，但是看到大家都吃得很高兴，他也就入乡随俗了。可是，饭都吃了一个小时了，大家也都差不多饱了，张莉莉的妈妈还是不停地给大家夹菜，让大家再多吃一点。艾杰森说了好几次"吃饱了"，可是看到张莉莉的妈妈这么热情，他也只好把夹给他的菜都吃了。最后因为吃得太饱，肚子都开始疼起来了，他有点不明白为什么自己已经说得很清楚了可张莉莉的妈妈还是给他夹菜。

思考与讨论：

1) 虽然客人说了"吃饱了"，为什么张莉莉的妈妈还是不停地给大家夹菜，让大家再多吃一点？
2) 如果你以后在中国家庭做客，碰到这样的情况，你该怎么办？

（二）文文在一所美国大学留学。第一次去美国的时候，她下了飞机，拉着两个大行李箱上了出租汽车，好不容易从机场到了公寓，已经累个半死。在公寓门口，文文正好碰到她的新室友Lisa从外面回来，她兴奋地跟Lisa打招呼，介绍自己。Lisa问文文，需要不需要帮忙把行李搬到文文的房间。文文客气了一下，说："不用了，不用了，我自己能行。"Lisa听了以后说："那好吧，欢迎你来到美国。"然后就回自己的房间去了。文文心想，这个Lisa真不礼貌，想想以前自己在中国是怎么帮助外国留学生的，她觉得又累又气。

思考与讨论：

1) 文文说"不用了，不用了，我自己能行"，可是后来她心里为什么不高兴呢？
2) 如果你以后碰到从中国来的朋友这样拒绝你的帮助时，你会怎么做呢？

（三）艾杰森和几个新认识的中国朋友一起打篮球。中场休息的时候，周强说要去旁边的小卖部买饮料喝，问大家都想喝什么。王大伟说要一瓶可乐，其他人都说不用了，说喝他们自己带来的水就行了。周强问艾杰森渴不渴，要不要喝点什么。艾杰森并不觉得渴，就说不用了。几分钟以后周强回来了，他给王大伟买了可乐，还给艾杰森买了一瓶水。艾杰森觉得有点奇怪，他没让周强帮他买水啊，就跟周强说"谢谢，我不渴"，而且也没有把水接过来。周强看了艾杰森一眼，觉得有点尴尬。

思考与讨论：

1) 为什么艾杰森跟周强说了不用帮他买水，可是周强还是帮他买了呢？
2) 如果你是艾杰森，周强把水给你的时候，你会怎么做？

（四）Scott来中国工作不久就有了女朋友，她叫丁宁宁。Scott第一次去宁宁家的时候，听了中国朋友的建议，给宁宁的爸爸妈妈买了礼物。宁宁的爸爸妈妈看起来很高兴，可是嘴上却说："来就来吧，还带什么东西啊，以后再来，什么都不要带。"两个星期后，宁宁的爸爸妈妈又请Scott来家里吃饭。这次Scott没有准备什么礼物，可是大家刚坐下来，宁宁就跟她爸妈说："爸妈，对不起，Scott太忙了，这次忘了给你们带礼物。" Scott听了以后觉得很奇怪，不知道宁宁为什么要那么说，是宁宁的爸爸妈妈不让他带礼物的呀。

思考与讨论：

1) 为什么宁宁跟她爸妈说："爸妈，对不起，Scott太忙了，这次忘了给你们带礼物"？
2) 如果你是Scott，再去宁宁家吃饭时你会怎么做？

二、口语交际练习 Oral communication exercises

1. 角色扮演 Role play

   Pair up with a peer and refer to one of the critical incidents in *Situation analysis* to create a five-minute skit with a similar storyline. Use new vocabulary and speech patterns that you have learned from this lesson in your skit. Perform the dialogue in class and discuss whether each skit properly reflects typical Chinese discourse behavior.

2. 思考与讨论 Reflection and discussion

   根据你对这一课内容的理解 (lǐjiě: understanding), 请你跟同学讨论下面这八个例子，想想:（i）哪个在中国文化里被认为是懂礼的做法，哪个不是？（ii）比较这些做法跟你国家的礼貌行为有什么一样或不一样的地方，这些行为后面的原因是什么。

   (1) 跟别人借了钱或东西，一定要记得还，因为中国有句老话说"有借有还，再借不难"。
   (2) 跟一个人认识，最好先问问这个人的年龄，然后选择一个合适的称呼。
   (3) 跟朋友在餐馆聚餐，轮到你点菜时，最好也问问别人都喜欢吃什么，有没有忌口 (jìkǒu: avoid certain foods)的。
   (4) 为了得到老板的赏识(shǎngshí: recognition)，你应该要处处表现(biǎoxiàn: show off)自己，而且不必在乎别人的感受(gǎnshòu: feeling)或别人对自己的看法。
   (5) 出进公共场所的大门时，不需要考虑后面有没有人， 你进去后关上门就好了。
   (6) 看到长辈要问好。
   (7) 去朋友家做客，最好要带上一点小礼物，表示对主人的尊敬和关心。
   (8) 如果你跟朋友出去玩儿，大家一起吃饭的时候， 谁愿意付钱就让谁付。

三、写作 Composition

1. 作文

你是中英文双语博客(blog)网站"行为文化笔记"的博主(blogger), 笔名叫"求知"。你写博客是为了帮助外国人了解中国人思考事情的方式和传统的价值观，同时也让中国人更多地了解外国人的想法。

最近你收到一位读者的来信。请根据你对中国人行为文化的认识提出建议，帮助她适应（shìyìng: adapt）在中国的生活。回信以前，可以在网上看一些相关资料(zīliào: information)，或者听听中国朋友的意见。

求知，

I am doing an internship in Beijing and have been living in China for almost three months. While I love my job and enjoy spending time with the Chinese friends that I have made here, sometimes I still feel there's a social distance between us, and I don't know how to bridge it. Last week, I was invited to Lili's (莉莉) birthday party at her house with two other Chinese coworkers. We had dinner with Lili's parents and her grandmother. While we were eating, her grandmother kept offering me more food than I could eat. By the end of the meal, I felt bad because I had a lot of food left on my plate. All of us brought Lili birthday presents, but she didn't open any of them in front of us, nor did she say anything about them afterwards. I'm a little disappointed, because I thought that Chinese people emphasize politeness (礼貌) and etiquette (礼节). I'm also confused. Was it impolite to leave so much food on my plate? Should I ask Lili if she liked my gift?

Samantha

- 用中文回信，至少写三段话。请注意中文书信的格式（géshì: format）。
- 尽量用下列句型和词语：首先……，其次……，最后…… / 在……上 / 对于 / 此外 / 往往 / 并 / 可见

2. 文化探索Cultural exploration: For learners who are currently studying or working in the target culture

Examine the merchandise in the stores of a shopping center 商场 or 大卖场GMS (General Merchandise Store) to learn about gift-giving in Chinese culture. Look at 4–6 items and find out when they are appropriate as gifts (e.g. occasion) and for whom they would be appropriate (e.g., age, gender, social relationship between the giver and the recipient) interviewing at least 3–5 sales clerks and/or customers. During your interviews, try to learn about any gift-giving taboos that may exist and whether special sayings should be used when giving presents for various occasions.

Make a copy of the table in *Appendix 1: cultural exploration* and record the information from your interviews in Chinese. Also, include a paragraph to reflect on the differences in gifting between Chinese and your own culture. Submit the completed assignment to your teacher.

第五课　中国人到底有没有礼貌？

行为聚焦：自谦敬人

Behavior highlighted: humble oneself and exalt others

课文 *Text*

在日常生活中，中国人常常把“客气”说成“礼貌”，把“礼貌”说成“客气”，这很容易让学习汉语的外国学生产生困惑。网上曾经有一篇博文，作者是一名刚从中国回来的美国学生，题目是《中国人到底有没有礼貌？》。他说，在没去中国以前，他经常在汉语课上听老师们说中国人很客气、很有礼貌，所学的汉语课本也都是这么说的。可是到了中国以后，他感到很困惑，因为他常常看到中国人没有礼貌的行为。他举例说，在饭馆，服务员端来饭菜以后，顾客很少说“谢谢”；超市里，收银员收了顾客的钱以后，也从来不说“谢谢”“再见”什么的。还有，有些人从你的旁边走过时，即使空间很小，也不会说“借过”或“麻烦让一下”，而往往是什么都不说，侧着身子就从你的身旁“挤”过去了。可是，中国人又是非常礼貌的。比如，你刚用汉语说了一个“你好”，他们就会热情地夸奖，说你的中文很棒。他们也会当着你的面夸你长得漂亮，叫你“帅哥”或“美女”，不管实际情况是不是这样。这位美国学生最后不解地问道，“中国人到底是有礼貌还是没有礼貌？”

其实，这个问题不是一个简单的“有”或者“没有”可以回答的，因为不同文化之间的礼节不同，人们对礼貌的理解也不同。此外，“礼貌”与“客气”两个词的混用也容易让人们产生误解。“礼貌”其实不等于“客气”，“客气”也不等于“礼貌”。“客气”一定是“有礼貌”的，可是“有礼貌”并不一定就是“客气”。前面说过，客气是中国礼文化的一部分，它的内容比礼貌丰富多了。除了“尊敬”“体贴”和“礼让”以外，“客气”还包含“谦虚”“热情”“慷慨”“为别人着想”等意思。就拿“为别人着想”这个意思来说，中国人在跟别人打交道时，为了让对方高兴，经常刻意地“抬高”对方。他们不但喜欢夸奖别人，而且还常常“贬低”自己，用降低自己的方式来抬高别人。

汉语里有很多的说法都是“谦辞”或“敬辞”。前者可以用来贬低自己，后者可以用来抬高别人。这样说来，很多中国人的客气行为和说法都是客套或客套话。比如，听到别人夸奖自己时，中国人会马上说“哪里，哪里”，或者“过奖了，跟你比还差得远呢。”不过，许多这样的客套或客套话一般都是发生在双方相识的人之间，而生人之间，中国人一般显得比较冷淡。前面讲到的美国学生的困惑，也许就是这个原因吧。有位美籍华人学者曾提出，美国人讲礼貌，不懂客气；中国人讲客气，不懂礼貌。一些中国人听了以后感到非常吃惊，认为这样说不符合事实。其实，从“礼貌”和“客气”这两个词的意思来看，这位华人学者的说法也有一些道理呢。

生词 New words

简体	繁體	拼音	词性	英文翻译
1. 到底		dàodǐ	adv	(who, when, what, why, how) on earth
2. 自谦	自謙	zìqiān	v/adj	humble oneself; self-effacing, self-deprecating
3. 困惑		kùnhuò	n/adj	perplexity; perplexed, puzzled
4. 博文		bówén	n	blog post
5. 题目	題目	tímù	n	title, topic
6. 感到		gǎndào	v	feel, sense
7. 端		duān	v	hold sth level with palm(s) facing upward
8. 举例	舉例	jǔ//lì	v	give an example
9. 顾客	顧客	gùkè	n	customer
10. 收银员	收銀員	shōuyínyuán	n	cashier [收: collect, receive; 银 (bf): silver (referring to money here)]
11. 借过	借過	jièguò	phr	excuse me [used when one tries to pass someone in a crowd]
12. 侧	側	cè	v	lean on one side, turn ... sideways
13. 挤	擠	jǐ	v	force others aside, squeeze
14. 热情	熱情	rèqíng	adj/n	cordial, enthusiastic, passionate; cordialness, enthusiasm, passion
15. 棒		bàng	adj	[colloquial] good, fine, strong
16. 不解		bùjiě	adj/v	puzzled; not understand
17. 道		dào	v	say [usu. used with direct quotations in literary or formal narratives, as in问道: asked, 说道: said, 解释道: explained]
18. 理解		lǐjiě	n/v	interpretation; interpret, understand
19. 混		hùn	v	mix, confuse
20. 误解	誤解	wùjiě	n/v	misunderstanding; misunderstand
21. 等于	等於	děngyú	v	equal to, tantamount to
22. 丰富	豐富	fēngfù	adj/v	rich, plentiful, abundant; enrich

简体	繁體	拼音	词性	英文翻译
23. 包含		bāohán	v	contain, include
24. 谦虚	謙虛	qiānxū	adj/v	modest; make modest remarks
25. 慷慨		kāngkǎi	adj	generous
26. 着想	著想	zhuóxiǎng	v	be considerate, give thought (to ...) [为……着想: be considerate towards ...]
27. 打交道		dǎ jiāo.dao	phr	interact with, have dealings with
28. 刻意		kèyì	adv	deliberately, purposefully
29. 抬高		tái//gāo	v	raise, exalt
30. 贬低	貶低	biǎndī	v	belittle, disparage, play down
31. 降低		jiàngdī	v	lower, cut down, drop, reduce
32. 谦辞	謙辭	qiāncí	n	humble language [a rhetoric device, and a type of Chinese honorific]
33. 敬辞	敬辭	jìngcí	n	respectful language [a rhetoric device, and a type of Chinese honorific]
34. 前者		qiánzhě	n	the former [后者: the latter]
35. 这样说来	這樣說來	zhèyàng shuōlái	phr	putting it this way, if so
36. 过奖	過獎	guòjiǎng	v	overpraise [您过奖了: You flattered me.]
37. 冷淡		lěngdàn	adj	cold, indifferent
38. 提出		tíchū	v	put forward, raise (an issue)
39. 籍		jí	bf	native place, membership [as in 国籍 (nationality, citizenship), 美籍, 外籍]
40. 华人	華人	huárén	n	people of Chinese descent
41. 讲	講	jiǎng	v	stress, pay attention to
42. 吃惊	吃驚	chī//jīng	v	be surprised, be shocked
43. 符合		fúhé	v	conform to, tally with
44. 事实	事實	shìshí	n	fact
45. 道理		dào.lǐ	n	reason, rationality [有道理: be reasonable, be convincing]

词语与句型 Expressions and sentence patterns

1. 到底 (who, when, what, why, how) on earth

课文例句1：中国人到底有没有礼貌？
课文例句2：中国人到底是有礼貌还是没有礼貌？

The adverb 到底can be used in an "A-not-A" question (example 1), an alternative question (example 2), or a wh-question (example 3) to push for a clear and definite answer.

It is ungrammatical to use 到底in a “statement吗” question. Moreover, 到底must precede the interrogative pronoun when the interrogative pronoun serves as the subject of the question (example 3).

- 你昨天说一定会跟我们去英国旅行，今天又说不去了。你到底去不去？
- 我们没时间了，红色的和绿色的都好看，你快点儿决定吧，到底买红的还是买绿的？
- 你说你去买菜，他说他去买，到底谁去买？ (谁到底去买 is incorrect.)

2. S 所 V 的（N） that which; those who

课文例句：在没去中国以前，他经常在汉语课上听老师们说中国人很客气、很有礼貌，所学的汉语课本也都是这么说的。

所 acts as a placeholder for the subject in a subordinate clause. It calls attention to the object of the clause, and its use makes the sentence more formal in tone.

- 王教授昨天所介绍的几个文化现象各有各的特点。
- 在不同的国家，人们所关心的问题也不完全一样。

3. 刚 VP1 就 VP2 VP2 as soon as VP1

课文例句：你刚用汉语说了一个“你好”，他们就会热情地夸奖，说你的中文很棒。

❖ S刚VP1就VP2
❖ S1刚VP1，S2就VP2

- 小李刚上大四就找到工作了。
- 昨天我刚把作业做完，我妹妹就来找我了。

4. ……。（就）拿……来说，…… ... (Just) Take ... (as an example),...

课文例句：除了“尊敬”“体贴”和“礼让”以外，“客气”还包含“谦虚”“热情”“慷慨”“为别人着想”等意思。就拿“为别人着想”这个意思来说，中国人在跟别人打交道时，为了让对方高兴，经常刻意地“抬高”对方。

- 中国人现在出国旅游的越来越多了。就拿2017年来说，出国旅游人次(man-times)多达1.3亿。
- 美国有些城市有“别称(biéchēng: another name)”。拿纽约市来说，人们都知道它又叫“大苹果”。再拿芝加哥来说，人们也把它称为“风城”。

5. ……。前者……，后者…… ... The former ... ; the latter ...

课文例句：汉语里有很多的说法都是“谦辞”或“敬辞”。前者可以用来贬低自己，后者可以用来抬高别人。

- “搭(dā)车(get a lift)”和“打车”不同，前者指的是坐别人的车，后者是指坐出租车。
- 北京和上海都是大城市，但前者是中国的政治中心，而后者是中国最大的金融 (jīnróng: finance)中心。

6. 跟B比，A…… Compared with B, A ...

课文例句：听到别人夸奖自己时，中国人会马上说“哪里，哪里”，或者“过奖了，跟你比还差得远呢。”

A, the subject or topic of the main clause, may be omitted when understood (such as in the sample sentence from the text). When the predicate of the main clause is relatively short, "A" may precede "跟B比" (example 2).

- 跟英国比，美国不但更大，而且人口也更多。
- 你中文说得真好，跟中国人一样！我的中文跟你的比还是不行。

> **语言练习** To practice and reinforce what you have learned from the Text, New Words, and the section "Expressions and sentence patterns" in this lesson, please visit the companion website to download a PDF version of the exercises.

交际情景 Communication scenarios

Study the following conversations between native speakers on the textbook companion website. Use the plug-in feature to find the definitions of the new words highlighted in orange. Try to visualize the scene as you read and listen to each dialogue. Discuss your reactions to these scenario dialogues with a classmate.

1. Wang Weimin and his wife Li Aihua are hosting a dinner party for the couple Zhao Xuedong and Liu Shaohong in their house. Pay attention to how the hosts use self-deprecation to deflect compliments from the guests about the dishes prepared by Li Aihua.

刘少红：（看着桌上的菜）李姐，您一定上午就开始忙了，做了这么多菜，我们几个人哪儿吃得了啊？
李爱华：哪儿多啊，我还怕不够吃呢。还有两个菜，马上就好了。
赵学东：还有两个菜啊，这都吃不完呢。你快坐下跟我们一块儿吃吧。
李爱华：就好了，马上来。

（一会儿，李爱华也坐下来跟大家一起开始吃饭。）

李爱华：我不太会做菜，都是些家常菜，大家多吃点儿啊。
刘少红：这么多好吃的菜，李姐，您太客气了。
赵学东：（看看王为民）老王，嫂子的厨艺真好，你太有口福了。
王为民：哪儿啊，都是些家常菜，跟你爱人比，水平差远了。

思考与讨论：

1）李爱华做了很多菜。客人跟她说了什么表示他们的感谢？请最少举两个例子。
2）为什么李爱华说她"不太会做菜""都是些家常菜"等等？在你的国家，主人做饭招待客人时也会这么说吗？
3）当客人称赞李爱华的厨艺时，王为民怎么回答？你对他的反应有什么看法？

2. Wang Weimin invites Xiao Zhang (小张), a new hire in his office, to play *ping pong* on a weekend. Observe closely how Xiao Zhang responds when Wang Weimin praises his *ping pong* skills.

王为民：听说你以前是学校乒乓球队的，今天我正好跟你学几招。
小　张：那都是好多年以前的事儿了，好久不打了，我都快忘了怎么发球了。

（打完球以后）

王为民：你打得真不错呀，不愧是专业水平的。
小　张：没有没有，现在胖了，跑不动了。
王为民：你就别谦虚了，刚才那个球打得多漂亮啊！
小　张：那算是今天的运气好。
王为民：不管怎么样，我就拜你为师了。
小　张：不敢当，不敢当，我们互相学习。

思考与讨论：

1）请解释“跟你学几招”“拜你为师”“不敢当”是什么意思。
2）王为民怎么称赞小张的球技？请最少举三个例子。
3）王为民称赞小张时，小张是怎么回应的？请最少举三个例子。
4）在你的国家，听到别人称赞时，人们一般会怎么回答？

3. Along with Ms. Li, Ms. Liu and her daughter Zhao Jing pay a New Year's visit to Ms. Qian. Pay attention to what Ms. Qian, Ms. Liu, and Ms. Li say when they praise each other's child and how they respond to the praise about their own child.

赵　静：钱阿姨过年好！
钱阿姨：刘姐，这是您女儿小静吧，越长越漂亮了，还这么懂事！
刘阿姨：（看看女儿）还说呢，越大越不听话了。还是你们家文文好，又聪明又用功，还是美国名牌大学的高材生。
文　文：刘阿姨过奖了。小静以后肯定也能金榜题名。
刘阿姨：她不像你那么让人放心，也不像人家李姐的儿子那么优秀，人家不但上的是名校，而且还没毕业就已经在一家世界500强公司找到实习工作了。
李阿姨：唉，别提了，上名校有什么好的，整天忙得要死，也不注意身体，忙的时候连饭都没时间吃。

思考与讨论：

1）钱阿姨夸奖刘阿姨的女儿小静时，刘阿姨为什么要说小静越大越不听话了？
2）刘阿姨夸奖钱阿姨的女儿文文时，为什么要提到李阿姨的儿子呢？
3）李阿姨真的觉得自己的儿子上名校不好吗？她为什么这么说？
4）别人在你父母面前夸奖你时，你父母一般会怎么说？

言语行为例说 Notes on discourse behavior

1. 对话例句：刘少红：（看着桌上的菜）李姐，您一定上午就开始忙了，做了这么多菜，我们几个人哪儿吃得了啊？
李爱华：哪儿多啊，我还怕不够吃呢。还有两个菜，马上就好了。

When Chinese people host a dinner party, they will often make or order more food than is needed. Making or ordering just enough food for everyone eating is considered stingy behavior. Though Chinese people may sound as if they are complaining when they say that they cannot eat everything, they are actually praising the host's generous hospitality. The host will often respond with “不多、不多” (“Not too much, not at all too much.”) or “哪儿多啊” (“Why would you think this is too much?”). The same is true when receiving presents.

Though a recipient may sound like if one is blaming the giver, that person is actually expressing appreciation.

- 甲：你点了这么多菜啊，太客气了，我们也吃不完啊。
  乙：没事儿，不多不多，这些菜都是这家饭馆儿的特色菜。你们跑了这么远来看我，一定要多吃点儿。
- 甲：小王，你来就来吧，怎么买东西啊？
  乙：阿姨，没买什么，只是一点水果，您慢慢吃。

2. 对话例句1：赵学东：（看看王为民）老王，嫂子的厨艺真好，你太有口福了。
   对话例句2：王为民：你打得真不错呀，不愧是专业水平的。
   对话例句3：钱阿姨：刘姐，这是您女儿小静吧，越长越漂亮了，还这么懂事！
   对话例句4：刘阿姨：……还是你们家文文好，又聪明又用功，还是美国名牌大学的高材生。
   对话例句5：刘阿姨：……人家不但上的是名校，而且还没毕业就已经在一家世界500强公司找到实习工作了。

Chinese people often demonstrate their regard by complimenting the other party. They often praise the children of the other party for being obedient (听话), responsible (懂事), studious (学习好), etc. To praise the children is actually meant as a compliment to the parent. Whether present or not, women are often praised in front of their husbands for being beautiful (漂亮), an ideal housewife in temperament and in capability (贤惠/贤慧: xiánhuì), or talented in cooking (厨艺好). Men are often praised in front of their wives for having the capacity to do great things (有本事), being capable (工作好/能干), making a good salary (收入高), and so on. As with the children, praising the person's spouse is actually meant as a compliment to that person.

- 甲：小王你真有福气，你看你老公又能干，收入又高，还在世界500强的大公司工作，我们几个人真羡慕你。
  乙：你们别开玩笑了，他哪有你们说的这么好！
- 甲：今天上午你儿子的报告做得真棒，不愧是从美国名校毕业的。
  乙：你过奖了，他还需要多练习。

3. 对话例句1：李爱华：我不太会做菜，都是些家常菜，大家多吃点儿啊。
   对话例句2：李爱华：哪儿多啊，我还怕不够吃呢。
   对话例句3：王为民：哪儿啊，都是些家常菜，跟你爱人比，水平差远了。
   对话例句4：小　张：那都是好多年以前的事儿了，好久不打了，我都快忘了怎么发球了。
   对话例句5：小　张：没有没有，现在胖了，跑不动了。
   对话例句6：小　张：那算是今天的运气好。
   对话例句7：小　张：不敢当，不敢当，我们互相学习。

A Chinese person will usually respond to praise in a self-deprecating manner. Common responses include "哪里哪里" (Where do you see that?), "哪儿……啊？" (Not at all), "比……差远了" (I'm so much worse than so-and-so), "不敢当" (I wouldn't dare), "运气

好" (Just lucky) "我不太会verb" (I don't really know how to ...), "过奖了" (you flatter me), "好久/好长时间不verb了，都忘了怎么verb了" (I haven't ... in a while and have almost forgotten how to do it), etc. In summary, the principle for Chinese people when interacting with others is to present a humble self while exalting the other party. Having said that, however, younger Chinese have been increasingly influenced by western customs, and it has become common for them to respond to a compliment by simply thanking the other party.

- 甲：这是你画的画吗？画得太好了，我看你都可以办画展了。
  乙：哪儿好啊？好久不画，我都忘了怎么画了。
- 甲：张教授，谢谢您给我们做的这个报告。我认为在中国您是这个专业中最有成就的教授，您的书对学生的影响也最大。
  乙：不敢当，不敢当。我的研究还有很多不足，欢迎大家批评。

4. 对话例句：刘阿姨：她不像你那么让人放心，也不像人家李姐的儿子那么优秀，人家不但上的是名校，而且还没毕业就已经在一家世界500强公司找到实习工作了。
   李阿姨：<u>唉，别提了</u>，上名校有什么好的，整天忙得要死，也不注意身体，忙的时候连饭都没时间吃。

"别提了" means "don't even mention it" or "let's not talk about it" (see the first example below). A common follow-up to this expands upon some circumstance that failed to live up to expectations. For example, in Dialogue 3, when Ms. Liu compliments Ms. Li's son for attending a top-ranking school, Ms. Li responds by recounting some of her son's shortcomings. She uses the phrase "别提了" not to refute Ms. Liu or to drop the topic but to display modesty.

- 甲：昨天下午的考试考得怎么样？
  乙：别提了，前天晚上没睡好，结果昨天下午考试的时候我都快睡着了，有的题没做完。
- 甲：老张，听说你儿子去美国做交换生了，真是太优秀了。
  乙：唉，别提了，我儿子说在美国每天都得读很多书，他天天待在图书馆，有时候都没时间睡觉。

体演情景 Perform the scenario

Select a dialogue from this section and listen to its recording several times. Imitate the speakers in pronunciation, intonation and discourse behavior in terms of both the words they use and the ways in which they carry themselves. Memorize the dialogue for performance in class.

跨文化交际 Cross-cultural communication

一、误解分析 Situation analysis

Break into groups and discuss the misunderstanding in each of the cross-cultural communication incidents below. For each incident, the group should generate an answer that best explains the cultural assumptions behind the ways in which the individuals say and do things. In addition, discuss possible strategies to avoid these misunderstandings in similar situations.

（一）艾杰森上中文课的时候听他的老师说，中国是“礼仪之邦”，到了中国一定要懂礼貌。可是艾杰森真的到了中国以后，发现有些事情跟老师说的不一样。比如，进商场的时候，他很有礼貌地给后面的人让门，可是很多人连“谢谢”都不说就过去了。再比如，在公交车上，有好几次他看到车上有空位，正想走过去坐下，没想到马上就有人抢先一步坐下了。可奇怪的是，他的中国同学对他总是很客气，而且每次看到老师也都会低头问好。这些现象让艾杰森很困惑，他不明白为什么中国人有的时候很讲礼貌，可是有的时候又好像什么礼貌都不讲。

思考与讨论：

1) 艾杰森为什么感到困惑？中国人有礼貌还是没有礼貌呢？
2) 如果你在中国，碰到人们上车抢座位，你会怎么办？

（二）学校请了国内著名的文学家周光教授来做一场有关明清小说的讲座。艾杰森早就听说过周教授的大名，所以那天早早地就来到了会场。讲座开始了，主持人花了很长时间介绍了周教授丰富的学术成果，可是周教授做开场白的时候却说，自己对今天要讲的课题研究得还很不够，希望大家对他的讲座多做批评。大家听了周教授的话好像没什么特别的反应，可是艾杰森觉得很奇怪，他不理解为什么像周教授这样的专家还会说自己的研究做得很不够，如果是这样，学校为什么要请他来做讲座呢？

思考与讨论：

1) 艾杰森觉得很奇怪，你能理解吗？为什么学校请周教授来做讲座，可是他却说自己对要讲的课题研究得还很不够？
2) 如果有人请你给中国人做一个讲座，你的开场白要说什么？

（三）艾杰森刚到中国的时候特别紧张，常常担心自己的中文不好，说错了话被别人笑话。可是他的中国朋友们都常常夸他，特别是周强。每当艾杰森说中文的时候，周强都说他说得好、说得地道。一年以后，艾杰森觉得自己的中文进步非常大，也越来越自信了，可是让他不理解的是，同学们不再常夸他了，周强有时候还会拿他的小错误开个玩笑。艾杰森觉得很困惑，他想：我现在的中文明明比以前好多了，可是我的中国朋友们为什么不但不夸我了，还开我的玩笑？

思考与讨论：

1) 你能帮艾杰森解除他的困惑吗？
2) 如果你的中国朋友也拿你说中文的小错误跟你开玩笑，你会生气吗？为什么？

（四）张莉莉得了全市大学生英文演讲比赛的冠军。回到学校后，同学们都祝贺她，并称赞她的英语水平。有的同学甚至跟她说：“你的英语真地道，说得跟美国人一样”。张莉莉说：“哪有啊？你这么说我都不好意思了。”这位同学说：“你不信，那我们问问我们的美国同学艾杰森。杰森，你说呢？”杰森说：“是啊，莉莉，你说得确实很地道，没有口音，音调也特别好。”张莉莉好像更不信了，说：“我哪有你说的那么好？你过奖了，杰森。”杰森听了以后一下子怔住了，不知道再说什么好。

思考与讨论：

1) 杰森为什么怔住不知说什么好了？张莉莉为什么要否定杰森的意见呢？
2) 如果你是杰森，听到张莉莉对你说的话以后，你应该怎么回答？

二、口语交际练习 Oral communication exercises

1. 角色扮演 Role play

   Pair up with a peer and refer to one of the critical incidents in *Situation analysis* to create a five-minute skit with a similar storyline. Use new vocabulary and speech patterns that you have learned from this lesson in your skit. Perform the dialogue in class and discuss whether each skit properly reflects typical Chinese discourse behavior.

2. 思考与讨论 Reflection and discussion

   第一题：在人际交往中，中国人往往在不同的场合(chǎnghé: occasion)有不同的客套和客套话。客套话不仅是一种说话的礼节，也能拉近人与人之间的关系。请(i) 查找并用中文解释下列客套话的意思和用法；(ii) 与你自己母语文化里的客套或客套话做比较，看看中国人说这些客套话时的原因和场合有什么相同或不同的地方; (iii) 与全班同学一起讨论你的发现和想法。

客套话	中文意思与用法	与你母语文化里的客套和客套话做比较
麻烦您……		
贵姓		
久仰(jiǔyǎng)		
慢走		
留步(liúbù)		
恭喜(gōngxǐ)		
您破费(pòfèi)了		
打扰(dǎrǎo)您一下		
拜托(bàituō)		
请多指教(zhǐjiào)		
您过奖了		

第二题：下面的例子代表了中国人一般的行为。 根据这些例子，谈谈你对中国人礼貌观念的理解。

- 跟朋友一起打车时，抢着坐前面的位子，下车时付钱。
- 跟家人、朋友或同事聚餐时, 把上座让给年纪比较大或地位比较高的人。
- 跟朋友在餐馆聚餐后，抢着付钱。
- 别人称赞自己时，一定要表示谦虚。
- 在饭馆吃饭时，大声招呼(zhāohu: call out to)服务员过来。
- 去别人家做客时一定要带礼物。

- 请别人来家里做客时，得多做几道菜。
- 进出商场、饭店或其他公共场所时，不必为走在你后面的陌生人(mòshēng rén: stranger)拉门。

三、写作 Composition

1. 作文题目：中国人的"礼"

   在第四课的课文里，我们学到中国人常把自己的国家称为"礼仪之邦"，而且有着"不学礼，无以立""礼多人不怪"等观念。在第五课中我们又学到了"客气"跟"礼貌"的差别，而且学了许多中国人自谦敬人的说法和做法。请你用3–4段话写出下面的内容：

   (1) 根据这两课的内容总结(zǒngjié: sum up)一下中国人"礼"的观念。"礼"都包含哪些内容？它的目的是什么？

   (2) 请你举2–3个例子说明中国人的礼貌和西方人的礼貌有什么相同和不同的地方。

   尽量 (jǐnliàng: as much as possible) 用本课的词语和句型：到底/ S所V的（N）/ 刚VP1就VP2 / (就) 拿……来说 / …… 前者……，后者…… / 跟B比，A……

2. 文化探索 Cultural exploration: For learners who are currently studying or working in the target culture.

"中国人的礼貌是什么？" Explore this question by doing 2–3 activities, such as taking a bus ride, shopping at a store, asking directions, or dining out in a Chinese restaurant. Observe how Chinese people interact with friends and acquaintances and contrast that with how they treat strangers in public spaces. Take note of their attitude, mannerisms, body language (including facial expressions), as well as the words they use when speaking. Note also their age, gender and attire. Make a copy of the table in *Appendix 1: cultural exploration* and fill in, in Chinese, the information that you gather. Also, write a paragraph to reflect on the information that you collect. When complete, submit both parts to your teacher.

第三单元 **Unit three**

文化视角：贵和思想

Cultural perspective: harmony orientation

第六课　礼之用，和为贵

行为聚焦：以和为贵
Behavior highlighted: harmony as priority

课文 *Text*

《论语》里说："礼之用，和为贵。"意思是说，礼的作用在于它能调节人与人之间的关系，使人们和睦相处，使社会和谐发展。中国文化自古以来就崇尚和谐。不仅儒家思想以和为贵，道家和其他的哲学思想也是这样。如果说儒家重视的是人与人、人与社会之间的和谐，那么道家更多关心的是人与自然的和谐共处。

和谐是中国人的世界观和最重要的价值观，也是中国人做人做事所遵守的基本原则。2008年北京奥运会开幕式上有这样一幕，令许多人至今难忘：扮演孔子三千弟子的演员们，用5897块字盘变换着不同字体的"和"字。他们通过这个汉字的历史演变，向全世界观众展示了中国文化传统中源远流长的和谐思想。

中国人有很多关于和谐的观念和说法：家庭方面的有"家和万事兴"；外交方面的有"和平共处"；经济方面的有"和气生财"；军事方面的有"天时地利人和"。"和"字的使用非常广泛，包括和气、和睦、和平、和好等。汉语里含有"和"字的成语也很多，比如和蔼可亲、心平气和，等等。这些都体现了中国人对和谐的追求，也反映了中国人的行为往往会受到以和为贵思想的影响。

中国土地面积广大，但是人口众多，生活资源相对有限。此外，中国人的人际关系主要是一种熟人关系，礼让和客气也主要发生在双方相识的人之间。由于这些原因，人们在中国常常可以看到有些人买东西时不排队，公共汽车上抢座位，公共场所抽烟和大声讲话等。在西方社会，这些行为都会被认为侵犯了他人的利益或空间，因此会引起他人的反感和批评。而在中国，人们对这些行为却表现出了极大的宽容和忍让。研究跨文化教育的Caryn Voskuil教授在她的《水与木：中国人的社会行为》一文中，用"木头"比喻西方人不忍让的行为，用"水"比喻中国人的妥协态度。Voskuil教授也许不知道，"水"正是中国和谐文化的高度象征。老子说："上善若水"。他还说，水造福万物而不与它们相争。中国人崇尚水的态度，主张遇到不顺心的事时要忍让。不过，令人遗憾的是，在经济发展越来越快、社会发展越来越不平衡的今天，人与人之间、特别是生人之间的矛盾和冲突也经常发生。

生词 New words

简体	繁體	拼音	词性	英文翻译
1. 礼之用，和为贵	禮之用，和為貴	lǐ zhī yòng, hé wéi guì		In practicing the rules of propriety, a natural ease is to be prized. [from *Analects of Confucius*; trans. James Legge]
2. 以和为贵	以和為貴	yǐhé-wéiguì	idiom	regard harmony as the most important [和 (n): harmony; 贵 (bf): highly valued]
3. 作用		zuòyòng	n	function, effect
4. 在于	在於	zàiyú	v	lie in, rest with, depend on
5. 调节	調節	tiáojié	v	adjust, regulate
6. 和睦		hémù	adj	harmonious [often interpersonal or familial]
7. 相处	相處	xiāngchǔ	v	get along [共处: co-exist]
8. 和谐	和諧	héxié	adj/n	harmonious [often international or societal]; harmony
9. 自古		zìgǔ	adv	since ancient times
10. 哲学	哲學	zhéxué	n	philosophy
11. 自然		zìrán	n/adj	nature, natural world; natural
12. 观	觀	guān	bf	outlook [世界观: worldview; 价值观: values]
13. 遵守		zūnshǒu	v	abide by, observe
14. 原则	原則	yuánzé	n	principle
15. 开幕式	開幕式	kāimùshì	n	opening ceremony [幕: curtain, screen]
16. 令		lìng	v	cause, make (something to happen) [more formal than 让 and 使]
17. 至今		zhìjīn	adv	to this day, up until now, as yet
18. 扮演		bànyǎn	v	play part of
19. 弟子		dìzǐ	n	disciple
20. 字盘	字盤	zìpán	n	type case
21. 变换	變換	biànhuàn	v	vary, alternate
22. 字体	字體	zìtǐ	n	calligraphic style, typeface, font
23. 演变	演變	yǎnbiàn	v	evolve, develop
24. 全		quán	adj/adv	entire, complete; entirely, completely [全世界: the whole world]
25. 观众	觀眾	guānzhòng	n	audience, spectators

简体	繁體	拼音	词性	英文翻译
26. 展示		zhǎnshì	v	reveal, display, show, exhibit
27. 源远流长	源遠流長	yuányuǎn-liúcháng	idiom	[of tradition, history, etc.] go back to the distant past, long-standing and well-established
28. 家和万事兴	家和萬事興	jiā hé wànshì xīng	idiom	Harmony in the family leads to prosperity in all undertakings. [万事: all things; 兴: prosper]
29. 外交		wàijiāo	n	diplomacy, foreign affairs
30. 和平	和平	hépíng	n	peace
31. 和气生财	和氣生財	hé.qi shēngcái	idiom	Geniality brings wealth. [和气: geniality; 生: generate; 财 (bf): wealth]
32. 军事	軍事	jūnshì	n	military affairs
33. 天时地利人和	天時地利人和	tiānshí dìlì rénhé	idiom	opportune time, advantageous terrain, popular support [origin: *Mencius*]
34. 包括		bāokuò	v	include
35. 和好		héhǎo	v	restore good relations, become reconciled
36. 和蔼可亲	和藹可親	hé'ǎi kěqīn	idiom	affable, genial
37. 心平气和	心平氣和	xīnpíng-qìhé	idiom	even-tempered and good-humored
38. 体现	體現	tǐxiàn	v	embody, give expression to
39. 土地		tǔdì	n	land, soil, territory
40. 面积	面積	miànjī	n	surface area
41. 资源	資源	zīyuán	n	resources
42. 相对	相對	xiāngduì	adj	relative [绝(jué)对: absolute]
43. 有限		yǒuxiàn	adj	limited, finite [无(wú)限: unlimited, infinite]
44. 熟人		shúrén	n	acquaintance [生人: stranger]
45. 抢	搶	qiǎng	v	fight over, snatch, loot
46. 场所	場所	chǎngsuǒ	n	venue, place
47. 反感		fǎn'gǎn	n/adj	dislike, antipathy; disgusted with
48. 宽容	寬容	kuānróng	v	tolerate, pardon
49. 忍让	忍讓	rěnràng	v	be conciliatory, exercise forbearance
50. 木头	木頭	mù.tou	n	wood, log, timber
51. 比喻		bǐyù	v/n	draw analogy; metaphor, analogy

简体	繁體	拼音	词性	英文翻译
52. 妥协	妥協	tuǒxié	v	compromise, come to terms
53. 态度	態度	tài.dù	n	attitude
54. 正		zhèng	adv	precisely
55. 高度		gāodù	adj/n	high-degree; height
56. 象征	象徵	xiàngzhēng	n/v	symbol, emblem; symbolize
57. 上善若水		shàng shàn ruò shuǐ		The highest excellence is like (that of) water. [from *Tao Te Ching*; trans. by James Legge]
58. 造福		zàofú	v	bring benefit to (society, people, things, etc.)
59. 万物	萬物	wànwù	n	all things in the universe
60. 争	爭	zhēng	v	contend, vie for, strive for [与⋯⋯ 相争: contend with ...]
61. 主张	主張	zhǔzhāng	v/n	advocate, maintain; proposition, position
62. 顺心	順心	shùn//xīn	adj	things going as one hopes, satisfactory
63. 遗憾	遺憾	yíhàn	adj/n	regretful; regret, pity
64. 平衡		pínghéng	adj/n/v	balanced; equilibrium, balance; balance
65. 矛盾		máodùn	n/adj	contradiction; contradictory
66. 冲突	衝突	chōngtū	n/v	clash; conflict

专有名词 Proper nouns

简体	繁體	拼音	英文翻译
1. 论语	論語	Lúnyǔ	*The Analects* ["edited conversations" literally], a collection of sayings and ideas attributed to Confucius and his contemporaries, including his disciples.
2. 道家		Dàojiā	Daoist School of the Warring States Period (475–221 BC) based on the teachings of Laozi or Lao Tze [老子, c. 6th century BC] and Zhuangzi or Chuang Tzu [庄子, 369–286 BC]
3. 奥运会	奥運會	Àoyùnhuì	Olympics [short for 奥林匹克运动会: Àolínpǐkè Yùndònghuì, Olympic Games]

词语与句型 Expressions and sentence patterns

1. 以 A 为 B　　regard A as B; take A as B; use A as B

课文例句：不仅儒家思想以和为贵，道家和其他的哲学思想也是这样。

"以 A 为 B" is a construction from classical Chinese that is still often found in formal writing and speech. Many four-character phrases are formed with this construction. For example:

❖ 以和为贵: regard harmony as the most important
❖ 以食为天: view food as the primary need
❖ 以民为本: put people first
❖ 以退为进: advance by retreating

This structure is also commonly used in the following patterns:

❖ 以……为主 consider ... as the main focus
❖ 以……为目标 take ... as the goal
❖ 以……为中心 regard ... as the center

- 自古以来，中国的老百姓就以食为天，认为能吃饱饭是最重要的事情。
- 不论政府制定什么样的政策 (zhèngcè: policy)，都要以民为本，这样才能得到人民的支持。
- 虽然打工能帮助大学生减轻经济负担，可是上学期间大学生还是应该以学习为主。
- 只有以经济发展为目标，才能让更多普通人过上好日子。

2. ……以来 since ...

课文例句：中国文化自古以来就崇尚和谐。

以来 is used to indicate the passage of time. It is generally preceded by an estimate of the amount of time that has passed (example 1), a reference to a past event (example 2), or a reference to a specific time in the past (example 3). 以来 can be accompanied by 自 or 自从。

- 两千多年以来，儒家思想一直影响着中国人和中国社会。
- 自从北京举办奥运会以来，想了解中国和中国文化的外国人越来越多了。
- 自 1978 年以来，中国社会和中国人的生活都发生了很大变化—那一年，中国开始改革开放 (gǎigé kāifàng: reform and open-up)。

3. 因此 therefore

课文例句：在西方社会，这些行为都会被认为侵犯了他人的利益或空间，因此会引起他人的反感和批评。

因此 literally means "because of this," and is used more frequently in formal writing or speech. The subject for the result clause can either precede or follow 因此 (example 1 and 2 below). However, when understood from the context, the subject of the result clause can be omitted (example 3: the subject 中国人 is omitted).

❖ ……，因此 (S) VP。
❖ ……，(S) 因此 VP。

- 中国人口众多，因此自然资源相对有限。
- 在中国，有的红绿灯给行人过马路的时间很短，很多人因此成为了闯灯大军中的一员。
- 中国人一般都很重视教育，因此都比较关心孩子的学习。

4. 正 precisely

课文例句：研究跨文化教育的Voskuil教授在她的《水与木：中国人的社会行为》一文中，用“木头”比喻西方人不忍让的行为，用“水”比喻中国人的妥协态度。Voskuil教授也许不知道，“水”正是中国和谐文化的高度象征。

When used as an adverb to strengthen the affirmative tone, 正 calls attention to the validity or truth of the assertion in a sentence.

- 中国文化的特点有哪些？正如易中天教授所说，中国文化最根本的特点就是群体意识。
- 在纽约市可以看到不同文化的影响，也可以吃到世界各地的美食，这正是很多人喜欢这座城市的主要原因。

5. ……的是……

课文例句：中国人崇尚水的态度，提倡遇到不顺心的事时要忍让。不过，令人遗憾的是，在经济发展越来越快、社会发展越来越不平衡的今天，人与人之间、特别是生人之间的矛盾和冲突也经常发生。

This construction acts as a shortened reference to something that has been raised earlier, allowing the speaker to introduce a direction for the discussion without having to repeat everything that preceded it. The “……的” portion of the construction is very versatile and can be completed with nouns, adjectives, verbs, as well as short complete sentences.

This structure is used in the following patterns:

- 令 someone + V 的是 what makes someone V is
- 让 someone + V 的是 what makes someone V is
- 受 someone + V 的是 what is V-ed by someone is

- 2010年以后，这个大学变化非常大，令人高兴的是学生们可以在全新的教室里上课了。
- 在北京，从2015年6月1日开始，在室内和一些室外公共场所都不许抽烟了。但让人生气的是，还是有人会在这些地方抽烟。
- 云南的不少小城都很有特点，其中最受游客欢迎的是大理。

> 语言练习 To practice and reinforce what you have learned from the Text, New Words, and the section “Expressions and sentence patterns” in this lesson, please visit the companion website to download a PDF version of the exercises.

交际情景 Communication scenarios

Study the following conversations between native speakers on the textbook companion website. Use the plug-in feature to find the definitions of the new words highlighted in orange.

Try to visualize the scene as you read and listen to each dialogue. Discuss your reactions to these scenario dialogues with a classmate.

1. The Wang family are having a family reunion dinner on the eve of Spring Festival, the Chinese New Year, to celebrate the holiday. Note how they propose toasts and express gratitude for each other.

王大伟：爷爷奶奶、爸爸妈妈，今天晚上是大年夜，我先来敬你们一杯，祝大家新年快乐！

李爱华：对，爸妈，我们俩也祝您二老身体健康。来，干杯！

（大家把酒喝下。）

奶　奶：这一年呀，咱们家的日子能过得这么红火，全靠为民和爱华。你们又要照顾我们和大伟，又要上班，真不容易。大伟也是好孩子，有时间就陪我和爷爷。

王为民：妈，看您说的，孝敬您二老不都是应该的嘛。我倒是觉得最辛苦的是爱华，她今年放弃了升职，就是为了多照顾家里，让我能在外面安心工作。来，老婆，我也敬你一杯。

（王为民敬了李爱华一杯酒。李爱华有点儿不好意思地喝下了。）

李爱华：都是一家人，说这些话干嘛呀？来，爸妈吃菜。

（李爱华给爸爸妈妈夹菜。）

思考与讨论：

1) 这个家庭是不是很和睦？对话中哪些行为和语言能表现出"家和万事兴"的观念来？
2) 根据这段对话，你可以看出中国人认为"家和"最重要吗？在你的国家有这样的观念吗？

2. Wang Weimin works at the Beijing office of a multinational corporation. His office plans to transfer an employee to its New York headquarters. However, Wang Weimin decided not to compete for this rare opportunity for professional development, surprising his colleague Zhao Xuedong. As you read the passage, identify the considerations that prompted Wang Weimin to make this decision.

赵学东：为民，听说你们部门今年要派一个人到纽约总部工作。我看一定是你。论专业，谁都比不了你。

王为民：这次机会是挺难得的，在总部一年比在国内三年学到的东西都要多。不过……，我没申请。

赵学东：你怎么没申请呢？这么好的机会放弃了多可惜啊！

王为民：我们部门有好几个比我早来的同事也想申请。他们工作都挺好的，我们关系也不错，没必要为了竞争弄得不愉快。都是在一个公司上班的，以和为贵嘛。

赵学东：说的也是，没事儿，以后你肯定还会有机会。

思考与讨论：

1) 王为民觉得这次去纽约的机会怎么样？但他为什么没申请？他担心什么？
2) 在你的国家，人们一般会不会为了别的同事放弃一个提高自己的机会？为什么？

3. Li Aihua is buying some red dates sold by a street vendor. Observe what the vendor says to please her other than giving her a good deal on the dates. Think about the reasons from cultural perspectives behind the conversation tactics used by the vendor and their effects on the customer.

李爱华：老板，你这个红枣怎么卖啊？
小　贩：十块钱一斤。大姐，您要是买五斤，算您九块五。
李爱华：能不能便宜点儿啊？
小　贩：我这是最好的新疆大红枣，您去别的店看看，他们都卖十五一斤呢。
李爱华：行，那给我来五斤。
小　贩：（一边称一边说）大姐，您看您气色这么好，皮肤也好，您今年最多四十吧？
李爱华：你可真会说话，我都快五十了。
小　贩：一点儿都看不出来，您真年轻。来，姐，这是您五斤枣。我再给您多抓一把。
李爱华：你真会做生意。
小　贩：（笑着对李爱华说）您慢走，以后常来！

思考与讨论：

1) 对话里哪些语言和行为表现出了"和气生财"的观念？请举例子说明。
2) 你觉得李爱华以后会再来这位小贩这儿买东西吗？为什么？

言语行为例说 Notes on discourse behavior

1. 对话例句1：王大伟：爷爷奶奶、爸爸妈妈，今天晚上是大年夜，我先来敬你们一杯，祝大家新年快乐！
李爱华：对，爸妈，我们俩也祝您二老身体健康。来，干杯！

对话例句2：王为民：……来，老婆，我也敬你一杯。
李爱华：都是一家人，说这些话干嘛呀？来，爸妈吃菜。

Toasting with alcohol is a common phenomenon at meals and banquets in China. To make a toast, the toaster usually must first name the person to be toasted, and then say "我敬你 / 您一杯" ("I propose a toast to you."). If the toaster means to toast all of the guests, s/he can say "我敬大家一杯" ("Here is a toast to everyone."). Following that statement, the toaster can express her/his appreciation, thanks or well wishes. The frequency of toasts at a Chinese banquet is much higher than that at a Western banquet. In addition, toasters would even get up and walk over to the seat of the person to be toasted and make a toast. Through these common acts, friends eating at the table become friendlier and the general atmosphere at a meal or banquet more harmonious.

- 甲：老王，我敬你一杯，你平时总是帮我、教我，我从你那儿学到了很多。干杯！
  乙：看你说的，咱们都是朋友了，你还这么客气。来，干杯。
- 甲：咱们公司今年的工作做得非常好，我敬大家一杯，谢谢大家一年来的努力。来，干杯。
  大家：谢谢张经理，干杯。

2. 对话例句：王大伟：爷爷奶奶、爸爸妈妈，今天晚上是大年夜，我先来敬你们一杯，祝大家新年快乐！
李爱华：对，爸妈，我们俩也祝您二老身体健康。来，干杯！

干杯 literally means “bottoms up.” As a set phrase, 干杯is often used similarly as the English phrase “cheers” without indicating that one must finish his drink completely. 干 is also used by itself, meaning drain the glass so nothing is left. There is a popular Chinese assumption, particularly in Northern China, that the more one drinks, the more one shows sincerity or respect for the other. Because of this popular assumption, it is common to see someone at a meal offer to empty his glass all at once, while asking the other party to do as he pleases (我先干为敬，你随意). Depending on the familiarity between the two parties, one can also urge the other to drink and demand that the latter drain his glass with the saying “干了，干了 (“Drink it up!”)”. Social and particularly business drinking in China can be seen to be excessive. However, depending on the circumstances, not everyone cares about how much the other party drinks, and under such circumstances there is little or no pressure on one to finish one’s drink completely. If the person being toasted can’t or doesn’t want to finish the drink, he can simply say“我喝不了了,” “我实在喝不了(“I can’t drink anymore.”),” or “再喝(我)就醉了(“Anymore and I’ll be drunk.”).”

- 甲：李经理，我先干为敬，您随意。
  乙：王经理，多谢您这么多年在生意上的照顾。您敬我，我怎么能不干？干杯。
- 甲：小王，大家都干了，你怎么没干啊？快干了。
  乙：不行了，我实在喝不了了，再喝就要醉了。明天早上还要早起上班呢。

3. 对话例句：奶　奶：……咱们家的日子能过得这么红火，全靠为民和爱华……
王为民：妈，看您说的，孝敬您二老不都是应该的嘛。

Disagreeing with what others have said may bring about unpleasant feelings. However, “看您/你说的” serves the function of disagreement without necessarily incurring bad feelings. On the contrary, it is often true that it may carry positive undertones depending on the circumstances. The implied meaning of“看您/你说的” is that the actual circumstance is nothing like what one has said. To respond with “看您/你说的” when being complimented means that the speaker does not think that he merits the compliment (at least he acts this way), and only uses these words as a way to express modesty. When discussing a negative event or unlucky circumstance for the other party, using “看您/你说的” as a response can comfort the other party by expressing the speaker’s view the actual circumstance is not as bad as it sounds.

- 甲：嫂子，你的厨艺真好，我看你都可以自己开一个饭馆儿了。
  乙：看你说的，都是家常菜，哪有那么好。爱吃的话就常来家里吃饭。
- 甲：我看这次升职是没有什么希望了。新来的两个研究生，专业比我好。
  乙：看你说的，也太悲观了。他们虽然是研究生，但是你比他们有经验啊。

4. 对话例句：赵学东：你怎么没申请呢？这么好的机会放弃了多可惜啊！
王为民：我们部门有好几个比我早来的同事也想申请。他们工作都挺好的，我们关系也不错，没必要为了竞争弄得不愉快。都是在一个公司上班的，以和为贵嘛。

Having a good long-term relationship is often viewed more important than a temporary personal gain or win, and so when a conflict occurs, such as an argument due to a difference of opinions, an individual may choose to back off, often by citing the expression "没有必要/不值得为了……弄得不愉快" ("There is no need/it's not worth it to make things unpleasant because of ..."), in order to preserve harmony in the relationship. If a third party is mediating, this person may often say "算了" ("Stop here."), "少说一句吧" ("Say no more.") and cite "(以)和为贵" "和气生财" as a reason for the two people in conflict to back off.

- 甲：奶奶，隔壁李阿姨又把垃圾放在我们家门口了。
  乙：算了，都是邻居，以和为贵嘛。不值得为了这一点儿小事弄得不愉快。
- 甲：开会的时候你怎么说是我把材料搞错了呢？你这样说太不负责任了。
  乙：不是你，那是谁？这些材料都是你一个人做的。我看，是你太不负责任了吧。
  丙：你们俩不要吵了，都少说一句吧。大家在一起工作要以和为贵，不值得为了这一点儿小事弄得不愉快。

5. 对话例句：小　贩：（一边称一边说）大姐，您看您气色这么好，皮肤也好，您今年最多四十吧？
   李爱华：你可真会说话，我都快五十了。

会说话 ("to know the right thing to say") describes a person who is able to establish or maintain a harmonious relationship with others by saying things in a tactful manner, as exemplified by the peddler in Dialogue 3 who complimented Li Aihua on looking younger than her actual age. Being fluent in the Chinese social code requires knowledge of the strategies that are considered to be part of 会说话, such as knowing how to take cues from somebody's words and facial expressions, avoiding direct criticism of someone or something whenever possible, knowing how to decline something in a tactful manner, etc. If you can master these tactics, you are considered to be 会说话; otherwise, you are judged to be 不会说话.

- 甲：我最近不知道怎么了，一下胖了六七斤。
  乙：哪有啊？一点儿都看不出来，还是跟以前一样苗条，你顶多一百斤吧。
  甲：你可真会说话。
- 甲：白云，我上次给你买的英语书你看了吗？
  乙：表姐，你那是什么破书啊？里面好多错误，我如果用那本书学英语，肯定考不好。
  丙：你这个孩子真不会说话，表姐给你买书是为了你好，快跟表姐说对不起。

体演情景 Perform the scenario

Select a dialogue from this section and listen to its recording several times. Imitate the speakers in pronunciation, intonation and discourse behavior in terms of both the words they use and the ways in which they carry themselves. Memorize the dialogue for performance in class.

跨文化交际 Cross-cultural communication

一、误解分析 Situation analysis

Break into groups and discuss the misunderstanding in each of the cross-cultural communication incidents below. For each incident, the group should generate an answer that best explains the cultural assumptions behind the ways in which the individuals say and do things. In addition, discuss possible strategies to avoid these misunderstandings in similar situations.

（一）艾杰森和同学张莉莉一起去饭馆儿吃饭。刚坐好就发现旁边一桌人一边抽烟一边聊天。艾杰森跟张莉莉说："我的中文不太好，你能不能跟他们说请他们别抽烟了？我真受不了这烟味儿，再说他们那桌还有孩子呢。"张莉莉站起来，在饭馆里看了一圈，然后对艾杰森说："我们换到门口那个位子吧。那儿有风，而且离他们远点儿。"艾杰森还是有点儿不高兴，他觉得在公共场合就是不应该抽烟啊，为什么张莉莉要换座位而不是去劝说他们呢？

思考与讨论：

1) 艾杰森为什么不高兴？张莉莉为什么不愿意劝说抽烟的人不要再抽烟了？
2) 如果你是艾杰森，听到张莉莉的建议以后，你会怎么想？

（二）文文在美国一所大学留学，她一个人住挺孤单的,就养了一条狗。有一天，文文带着狗去朋友家玩儿，路过超市想买瓶水喝。她想可以快去快回，就把狗留在了车上。没想到回来的时候看见有人在她的车上留了张纸条。纸条上写着："天气很热，把狗留在车上是很危险的，这样做特别不负责任。"文文心里想，这个人真爱管闲事，哪有这么不客气地批评人的，我不是马上就回来了嘛。

思考与讨论：

1) 文文为什么觉得留纸条的人多管闲事而生这个人的气？
2) 如果你在中国，碰到有人做了你认为不对的事，你会怎么做？

（三）Patrick在北京工作的时候很喜欢坐地铁，他觉得又方便又环保。周五晚上，Patrick跟平时一样坐地铁回家。车上有一位妇女，一直捂着肚子，好像身体很不舒服。Patrick马上站起来，想把座位让给她。就在Patrick刚站起来的时候，旁边的一个小伙子却先坐下了。Patrick有点儿生气地对小伙子说："座位是让给这位大姐的，不是给你的。"小伙子瞪了Patrick一眼，没说话，很不情愿地站了起来。但更让Patrick没想到的是，这位女士没有坐下反而连连摆手说："没事儿，没事儿，我站一会儿没事儿。谢谢你啊。"

思考与讨论：

1) Patrick 为什么感到惊讶？这位妇女为什么说站一会儿没事儿，她不想坐下吗？
2) 如果你是这位妇女，有人给你让座，又有人抢了你的座，你会怎么办？

（四）Peter的太太是中国人，结婚以后，他跟太太一起住在太太父母家。上个周末，居委会张大妈到Peter家告诉他们一个好消息，他们家被选为“五好家庭”了。Peter问什么是“五好家庭”，他太太解释说：“五好家庭最重要的就是夫妻和睦，孝敬老人，团结邻居。”张大妈还说下个星期她会把“五好家庭”的牌子贴在他们家的门上。Peter听了以后觉得非常奇怪，他觉得他们家的情况为什么要让别人知道呢？可是他太太的父母却觉得这是一个荣誉，应该让邻居都知道。

思考与讨论：

1) Peter 为什么觉得奇怪？中国小区为什么要评选“五好家庭”呢？
2) 如果你是Peter，遇到类似的情况会怎么想？

二、口语交际练习 Oral communication exercises

1. 角色扮演 Role play

   Pair up with a peer and refer to one of the critical incidents in *Situation analysis* to create a five-minute skit with a similar storyline. Use new vocabulary and speech patterns that you have learned from this lesson in your skit. Perform the dialogue in class and discuss whether each skit properly reflects typical Chinese discourse behavior.

2. 观察与比较 Observation and comparison

   2004年，中国政府提出“构建 (gòujiàn: construct) 和谐社会”的口号 (slogan)。请你上维基百科 (wéijī bǎikē: Wikipedia) 网站用英文或中文读一篇介绍“和谐社会”的文章, 然后完成下面的活动：

   - 上网用中文输入(shūrù: input)关键词(guānjiàn cí: keyword)“和谐社会图片”，看看网上有多少相关的图片或海报(poster)。注意这些海报包括了哪些内容。
   - 选出3–4张你认为最有意思的海报，用手机或电子邮件转发给2–4位中文母语者，并告诉他们你为什么选这几张海报。请跟这几位朋友谈谈：

     (1) 这几张海报的目的(mùdì:purpose)是什么？
     (2) 你们对海报和口号的内容有什么看法？
     (3) 这些海报和口号反映出中国文化和社会的那些价值观？
     (4) 这些海报和口号对中国社会可能会产生什么影响？
     (5) 中国政府使用海报和口号的方式跟你国家的情形有什么相同或不同的地方？

   - 把这几张海报和你跟朋友们(中文母语者)的看法做成PPT，用小组的方式跟同学们分享。

三、写作 Composition

1. 作文 （两题选一题）

题目1：做了上面“观察与比较”的活动后，请把访谈的内容写成作文，并自己为作文定一个题目。写作时请尽量使用这一课的生词和句型。

提示：
- 中国政府于2004年提出了什么口号？目的是什么？
- 你选的海报包括什么内容？你为什么选这几张海报？（把图片放在作文里。）
- 总结(zǒngjié: summarize)一下那几位中文母语者的看法，并跟你自己的看法做一个比较。

题目2：我对忍让的看法

课文里提到，Caryn Voskuil女士用“木头”比喻西方人不忍让的行为，用“水”比喻中国人的妥协态度。你同意她的看法吗？你怎么看中国人忍让的行为？请提出你自己对忍让的看法。

2. 文化探索 Cultural exploration: For learners who are currently studying or working in the target culture.

In this lesson we have learned several idioms or set phrases related to 和 or 和谐 in Chinese. When you are out on the street, pay particular attention to slogan posters (标语) and commercial advertisements that deliver messages related to the concept of 和. Take pictures of them and make sure that these slogans and advertisements are from at least five different sources. Record where you took the pictures and pay attention to the key words of the slogans or advertisements. Make a copy of the table in *Appendix 1: cultural exploration* of this book and fill it in with the information from your notes. Also, include a paragraph of your reflection on the data collected. Submit your table and reflections to your teacher after completion.

第七课　忍字头上一把刀

行为聚焦：忍字当头
Behavior highlighted: forbear and forgive

课文 *Text*

来自不同文化的人们发生冲突时，很可能常常分不清到底是谁对谁错。在全球化背景下，管理学学者越来越清楚地认识到，文化不同，其企业管理的方式也有所不同。因中西文化差别而引起的冲突，可能是外籍高管在与中国同事沟通时遇到的最大问题。

德勤亚太及中国区一位负责人认为，中西企业管理的差别主要是因为不同的思维方式和沟通方式。他说，中国人常常从整体上思考问题，在与别人说话时也比较含蓄。他们更关心的是交谈后双方是否和谐，所以说话时特别关注对方的反应和感受。西方人的思维比较具体，而且，他们习惯明确地表达自己的观点，一般不会像中国人一样总是考虑我这样说，对方会怎么想。

为了避免冲突，保持人际关系的和谐，中国人对自己认识的人常常采取忍让的态度，即使这个人说了不合适的话、做了让自己不高兴的事也是一样。因为不忍让就会引起面对面的争吵，而一旦发生争吵，伤了和气，两个人以后就很难继续做朋友，甚至很难继续说话或打交道了。交一个朋友很难，而失去一个朋友很容易，所以中国人常常提醒自己说“忍一时风平浪静”，或“忍字头上一把刀”。另外，为了保持熟人之间的和气，中国人在与朋友交往时，还常常喜欢将心比心。他们认为只有遇到问题时先为他人着想，朋友之间才能和睦相处。可是，这个“以己度人”的习惯到了注重个人自由的西方文化里，却可能容易引起他人的误会。下面的故事就是一个很好的例子。

这是一个真实的故事，发表在英国《金融时报》的中文网上。文章讲的是作者刚到美国读博士时与美国室友发生的文化冲突。在美国室友搬进来的第一天，两人之间就发生了一件不愉快的事情。那天，室友在往屋子里搬东西，她的东西特别多。作者想，从今天起她们就要成为室友了，不帮忙搬东西不好意思，所以她对室友说：“让我帮你吧。”对方回答说：“不用了，不过真的很谢谢你。”作者觉得她只是在客气，所以就一边跟着她下楼一边说：“没关系，我反正也没什么事。”美国室友突然不高兴了，回过头来严肃地对她说：“我说了不用就是不用。你难道不知道‘不’的意思吗？”作者一下子愣住了，她完全没有想到自己的一片好心会引来室友这样的反应。后来，美国室友送给她一本书，并且向她道了歉，可是在很长的时间里，作者心里还在想着室友生气时喊出来的“No means No!”

生词 New words

简体	繁體	拼音	词性	英文翻译
1. 忍字头上一把刀	忍字頭上一把刀	rěn zì tóu .shang yì bǎ dāo	proverb	"The top portion of the character *ren* is a knife."/ Practice forbearance as if there were a knife hanging above the head.
2. 忍字当头	忍字當頭	rěn zì dāngtóu	phr	Forbearance is the most important principle. [当头: put ahead of everything else]
3. 分清		fēn//qīng	v	distinguish; draw a clear distinction between
4. 全球		quánqiú	n	whole world [全球化: globalize; 地球: the Earth]
5. 背景		bèijǐng	n	background, backdrop
6. 管理		guǎnlǐ	v	manage [管理学: management science]
7. 企业	企業	qǐyè	n	enterprise, corporation
8. 差别	差別	chābié	n	difference
9. 高管		gāoguǎn	n	high-rank managerial personnel, senior executive [short for高级管理人员]
10. 沟通	溝通	gōutōng	v	communicate
11. 区	區	qū	n	region, district
12. 负责	負責	fùzé	v	be in charge of, take responsibility for; [负责人: person in charge]
13. 思维	思維	sīwéi	n/v	thinking, thought; think
14. 含蓄		hánxù	adj	implicit, reserved, veiled
15. 交谈	交談	jiāotán	v	converse
16. 是否		shìfǒu	adv	whether or not [more formal than 是不是; 能否: 能不能; 可否: 可不可以]
17. 关注	關注	guānzhù	v	pay close attention to, follow with interest
18. 反应	反應	fǎnyìng	n/v	reaction; react
19. 感受		gǎnshòu	n/v	a feeling; experience, feel
20. 具体	具體	jùtǐ	adj	concrete, specific
21. 表达	表達	biǎodá	v	voice (opinion, feelings), express, convey
22. 避免		bìmiǎn	v	avoid, avert, refrain from
23. 保持		bǎochí	v	maintain, keep, preserve

简体	繁體	拼音	词性	英文翻译
24. 采取	採取	cǎiqǔ	v	adopt
25. 面对面	面對面	miànduìmiàn	phr	face-to-face
26. 争吵	爭吵	zhēngchǎo	v	quarrel, dispute, argue
27. 一旦		yídàn	adv	if one day (something happens)
28. 伤	傷	shāng	v	hurt, do harm to, injure, wound
29. 继续	繼續	jìxù	v	continue
30. 失去		shīqù	v	lose
31. 提醒	提醒	tíxǐng	v	remind, call attention to
32. 忍一时风平浪静	忍一時風平浪靜	rěn yìshí fēngpíng-làngjìng	proverb	"Practice forbearance for a short while, and the winds and waves will subside."/ Practicing forbearance for a short while will bring about tranquility.
33. 将心比心	將心比心	jiāngxīn-bǐxīn	idiom	judge another's feelings by one's own, put oneself in somebody else's shoes
34. 以己度人		yǐjǐ-duórén	idiom	place oneself in another's position, judge others by oneself
35. 注重		zhùzhòng	v	emphasize, lay stress on
36. 误会	誤會	wùhuì	n/v	misunderstanding; misunderstand
37. 真实	真實	zhēnshí	adj	true, real
38. 博士		bóshì	n	Ph.D.
39. 愉快		yúkuài	adj	pleasant, joyful
40. 突然		tūrán	adj	sudden, abrupt, unexpected
41. 严肃	嚴肅	yánsù	adj	serious, solemn
42. 难道	難道	nándào	adv	do you really mean to say that ...; could it be that ...
43. 一下子		yíxià.zi	n	a short while
44. 愣		lèng	v	be stupefied, be distracted
45. 好心		hǎoxīn	n	good intention, kind heart [一片好心: the best of intentions]
46. 并且	並且	bìngqiě	conj	and, besides, moreover
47. 道歉		dào//qiàn	v	apologize
48. 喊		hǎn	v	cry out, yell

专有名词 Proper nouns

简体	繁體	拼音	英文翻译
1. 德勤		Déqín	Chinese translation of Deloitte, a company that provides accounting and consulting services [德: virtue; 勤: diligence]
2. 亚太	亞太	Yà Tài	Asia-Pacific [亚洲: Asia; 太平洋: Pacific Ocean]
3. 金融时报	金融時報	Jīnróng Shíbào	*Financial Times*, a British newspaper

词语与句型 Expressions and sentence patterns

1. 因(为)……而VP due to ..., VP

课文例句：因中西文化差别而引起的冲突，可能是外籍高管在与中国同事沟通时遇到的最大问题。

因 or 因为 introduces the cause; 而 introduces the effect in the form of a verb phrase.

The "因(为)……而VP" pattern can only have one subject. In contrast, the two clauses in the "因为……，所以……" pattern may each have a subject. For example, "他 (S) 因为病了，所以没去看球赛" has only one subject, while "因为他的车 (S1) 坏了，所以他 (S2) 没去看球赛" has a subject in each clause.

❖ S 因(为) NP 而VP
❖ S 因(为) VP1 而VP2

- 在中国，某些行人会因"法不责众"的心理而闯红灯。
- 小李因为在北京生活过十多年而对这座城市十分了解。

2. 一旦……，…… if one day (something happens), (then) ...

课文例句：因为不忍让就会引起面对面的争吵，而一旦发生争吵，伤了和气，两个人以后就很难继续做朋友，甚至很难继续说话或打交道了。

一旦 is used in the first clause to introduce a condition. 就 is often added to the second clause to emphasize the fact that if one day something happens (indicated by the verb phrase following 一旦), something else (indicated by the verb phrase following 就) would or should also happen.

- 汉字刚开始学比较难，但是一旦认识了四五百个字，后面学起来就容易了。
- 你现在比昨天好多了，但是一旦再发烧，一定要马上去医院看病。

3. 只有……才VP only ... VP

课文例句：他们认为只有遇到问题时先为他人着想，朋友之间才能和睦相处。

才 introduces a situation that will take place only if the situation introduced by 只有happens.

❖ (S) 只有 VP1，(S) 才VP2
❖ 只有S1 VP1，S2才VP2
❖ 只有NP (才) VP

- 学习汉字只有常读、常写才不会忘记。
- 很多中国人认为，只有家庭和睦，国家才能和谐。
- 这个宿舍楼只有新生 (才) 能住。

4. 从event/time point起 starting from event/time point

课文例句：作者想，从今天起她们就要成为室友了，不帮忙搬东西不好意思，所以她对室友说："让我帮你吧。"

- 实习对大学生很重要，所以从上大学起，小王每年暑假都找一家公司实习。
- 这个学校的新校区从明年九月起开始使用，听说大三的学生都要搬过去。

5. 难道……？ Do you really mean to say that ...? Could it be that ...?

课文例句：美国室友突然不高兴了，回过头来严肃地对她说："我说了不用就是不用。你难道不知道'不'的意思吗？"

The adverb难道 can be used before or after the subject of a rhetorical question that takes the form of "statement + 吗" to strengthen the tone of disbelief (example 1), or to strengthen the conjectural tone (example 2).

- 你没有去过中国，但是你难道不知道上海不是中国的首都，北京才是吗？
- 小王怎么还没来？难道他不知道我们下午要开会吗？

6. 一下子 a short while

课文例句：美国室友突然不高兴了，回过头来严肃地对她说："我说了不用就是不用。你难道不知道'不'的意思吗？"作者一下子愣住了，她完全没有 想到自己的一片好心会引来室友这样的反应。

When followed by a verb phrase, 一下子 can mean "instantaneously," "all at once," "all of a sudden", etc. The exact translation will depend on the context.

- 这些孩子都很聪明，不管老师教什么，他们总是一下子就学会了。
- 昨天李老师问人生的意义到底是什么时，很多学生一下子不知道该怎么回答。

7. 并且 and, in addition, moreover

课文例句：后来，美国室友送给她一本书，并且向她道了歉，可是在很长的时间里，作者心里还在想着室友生气时喊出来的"No means No!"

The conjunction 并且is more formal than 而且. Though both can be used between two verb phrases, 而且 is preceded by不但 or 不仅 in a pattern that means "not only ... but also" to connect two sentences. In contrast, 并且 is predominantly used to connect clauses (example 1) or verb phrases (example 2 and 3), to show that actions or events are happening or in sequence, possibly with increasing intensity.

并且 is a disyllabic variant of 并. Unlike 并且, 并 is used primarily in written form or with literary Chinese and cannot be used to join clauses that contain different subjects (example 1).

- “中国菜”的内容很丰富，“八大菜系”代表着中国八个比较大的地区，每个菜系都有各自的特点，并且，“八大菜系”以外的很多地方也有自己的名菜。
- 去外国留学，可以在语言学习上有所提高，并且能更好地了解当地的文化。
- 黄老师上课时总能简单并且清楚地介绍学习内容，因此很受学生欢迎。
- Tom的中文发音标准并且自然，很多人听到他说中文都夸奖他。

语言练习 To practice and reinforce what you have learned from the Text, New Words, and the section “Expressions and sentence patterns” in this lesson, please visit the companion website to download a PDF version of the exercises.

交际情景 Communication scenarios

Study the following conversations between native speakers on the textbook companion website. Use the plug-in feature to find the definitions of the new words highlighted in orange. Try to visualize the scene as you read and listen to each dialogue. Discuss your reactions to these scenario dialogues with a classmate.

1. A neighbor of Li Aihua and Wang Weimin often blocks the entrance when he parks his car on the neighborhood street. While Weimin is losing his patience with the person, Aihua holds a different opinion. Take note of the rationale behind Aihua’s suggestion as to what Weimin should do.

   王为民：楼上小赵的车又随便停在路口，没停到车位上。
   李爱华：你就从旁边绕过去嘛。
   王为民：他这么停车，别人出来进去都不方便。我得给物业打电话投诉。这都好几 次了，我们不能一直这么忍着。
   李爱华：不忍怎么办？小赵要是知道是我们投诉的，肯定要来跟我们吵架。要是伤了和气，以后还怎么当邻居啊？他可能是有急事，要不然不会停在路口的。
   王为民：你怎么帮他说话呢？
   李爱华：我不是帮他说话，只是不想把事情闹大。都是邻居，最好大事化小、小事化了。

   ### 思考与讨论：

   1) 对于小赵乱停车的行为，李爱华为什么采取忍让的态度？
   2) 如果这件事发生在你的国家，人们一般会怎么做？

2. Wang Weimin, who is a manager in his company, was asked to lower the prices of their products by its regular customer Da Fa Company, although they have signed a three-year contract last year. Pay attention to how Weimin sorts out his rationale when making a decision.

   李秘书：王经理，今天大发公司打电话问我们卖给他们的机器能不能降价？
   王为民：去年签合同的时候，他们对价格不是很满意吗？怎么又要降价呢？

李秘书：是啊，太过分了，我们签的还是三年的长期合同呢。但是大发说他们最近资金出了问题，也没办法。不过如果降价，我们就受损失了。您能忍下这口气吗？我们要不要找律师出面处理这件事？
王为民：唉，算了算了，我们损失就损失一点儿吧，谁让他们是老客户呢？如果我们告他，先不说要花多少时间和精力，更重要的是损失了这样一个大客户，以后就没法继续合作了。忍一时风平浪静，还是和气生财吧。

思考与讨论：

1) 你觉得大发公司的要求合理吗？王为民为什么接受了降价的要求？
2) 根据对话，王为民更重视合同还是跟客户之间的关系？为什么？
3) 这种情形如果发生在你的国家，一般商人可能会怎么做？

3. Zhao Xuedong feels that his department's decision on promotion is unfair to him. Observe how Wang Weimin comforts him and why Zhao Xuedong does not complain to the CEO of the company.

王为民：学东，怎么了？看你愁眉苦脸的。
赵学东：唉，别提了。最近我们部门选副经理，又不是我。
王为民：那你跟你们部门经理谈了吗？他怎么说？
赵学东：他说我工作上的表现他都知道，不过这次升职只有一个名额，他还说让我别着急，再等等，以后肯定有机会。可他虽然这么说，我还是觉得有点不公平。
王为民：那怎么办？要不要再跟总裁谈谈？
赵学东：唉，算了，我还是忍忍吧。我以后还要在他手下工作，把关系搞僵了，对我也没好处。

思考与讨论：

1) 部门经理跟赵学东谈话时，语言上是否含蓄？请举例说明。在你的国家，人们会不会这样说？
2) 赵学东觉得不公平，但他为什么不想跟总裁谈这件事？在你的国家，如果人们碰到这样的事，会有赵学东这样的想法吗？如果没有，他们会怎么想？怎么处理？

言语行为例说 Notes on discourse behavior

1. 对话例句：王为民：你怎么帮他说话？
李爱华：我不是帮他说话，只是不想把事情闹大。都是邻居，最好大事化小、小事化了。

The saying 大事化小、小事化了(liǎo) (a.k.a. 大事化小、小事化无) means to turn big problems into small ones, and to turn small ones into nothing. The priority is to find a peaceful resolution that makes the least amount of trouble for everyone involved, achieved usually by making compromises by some or all parties.

- 甲：张老师，李小朋在班上打了我儿子，您看这得怎么惩罚？
乙：李小朋的家长已经把他带回家教育了，也付了您儿子的医药费。还是大事化小、小事化了吧。再给他一个机会，他还是一个孩子，而且以后您儿子还要跟他一起上课呢。

- 甲：新来的小王把实验的数据搞错了，这事我们是不是应该报告给主任？
  乙：我看还是大事化小、小事化无吧。这事说出去也影响我们整个实验室的声誉。

2. 对话例句：李秘书：……不过如果降价，我们就受损失了。您能忍下这口气吗？
   王为民：……我们损失就损失一点儿吧，谁让他们是老客户呢？

The saying 忍下这口气 means "swallow the indignity." It is a reminder to oneself or to another person who is involved in an unpleasant situation. In Dialogue 2, Secretary Li asks "你能忍下这口气吗 (Can you swallow the indignity?)" when she asks Manager Wang how he plans to handle a breach of contract by one of their customers.

- 甲：我们的孩子被同学欺负，老师还劝我们忍忍算了，你能忍下这口气吗？
  乙：当然不行，明天我去学校找校长解决这个事情。
- 甲：我明明做得比小赵好，但是老板却给小赵升职，真忍不下这口气。
  乙：那有什么办法呢，要不你找老板谈谈？

3. 对话例句：李秘书：……不过如果降价，我们就受损失了。您能忍下这口气吗？
   王为民：唉，算了算了，我们损失就损失一点儿吧……<u>忍一时风平浪静</u>，还是和气生财吧。

Like 忍字头上一把刀, the saying 忍一时风平浪静 (rěn yìshí fēngpínglàngjìng), meaning "find peace with a little forbearance," is a reminder to practice self-control rather than acting on impulse. 退一步海阔天空(tuì yí bù hǎikuòtiānkōng), meaning "find more space by taking a step back," is often used to complete the saying to form a couplet.

- 甲：老王，我们都觉得经理对你的惩罚很不公平，你明明没有做错什么，你可以写邮件到总公司投诉啊。
  乙：算了，忍一时风平浪静，我以后还要在他手下工作，该忍的时候还是要忍。
- 甲：我老板对我们这几个实习生非常不公平，给我们的工作特别多，我都没时间睡觉。而且即使我们花了很长时间完成工作，他还是批评我们。我真忍不下去了。
  乙：忍一时风平浪静，能忍就忍了吧。再过一个星期，实习也就结束了。

4. 对话例句：王为民：那你跟你们部门经理谈了吗？他怎么说？
   赵学东：<u>他说我工作上的表现他都知道，不过这次升职只有一个名额，他还说让我别着急，再等等，以后肯定有机会</u>。

Out of consideration for social harmony and the desire not to hurt anyone's feelings, Chinese speakers often couch refusals or bad news in euphemisms. When delivering very bad news, such as Zhao Xuedong's situation in Dialogue 3, the speaker will often offer complement before using 不过 (nonetheless) or 可是to transition to the bad news. It is very rare for a Chinese person to make an explicit refusal to a request; instead s/he may push the decision to a future time with "好，到时候再说 (we'll see)," "我再考虑考虑 (I'll think about it some more)," "我再给你打电话 (I'll call you later)," or "行，看情况吧 (it'll depend on the circumstances)." Though non-committal in tone, all these expressions actually imply rejection.

- 甲：我们已经认识这么久了，你可以考虑做我的女朋友吗？
  乙：你真是一个好人，我们也是好朋友。可是我觉得现在学习比较重要，还不想太早谈恋爱。
- 甲：老张，下个月我搬家，家具太多了，你得来帮我搬东西啊。
  乙：噢，行，下个月我也不知道哪天有空，咱们到时候再说吧。

体演情景 Perform the scenario

Select a dialogue from this section and listen to its recording several times. Imitate the speakers in pronunciation, intonation and discourse behavior in terms of both the words they use and the ways in which they carry themselves. Memorize the dialogue for performance in class.

跨文化交际 Cross-cultural communication

一、误解分析 Situation analysis

Break into groups and discuss the misunderstanding in each of the cross-cultural communication incidents below. For each incident, the group should generate an answer that best explains the cultural assumptions behind the ways in which the individuals say and do things. In addition, discuss possible strategies to avoid these misunderstandings in similar situations.

（一）周强这个学期在美国的一所大学做交换生。上周六晚上，他找了几个国内来的同学到自己的公寓包饺子。七八个人围着桌子吃吃喝喝，说说笑笑。大伙玩儿得特别开心，都忘了时间。突然，有人敲门并大声地说"开门，开门，警察！"周强打开门一看，真的是警察！警察说："有人报警，说你们太吵了，晚上12点以后必须安静，知道吗？"周强连忙道歉说："对不起，我们会注意的。"警察离开后，周强觉得很奇怪，他那层楼只住了一个叫Penny的租客，其他邻居都住得挺远的。平常Penny跟他的关系挺好的，她为什么要为了这么一点小事报警呢，真让人生气。第二天，周强看见Penny，她向他点头微笑，周强却假装没看见就走开了。

思考与讨论：

1) 周强的行为影响了邻居，为什么他不觉得自己不对，反过来还生邻居的气呢？
2) 如果你是周强的邻居，碰到这种情形，你会怎么做？

（二）Tiffany在重庆的一家中国公司上班。重庆的夏天特别热，可是Tiffany却发现中国同事李书静在自己的办公室里有时披着一件外套。Tiffany觉得很奇怪就问李书静："你披着外套不热吗？"书静回答说："跟我一个办公室的王姐特别怕热，每天都把空调开得很低很低，我在办公室里觉得冻死了，就找了件外套披上。"Tiffany又接着问："你觉得空调温度太低，怎么不跟王姐说一下呢？"书静说："还是别说了。如果说了以后她不愿意调高温度，那多尴尬。我忍几天就过去了。再说，披件外套也不麻烦，我每天都把外套放办公室里。"Tiffany还是不能理解书静的做法，她想，书静还没有问过王姐，她怎么知道王姐同意不同意呢？

思考与讨论：

1) 李书静为什么忍着不跟王姐说空调温度的事情？她的顾虑是什么？
2) 如果你是李书静，碰到这样的情况你会怎么做？

（三）Olivia在中国的一家公司工作。周四下午开会时，部门经理简单地讲了一下本周的工作情况，然后说，“明天有领导来检查工作，有个项目需要大家今天晚一点下班把它完成，有人有问题吗？” Olivia想到自己晚上约了朋友一起吃饭，刚想说不能加班，但听到周围的同事都说“没问题，没问题”她就没说。让Olivia惊讶的是，开完会经理刚走，大家就开始你一句我一句地抱怨起来。有的说自己约了朋友要去健身，有的说晚上要回家看父母，好像并没有人愿意留下来加班。Olivia不解地问，“既然你们都不愿意加班，刚才经理问有没有意见时，怎么没有人说话呢？”大家互相看了一下，没有人回答她的问题。

思考与讨论：

1) Olivia 的不解是什么？为什么中国同事们等经理走了以后才开始抱怨加班呢？
2) 如果你是 Olivia，以后再碰到这种情形，你会怎么做？

（四）Jack和李明是同屋，昨晚宿舍里的空调又坏了，于是两人一起去找宿舍管理员。管理员听了以后说：“你们先回去吧，我会找人去修。”可是Jack和李明没走，他们请求说：“这个空调已经修了好几次了，上个星期才刚修过，现在又坏了。你们能不能就别修了，给我们换新的吧！”管理员看了他们一眼说：“一个空调不少钱呢！怎么能说换就换呢？这样吧，今天先找人来修。回头我跟学校申请一下，我们研究研究。” Jack着急地问，“那到底能不能换？什么时候能换？”管理员说，“这不好说。等有了消息我告诉你们，过几天再说吧。”Jack还想问要等几天，可是李明拉着他就出去了。Jack问李明：“你怎么拉我出来了，我还没问他要等几天呢？”李明失望地说：“算了，我看咱们的新空调没戏了。忍忍吧，反正再过两个星期就放假了。”Jack不明白李明怎么已经知道不行，管理员刚才没拒绝他们啊，不是说要研究一下吗？

思考与讨论：

1) 管理员说“我们研究研究”“不好说”“过几天再说吧”，你觉得这是什么意思？
2) 如果你是Jack，这时候还会继续追问管理员吗？为什么？

二、口语交际练习 Oral communication exercises

1. 角色扮演 Role play

   Pair up with a peer and refer to one of the critical incidents in *Situation analysis* to create a five-minute skit with a similar storyline. Use new vocabulary and speech patterns that you have learned from this lesson in your skit. Perform the dialogue in class and discuss whether each skit properly reflects typical Chinese discourse behavior.

2. 观察与比较 Observation and comparison

画家刘扬(Liú Yáng)在中国出生，但是十四岁时跟着父母搬到德国的去居住，因此她对中西文化差别有着特别的感受。通过一系列(xìliè: series)的图片，刘扬表达了她对两个国家和两种文化的看法。请跟一位同学一起看看下面两组图片，并讨论下列问题。

处理问题（problem-solving approach）:

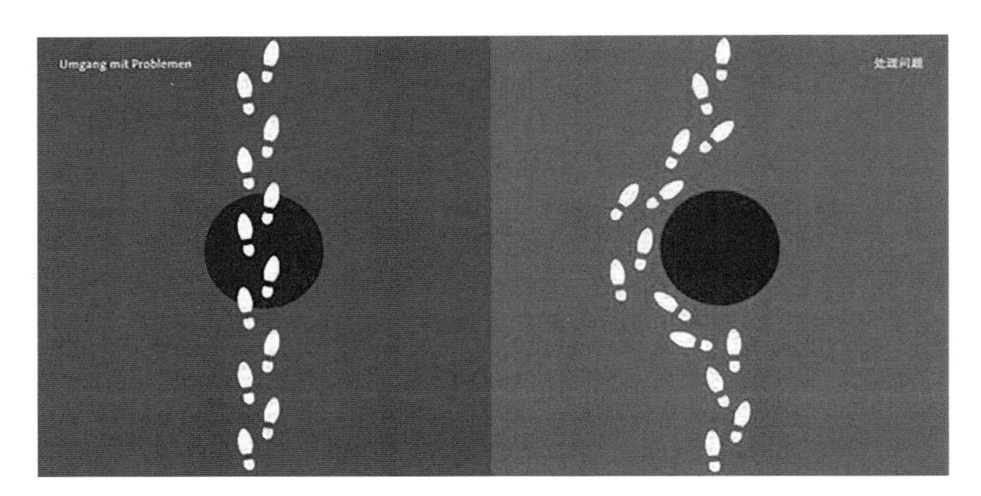

表达意见（complexity of self-expression）:

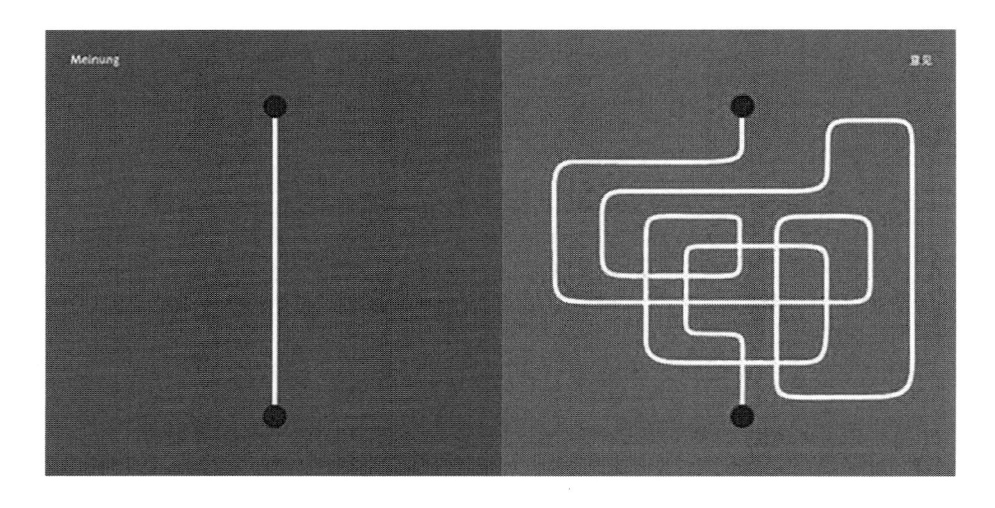

(1) 每组图片中的左右两张图片，哪个代表德国人或西方人的思考方式，哪个代表中国人的思考方式？
(2) 解释每组图片所表达的意思，并举例说明西方人和中国人因为思考方式不同，可能有什么不一样的做法。
(3) 他们会不会因为做法不一样而产生误解？请举例说明。
(4) 你们认为怎么做，可以减少误解？
(5) 请上网查看更多的图片， 选1–2组你们认为最有意思的，讨论你们的看法。

网站：（二选一）

- "East Meets West: An Infographic Portrait by Yang Liu" (http://bsix12.com/east-meets-west/)
- "华裔设计师刘扬：东西相遇" (http://works.ccsph.com/detail_6534.html)

跟全班同学介绍你们挑选的图片是什么，并分享你们的讨论内容。

三、写作 Composition

1. 作文 （两题选一题）

题目1：上一题"观察与比较"中介绍了刘扬"东西相遇"的图片。请从网站上选出2–3组你认为最有意思，或者最能反映你自己生活经验的图片。完成以下几个步骤(bùzhòu: step)：

- 根据你对中西文化的理解，解释并比较每组图片所表达的内容。
- 谈谈你的看法跟刘扬有什么一样或不一样的地方并举例说明。
- 请用其中一个例子说明你认为怎样可以增加双方之间的了解。
- 自己为作文定一个题目。

写作时请尽量使用这一课的生词和句型。

题目2：将心比心

- "将心比心"指的是为他人着想。虽然这个观念在每一个文化中都存在，但它是中国人崇尚的做事原则。请你谈谈：(1)"将心比心"的做法在中西方跨文化交际中可能产生的影响；(2)根据课文，为什么有时"一片好心"反而会引起误解？(3)在你看来，"将心比心"会让双方的关系更加友好，还是更容易引起误会，使对方反感？为什么？请举例说明你的观点。(4)总结你的看法。
- 写作时请尽量使用新学的生词和句型。

2. 文化探索 Cultural exploration: For learners who are currently studying or working in the target culture.

In this lesson, you have learned what Chinese people would say and do in order to avoid conflicts and maintain harmony in relationships. When you are out in public, either with

Chinese friends or by yourself, notice (1) what Chinese people would say when apologizing and (2) how they couch refusals in different situations. Pay attention to the social position of the speaker, such as their age and job, as well as how their language changes as a function of the closeness (or absence) of the relationship with the other party. Discuss your observations with Chinese friends and record them in the table in *Appendix 1: cultural exploration*. Compose a journal that include your own reflection on the experience of this activity.

第八课　保持中道

行为聚焦：中庸之道
Behavior highlighted: (take) the middle road

课文 *Text*

中国文化中以和为贵的思想，是与中国人的"中庸"观念联系在一起的。儒家经典《中庸》说："中也者，天下之大本也；和也者，天下之达道也。致中和，天地位焉，万物育焉。"[1] 这段话的意思是说，"中"是天下万事万物的根本，"和"是天下万事万物所共同遵守的规则。只有保持"中和"，天与地才能各得其位，天地之间的万物才能蓬勃生长。

20世纪初，《中庸》被儒家学者辜鸿铭翻译成了英文，传到西方后引起了不小的轰动。人们是看了标题去读这篇文章的，因为辜先生把《中庸》的标题翻译成了"普遍秩序或人生准则"。一篇几千字的文章为什么采用这样高深的题目呢？这是因为中庸之道在儒家思想中代表着最高的智慧和真理，被认为是解决一切问题的最好方法。中庸之道的核心是"中"。"中"有两个基本意思：一是保持中道，二是调和两端。前者讲的是做任何事情都应该做到正好，既不应该做过了头，也不应该做得不够；后者讲的是不同事物之间，应该追求大方面的相同，忽略小方面的不同，做到"和而不同"。

儒家的中庸思想其实与古希腊哲学中mean（常译为"中道"或"适度"）的意思差不多相同。但与后者不同的是，几千年以后，中庸之道并没有随着时间的过去成为历史，而是作为一种高级智慧深深地渗入了中国人的血液中，已成为中国人做人做事的普遍规则。中国人崇尚中庸，对"中"有着特殊的喜好。有人开玩笑说，中国人坐位子喜欢坐中间，住房子喜欢住中层，就连吃东西，很多人也是喜欢吃中间的部分。中国人说话常常喜欢说"适中"的话，朋友之间遇到问题发生矛盾，也常会找个"中间人"帮助解决。一般来说，中国人不喜欢出风头，认为"枪打出头鸟"；很多人更不喜欢发了财以后炫富，因为"树大招风"。

中庸之道这一古老智慧，既可以用于做人做事，也可以用于治理国家。它既是人与人之间的求和之道，也是国与国之间和平相处的法则。有人认为，中国"和平共处、互不干涉"的外交理念就体现了中国人的中庸思想。还有人把

---

1 Zhōng yě zhě, tiān xià zhī dà běn yě; hé yě zhě, tiān xià zhī dá dào yě. Zhì zhōng hé, tiān dì wèi yān, wàn wù yù yān. This Equilibrium is the great root from which grow all the human actings in the world, and this Harmony is the universal path which they all should pursue. Let the states of equilibrium and harmony exist in perfection, and a happy order will prevail throughout heaven and earth, and all things will be nourished and flourish. (*Trans.* James Legge)

中国在联合国安理会投票的规律也解释为中庸思想的表现。对于没有什么争议的问题，中国基本上投赞同票，涉及自己利益的问题，中国会投反对票，其它的一律投弃权票。在2014年发生的有关乌克兰问题的重大事件上，中国又投了弃权票。因为对立的两端一方是美国，一方是俄罗斯，作为三个大国之一，中国似乎只有保持中道，投个弃权票。

生词 New words

简体	繁體	拼音	词性	英文翻译
1. 中庸之道		zhōngyōng zhī dào	idiom	the golden mean (of the Confucian school) [中庸: Mean; 道: the Way]
2. 经典	經典	jīngdiǎn	n/adj	classics, canons; classical
3. 天下		tiānxià	n	everywhere under heaven, world, China
4. 共同		gòngtóng	adv/adj	jointly, together; common, mutual
5. 各得其位		gèdé-qíwèi	phr	Each is in its proper place./Each has a role to play.
6. 蓬勃		péngbó	adj	vigorous, full of vitality
7. 生长	生長	shēngzhǎng	v	grow, develop
8. 世纪	世紀	shìjì	n	century
9. 初		chū	n	the beginning of (a period of time)
10. 翻译	翻譯	fānyì	v/n	translate; translator, translation
11. 传	傳	chuán	v	spread, pass on, circulate
12. 轰动	轟動	hōngdòng	v	cause a great sensation
13. 标题	標題	biāotí	n	(book, article) title, (news) headline
14. 秩序		zhìxù	n	order, sequence
15. 人生		rénshēng	n	human life, one's lifetime
16. 采用	採用	cǎiyòng	v	select, employ, adopt
17. 高深		gāoshēn	adj	profound [深: deep]
18. 智慧		zhìhuì	n	wisdom
19. 真理		zhēnlǐ	n	truth
20. 解决	解決	jiějué	v	solve, resolve
21. 一切		yíqiè	pron	all, everything
22. 调和	調和	tiáohé	v	mediate, reconcile
23. 端		duān	bf	end, extremity [两端: two ends]
24. 任何		rènhé	pron	any
25. 正好		zhènghǎo	adj/adv	just right; precisely
26. 过头	過頭	guò//tóu	adj	going too far

简体	繁體	拼音	词性	英文翻译
27. 忽略		hūlüè	v	ignore, overlook
28. 和而不同		hé ér bùtóng	idiom	harmony without uniformity
29. 适度	適度	shìdù	adj	moderate, appropriate
30. 作为	作為	zuòwéi	prep/v	as; regard as, take for
31. 高级	高級	gāojí	adj	supreme, advanced
32. 渗入	滲入	shènrù	v	enter, penetrate
33. 血液		xuèyè	n	blood
34. 特殊		tèshū	adj	special, unusual
35. 喜好		xǐhào	n/v	preference, fondness; love, like, be fond of
36. 适中	適中	shìzhōng	adj	appropriate, moderate
37. 中间人	中間人	zhōngjiānrén	n	mediator, middleman
38. 出风头	出風頭	chū fēng.tou	phr	seek the limelight
39. 枪打出头鸟	槍打出頭鳥	qiāng dǎ chūtóuniǎo	idiom	The shot hits the bird that pokes its head out./Nonconformity gets punished.
40. 发财	發財	fā//cái	v	make a fortune
41. 炫富		xuàn//fù	v	flaunt wealth
42. 树大招风	樹大招風	shùdà-zhāofēng	idiom	A tall tree catches the wind./A prominent person attracts attention [i.e., criticism].
43. 用于	用於	yòngyú	v	use in/on [于: more formal than "在……上/中"]
44. 法则	法則	fǎzé	n	law, rule, principle
45. 理念		lǐniàn	n	concept, notion, idea
46. 投票		tóu//piào	v	cast vote
47. 规律	規律	guīlǜ	n/adj	pattern; regular
48. 基本上		jīběn.shàng	adv	basically, primarily
49. 赞同	贊同	zàntóng	v/n	approve of, agree with, endorse; approval, endorsement
50. 涉及		shèjí	v	involve, relate to
51. 反对	反對	fǎnduì	v/n	oppose, disagree; disagreement
52. 一律		yílǜ	adv	without exception
53. 事件		shìjiàn	n	event, incident
54. 弃权	棄權	qì//quán	v/n	abstain from voting; abstention
55. 对立	對立	duìlì	v/n	oppose, be antagonistic to; opposition
56. 似乎		sìhū	adv	seemingly

专有名词 Proper nouns

简体	繁體	拼音	英文翻译
1. 《中庸》		Zhōngyōng	*The Doctrine of the Mean*, one of the Four Books of the Confucian philosophy. Originally published as a chapter in the *Classic of Rites*, the text is attributed to Zisi or Kong Ji, the grandson of Confucius.
2. 辜鸿铭	辜鴻銘	Gū Hóngmíng	Hung-ming Ku or Hongming Gu (1857–1928), a Malaysian Chinese man of letters known for his monarchist views and highly regarded for his works in English.
3. 联合国	聯合國	Liánhéguó	United Nations
4. 安理会	安理會	Ānlǐhuì	UNSC [short form of 联合国安全理事会, United Nations Security Council]
5. 乌克兰	烏克蘭	Wūkèlán	Ukraine
6. 俄罗斯	俄羅斯	Éluósī	Russia [short form of 俄罗斯联邦: Éluósī Liánbāng; the Russian Federation]

词语与句型 Expressions and sentence patterns

1. V 成 — V into

课文例句：20世纪初，《中庸》被儒家学者辜鸿铭<u>翻译成</u>了英文，传到西方后引起了不小的轰动。

成 means “become” or “change into.” “V成” can be used to describe a factual change, as seen in 翻译成, 做成, 换成, 切成 (example 1), or a situation that has come into being due to an error, with 成 often found in combination with听, 读, 看, 当, or 打 (example 2).

- 做青菜豆腐汤需要把豆腐<u>切成</u>小块儿。
- 有些人分不清in和ing，所以打字时会把“因为”<u>打成</u>“应为”，或者把“应该”<u>打成</u>“因该”。

2. ……，一是……，二是…… — ... the first (reason) is ..., the second (reason) is ...

课文例句：“中”有两个基本意思：<u>一是</u>保持中道，<u>二是</u>调和两端。

This structure is mostly used when presenting a list of reasons or supporting evidences.

- 一些不怎么了解中国的外国人只知道两个中国城市，<u>一是</u>北京，<u>二是</u>上海。
- 不少学生喜欢通过看电影来学习外语，<u>一是</u>比较轻松有趣，<u>二是</u>可以听到地道的语言。

3. 既 VP1，也/又 VP2 — not only VP1, but also VP2

课文例句1：前者讲的是做任何事情都应该做到正好，<u>既</u>不应该做过了头，<u>也</u>不应该做得不够；后者讲的是不同事物之间，应该追求大方面的相同，忽略小方面的不同，做到“和而不同”。

课文例句2：中庸之道这一古老智慧，<u>既</u>可以用于做人做事，<u>也</u>可以用于治理国家。它<u>既</u>是人与人之间的求和之道，<u>也</u>是国与国之间和平相处的法则。

- 学中文的学生多看一些中国电影既能学习语言，也能了解文化。
- "以和为贵"既可以用于人与人之间的相处，又可以用于商家之间的合作。

4. …… (A)与B不同的是，A…… ... what makes A different from B is that A ...

课文例句：儒家的中庸思想其实与古希腊哲学中mean（常译为"中道"或"适度"）的意思差不多相同。但与后者不同的是，几千年以后，中庸之道并没有随着时间的过去成为历史，而是作为一种高级智慧深深地渗入了中国人的血液中，已成为中国人做人做事的普遍规则。

After stating the similarities between A and B, this structure is often used to point out the differences between them by highlighting the unique features or characteristics of A.

- 华盛顿特区(Huáshèngdùn Tèqū: Washington D.C.)和北京都是首都，但与北京不同的是，华盛顿的高楼比北京少得多，人口也只有60多万。
- 中国人和西方人都很重视礼貌。但中国人与西方人不同的是，中国人对"客气"也很讲究。

5. V为NP V as NP

课文例句1：儒家的中庸思想其实与古希腊哲学中mean（常译为"中道"或"适度"）的意思差不多相同。

课文例句2：还有人把中国在联合国安理会投票的规律也解释为中庸思想的表现。

Unlike "V成", which entails change or transformation (see the first entry), "V为" is a formal construction that provides information on how a certain person or object should be called, regarded, interpreted, or selected to be (depending on the meaning of the verb). Commonly usages include 称为 (referred to as), 视为 (to regarded as), 选为 (elected or selected to be), etc.

- 在中国，有钱人家的孩子也被称为"富二代"。
- 儒家把"中"视为天下万事万物的根本。
- 小李被选为学生会主席(zhǔxí: chairperson)后，校报发表了一篇介绍她的文章。

In the first example from the text, 译为 can be changed to 译成 or 翻译成 without affecting the meaning of the sentence. However, the construction becomes less formal after making the change.

6. 作为NP as NP

课文例句1：几千年以后，中庸之道并没有随着时间的过去成为历史，而是作为一种高级智慧深深地渗入了中国人的血液中，已成为中国人做人做事的普遍规则。

课文例句2：因为对立的两端一方是美国，一方是俄罗斯，作为三个大国之一，中国似乎只有保持中道，投个弃权票。

The subject of the sentence can be placed before or after the "作为 NP" segment.

- 在过去三四十年中，可口可乐常常出现在人们的餐桌上，作为典型的西式饮料进入了普通中国人的生活。
- 作为一个在中国生活过很多年的外国人，John觉得中国的老百姓都挺热情的。

语言练习 To practice and reinforce what you have learned from the Text, New Words, and the section "Expressions and sentence patterns" in this lesson, please visit the companion website to download a PDF version of the exercises.

交际情景 Communication scenarios

Study the following conversations between native speakers on the textbook companion website. Use the plug-in feature to find the definitions of the new words highlighted in orange. Try to visualize the scene as you read and listen to each dialogue. Discuss your reactions to these scenario dialogues with a classmate.

1. Professor Lin's TV show on *The Dream of the Red Chamber* made him very popular. However, he has decided to quit the show at the height of his popularity. Pay attention to the stated concerns that may have prompted him to do so.

王大伟：林老师，您在电视上讲《红楼梦》的节目太火了。我好几个亲戚朋友都看了，都说您讲得特别好。
林老师：哪里，哪里。我也没想到这么受欢迎。
王大伟：那接下来您还要讲其他名著吗？
林老师：《红楼梦》讲完就不再讲了，现在观众反应不错，我也就见好就收吧。讲得多了，说不定观众就不爱看了。
王大伟：那不是太可惜了？现在这个节目特别火，您要是接着讲，肯定能成电视明星。
林老师：俗话说"人怕出名猪怕壮"，还是低调点儿好。如果出了名，一定会有人找我麻烦，说我不好好教书什么的。再说，我上电视也不是为了出名和赚钱，我的收入比上不足比下有余，已经很好了。

思考与讨论：

1) 请解释"人怕出名猪怕壮"是什么意思。
2) 林老师崇尚中庸吗？对话中他的哪些行为和语言表现了这一点？
3) 根据这段对话，林老师为什么担心出名？在你的国家人们会有这样的担心吗？

2. Wang Dawei would like to drive his mother's new car to a class reunion, but his mother disapproves of this idea. Think carefully about the reasoning behind his mother's edict.

王大伟：妈，晚上同学聚会，我能开咱家的新车去吗？
李爱华：坐地铁去不是挺方便的吗？开什么车啊！
王大伟：妈，我刚拿了驾照，咱家又买了那么好的车，我想开出去转转。
李爱华：不行。你是个大学生，不要老想着出风头。同学都不开车去，就你开，这样大家可能会在背后议论你、疏远你的。还是坐地铁去吧。
王大伟：您想得太多了，妈。
李爱华：不是我想得多，这是做人的道理。别人怎样，你就怎样，要尽量跟大家一样。"树大招风"的道理，你懂吧？
王大伟：那好吧。

思考与讨论：

1) 李爱华为什么不愿意让儿子开新车去参加同学聚会？
2) 在你的国家，"树大招风"是做人做事的重要道理吗？父母会不会教给孩子这样的观点？

3. Wang Weimin's subordinates disagree with each other about how to organize a training session for new staff. Observe how Wang Weimin comes up with a compromise arrangement to solve the problem.

王为民：明天的培训，你们准备得怎么样了？
小　张：差不多了，但是要不要按照不同的部门让新员工分组培训，我们俩的看法不一样。
王为民：怎么不一样？说来听听。
小　张：我觉得应该分开，每个部门的工作不一样，而且我已经做好分组培训计划了。
李秘书：可是大家在一起培训可以互相认识，更了解公司的情况。这个培训我已经做过好几次了，一直都不分组，也都挺好的。王经理，您说怎么办？
王为民：这个嘛……你们说的都有道理。咱们折中一下。既然小张做好计划了，那我们就分组试一试。但是开头的介绍和最后的总结不分组。李秘书，你经验多，重要的部分还是你来讲。

思考与讨论：

1) 面对不同意见的时候，王为民是怎么解决的？他为什么要找一个折中的办法？
2) 你觉得小张和李秘书会不会接受王为民的决定？为什么？

言语行为例说 Notes on discourse behavior

1. 对话例句：王大伟：那接下来您还要讲其他名著吗？
林老师：《红楼梦》讲完就不再讲了，现在观众反应不错，我也就见好就收吧。讲得多了，说不定观众就不爱看了。

The idiom 见好就收 ("knowing when to stop") suggests moderation, cautioning against being greedy (贪心) and by doing so risking the possible future benefits or profits possibly greater.

- 甲：最近我们买的股票都赚了不少钱，我们再多买点儿吧。
乙：还是见好就收吧，买股票风险太大了。
- 甲：我们的产品在东南亚这么受欢迎，应该马上发展欧美市场。
乙：我看现在我们还是见好就收吧，先把东南亚市场做好。欧美市场我们还不了解，不要冒险。

2. 对话例句：王大伟：……现在这个节目特别火，您要是接着讲，肯定能成电视明星。
林老师：俗话说"人怕出名猪怕壮"，还是低调点儿好。

人怕出名猪怕壮 (rén pà chū míng zhū pà zhuàng) originates from *The Dream of the Red Chamber*, one of China's greatest classical novels. The phrase literally means that fame portends trouble for humans, just as weight does for pigs. For the sake of self-protection, it is better to maintain a low profile (低调) and practice见好就收. This expression is similar to树大招风 in meaning (discussed in the next entry), but it is more informal in usage.

- 甲：小林，大家都希望你当学生会主席，你怎么不愿意？
乙：俗话说人怕出名猪怕壮，我可不想给自己找麻烦。快毕业了，我还是好好找工作吧。

- 甲：你那篇文章发表以后，好几个电视台要采访你，你怎么都不去？
  乙：我想当作家，而不是明星，还是低调一点儿好。中国有句俗话：人怕出名猪怕壮。出了名以后就没有办法安安静静地写文章了。

3. 对话例句：李爱华：不行。你是个大学生，不要老想着出风头……
   王大伟：您想得太多了，妈。
   李爱华：……别人怎样，你就怎样，要尽量跟大家一样。"树大招风"的道理，你懂吧？

The thinking behind 出风头is that a person who enjoys showing off or being different will not get along well with others. Thus, parents usually discourage their children from doing so and instead urge them to blend in with others by doing what others do. The expression 树大招风 ("A big tree catches the wind") similarly cautions people against behaviors that attract notice, as they will also provoke criticism or trouble. For all these reasons, it is common in China that when people become rich, they generally do their best not to display their wealth in public.

- 甲：高小朋开会的时候跟经理说他今年的销售量要提高30%，可别人都说只能提高 5%。你说他做得到吗？
  乙：他呀，就爱出风头。我们就等着看吧，看他做不到怎么办。
- 甲：淘宝已经成了中国最大的网上商城，谁能跟它竞争？
  乙：没错，可是树大招风，你看现在很多人在批评淘宝的商品质量问题。

4. 对话例句：小 张：……我们俩的看法不一样。
   ……
   王为民：这个嘛……你们说的都有道理。咱们折中一下。

折中means to compromise by taking the middle road. The rationale behind the expression is that the best way to resolve disagreements is for parties at odds to take the middle-ground and compromise on a solution.

- 甲：你们能不能吃辣的菜？我最喜欢辣的，越辣越好！
  乙：太辣的我吃不了。
  丙：那咱们折中一下，服务员，这个菜做成微辣的。
- 甲：你们的两个产品，一个价格太高，一个质量太差。我们都不能用。
  乙：对不起，那我们来想一个折中的办法，给你们提供一个既质量好、价格又不太贵的产品。

体演情景 Perform the scenario

Select a dialogue from this section and listen to its recording several times. Imitate the speakers in pronunciation, intonation and discourse behavior in terms of both the words they use and the ways in which they carry themselves. Memorize the dialogue for performance in class.

跨文化交际 Cross-cultural communication

一、误解分析 Situation analysis

Break into groups and discuss the misunderstanding in each of the cross-cultural communication incidents below. For each incident, the group should generate an answer that best explains the cultural assumptions behind the ways in which the individuals say and do things. In addition, discuss possible strategies to avoid these misunderstandings in similar situations.

（一）张明明大学毕业不久就在一家美国公司工作。这个月她们公司要招聘一名会计，因为这跟明明的工作有关系，经理John和副经理Chris也让她参加了面试。面试以后，John说："我觉得两位应聘者都很好，但是我更喜欢第一位，经验比较多。"这时，Chris却说："但是我们需要员工能用英文沟通，第二位的英文比第一位好。明明，你怎么看？"明明想了想说："我都同意，经验非常重要，英文沟通能力也是必须要有的。我还没想好谁更合适，我再考虑考虑。" John和Chris感觉明明不太想说出她的看法，但是却不知道为什么。

思考与讨论：

1) 张明明是真的没有想好谁更合适吗，还是有可能有别的考虑？
2) 如果你是John或Chris，为了听到张明明的真实看法，你会怎么安排面试和面试后的讨论？

（二）James夏天在中国参加了一个关于环境保护的夏令营。他的同学都来自中国和一些其他亚洲国家。James最喜欢讨论课，老师每次提问他都会抢着回答，说得最多，表现得特别积极。但是他注意到有些同学总等着老师叫他们回答，如果老师不叫他们的名字，他们就不会参加讨论。开始时James 以为这些同学性格内向，但是下课以后一起玩儿的时候发现他们都很活泼，爱说爱笑。James特别不理解，为什么这些同学上课时好像变了一个人一样。

思考与讨论：

1) James的困惑是什么？为什么他的同学上课时表现得都很安静？
2) 如果你是James，别人都很安静时，你会怎么做？

（三）Emma跟男朋友张文天住在北京，他们也在同一家公司工作。新年快到了，公司照例要举行年会，但Emma和张文天却为了年会的事有点不开心。原来，公司打算在年会上让张文天作为员工代表讲话，但张文天却不愿意。Emma开始以为是张文天不自信就鼓励了他几次，可他还是不愿意，他说："我就是个普通员工，有什么好讲的？我们部门比我资深的人不少，比我年轻优秀的人也不少，我可不想出这个风头。" Emma想，做员工代表是一个荣誉，她不明白张文天为什么不愿意，这跟"出风头"又有什么关系。

思考与讨论：

1) 张文天不想做员工代表，是因为不自信吗？
2) 如果你是Emma，你会继续鼓励张文天作为员工代表讲话吗？

（四）Tyler在一家中国公司做新产品的研发工作。Tyler喜欢创新，而同一部门的其他同事却觉得保持传统非常重要，因此在工作中有时会发生一些小矛盾。最近一次开会时又发生了意见不同的情况。这时经理站出来对大家说："我们太需要创新了，有些落后的传统早就不应该要了。但是话又说回来，传统代表了稳定，保持传统不是没有道理。"经理就这样说回来说回去，讲了好长时间。Tyler越听越糊涂，他听不懂领导的意思，到底应该尽量创新还是应该尽量保持传统呢？

思考与讨论：

1) Tyler为什么糊涂了？经理为什么这样说回来说回去，他的意思到底是什么？
2) 如果你是经理，你在工作中会怎么处理这个问题？

二、口语交际练习 Oral communication exercises

1. 角色扮演 Role play

   Pair up with a peer and refer to one of the critical incidents in *Situation analysis* to create a five-minute skit with a similar storyline. Use new vocabulary and speech patterns that you have learned from this lesson in your skit. Perform the dialogue in class and discuss whether each skit properly reflects typical Chinese discourse behavior.

2. 辩论 (biànlùn) Debate

   题目：中庸思想应不应该提倡？
   正方：应该提倡中庸思想　　　　反方：不应该提倡中庸思想

通过这一课的学习，我们了解到中庸思想对中国人的思维和行为方式有很大的影响。但是，有些人认为这些影响对中国人和中国社会并没有好处，因此不应该提倡中庸思想。请分成两个小组，辩论中庸思想对中国社会到底有什么正面和负面(fùmiàn: negative side)的影响。

辩论以前，请大家：(1) 上网查找有关的信息(xìnxī: information)；(2) 跟几位中文母语者聊聊这个问题；(3) 上YouTube或优酷网站看看中国大学生怎么做"辩论赛"。辩论赛的话题和场合都比较正式。为了表示礼貌，辩论时请用以下这些词语：

- 介绍自己这一方的看法：我方的观点是……
- 表达看法：对方（同学）说……，而我方认为……　/　对于……，我方的看法是……
- 具体说明自己的观点：一是……，二是…… / 首先，其次，最后 / 第一，第二，第三
- 其他词语/句型：既……，也/又…… / S随着……而…… / ……，与……不同的是…… / S作为……

三、写作 Composition

1. 作文　（两题选一题）

   题目1：我对中庸之道的看法

   - 中庸之道对中国人的生活行为、人际关系、企业甚至国家管理方式都有很大的影响。请你：(1) 解释什么是中庸之道；(2) 中庸之道跟你母语文化的价值观有什么一样或不一样的地方；(3) 你认为应不应该提倡中庸之道；(4) 从最近的社会现象、经济发展、环境保护或政治等方面，选

择一个话题并从中庸思想的角度谈谈你认为应该怎么看待(kàndài: look upon)或解决这个问题；(5) 总结你对中庸之道的看法。

- 写作时请尽量用新学的生词和句型。

题目2：谈“出风头”

- 请你用自己的话解释“出风头”是什么意思。
- 中国人对“出风头”的看法是什么？这种思想跟你的文化背景有什么类似或不同的地方？请举例说明。
- 你认为强调“枪打出头鸟”和“树大招风”这种观念有什么好处与坏处？
- 经过前面的分析跟比较后，当你有“出风头”的机会时，你会用什么样的态度面对？总结你的看法。

2. 文化探索 Cultural exploration: For learners who are currently studying or working in the target culture.

This lesson introduced several common expressions that advocate behaving in accordance with the philosophy of 中庸. Make a table (example below) for at least four related sayings. Interview 3–4 native speakers and discuss the following questions with them:

1) What kind of ideology or cultural value do these sayings promote?
2) How do these values influence Chinese behavior in general?
3) Do they observe these values in their own lives?

Record the answers in the table, then write a paragraph to reflect on your findings. Submit the table and your reflections to your instructor.

Examples：

俗语 (súyǔ: folk saying)	*俗语的观念*	*个人的经验*
人怕出名猪怕壮。		

第四单元 **Unit four**

文化视角：面子心理

Cultural perspective: face psychology

第九课　面子——打开中国人性格之锁

行为聚焦：保全面子
Behavior highlighted: saving face

课文 *Text*

一个文化的深层结构往往是通过一些世俗观念对人们产生影响的。这些世俗观念并不一定在哲学经典里找得到，但它们的意义更实际、更具体，因此对人们的影响也更直接。中国文化里的"面子""人情""关系"等，就是这样一些既实际又具体的世俗化观念。

众所周知，中国人"爱面子"。事实上，许多中国人不仅是"爱面子"或"要面子"，而且是"死要面子"。所谓"死要面子"，就是说一个人宁可委屈自己，甚至宁可受罪也要保全自己的面子。最早发现中国人这个特点的西方人，是一百多年前到中国传教的美国人亚瑟·史密斯。他在中国生活了二十二年，并根据自己的生活经历写了一本书，叫《中国人的性格》。在这本书里，史密斯总结了中国人的二十多种性格特点，其中第一种就是"保全面子"。他说，面子好像是一把钥匙，如果掌握了中国人面子的秘密，你就能够打开中国人性格的这把锁。

中国人的面子是什么？它跟西方人的面子观念又有什么不同？一般来说，面子指的是一个人在别人眼中的形象或尊荣。可是，中国人的面子有些复杂，一个主要的原因在于它是由"脸"和"面"两个部分组成的。从这两个词的基本意义来看，"脸"指的是头的前面，即面孔；"面"说的是一个物体的表面。两者指的都是表面，所以中国人用这两个词来形容面子心理时常常混用。很多情况下，"有面子"也可以说是"有脸"，"丢面子"也可以说是"丢脸"。可是，"脸"和"面子"的意思又不完全相同。人类学家胡先缙女士早在上世纪四十年代就指出，"脸"含有很强的道德意义，而"面子"主要指的是一个人在他人眼里的地位和尊荣。所以，"不要面子"也许是说一个人对自己在别人眼里的形象不那么在乎，而"不要脸"则有可能说一个人做了什么不光彩的事，是一个道德问题了。

"脸"和"面"不仅常常混用，而且还可以连用（如"要脸面""丢脸面"等），这使得中国人的面子在很多情况下带有道德的色彩。所谓中国人爱面子，其实主要是说中国人在做人做事时努力保全自己的形象，不让自己丢脸。此外，由于中国人的群体意识，生活在这种环境里的人必须时时面对他人，并通过他人来评价自己，中国人面子里的他人因素也非常的强。如果说在西方，一个人的面子是通过积极地表现自己而赢得的，那么在中国文化里，一个人的面子则常常是由他人给的、伤害的，甚至拿去的。最后，也是由于群体意识的文化原因，中国人的面子不仅包括“我的面子”“你的面子”，而且还包括“我们大家的面子”。

中华民族自古以来就是一个爱面子的民族。到了今天，中国人还是一样地爱面子，要面子，甚至想方设法争面子。多年前，央视春晚有个小品叫《有事您说话》。小品里的主人公为了有个好人缘，宁可夜里不睡觉在火车站排队帮人买车票。他不想让人知道这个秘密，所以回来后跟别人说票都是自己通过关系拿到的。这个小品虽然是为了搞笑，可是它传递的信息，即面子问题的严重性，却值得广大观众思考。有人说，随着中国商品经济的进一步发展，中国人的面子问题现在变得越来越严重、越来越不正常了。“美女经济”“面子消费”“形象工程”等等，这些都是面子心理在当今物质化社会的表现。难怪网上有人把目前中国所处的时代叫做“眼球时代”！

生词 New words

简体	繁體	拼音	词性	英文翻译
1. 性格		xìnggé	n	character, temperament
2. 锁	鎖	suǒ	n/v	lock; lock
3. 保全		bǎoquán	v	keep ... intact, safeguard
4. 深层	深層	shēncéng	adj/n	deep, deep-seated; deep layer
5. 结构	結構	jiégòu	n	structure, construction
6. 世俗		shìsú	adj/n	earthly, secular; the worldly [世俗观念: worldly views, common views]
7. 意义	意義	yìyì	n	meaning, significance
8. 直接		zhíjiē	adj	direct [间接 (jiànjiē): indirect]
9. 人情		rénqíng	n	human feelings, favor
10. 众所周知	眾所周知	zhòngsuǒzhōuzhī	idiom	as everybody knows, as it is known
11. 事实上	事實上	shìshí.shàng	adv	in reality, in fact
12. 宁可	寧可	nìngkě	adv	would rather
13. 委屈		wěi.qu	v/adj	resign oneself to; feeling wronged
14. 受罪		shòu//zuì	v	endure hardship, suffer
15. 传教	傳教	chuán//jiào	v	spread a religion, preach
16. 根据	根據	gēnjù	prep/v/n	based on; base ... on; basis
17. 经历	經歷	jīnglì	n/v	experience; go through (event, era)

简体	繁體	拼音	词性	英文翻译
18. 总结	總結	zǒngjié	v/n	summarize, sum up; summary
19. 钥匙	鑰匙	yào.shi	n	key [classifier: 把]
20. 掌握		zhǎngwò	v	master
21. 秘密		mìmì	n/adj	secret, secrecy; secret
22. 尊荣	尊榮	zūnróng	n	dignity and honor
23. 复杂	複雜	fùzá	adj	complicated, complex
24. 面孔		miànkǒng	n	face
25. 物体	物體	wùtǐ	n	object
26. 表面		biǎomiàn	n	surface
27. 形容		xíngróng	v	describe
28. 人类学	人類學	rénlèixué	n	anthropology [人类: mankind; 人类学家: anthropologist]
29. 地位		dìwèi	n	rank, social status
30. 光彩		guāngcǎi	adj/n	glorious, honorable; glory, luster, splendor
31. 使得		shǐ.de	v	(intentions, plans, things) cause (a result) [more formal than 让]
32. 色彩		sècǎi	n	color, hue
33. 时时	時時	shíshí	adv	frequently, constantly
34. 面对	面對	miànduì	v	face, confront
35. 评价	評價	píngjià	v/n	appraise, evaluate; evaluation
36. 因素		yīnsù	n	factor, element
37. 积极	積極	jījí	adj	positive, proactive
38. 赢得		yíngdé	v	win
39. 伤害	傷害	shānghài	v	harm, hurt
40. 民族		mínzú	n	nation-state, ethnic group
41. 想方设法	想方設法	xiǎngfāng-shèfǎ	idiom	try every means, leave no stone unturned
42. 春晚		chūnwǎn	n	Chinese New Year's eve gala [short for 春节联欢晚会]
43. 小品		xiǎopǐn	n	skit, short act
44. 主人公		zhǔréngōng	n	protagonist
45. 人缘	人緣	rényuán	n	relations with other people, popularity among people
46. 搞笑		gǎo//xiào	v/adj	make people laugh, entertain; hilarious
47. 传递	傳遞	chuándì	v	transmit, pass on
48. 信息		xìnxī	n	information, message

简体	繁體	拼音	词性	英文翻译
49. 值得		zhí//.dé	v	merit, be worthy of
50. 进一步	進一步	jìnyíbù	adv	one step further, further onward
51. 正常		zhèngcháng	adj	normal
52. 工程		gōngchéng	n	project, engineering [形象工程: vanity project]
53. 当今	當今	dāngjīn	n	present time
54. 物质	物質	wùzhì	adj/n	materialistic; material, matter
55. 处	處	chǔ	v	be situated at, be in a position of [所处的时代: the era that people live in]
56. 时代	時代	shídài	n	times, age, epoch, era
57. 难怪	難怪	nánguài	adv	no wonder
58. 眼球		yǎnqiú	n	eyeball, [*fig.*] attention

专有名词 Proper nouns

简体	繁體	拼音	英文翻译
1. 亚瑟•史密斯	亞瑟•史密斯	Yàsè Shǐmìsī	Arthur Henderson Smith (1845–1932), Chinese name 明恩溥 (Míng Ēnpǔ), a missionary of the American Board of Commissioners for Foreign Missions. His *Chinese Characteristics* (1894) was the most widely read book on China by foreigners living in the country through the 1920s.
2. 胡先缙	胡先縉	Hú Xiānjìn	Hsien Chin Hu, a pioneering Chinese anthropologist
3. 央视	央視	Yāngshì	CCTV [short for 中国中央电视台, China Central Television]

词语与句型 Expressions and sentence patterns

1. 宁可VP would rather VP

课文例句：所谓"死要面子"，就是说一个人宁可委屈自己，甚至宁可受罪也要保全自己的面子。

宁可 introduces an undesirable course of action that the subject settles on doing after assessing other, more undesirable options.

The 宁可 clause can be followed by the 也 clause. However, the sentence can convey two very different meanings, depending on whether the 也 clause contains negation. Without negation (example 1), the sentence emphasizes that the subject will commit to the action described in VP1 in order to achieve the outcome described by VP2. In contrast, the presence of negation (example 2) draws attention to the action in VP1 that the subject would rather suffer the action described in VP1 rather than endure the consequences described in VP2.

The 也 clause does not need to be included if the alternate scenario is clear from context (example 3).

❖ S宁可 VP1，也 + 要/会 VP2 S would rather VP1 in order to VP2
❖ S 宁可 VP1，也 + 不 VP2 S would rather VP1 than VP2

- 中国人重视教育，很多家长宁可自己辛苦一点，也会把钱花在孩子的教育上。
- 小王上大学时有室友，觉得很不方便。工作以后，他宁可多花钱自己租房也不愿意找室友合住了。
- 如果这次足球赛的门票太贵，那我宁可不去看。

2. 早在 + time point + 就 VP VP as far back as + time point

课文例句：人类学家胡先缙女士早在上世纪四十年代就指出，"脸"含有很强的道德意义，而"面子"主要指的是一个人在他人眼里的地位和尊荣。

早在usually precedes the description of a specific time period in the past.

- 丝绸(sīchóu: silk)之路早在2000多年前就已存在。
- 早在19世纪就有中国人到欧美留学，把西方思想带回了中国。

3. A……，(而)B则…… A ...; in contrast, B ...

课文例句："不要面子"也许是说一个人对自己在别人眼里的形象不那么在乎，而"不要脸"则有可能说一个人做了什么不光彩的事，是一个道德问题了。

In formal language, the use of 则 draws attention to the differences in the content of the two clauses. 而 may be included at beginning of the second clause without changing the sentence's meaning.

- 约会总是迟到也许是个人习惯问题，(而)上班经常迟到则是工作态度问题。
- 一般来说，中国人比较重视集体的利益，(而)西方人则更重视个人的利益。

4. 而③

课文例句：如果说在西方，一个人的面子是通过积极地表现自己而赢得的，那么在中国文化里，一个人的面子则常常是由他人给的、伤害的，甚至拿去的。

When used with 通过, 为了, 由于, etc., 而③ introduces the result or outcome that was achieved due to the means or reasons that had been introduced by 通过, 为了, 由于, etc.

❖ S 通过……而 VP [通过: through (method/process)]
❖ S 为了/为……而 VP [为了/为: in order to (achieve a purpose)]
❖ S 因为/因/由于……而 VP [因为/因/由于: because of (reason)]
❖ S 根据 NP 而 VP [根据: based on (judgement)]

- 小李通过努力工作而引起了董事长的注意。
- 中国人经常为了客气而刻意贬低自己、抬高对方。
- 微信由于方便易用而被人们所喜爱，成为中国人广泛使用的社交工具。
- 在是否建海外分公司的问题上，张经理根据经验和自己对经济规律的认识而投了反对票。

而③ can be omitted without changing the meaning. However, its presence makes the language more formal.

For other usage of 而, see 而① in Lesson One and 而② in Lesson Two.

5. 由…… V　　be V-ed by ...

课文例句1：中国人的面子有些复杂，一个主要的原因在于它是由"脸"和"面"两个部分组成的。
课文例句2：如果说在西方，一个人的面子是通过积极地表现自己而赢得的，那么在中国文化里，一个人的面子则常常是由他人给的、伤害的，甚至拿去的。

When used as a preposition, 由 introduces the components that make up an entity or the factor(s) that brought about a certain outcome. It can also be used introduce the person who performs an action. In example 1 below, 由 describes the components that make up a university, the sentence subject, while in example 2 below, 由 introduces the parents who made marriage decisions for their children in traditional China.

- 这个大学是由八个学院组成的。
- 在中国传统社会中，子女和什么人结婚一般是由父母决定的。

语言练习 To practice and reinforce what you have learned from the Text, New Words, and the section "Expressions and sentence patterns" in this lesson, please visit the companion website to download a PDF version of the exercises.

交际情景 Communication scenarios

Study the following conversations between native speakers on the textbook companion website. Use the plug-in feature to find the definitions of the new words highlighted in orange. Try to visualize the scene as you read and listen to each dialogue. Discuss your reactions to these scenario dialogues with a classmate.

1. Wang Dawei and Zhang Lili have been dating for some time. They want to hold a small destination wedding after graduation. His parents disagree, instead insisting on holding a lavish wedding banquet to celebrate the occasion. Pay attention to his parents' reasoning as well as to Dawei's concerns.

王大伟：爸、妈，我跟莉莉打算毕业以后旅行结婚。你们就不用帮我们摆酒席了。
李爱华：旅行结婚？那可不行。酒席一定要摆，而且得订最好的酒店，订三十桌，把亲戚朋友还有我和你爸的同事都请来。
王为民：对，菜和酒都要最好的，这钱不能省。如果让人笑话我们小气，那多没面子。

王大伟：可是你们请的那些同事我和莉莉都不认识，这有什么意义？
李爱华：你懂什么？婚礼就是人多热闹，我们家才有面子。
王大伟：妈，我们家哪有那么多钱啊？
李爱华：你放心吧，我们虽然工资不多，但是平时一直很省，就是为了攒钱给你结婚。
王大伟：你们这不是死要面子活受罪吗?!

思考与讨论：

1） 王大伟的父母爱面子吗？对话中哪些行为和语言能表现出来？在你的国家父母也会这样做吗？
2） 根据这段对话，王大伟为什么不愿意父母为他摆酒席？

2. At a teacher-parent conference, Zhou Qiang's father is greatly embarrassed when he finds out that his son has been cheating on exams. Take note of the reasons other than the cheating itself that may have upset his father.

周强父亲：今天开完家长会，老师就把我叫到办公室，把周强考试作弊的事说了一遍。
周强母亲：就是那个年轻的小王老师吗？
周强父亲：对啊，她才刚毕业，工作不到一年，就当着别的老师的面，一点儿都不客气地批评我没把孩子教育好，真是把我的脸都丢光了。
周　　强：爸，是我错了。对不起。
周强父亲：说对不起有什么用？你不要脸，我还要脸呢。以后我有什么脸去学校，跟老师和别的同学家长见面？

思考与讨论：

1） 对话中哪些事情让周强的父亲觉得特别丢脸？
2） 周强父亲批评儿子时为什么只强调丢脸，而不是作弊本身的问题？
3） 在你的国家，有没有老师批评家长的情况？被批评的家长的想法跟周强父亲一样吗？

3. Wang Dong represented China at an international athletic competition. Though he had a fever on the night before the event, Wang decided not to withdraw and ended up winning the title. Identify the considerations that motivated him to persevere through the hardship.

记者：祝贺你得了冠军!
王东：谢谢。
记者：听说你比赛前发烧了，是吗？
王东：对，比赛前一天烧到38度。本来想过放弃比赛，但是后来想到只有我一个中国人进了决赛，不能给祖国和人民丢脸，我就坚持参加了比赛。
记者：比赛中有没有不舒服？
王东：是挺不舒服的，但是一想到我在为国争光，就不管这些了。
记者：现在有什么要对观众说的吗？
王东：谢谢大家支持我，我以后会更努力，为国家和人民赢得更多比赛。

思考与讨论：

1） 是什么原因让王东带病坚持参加了比赛？
2） 如果他放弃了比赛，他自己和观众有可能会怎么想？在你的国家，碰到这样的情况，运动员和观众也会这么想吗？

言语行为例说 Notes on discourse behavior

1. 对话例句1：李爱华：酒席一定要摆，而且得订最好的酒店……
   王为民：……如果让人笑话我们小气，那多没面子。

   对话例句2：王大伟：可是你们请的那些同事我和莉莉都不认识……
   李爱华：……婚礼就是人多热闹，我们家才有面子。

   An individual does not earn, have, or lose 面子 in isolation. It will also be affected by the social status and public actions of one's family and friends. For example, parents gain face if their children are exemplary students. A man can gain face from having rich and powerful friends or by marrying a beautiful woman.

   - 儿子：人家都有车了，咱家也得买。您说买国产的好还是进口的好？
     父亲：当然买进口的，开国产车咱多没面子。
   - 甲：马上要毕业了，我还没想好是去美国读博士，还是留在中国工作。
     乙：去美国吧，读个美国博士让你父母亲戚都有面子。

2. 对话例句：李爱华：……我们虽然工资不多，但是平时一直很省，就是为了攒钱给你结婚。
   王大伟：你们这不是死要面子活受罪吗?!

   死要面子活受罪 means that one would rather suffer horribly rather than to lose face. Though this scenario can be often observed in Chinese society, a speaker usually invokes this saying to reproach or disapprove of the phenomenon.

   - 甲：为了还车贷，我每个月得打三份工，真有点儿受不了了。
     乙：你明明负担不起，却买那么贵的车，不是死要面子活受罪吗？
   - 甲：你为什么要帮小李做PPT？你自己的工作不是还没做完吗？
     乙：我看她做了那么久还不对，挺可怜的，就答应帮她了。都已经答应帮忙了，如果再告诉她不帮了，那多没面子。
     甲：今天晚上别睡觉了，你真是死要面子活受罪。

3. 对话例句1：周强母亲：就是那个年轻的小王老师吗？
   周强父亲：对啊，她才刚毕业，工作不到一年，就当着别的老师的面，一点儿都不客气地批评我没把孩子教育好，真是把我的脸都丢光了。

   对话例句2：周　强：爸，是我错了。对不起。
   周强父亲：说对不起有什么用？你不要脸，我还要脸呢。以后我有什么脸去学校，跟老师和别的同学家长见面？

   对话例句3：记者：听说你比赛前发烧了，是吗？
   王东：……本来想过放弃比赛，但是后来想到只有我一个中国人进了决赛，不能给祖国和人民丢脸，我就坚持参加了比赛。

   不要脸, literally "don't want face," actually means that a person is "shameless" containing a strong moral implication. To say that someone 不要脸, "有什么脸……?", "把 someone 的脸都丢光了" or "给……丢脸" is a very strong accusation.

   - 甲：没想到张秘书居然是王经理的小三，现在全公司都知道了。
     乙：真不要脸！她还有什么脸来上班，应该辞职回家！
     甲：是啊，就算不辞职，她也没脸来见同事了吧。

- 甲：最近电视报道了三亚一家饭馆骗客人钱的事，一条鱼卖两千块！
  乙：这样不道德的商人把我们三亚人的脸都丢光了，应该在电视上多报道，让他们没脸在三亚做生意!

4. 对话例句：记者：比赛中有没有不舒服？
   王东：是挺不舒服的，但是一想到我在为国争光，就不管这些了。

The idea of 面子 applies to groups as well as to individuals. 面子 is also transferrable; personal glory or disgrace affects the individual as well as to his or her group. This has resulted in a strong sense of nationalism, as seen in Dialogue 3. 为/给 sb 争光/争面子 means to win glory/gain face for someone/someone's group, including one's country. When acting as a representative in competition, that person would not dare to give up easily for fear of facing collective disapproval from the group.

- 甲： 老李，你女儿真给你们家争面子，考了全市第一，这下你们全家都脸上有光了。
  乙： 是啊，我这个女儿算是没白养。
- 甲： 你这两个月天天为演讲比赛做准备，累不累啊？
  乙： 校长说了这是给学校争光的大事，不能马虎啊。

体演情景 Perform the scenario

Select a dialogue from this section and listen to its recording several times. Imitate the speakers in pronunciation, intonation and discourse behavior in terms of both the words they use and the ways in which they carry themselves. Memorize the dialogue for performance in class.

跨文化交际 Cross-cultural communication

一、误解分析 Situation analysis

Break into groups and discuss the misunderstanding in each of the cross-cultural communication incidents below. For each incident, the group should generate an answer that best explains the cultural assumptions behind the ways in which the individuals say and do things. In addition, discuss possible strategies to avoid these misunderstandings in similar situations.

（一）Leila在中国教英语一年了，认识了不少中国朋友。其中有几个朋友的家境很好。这一天，她的好朋友Rebecca去中国看她。Leila约了七八个中国朋友再加上Rebecca一起去餐馆吃饭。他们点了一大桌子菜，吃得很开心。王明是他们当中最有钱的。吃完饭，服务员送来账单的时候，他就抢着付钱。Rebecca不习惯让陌生人付钱，说什么也要付自己那份，她问Leila该怎么办。Leila比较熟悉这种做法，就说："既然王明坚持，那就让他付吧。"王明说："就是啊，这是小意思，总得给我个面子吧。" Rebecca听了以后觉得很奇怪，她心想，你花钱买面子吗？

思考与讨论：

1) Rebecca为什么不理解王明的做法？王明抢着付钱的原因是什么？
2) 如果你是Rebecca，听到Leila和王明的看法以后，你还会坚持付钱吗？

（二）文文在美国一所大学念书。一天，她和语伴Anna约好，一起去奥特莱斯买东西。Anna找到一件T恤衫和一条裤子，牌子很普通但都很适合她，而且是半价，就高高兴兴地买了下来。文文不太在乎价格，只是很讲究牌子。她买了一双UGG靴子，一个寇驰包和好几样雅诗兰黛化妆品。Anna说："你平常不是总说我们是穷学生吗？怎么一下子买了这么多这么贵的东西啊？"文文说："这里的每个牌子都比中国便宜多啦。再说，个人形象很重要，没钱就先用信用卡，然后想办法再还。"Anna心想，文文这样做值得吗？

思考与讨论：

1) 文文好像平时很节省，可为什么愿意花大价钱买很贵的名牌？
2) 如果你是Anna，听到文文的想法后，你的看法是什么？

（三）Tim 从美国给他的中国寄宿家庭带了一袋咖啡。周日晚上Tim的中国爸爸请了几个亲戚和Tim吃晚饭，饭后他把咖啡拿出来，跟大家说："这可是美国最好的咖啡，特别贵，Tim专门从美国带给我的。"Tim听了本来想说这咖啡并不是特别贵，可是刚开口他的中国爸爸就让他打住了。接着，Tim的中国爸爸给大家冲了咖啡，他一边喝一边跟Tim说好喝好喝。客人都走了以后，Tim也回到了自己的房间，他听见客厅里中国爸爸跟中国妈妈说："这个咖啡的味道实在太苦了，不好喝。"Tim不明白既然中国爸爸不喜欢，为什么还一直跟他说好喝？他更不明白的是，他没说过这咖啡多少钱，中国爸爸怎么知道这是最好的而且还特别贵？

思考与讨论：

1) 为什么Tim的中国爸爸跟客人说Tim给他买的咖啡是最贵最好的，而且明明不喜欢喝咖啡还说咖啡好喝？
2) 如果你是Tim，碰到这样的情况你会怎么办？会不会也像Tim一样想要纠正他中国爸爸的说法？

（四）Harvey在一家跨国公司的中国分公司负责计算机部门。他经常组织一些计算机方面的培训，而参加培训的都是各个部门的中国员工。上课的时候，员工们都坐得端端正正的，没有人吃东西或上厕所，有的人还努力地做笔记。Harvey也总是给员工一些互动和提问的机会，并且总是一遍又一遍地问参加培训的员工"是不是都懂了？有没有什么问题？"员工们总是点头表示懂了。可是 Harvey一问到具体的问题，就发现没有一个人可以回答。这样的情况经常发生，让Harvey感到很困惑。他想，员工们明明不懂，为什么都点头表示懂了呢？

思考与讨论：

1) 中国员工听懂 Harvey 的讲座了吗？如果没有，为什么他们不问 Harvey 问题，反而还点头表示懂了？
2) 如果你是 Harvey，你会用什么样的方式检查员工到底懂没懂？

二、口语交际练习 Oral communication exercises

1. 角色扮演 Role play

Pair up with a peer and refer to one of the critical incidents in *Situation analysis* to create a five-minute skit with a similar storyline. Use new vocabulary and speech patterns that you have learned from this lesson in your skit. Perform the dialogue in class and discuss whether each skit properly reflects typical Chinese discourse behavior.

2. 观察与比较 Observation and comparison

请在YouTube或优酷网站上用关键词 (guānjiàn cí: keyword) 搜索(sōusuǒ: search)，找到课文中提到的央视春晚小品。观看时，也注意听听小品中不同人物的口音，然后完成下面的活动：

- 请一位中国朋友也看看这个小品，然后一起讨论以下几个问题并做笔记。如果你对这个小品有什么问题，比方说有什么地方看不懂的，请中国朋友先跟你解释一下。

  (1) 中国朋友对这个小品所传达的信息有什么看法？
  (2) 他/她怎么看中国人面子的问题？
  (3) 你的母语文化里也有面子这个观念吗？跟中国人的面子有什么相同或不同的地方？
  (4) 面子观念对中国社会有什么影响？在你的国家呢？请举例说明。

- 把你们讨论的内容用下面表格(biǎogé: table)的形式记录下来。讨论时请尽使用下列词语和句型：宁可……也…… / 事实上 / 早在……就…… / S所处的N / 想方设法 / 使得 / 传递 / 信息 / 人缘 / 丢脸 / (没)有面子 / 难怪。

	中国人的面子观念	我母语文化中的面子观念
相同的地方		
不同的地方		
举例说明		
面子的影响		

- 总结访谈的内容，做成 3–5 分钟的口头报告并录音，然后把录音和表格一起交给老师。

三、写作 Composition

1. 作文 （两题选一题）

题目1：我对“面子”的看法

- 面子观念在许多国家和不同的文化传统中都存在。但相对来说，中国人更好面子。通过这一课的内容，请你：(1)用自己的话解释中国人的面子观是什么？(2)这个观念跟你母语文化的传统有什么相似或不同的地方？(3)比方说，如果你的中文老师周五要请全班同学们聚餐，但是你已经跟朋友约好了那天要去看电影，你参不参加这个聚餐呢？请最少列出三个你做决定的理由。(4) 根据前面的例子或者类似的例子，你认为面子观对人际关系有什么影响？有什么好处与坏处？(5) 总结你对中国人面子观的看法。

- 建议使用的词语和句型：……，（而）……则……/宁可……也……/在……，情况下/因为……而/S所处的N

题目2：一件让你觉得最丢面子的事

- 请你说说这件事是怎么发生的，为什么让你觉得没有面子？你当时是怎么处理这件事的？你从这件事得到了什么经验或教训 (jiào.xùn: lesson; moral)?
- 写作时请尽量用新学的生词和句型。

2. 文化探索 Cultural exploration: For learners who are currently studying or working in the target culture.

After finishing this lesson, you should now be more attuned to situations in which Chinese people are fighting to earn (争 zhēng) face, giving face to others, or trying to save face. These situations are more likely to happen at public and formal occasions, such as a wedding, a formal dinner, a school reunion, etc. If you observe such an event happening in real life or being portrayed in the media, pay attention to what people say and how they say it (e.g. body language, tone of voice). Make note of the setting, such as the location and the nature of the event, in which it occurs. Copy the table in *Appendix 1: cultural exploration* and record your observations in Chinese. Write a paragraph to reflect on what you have observed. Submit the table and your reflections to your instructor.

第十课　伤什么也不能伤面子

行为聚焦：面子运作
Behavior highlighted: face work

课文 *Text*

简单地说，“有面子”其实就是受他人的尊重。人们都希望别人尊重自己，不分种族和国籍。可是在中国，由于儒家的道德观念和“耻感文化”的影响，人们特别在乎自己的公众形象，也十分期望得到周围人的尊重。中国有句俗话说，“人活一张脸，树活一张皮”，面子被看得跟生命一样重要。正因如此，中国人认为，在与自己相识的人交往中，伤什么也不能伤面子。特别是当对方是自己的领导时，说话做事更要小心。因为地位越高，面子也越大，如果领导的面子伤了，有时后果会很严重。

端传媒网站上有一篇文章，讲的是加拿大人 John 在中国成功创业的经历。John 在中国生活了很多年，现在已是两个公司的老板。他对记者说，他的成功得益于自己对中国面子文化的深入了解。他还清楚地记得自己过去由于无知犯的一个错误。1998 年，John 辞去外教工作，到青岛的一家五星级酒店负责开发国际业务。他工作得很认真，又做市场调查，又找员工谈话，对酒店在运营和管理方面的问题进行了深入的研究。他花了很长时间向董事会汇报了他的研究结果，并把自己的改进意见详详细细地讲了一遍。听完他的报告，董事们无不称赞，并说可以马上开始行动。

可是散会以后，什么也没有发生。不仅 John 的计划一个都没有得到实施，而且更糟糕的是，他被告知以后不要再做相关的工作了。后来 John 明白了，自己犯了一个“严重”的错误。他对记者说，董事们都是五六十岁的领导，有二三十年酒店工作的经历，而他那时35岁，并且没有在酒店工作过。可是他的做法似乎是在告诉领导，他们做错了，现在应该按照他的建议重新开始。这对于中国领导来说是不可接受的。如果他的方案被采用，问题得到解决，别人就会认为那是 John 的功劳而不是领导们的，这会让领导很没有面子。如果领导不采用 John 的方案，即使工作没有得到改善，他们也不会丢面子。John 强调说，“在中国面子比成功重要”。

半年以后，John 去了上海一家五星级酒店工作，还是负责国际业务的开发。但这一次，John 没有把自己发现的问题直接向董事会汇报，而是先私下找到了董事会主席，提出自己的想法并征求他的意见。主席同意的方案就留下，不同意的就放到了一边。这些主席同意了的方案最后再由主席自己向董事会汇报。这一次，董事会采纳了John 的建议，他成功了。

John 的故事是一个很好的案例，它告诉我们，在中国面子不仅仅是一个心理现象，而且还代表着一套重要的行为规则。这个案例还告诉我们，跟中国人打交道，考虑怎样保全自己的面子固然很重要，但考虑怎样保全对方的面子更重要。知道怎样给别人留面子，甚至知道怎样帮别人挽回面子，其实是中国面子文化最重要的内容。

那么，怎么给别人留面子呢？首先不要当着众人的面批评一个人，这会让人感到下不来台。其次，千万不要证明别人错了。如果需要表达自己的看法，话要讲得委婉、含蓄。此外，如果对方做了什么丢面子的事，比如说借了你的钱忘了还，最好不要当面提醒他，发个委婉的短信或请个中间人帮帮忙都是不错的办法。最后，如果一个人遇到了尴尬的情况，比如当众说错了话，如果你能说点什么帮他解围，在很长的时间里，这个人都会对你非常感激。

总之，按照面子规则做事是中国人的做人之道和处世之道。这不仅在人际交往中，而且在企业的商务来往中，甚至在国家之间的政治谈判中都非常重要。面子是一门深奥的学问，虽然在学校里学不到，但却是中国人在一生中都必须努力掌握的。

生词 New words

简体	繁體	拼音	词性	英文翻译
1. 运作	運作	yùnzuò	n/v	operation [面子运作: face operation, face work]; operate
2. 尊重		zūnzhòng	v/n	respect; respect, esteem, honor
3. 种族	種族	zhǒngzú	n	race
4. 耻感文化	恥感文化	chǐ gǎn wénhuà	phr	shame-based culture [耻 (bf): shame, disgrace]
5. 期望		qīwàng	v	expect, earnestly hope
6. 人活一张脸，树活一张皮	人活一張臉，樹活一張皮	rén huó yì zhāng liǎn, shù huó yì zhāng pí	proverb	Humans depend on their face just as trees depend on their bark for life. [皮: (tree) bark, skin]
7. 生命		shēngmìng	n	life
8. 领导	領導	lǐngdǎo	n/v	leader, leadership; lead
9. 后果	後果	hòuguǒ	n	consequence, aftermath
10. 创业	創業	chuàngyè	v	begin an undertaking, start a venture

简体	繁體	拼音	词性	英文翻译
11. 记者	記者	jìzhě	n	reporter, journalist
12. 得益于	得益於	déyìyú	phr	benefit from, be the beneficial result of
13. 深入		shēnrù	adj/v	thorough; go deep into
14. 了解		liǎojiě	n/v	understanding, comprehension; understand
15. 无知	無知	wúzhī	n/adj	ignorance; ignorant
16. 犯		fàn	v	commit [犯错误: commit an error, make a mistake, 犯罪(zuì): commit a crime, 犯法: break the law]
17. 错误	錯誤	cuòwù	n/adj	mistake, error; erroneous, incorrect
18. 辞	辭	cí	v	resign (from a job), quit (a job) [辞去工作 or 辞职 (cí//zhí): resign from a job]
19. 外教		wàijiào	n	foreign teacher [abbr. for 外国教师]
20. 开发	開發	kāifā	v	develop, exploit (a resource)
21. 业务	業務	yèwù	n	business, service
22. 调查	調查	diàochá	n/v	investigation; investigate [市场调查: market research]
23. 员工	員工	yuángōng	n	employee, staff
24. 运营	運營	yùnyíng	n/v	operation; operate
25. 进行	進行	jìnxíng	v	carry out, execute
26. 董事会	董事會	dǒngshìhuì	n	board of directors [董事: board member] [董事长: chairman of board]
27. 汇报	匯報	huìbào	v	collect information and report (to an authoritarian figure)
28. 改进	改進	gǎijìn	v	improve
29. 意见	意見	yìjiàn	n	opinion, suggestion, complaint
30. 无不	無不	wúbù	adv	without exception, invariably
31. 称赞	稱讚	chēngzàn	v	praise, acclaim, commend, compliment

简体	繁體	拼音	词性	英文翻译
32. 散会	散會	sàn//huì	v	disperse a meeting
33. 实施	實施	shíshī	v	implement
34. 告知		gàozhī	v	inform
35. 相关	相關	xiāngguān	adj/v	related, relevant; be interrelated
36. 明白		míng.bai	v/adj	realize, understand; clear, obvious
37. 重新		chóngxīn	adv	once more
38. 方案		fāng'àn	n	plan, proposal
39. 功劳	功勞	gōngláo	n	meritorious service, achievement, credit
40. 改善		gǎishàn	v	make better, improve
41. 强调	強調	qiángdiào	v	emphasize, stress
42. 私下		sīxià	adv	in private, privately
43. 主席		zhǔxí	n	chairperson
44. 征求	徵求	zhēngqiú	v	seek (opinions, feedback, etc.)
45. 采纳	採納	cǎinà	v	adopt
46. 案例		ànlì	n	case for study
47. 固然		gùrán	conj	admittedly, it's true that
48. 挽回		wǎnhuí	v	redeem, retrieve
49. 下不来台	下不來臺	xià .bu lái tái	phr	in an awkward situation that is hard to escape from [下台: get off the stage]
50. 千万	千萬	qiānwàn	adv	by all means
51. 证明	證明	zhèngmíng	v/n	prove; proof
52. 委婉		wěiwǎn	adj	tactful, indirect, euphemistic
53. 尴尬	尷尬	gān'gà	adj	embarrassed, awkward
54. 解围	解圍	jiě//wéi	v	help someone out of embarrassment, lift a siege
55. 感激		gǎnjī	v	be grateful, appreciate
56. 处世	處世	chǔshì	v	conduct oneself in society
57. 商务	商務	shāngwù	n	business affairs
58. 政治		zhèngzhì	n	politics, political affairs
59. 谈判	談判	tánpàn	n/v	negotiation; negotiate

简体	繁體	拼音	词性	英文翻译
60. 深奥	深奧	shēn'ào	adj	profound, abstruse
61. 学问	學問	xué.wen	n	learning, knowledge, scholarship [classifier: 门]

专有名词 Proper nouns

简体	繁體	拼音	英文翻译
1. 端传媒	端傳媒	Duān Chuánméi	Initium Media (https://theinitium.com), Hong Kong-based digital media outlet launched in August, 2015 [端: beginning, *initium*; 传媒: media]
2. 青岛	青島	Qīngdǎo	Qingdao, sub-provincial city in Shandong Province [a.k.a. Tsingtao]

词语与句型 Expressions and sentence patterns

1. 正因如此 precisely because of this

课文例句：中国有句俗话说，"人活一张脸，树活一张皮"，面子被看得跟生命一样重要。正因如此，中国人认为，在与自己相识的人交往中，伤什么也不能伤面子。

正因如此 calls attention to the causal relationship that exists between two statements linked by the phrase. The sentence preceding 正因如此 discusses the cause, while the sentence following it discusses the effect.

❖ S VP1，正因如此，(S) VP2
❖ S1 VP1。正因如此，S2 VP2

- 小李在北京的两家公司做过管理工作，很有经验，正因如此，在上海找新工作时也相对顺利。
- 中文有声调，而很多其它语言没有。也正因如此，对不少外国学生来说，声调较难掌握。

2. 得益于 benefit from

课文例句：他对记者说，他的成功得益于自己对中国面子文化的深入了解。

❖ S得益于 NP — S has benefited from NP.
❖ 得益于 NP，S VP — Having benefited from NP, S VP.

- 小美经常说，她的中文发音好是得益于她一年级中文课的老师教得好。
- 得益于多年的管理经验，公司的董事们在公司面临问题时很快就找到了解决方法。

3. 固然……，但…… admittedly (it is true that) ..., but ...

课文例句：这个案例还告诉我们，跟中国人打交道，考虑怎样保全自己的面子固然很重要，但考虑怎样保全对方的面子更重要。

This construction is relatively formal in usage. The speaker first acknowledges the validity of the information presented in the 固然 clause, then moves on to discuss additional information that is also true and/or even more important. The information in the two clauses is not in conflict, and the transition signified by 但(是) or 可(是) is only used to highlight the content presented in the second clause.

- 昨天董事会没有通过John提出的方案。在我看来，他的方案固然存在一些问题，但里面的一些建议还是不错的。
- 央视春晚小品《有事您说话》反映的是死要面子的问题。保全自己在他人眼中的形象固然重要，但如果帮助他人只是为了争面子，那也值得人们思考。

4. 千万 by all means, by any means

课文例句：那么，怎么给别人留面子呢？首先不要当着众人的面批评一个人，这会让人感到下不来台。其次，千万不要证明别人错了。

In an imperative sentence, 千万 is usually used in combination with 不能, 别, 不要, 要, 得(děi) to add a tone of urgency to the command or advice given.

❖ S千万 +不能/别/不要 + VP S must not VP by any means.
❖ S千万 + 要/得 + VP S must VP by all means.

- 这件事老李还不知道，你们千万别告诉他。
- 下次考试很重要，你千万要好好复习，做好准备。

语言练习 To practice and reinforce what you have learned from the Text, New Words, and the section "Expressions and sentence patterns" in this lesson, please visit the companion website to download a PDF version of the exercises.

交际情景 Communication scenarios

Study the following conversations between native speakers on the textbook companion website. Use the plug-in feature to find the definitions of the new words highlighted in orange. Try to visualize the scene as you read and listen to each dialogue. Discuss your reactions to these scenario dialogues with a classmate.

1. The CEO of Wang Weimin's company gave a presentation to the general managers right after returning from a leadership-training workshop in the United States. Weimin had questions about some data but did not ask during the presentation. Pay attention to his reasons while talking to his colleagues and how he decides to handle the situation later.

李秘书：总裁今天的报告真不错，去了一趟美国，看来收获挺大。
王为民：是啊。可是今天他提到的一些数据，跟我以前看到的好像有点儿不一样，可能再确认一下比较好。
赵学东：开会的时候你怎么不提出来？
王为民：（看了看赵学东和李秘书）各个部门的负责人都在，这时候提出来，总裁一定觉得下不来台。
赵学东：那怎么办？这些数据还挺重要的。

李秘书：是啊，要是搞错了，影响可不小。
王为民：说不定是我记错了，我回去再好好查查。如果真是总裁错了，我回头让他的秘书跟他说吧。

思考与讨论：

1) 对话中哪些行为和语言表现出王为民为总裁留面子？请举三个例子。
2) 王为民为什么要努力为总裁留面子？在你的国家，人们在这样的情况下会怎么做？

2. Each day when they are about to go to bed, Li Aihua and Wang Weimin hear piano music coming from the apartment of Xiao Zhao, their neighbor upstairs. Despite her husband's reservations, Li decides to talk to Xiao Zhao in an effort to stop the noise at their bedtime. Observe what she says and how effectively she gets the message across.

王为民：爱华，你听，是不是楼上小赵家的儿子又在弹钢琴啊？
李爱华：是啊，都快十一点了，还让不让人睡觉了？他最近天天晚上弹琴。不行，明天我得找小赵说说这事儿。
王为民：算了，都是邻居，伤什么不能伤面子，要不以后怎么相处啊？
李爱华：你放心，我知道怎么说，会给他留面子的。

（第二天）

李爱华：小赵，你儿子真刻苦，每天晚上十一点多，我们都睡觉了，还听见他在弹琴。孩子刻苦是件好事儿，但是身体还是很重要的。
小　赵：是，你说得对。是不是影响你们休息了？以后我让他早点儿练习，早点儿睡觉 。
李爱华：没有没有，孩子弹得挺好的。

思考与讨论：

1) 对于小赵儿子晚上弹钢琴太吵的事儿，王为民跟李爱华的态度有什么不一样？为什么？
2) 小赵问李爱华是不是影响她休息了，李爱华为什么说"没有没有"？
3) 李爱华为什么不想直接跟小赵抱怨？在你的国家，人们在这样的情况下会怎么 做？

3. It has been more than three months since Liu Shaohong's colleague borrowed some money from her. Liu Shaohong asks Li Aihua for advice on how to remind her colleague about the loan. Take note of the tactics that the two discuss and the reasoning behind each tactic.

刘少红：我们办公室一个同事跟我借了两千块钱，三个多月了还没还。李姐，你说我要不要直接开口跟她要？
李爱华：别直接说。人活一张脸，树活一张皮。都是同事，得给她留点儿面子。我看，你最好暗示她一下。
刘少红：那我就跟她说我们全家要去旅游，手头紧，你看怎么样？
李爱华：行啊，如果她想起来了，你也别忘了给她个台阶下。
刘少红：怎么给她台阶下呢？
李爱华：你可以跟她说，没事儿，其实你也忘了这两千块钱的事儿了，不着急，慢慢还。

思考与讨论：

1) 刘少红想通过什么方式既提醒同事欠钱的事，又给同事留面子？请举两个例子。
2) 在你的国家，人们在这样的情况下会怎么做？

言语行为例说 Notes on discourse behavior

1. 对话例句1：李秘书：总裁今天的报告真不错，去了一趟美国，看来收获挺大。
   王为民：是啊。可是他今天提到的一些数据，跟我以前看到的好像有点儿不一样，可能再确认一下比较好。

   对话例句2：李秘书：是啊，要是搞错了，影响可不小。
   王为民：说不定是我记错了，我回去再好好查查。……

   Words like 可能, 也许, 好像 are often used when the speaker wants to save face while making suggestions, refuting something, or refusing to accept something. For instance, in order to save face for the other party, you may want to say "这好像不太好 (this does not seem to be appropriate)", "可能需要再重新查查 (you might want to check it again)", "也许再确定一下比较好 (it would be better to confirm it again)", "说不定是我记错了(maybe I remembered it wrong)". When making a suggestion, you may want to phrase it as "也许这样做更好 (doing it this way might be better)", "可能……更合适 (doing ... may be more suitable)". When you wish to refute someone's idea and bring up a different point of view, you should first try to save the other party's face by validate their views. For example, you may want to say "你说的都很有道理，但是可能要再好好想想 (what you said sounds very reasonable, but we may want to give it further consideration)" or "你的建议很有用，不过也许需要再讨论讨论 (your suggestion is very helpful, but we should probably discuss it again)".

   - 甲：李编辑，我寄给您的文章您看了吗？
     乙：高老师，您的文章我看了。整体上看真不错，但是里面有一段好像有点儿重复，可能需要您再看看。
   - 甲：张经理，您看，这次的活动这样安排可以吗？
     乙：你的安排挺好的，不过也许要再好好想想怎么能更突出活动的主题。

2. 对话例句1：赵学东：开会的时候你怎么不提出来？
   王为民：……各个部门的负责人都在，这时候提出来，总裁一定觉得下不来台。

   对话例说2：李爱华：行啊，如果她想起来了，你也别忘了给她个台阶下。
   刘少红：怎么给她台阶下呢？
   李爱华：你可以跟她说，没事儿，其实你也忘了这两千块钱的事儿了，不着急，慢慢还。

   In social situations, criticizing someone in public, even if it's as innocuous as pointing out an unintended error, may make that person lose face without a way out and make that person feel 下不来台. Thus, you may want to "给sb (一) 个台阶下", i.e., to give a person a way to save face or to regain face in order to avoid embarrassment.

   - 甲：小高说他一年赚一百万，我看他在吹牛，晚上同学会上我要问问他，这一百万是怎么赚的？
     乙：你知道他在吹牛就行了，何必让他在同学们面前下不来台？
   - 甲：昨天王教授的讲座怎么样？
     乙：他讲完以后台下一位教授提出了PPT上一些数据有错，王教授回答不出来，弄得挺下不来台的。好在另一位教授给了王教授一个台阶下，问这个PPT是不是王教授的秘书帮忙准备的，不小心把数据打错了。

3. 对话例句：王为民：算了，都是邻居，伤什么不能伤面子，要不以后怎么相处啊？
   李爱华：你放心，我知道怎么说，会给他留面子的。

   伤什么不能伤面子 highlights the extent to which a Chinese person wants to maintain his or her public image and his or her desire to receive respect from other people. Being fully mindful of what you say and how you act will help you avoid damaging the other person's face. Failing to do so will make that person much more reluctant to interact with you in the future.

   - 甲：你不是不喜欢喝酒吗？为什么他送你酒，你还收下了？
     乙：他送我东西，我怎么能让他拿回去？如果不收就太伤他的面子了。
   - 甲：你不是不喜欢出差吗？怎么还去面试销售员的工作？
     乙：这个工作是我以前公司的经理介绍的。伤什么不能伤面子，喜欢不喜欢都得去面试一下。

4. 对话例句：刘少红：我们办公室一个同事跟我借了两千块钱，三个多月了还没还。李姐，你说我要不要直接开口跟她要？
   李爱华：别直接说。人活一张脸，树活一张皮。都是同事，得给她留点儿面子，我看，你最好暗示她一下。

   In conversations, a Chinese person often cites the saying "人活一张脸，树活一张皮" for justifying an action he or she is going to take, or as a precaution for preventing another person from doing something that would cause other people to lose face, as seen in Dialogue 3 above.

   - 甲：什么？这个出国访问的机会你不要了？
     乙：同学们讽刺我说我能得到这个机会是因为我爸爸是校长。人活一张脸，树活一张皮，我决定自己申请，不用学校的机会。
   - 甲：你决定辞职了？不再考虑考虑？
     乙：公司里有人说项目没成功是因为我的原因。人活一张脸，树活一张皮，我也没有脸再在这儿工作下去了。

体演情景 Perform the scenario

Select a dialogue from this section and listen to its recording several times. Imitate the speakers in pronunciation, intonation and discourse behavior in terms of both the words they use and the ways in which they carry themselves. Memorize the dialogue for performance in class.

跨文化交际 Cross-cultural communication

一、误解分析 Situation analysis

Break into groups and discuss the misunderstanding in each of the cross-cultural communication incidents below. For each incident, the group should generate an answer that best explains the cultural assumptions behind the ways in which the individuals say and do things. In addition, discuss possible strategies to avoid these misunderstandings in similar situations.

（一）Judy在南京的一个中国家庭里住了好几个月了。上个周末，她的中国爸爸的亲戚从农村老家来南京探亲。Judy听到中国爸爸叫他二伯。二伯的身体好像不太好，穿的衣服也很破旧，虽然是长辈，但是对中国爸爸说话却非常客气。他们聊了好长时间老家的事情。晚饭后，中国爸爸把二伯送去了火车站，回到家以后，又给二伯打了一个电话。电话里中国爸爸对二伯说，他把一个信封放在二伯的包里了，里面有三千块钱，快过年了，这些钱是给二伯买年货的。Judy不理解为什么中国爸爸不当面把钱给二伯，而且现在是十一月，离过年还有好久呢，为什么说这是过年买年货的钱？

思考与讨论：

1) Judy的中国爸爸为什么不当面把钱给二伯，而且说这是买年货的钱呢？
2) 如果你是中国爸爸，你会不会这么做？

（二）Justin在广州一家IT公司实习。到了周末同事们常常一起聚餐唱KTV。吃饭的时候，热情的中国同事总是要劝酒，而Justin不习惯喝中国的白酒，每次喝完都觉得很不舒服。有时候Justin会直接告诉同事他不喜欢喝白酒，可同事们却还是常常说"给我们个面子，喝一杯""不喝太不给面子了"这样的话，一边说还一边把酒倒在Justin的杯子里，甚至把酒送到他的嘴边。这时候Justin觉得非常为难，不知道应该喝还是不应该喝，更不明白自己不习惯喝白酒跟给同事面子有什么关系。

思考与讨论：

1) 在这样的场合，喝下同事敬的白酒代表了什么？如果不喝，同事为什么不高兴？
2) 如果你是 Justin，在这样的情况下你是喝还是不喝同事们敬你的酒？

（三）中国留学生文文跟美国学生Lisa是室友。快过暑假了，文文计划回中国探亲。Lisa发现文文买了很多东西，就好奇地问文文原因。原来这些东西都是文文在国内的亲戚朋友请她代购的。文文告诉Lisa代购要花很多时间和精力，再说她自己的东西已经很多了，担心行李超重。其实她很不愿意这样做，但又不知道怎么拒绝。Lisa回答说："这有什么难的？如果我是你，我就直接拒绝他们。不想做就不做嘛。"文文不知道怎么跟Lisa解释，只是说："事情不像你说的那么简单。"Lisa不懂为什么这不是一件简单的事。

思考与讨论：

1) 在中国拒绝亲朋好友的请求是不是一件简单的事？为什么？
2) 如果你是文文，你会怎样处理你中国亲戚朋友的请求？

（四）Austin 在北京一家公司工作，负责销售部门。快过年了，公司的总经理请销售部门吃饭，并且庆祝这一年的销售成绩提高了百分之十。饭桌上，几位员工在总经理面前敬了Austin一杯酒，他们说销售部的成功都是因为Austin领导得好，而且大家也跟Austin学到了很多东西。Austin 听了以后觉得有点尴尬。其实他是八月才到这家公司的，花了很长时间才了解和适应了新工作，对公司没做多少贡献。他很感谢他的员工，但不知道为什么大家要这样说。他喝下了员工敬给他的酒，不知道应该说点儿什么好。

思考与讨论：

1) Austin 为什么觉得尴尬？几位员工为什么在总经理面前称赞 Austin？
2) 如果你是 Austin，你会怎么回应员工在领导面前对你的称赞？

二、口语交际练习 Oral communication exercises

1. 角色扮演 Role play

   Pair up with a peer and refer to one of the critical incidents in *Situation analysis* to create a five-minute skit with a similar storyline. Use new vocabulary and speech patterns that you have learned from this lesson in your skit. Perform the dialogue in class and discuss whether each skit properly reflects typical Chinese discourse behavior.

2. 思考与访谈 Reflection and interview

   (1) 课前准备

   - 老师：

     请2–4位中文母语者到班上来跟同学们讨论“耻感文化与面子运作的关系”。这几位客人的年龄最好都不一样（比方说，包括二十岁到五十岁以上的人），他们的工作背景也最好都不相同。

   - 学生：

     本课课文的第一段中谈到儒家的道德观念和“耻感文化”对中国社会和人们思考方式的影响。但是，什么是耻感文化呢？除了耻感文化以外，还有什么样的文化观念对其他国家的人会产生不同的影响？请你上英文的维基百科(wéijī bǎikē: Wikipedia)网站读“Guilt-Shame-Fear spectrum of cultures”这篇文章。读完以后，请完成下面的活动：

   1) 请试着用中文做笔记，解释什么是“耻感文化”“罪 (zuì: guilt) 感文化”和“恐惧(kǒngjù: fear)文化”。
   2) 许多专家学者认为，西方社会因为受了宗教 (zōngjiào: religion) 的影响，因此多半以“罪感文化”为主。你同意这个看法吗？为什么？ 请举例说明，并跟中国的“耻感文化”做一个比较。
   3) 请每位同学根据第十课的内容和 “Guilt-Shame-Fear spectrum of cultures” 这篇文章，课前准备三个问题，下节课跟老师请来的嘉宾 (jiābīn: honored guest) 们讨论。

   (2) 课堂活动

   - 请每一位嘉宾谈谈“耻感文化”与“面子运作”的关系，然后跟同学们进行讨论。
   - 同学们跟嘉宾分享你们的母语社会是不是也受了“耻感文化”的影响。谈谈你们对“罪感文化”“恐惧文化”的看法，并探讨你们的母语社会里，“面子运作”的方式跟中国的有什么相同或不同的地方。

- 大家一起总结“耻感文化”与“面子运作”有什么关系、如何增进对文化差异(chāyì: difference)的理解。

讨论时请做笔记，并尽量使用本课的生词和下列的句型与词语， 例如：正因如此 / 得益于 / 固然……，但…… / 千万 / 公众形象 / 后果 / 改善 / 当众 / 总之。

三、写作 Composition

1. 作文 （两题选一题）

   题目1：谈“耻感文化与面子运作的关系”

   做了上面“思考与访谈”的活动后，请把自己最有兴趣的一部分讨论内容写成作文（最少分成3段）。写作时请尽量用这一课的生词和句型。

   题目2：谈“留面子”

   通过本课John的故事，我们学到“在中国，面子不仅仅是一个心理现象，而且还代表着一套重要的行为规则”。请你：(1)用自己的话解释什么是“留面子”；(2)这个观念跟你母语文化的传统有什么相似或不同的地方？(3)比方说，有一个朋友借钱总是不还，最近他又要跟你借钱了。你要怎么委婉地拒绝他，而且还要保全对方的面子？(4)根据前面的例子或者类似的例子，你认为给人留面子对人际关系有什么影响或帮助？(5)总结你对留面子的看法。

2. 文化探索 Cultural exploration: For learners who are currently studying or working in the target culture.

In general, Chinese culture emphasizes the importance of preserving face for everyone in interpersonal and social communication. Look for the following circumstances and pay attention to what is being said, how it is said, and the body language that accompanies the speech:

(1) When dinner toasts are being made, take note of what the host and the person(s) being toasted say to each other. In particular, if the guest indicates that s/he cannot drink anymore, listen to what the person or his/her neighbors will say.
(2) Observe the body language of a smoker when greeting someone. What is proper smoking etiquette between a smoker and a non-smoker? Take note of the verbal, non-verbal, and physical responses from non-smokers who stand or sit close to the smoker.
(3) Pay attention to how others will respond when someone makes a mistake in a formal public setting.

Make a four- to six-minute audio recording to reflect on your observation of everyone's behavior. Submit the completed recording to your instructor.

第五单元 **Unit five**

文化视角：人情法则

Cultural perspective: rules of *renqing*

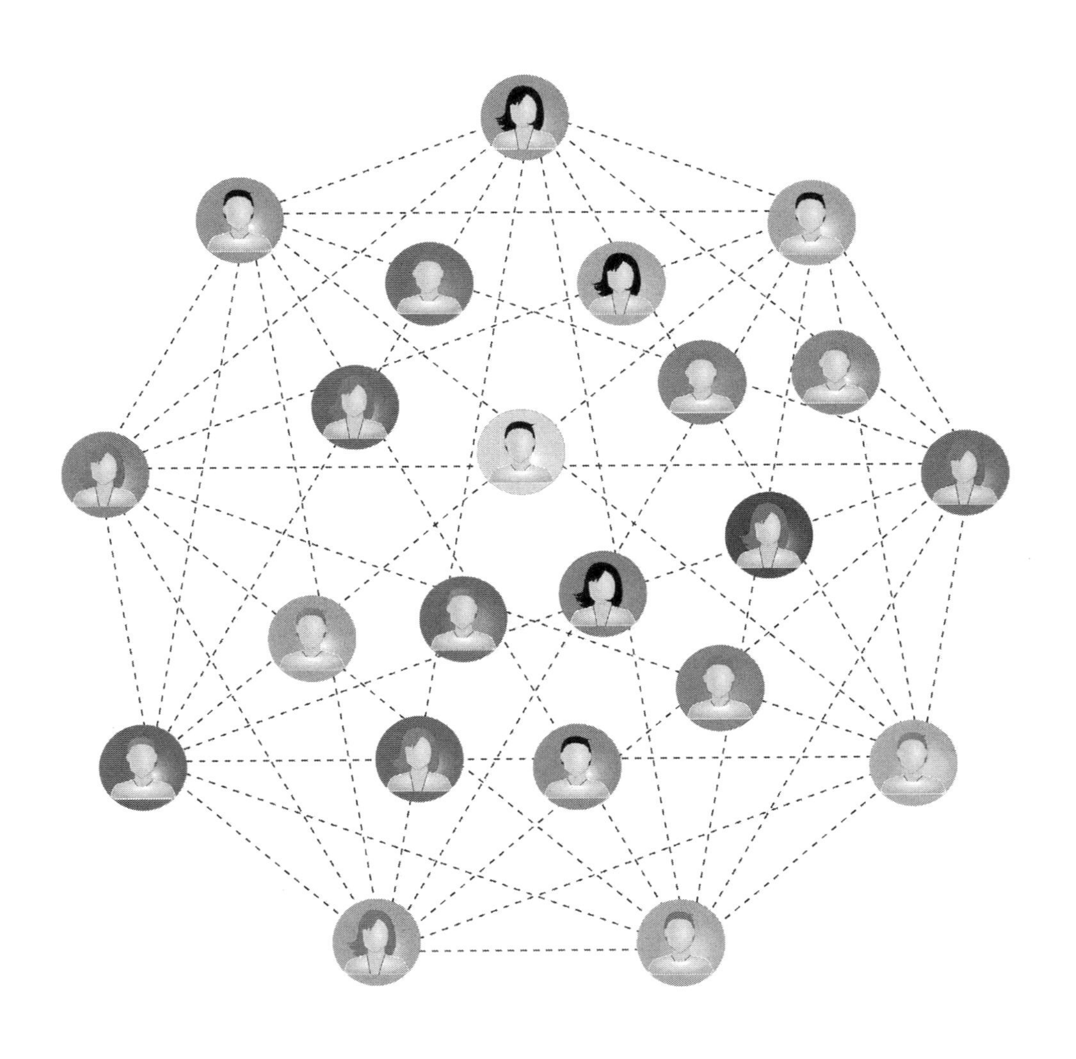

第十一课　来而不往非礼也

行为聚焦：礼尚往来
Behavior highlighted: reciprocation

课文 *Text*

除了面子以外，“人情”和“关系”是另外两个对中国人的行为方式有着直接影响的世俗化观念。

中国社会是一个人情社会，讲人情、重关系是中国文化的一个重要特征。中国的人情社会是建立在传统的熟人社会基础上的。最早提出“熟人社会”这个概念的是著名社会学家费孝通。在其《乡土中国》一书中，费先生讲述了中国传统乡土社会的种种特点，其中最主要的是人与人之间的关系网：人们通过血缘和地缘，把各种人际关系像网一样联系起来。关系网不断扩大，就形成了带有中国特色的熟人社会。

中国传统农业是熟人社会形成的最根本原因。在传统农业社会中，商品经济不发达，人口流动较少。人们受到土地的束缚，长期生活在某个固定的地方，过着自给自足、封闭保守的农耕生活。家是人们生活的最小单位，其次是家族和邻里。在这样的生活环境里，人们相互熟悉并且关系稳定，人与人交往或处理问题时，亲缘或情感的作用很大。

儒家思想也促进了中国人情社会的形成和发展。儒家把社会中人与人的关系视为人伦关系，把夫妇、父子、兄弟、君臣、朋友这五种最基本的人际关系称为“五伦”[1]。儒家思想提倡“君义、臣行、父慈、子孝、兄爱、弟敬”。这些人伦关系不仅井然有序，而且也充满了浓厚的人情味，因为维护这些关系的不是法律，而是伦理和情感。

作为一个词语，“人情”首先指的是人的感情。中国人十分看重人与人之间的感情，所以有着爱情、亲情、父母情、儿女情、兄弟情、姐妹情、邻里情、乡情、同学情、战友情等等许多说法。但在实际生活中，人与人之间的情感常常表现为各种各样的互助或互惠活动，因此，“人情”一词在实际使用中更多指的是这些互助互惠活动。这些活动可以是物质的（如给他人金钱和礼品），也可以是

---

1 五伦 refers to the five cardinal Confucian relationships, i.e. 夫妇(fūfù: husband-wife), 父子, 兄弟, 君臣(jūnchén: ruler-subject), and 朋友. 君义: righteousness on the part of the ruler; 臣行: loyalty on the part of the minister; 父慈(cí): kindness on the part of the father; 子孝: filial piety on the part of the son; 兄爱: gentleness on the part of the elder brother; 弟敬: respect on the part of the younger brother.

非物质的（如给他人提供一次方便的机会）。同时，这些活动又遵循着一套约定俗成的规则，人们是根据这些规则做人做事并把握关系和交往的。

“知恩图报”和“礼尚往来”是人情的两个基本法则。“报”即“报恩”，指的是报答别人对自己的恩情，比如父母的养育之恩、学校老师的培育之恩、朋友的知遇之恩，等等。知恩图报是儒家“礼”的重要内容，而礼注重有来有往，即所谓“礼尚往来”。所以，知恩而不报，就如有来而无往，这样做不仅违反了礼的规范，而且也会伤害人与人之间的感情。人们有来有往，而且常来常往，这样既可以加深彼此之间的感情和友谊，同时也反映了人情的道德约束及其背后的公平法则。

《新京报》有一篇文章，作者谈到他与其它国家的人打交道时所遇到的相互不理解。有一次，他的一位欧洲朋友问他，中国人忌讳当面谈钱的问题，认为谈钱伤感情，可是为什么春节时长辈要给晚辈钱，为什么亲人和朋友结婚时，人们也要送钱呢？作者解释说：春节发红包和婚礼随份子钱背后其实存在着一个公平系统。你的小孩收了人家多少压岁钱，你以后也要把这些钱以压岁钱或其它的方式还给人家；别人的婚礼你随了多少份子钱，你结婚的时候人家也会还回来。这样，彼此之间既没有经济损失，还在这一来一往的过程中体现了人情并加深了双方的感情。作者的解释让他的外国朋友更糊涂了。对方问，人们非要这样做吗？难道他们没有选择的自由吗？作者愣了一下，最后只好说，在大多数情况下是没有的。

生词 New words

简体	繁體	拼音	词性	英文翻译
1. 来而不往非礼也	來而不往非禮也	lái ér bù wǎng fēi lǐ yě		Courtesy demands reciprocity./Respond in kind. [This expression has its origin in *The Book of Rites*.]
2. 礼尚往来	禮尚往來	lǐshàngwǎnglái	idiom	What the rules of propriety value is reciprocity. [trans. by James Legge]
3. 特征	特徵	tèzhēng	n	distinctive feature, trait
4. 建立		jiànlì	v	found, establish
5. 概念		gàiniàn	n	concept, notion
6. 著名		zhùmíng	adj	renowned, celebrated
7. 讲述	講述	jiǎngshù	v	narrate, tell about, describe
8. 血缘	血緣	xuèyuán	n	consanguinity, ties of blood
9. 地缘	地緣	dìyuán	n	regional ties

简体	繁體	拼音	词性	英文翻译
10. 不断	不斷	búduàn	adv	unceasingly, continuously
11. 扩大	擴大	kuòdà	v	expand, enlarge, broaden, extend
12. 形成		xíngchéng	v	form, develop into, take shape
13. 特色		tèsè	n	unique feature, distinguishing quality
14. 发达	發達	fādá	adj	developed
15. 流动	流動	liúdòng	v	flow
16. 束缚	束縛	shùfù	n/v	restriction, fetters; tie up, fetter, restrict
17. 固定		gùdìng	adj/v	fixed, regular; fasten, set rigidly in place
18. 自给自足	自給自足	zìjǐ-zìzú	idiom	self-sufficient; maintain self-sufficiency
19. 封闭	封閉	fēngbì	adj/v	enclosed, confined; seal off, close down
20. 保守		bǎoshǒu	adj	conservative
21. 农耕	農耕	nónggēng	n/v	farming; practice farming [耕: till (fields)]
22. 单位	單位	dānwèi	n	unit (in measurement or organization)
23. 家族		jiāzú	n	clan, family
24. 邻里	鄰里	línlǐ	n	neighbors, neighborhood
25. 稳定	穩定	wěndìng	adj/v	stable, steady; stabilize
26. 处理	處理	chǔlǐ	v	handle, deal with, process
27. 亲缘	親緣	qīnyuán	n	family ties
28. 情感		qínggǎn	n	feeling [same as 感情], emotion
29. 促进	促進	cùjìn	v	accelerate, promote
30. 人伦	人倫	rénlún	n	ethical relations, human relationship according to the Confucian ethics [伦理: ethics]
31. 井然有序		jǐngrán-yǒuxù	idiom	in order, orderly
32. 充满	充滿	chōngmǎn	v	be brimming/permeated with
33. 浓厚	濃厚	nónghòu	adj	strong, deep, dense, pronounced

简体	繁體	拼音	词性	英文翻译
34. 感情		gǎnqíng	n	feeling [爱情: romantic love; 亲情: family love; 乡情: affection for native place; 战友情: friendship between or among fellow soldiers]
35. 十分		shífēn	adv	very, extremely
36. 看重		kànzhòng	v	value
37. 互惠		hùhuì	v	mutually benefit
38. 金钱	金錢	jīnqián	n	money, wealth
39. 礼品	禮品	lǐpǐn	n	gift, present
40. 非		fēi	bf/adv	non- [非物质: non-material, intangible]; have got to, simply must
41. 提供		tígōng	v	supply, provide, furnish
42. 把握		bǎwò	v/n	grasp firmly, command; assurance, certainty
43. 知恩图报	知恩圖報	zhīēn-túbào	idiom	be grateful for a kind act and seek ways to repay it [恩 or恩情: favor, kindness] [图: seek] [报 or 报答: repay]
44. 养育	養育	yǎngyù	v	rear (child), bring up
45. 培育		péiyù	v	cultivate, foster, breed
46. 知遇		zhīyù	v	recognize someone's worth
47. 违反	違反	wéifǎn	v	violate (law, regulation, principle, etc.)
48. 规范	規範	guīfàn	n/adj/v	norm; standard; regulate, standardize
49. 加深		jiāshēn	v	deepen
50. 彼此		bǐcǐ	pron	each other, one another
51. 友谊	友誼	yǒuyì	n	friendship
52. 约束	約束	yuēshù	n/v	restriction; restrain, bind
53. 背后	背後	bèihòu	n	back, rear
54. 公平		gōngpíng	adj/n	fair, just, impartial; fairness
55. 忌讳	忌諱	jìhuì	v/n	avoid as a taboo, abstain from; taboo
56. 婚礼	婚禮	hūnlǐ	n	wedding ceremony
57. 随	隨	suí	v	go along with (some action)
58. 份子钱	份子錢	fèn.ziqián	n	share for a joint undertaking [as in buying a gift; a.k.a. 份子]

简体	繁體	拼音	词性	英文翻译
59. 系统	系統	xìtǒng	n/adj	system; systematic
60. 压岁钱	壓歲錢	yāsuìqián	n	lunar New Year gift money given to children for luck and good health
61. 损失	損失	sǔnshī	n/v	loss, damage; lose
62. 过程	過程	guòchéng	n	course of events, process, procedure
63. 糊涂	糊塗	hú.tu	adj	muddled, confused

专有名词 Proper nouns

简体	繁體	拼音	英文翻译
1. 费孝通	費孝通	Fèi Xiàotōng	Fei Xiaotong or Fei Hsiao-Tung (1910–2005), a renowned scholar and professor of sociology and anthropology. His famous work 《乡土中国》, translated as *From the Soil: The Foundations of Chinese Society*, was first published in 1948 and widely referenced by Chinese sociologists and anthropologists.
2. 新京报	新京報	Xīn Jīng Bào	*The Beijing News* [www.bjnews.com.cn/]
3. 欧洲	歐洲	Ōuzhōu	Europe

词语与句型 Expressions and sentence patterns

1. 以……VP　　　　VP with ...

课文例句1：久而久之，人情成为中国人的潜意识，并以一套"潜规则"的形式指导着中国人的人际关系与行为方式。
课文例句2：你的小孩收了人家多少压岁钱，你以后也要把这些钱以压岁钱或其它的方式还给人家。

The 以 here is a formal preposition from classical Chinese that roughly translates to 用 or 通过.

- 中国人在跟别人打交道时，经常以自贬来抬高对方，让对方高兴。
- 易中天教授在他的《闲话中国人》一书中举了一个中国人请外国朋友吃饭的例子，并以此说明中西文化的不同。

2. Sentence 1。这样(，) sentence 2　　　　... By doing so, ...

课文例句1：人们有来有往，而且常来常往，这样既可以加深彼此之间的感情和友谊，同时也反映了人情的道德约束及其背后的公平法则。
课文例句2：你的小孩收了人家多少压岁钱，你以后也要把这些钱以压岁钱或其它的方式还给人家；别人的婚礼你随了多少份子钱，你结婚的时候人家也会还回来。这样，彼此之间既没有经济损失，还在这一来一往的过程中体现了人情并加深了双方的感情。

这样 elaborates on the scenario discussed in the first sentence by clarifying the speaker's intentions or explaining potential consequences. When the clause following 这样 has its own subject (example 1), the two segments may be separated by a comma.

- 在上海留学期间，小李经常去公园跟中国人学打太极拳(tàijíquán: shadow boxing [*tai chi*])。这样，他既可以锻炼身体，还可以练习中文。
- 去外国留学应该多交一些当地朋友，这样不仅能练习口语，而且也能通过他们更好地了解当地的社会和文化。

In contrast, 所以 or 因此 indicates a causal relationship. It is incorrect to use 这样 in the following sentence.

- 小王相信，中国在21世纪会是一个十分重要的国家，所以高中就开始学中文了。

3. 而④ but; and

课文例句：知恩而不报，就如有来而无往。

The conjunction 而 can connect verb phrases or adjectival phrases. It indicates a transition to a piece of contradictory information (examples 1, 2), or represents a mutually complimentary relationship between the two phrases connected by 而 (examples 3, 4).

- 等待比赛的时候，我感到紧张而又兴奋。
- 这家酒店位置 (wèi.zhì: location)好而服务差，董事会正在研究改进方案。
- 委婉而含蓄是很多中国人说话的特点之一。
- 如果发生了让某人丢面子的事情，怎样挽回面子而不使人下不来台是一门深奥的学问。

[See 而① in Lesson one, 而② in Lesson three, 而③ in Lesson nine.]

4. 非 has got to; must

课文例句：作者的解释让他的外国朋友更糊涂了。对方问：人们非要这样做吗？

Before verb phrases, 非 can be used as an adverb to emphasize the subject's strong determination to do something (example 1) or the subject's obligation to do something (examples 2, 3). More often than not, 非 is used with 不可 for added emphasis.

❖ S 非VP (不可)
❖ S非要/得VP (不可)

- 昨天下午下雨了，可他还是非出去跑步(不可)，晚上就发烧了。
- 在中国，亲友结婚时，人们不是非要送礼物(不可)，但一般来说都要给红包。
- 我小时候，每次要看电视都非得先做完作业(不可)，否则我父母不让我看。

非 functions differently in 来而不往非礼也 and 非物质. In 来而不往非礼也, 非 is a verb meaning "to violate, not conform," while in 非物质, it corresponds to the suffix "non".

语言练习 To practice and reinforce what you have learned from the Text, New Words, and the section "Expressions and sentence patterns" in this lesson, please visit the companion website to download a PDF version of the exercises.

交际情景 Communication scenarios

Study the following conversations between native speakers on the textbook companion website. Use the plug-in feature to find the definitions of the new words highlighted in orange. Try to visualize the scene as you read and listen to each dialogue. Discuss your reactions to these scenario dialogues with a classmate.

1. A recruiter contacted Zhao Xuedong, Wang Weimin's colleague, and offered him a job with a salary higher than at his current company. Zhao Xuedong talks to Weimin about it. Pay attention to Zhao Xuedong's thinking behind his decision not to take the offer.

赵学东：为民，我跟你说个事儿。最近好几个猎头联系我，问我有没有兴趣跳到利金公司去。而且利金给的工资还挺高的，比我们这儿要高百分之三十。
王为民：那你动心了吗？我知道你父亲生病，家里需要钱，你就是跳槽过去我也能理 解，这也是人之常情嘛。
赵学东：但张总对我这么好，利金给再高的工资，我都不会跳的。去年我父亲生病住院，张总给我放了好几个月的假，我迟到早退，他也是睁一只眼闭一只眼。现在我父亲好多了，我不能翻脸不认人啊。
王为民：你说的对，人活着也不能只是为了赚钱吧。

思考与讨论：

1） 请解释"翻脸不认人"是什么意思。
2） 赵学东为什么不愿意离开现在的公司？在你的国家，人们在这样的情况下会怎么做？

2. Wang Weimin's mother hopes that Wang Weimin will help a cousin find a job at his company. Observe how she convinces Weimin to help, and take note of why Weimin thinks that Old Lee in Personnel will do him a favor.

母　亲：今天你舅舅来电话，说你表弟丢了工作，让你想办法在你们公司给他找个工作。
王为民：妈，公司有公司的规定，我也不能随便安排人进公司啊。
母　亲：你不帮忙就太不讲人情了，那是你亲舅舅的儿子。你刚从老家到北京的时候，你舅舅帮你买东西、找房子、介绍工作，帮了多少忙啊！
王为民：妈，我知道该知恩图报。这样吧，明天我问问人事部的老李。老李应该能帮忙，去年我帮他争取到了出国培训的机会。

思考与讨论：

1） 王为民的母亲是怎么说服王为民为舅舅的儿子找工作的？
2） 王为民为什么相信人事部的老李应该能帮忙？
3） 在你的国家，人们在这样的情况下会怎么做？

3. Weimin has severe headaches and needs to see a doctor. Li Aihua calls Xiao Yang and asks her to help Weimin get an appointment at the hospital where Xiao Yang's husband works. Pay attention to why Xiao Yang is willing to help.

李爱华：喂，小杨啊，我是你李姐。现在忙吗？
小　杨：李姐，不忙不忙，什么事儿啊？
李爱华：你爱人是不是在中心医院工作啊？
小　杨：是啊，怎么了？

李爱华：我家老王最近头疼得厉害，我们想挂中心医院的号挂不上，请你爱人帮个忙挂个号，行吗？

小　杨：李姐你放心，没问题。前两年我们家买房子，你们借给我们好几万，我们欠了你们这么大的人情，不知道怎么还。挂号这点儿小事，一点儿问题都没有。

李爱华：那就太感谢了。等老王好一点儿，一定请你们吃饭。

思考与讨论：

1）小杨欠了李爱华什么人情？她打算怎么还？
2）在你的国家，人们会不会也像李爱华和小杨这样想这样做？

言语行为例说 Notes on discourse behavior

1. 对话例句：赵学东：……利金给的工资还挺高的，比我们这儿要高百分之三十。

王为民：……我知道你父亲生病，家里需要钱，你就是跳槽过去我也能理解，这也是人之常情嘛。

Roughly translated, 人之常情 means "such is human nature". This phrase refers to the true feelings or natural reactions that a person has. Because the Chinese attach more importance to feelings and relationships than to contracts and rules, behaviors that violate rules but are motivated by 情理 are often deemed to be acceptable. In everyday speech, people invoke the phrase to justify what has been done as being natural.

- 甲：他父母不让他出国留学，还要求跟他住一起，这样他一点儿自由都没有了。
  乙：父母年纪大了，害怕寂寞，想跟孩子在一起住也是人之常情，可以理解。
- 甲：这个人人品真差，看到我们赚钱了，就要参加，现在我们亏钱了，他就跑得远远的。
  乙：这是人之常情嘛，也不能怪他。

2. 对话例句：赵学东：去年我父亲生病住院，张总给我放了好几个月的假，……现在我父亲好多了，我不能翻脸不认人啊。

王为民：你说的对，人活着也不能只是为了赚钱吧。

翻脸不认人 (fān liǎn bú rèn rén) is a vernacular saying that means "to become hostile after falling out with somebody." 翻脸, literally meaning "to turn the face", refers to a conflict that has arisen between parties. 不认人, literally "to not recognize someone", means that the parties no longer recognize that social ties exist between them. Taken together, the phrase describes the situation in which previously close parties have turned hostile due to a conflict. This is considered cold-blooded and ruthless behavior, and people invoke this saying either to warn against acting this way or to criticize it when they see it happening.

- 甲：你今天必须把欠我的钱还给我。
  乙：我们是十几年的同学，上学的时候我也没少帮你，你不能这么翻脸不认人吧。

- 甲：小刘，原来公司生意好的时候，给了你那么多奖金。没想到现在公司有一点儿小问题，你马上就翻脸不认人，还去法院告我们欠工资。你就不能等等吗？
  乙：老板，我也要生活，不能一直等下去啊。

3. 对话例句1：王为民：妈，公司有公司的规定，我也不能随便安排人进公司啊。
   母　亲：你不帮忙就太不讲人情了，那是你亲舅舅的儿子。
   对话例句2：李爱华：我家老王最近头疼得厉害，我们想挂中心医院的号挂不上，请你爱人帮个忙挂个号，行吗？
   小　杨：……前两年……你们借给我们好几万，我们欠了你们这么大的人情，不知道怎么还。挂号这点儿小事，一点儿问题都没有。

人情 means "human feelings," but more often than not, it refers to the currency of human capital that is created through the doing of favors or the giving of gifts between parties that are in a social relationship of some kind. 讲人情 implies that social relationships or even organizational responsibilities should be handled with sensitivity rather than strictly according to rules or principles. To say 太不讲人情了to someone or an organization is to criticize them for being inflexible and lacking basic consideration for human feelings or relationships (重情).

In addition, 人情 is a continuous process of granting favors (做人情) and being repaid in kind. To engage in 人情, the rules require that a person must "return (还 huán)" a favor when that person "owe(s) (欠 qiàn)" someone for a previous favor. The process of owing and returning favors maintains and reinforces the relationship between the involved parties.

- 甲：你晚上为什么要请李天明吃饭啊？
  乙：他帮我弟弟找了一个工作，这个人情我得想办法还。
- 甲：我昨天交通违章，被警察抓到了，可能要扣分。
  乙：你找王明啊，他是我们的老同学，又是交通队的大队长。
  甲：算了，他这个人一点儿人情都不讲，找他也没用。

4. 对话例句：母　亲：你刚从老家到北京的时候，你舅舅……帮了多少忙啊！
   王为民：妈，我知道该知恩图报。这样吧，明天我问问人事部的老李。

Chinese social traditions place a strong emphasis on 知恩图报, which comes from the original saying 知恩图报, 善莫大焉 (shàn mò dà yān)—"there is nothing better than to return a kindness." Using 知恩图报 in conversation acts as a reminder to act in accordance with this ethical value.

- 甲：你为什么要为张教授免费提供实验室呢？
  乙：我以前是他的学生，我有今天的成绩都是因为他的帮助。做人要知恩图报, 他需要借用我们的实验室，我怎么能收钱呢？
- 甲：你实习结束，马上就要成为正式的员工了，在这儿工作有什么感受？
  乙：公司给了我很多机会，我会知恩图报，努力为公司服务。

体演情景 Perform the scenario

Select a dialogue from this section and listen to its recording several times. Imitate the speakers in pronunciation, intonation and discourse behavior in terms of both the words they use and the ways in which they carry themselves. Memorize the dialogue for performance in class.

跨文化交际 Cross-cultural communication

一、误解分析 Situation analysis

Break into groups and discuss the misunderstanding in each of the cross-cultural communication incidents below. For each incident, the group should generate an answer that best explains the cultural assumptions behind the ways in which the individuals say and do things. In addition, discuss possible strategies to avoid these misunderstandings in similar situations.

（一）住在南京的高明最近收到了研究生同学 Monica 的电子邮件，说她们一家要从美国到南京来玩儿，邮件里问了高明许多关于旅行安排的问题。高明想着两个人当年是同班同学，老同学要来了，当然要好好照顾。于是就详细地回答了 Monica 的问题，还帮她订了旅馆。Monica 一家三口人到了南京以后又联系高明，高明和家人就请他们在一家不错的饭馆儿吃了饭。但是这顿饭吃完以后，高明心里有点儿不太高兴了。他想，Monica 怎么连一个小小的纪念品都没有从美国带给他的家人，哪怕给他女儿买个小玩具也行啊。另外，她也没提出要回请一顿饭。自己忙前忙后帮了不少忙，Monica 也太不懂人情了。

思考与讨论：

1) 高明不高兴的原因是什么？他为什么觉得 Monica 不懂人情？
2) 如果你是 Monica，你会怎么做？

（二）Tom 和中国姑娘叶明结婚以后一直住在西安。最近叶明的表哥要买房子，还需要二十万。叶明跟Tom商量能不能拿出五万块借给表哥。Tom问叶明："你表哥需要钱为什么找我们借？"叶明回答说："不是只找我们借，他也找了其他亲戚，每家都借一点儿，就能凑够二十万了。"Tom还是不明白，他问："如果他的钱不够，可以等将来再买房子或者去银行贷款啊。"叶明说："找银行贷款还要付好多利息，我们都是亲戚，互相帮帮忙，就省下不少钱呢。以后我们需要钱，他们也会帮我们的。"Tom 还是坚持自己的看法，最后叶明生气地说："你这个人真没有人情味儿。"

思考与讨论：

1) 为什么叶明愿意借给表哥钱，而不让表哥去银行贷款？为什么她认为 Tom 没有人情味儿？
2) 如果你是 Tom，会不会借钱给叶明的表哥？如果不会，你会怎么跟叶明解释？

（三）Andy暑假住在北京的一个中国家庭里。他的中国爸爸和中国妈妈周末要去参加他们大学同学儿子的婚礼。出发以前，Andy看见他们在为同学准备份子钱。中国爸爸问："我们出多少份子钱合适啊？"中国妈妈回答说："你等一下，我查查。"然后，她拿出了一个笔记本查找起来。过了一会儿，她对中国爸爸说："我们女儿结婚的时候，他们家给了我们六百块的红包。那我们就给她八百吧。"Andy在心里好奇地想，中国爸爸和妈妈去参加婚礼是为了祝福同学的儿子婚后幸福呢，还是为了"还账"呢？

思考与讨论：

1) 中国爸爸妈妈参加婚礼的目的是为了"还账"吗？他们出于什么考虑决定给同学八百块的红包？
2) 如果你要参加中国同学的婚礼，会根据什么准备礼物或者红包？

（四）孙艺家最近住进来一个到中国留学的美国小伙子，叫Peter。孙艺为了表现她很好客，经常请Peter去饭馆儿吃饭，周末也带他到有名的地方玩儿，甚至还帮Peter把脏衣服都洗了。Peter虽然觉得有点儿不好意思，但还是很感谢孙艺一家人。有一天，孙艺找到Peter问："我女儿正在学英文，你能跟她练习对话吗？" Peter很抱歉地说："对不起，孙阿姨，我的中文课有语言誓约，不能说英文。"孙艺说："没事儿，你跟我女儿在家里练英文，你的老师也不知道，我也不会告诉老师的。"Peter再次道歉说："我还是想利用在中国的时间多学中文。"孙艺嘴上说"那好吧，没关系"，但是心里却非常别扭，她不明白自己对Peter这么好，Peter怎么连这么小的忙都不愿意帮。

思考与讨论：

1) 为什么孙艺心里觉得非常别扭？
2) 如果你是Peter，遇到这个两难的问题你该怎么办？

二、口语交际练习 Oral communication exercises

1. 角色扮演 Role play

   Pair up with a peer and refer to one of the critical incidents in *Situation analysis* to create a five-minute skit with a similar storyline. Use new vocabulary and speech patterns that you have learned from this lesson in your skit. Perform the dialogue in class and discuss whether each skit properly reflects typical Chinese discourse behavior.

2. 思考与讨论 Reflection and discussion

   礼尚往来是中国人情社会的特点之一，而"送礼"是维护关系、增进感情最常见的方式。中国人有很多送礼的讲究。请通过下面的活动，学习这些讲究和礼仪有什么关系，并探讨 (tàntǎo: inquire into)它们对维护人情有什么帮助。

   (1) 课前准备：请上网查找或请教 (qǐngjiào: ask for guidance)中国朋友下列问题的答案(dá'àn: answer)，并了解它们背后的原因。

   - 中国人包装(bāozhuāng: wrap)礼品喜欢用什么颜色？
   - 中国人送礼金或礼物时喜欢单数 (odd number) 还是双数 (even number)？
   - 中国人送礼有什么忌讳(jìhuì: taboo)？
   - 中国人送礼和接受礼物时会说什么客套话？会有什么特别的肢体(zhītǐ: body)语言？

(2) 课堂活动：2–3名同学一组，讨论下列问题并做笔记。讨论时，请尽量使用本课生词和句型。

- 讨论“课前准备”活动的问题，并解释背后的原因。
- 你的国家有没有什么送礼的讲究？大家也注重礼尚往来吗？请举例说明。
- 你的母语文化传统也重视“人情”吗？平常大家怎样维护关系、增进感情？请举例说明。
- 在国际商务交往中，你认为中国的“人情”和“礼尚往来”的文化传统可能有什么好处与坏处？怎样避免坏处？
- 总结“礼尚往来”与“人情”的关系、不同文化之间的差异与类似的地方，以及如何彼此促进了解。

三、写作 Composition

1. 作文（两题选一题）

题目1：谈礼尚往来与人情的关系
做了上面“思考与讨论”的活动后，根据你所做的笔记写一篇作文（最少分成三段）。尽量使用本课的生词和句型。

题目2：西方人讲不讲人情？
提示：

- 有人说西方社会不讲人情，只讲法律，你同意这个说法吗？为什么？
- 在你的母语文化环境中，什么时候讲人情，什么时候不讲？跟中国社会有什么相似或不同的地方？
- 讲人情有什么好处与坏处？礼尚往来呢？请举例说明。
- 总结你对“西方人讲不讲人情”的看法。
- 也许用得上的词语和句型：因此/这样/以/非/难道/自给自足/约定俗成/亲缘/(重)感情/互助/互惠/契约(qìyuē: contract, deed)。

2. 文化探索 Cultural exploration: For learners who are currently studying or working in the target culture.

Chat with three to five Chinese adults of varying ages and from different socioeconomic backgrounds about their experiences navigating social relationships (人情). Ask them when and with whom they normally carry out social rituals such as bringing a present (送礼), hosting a dinner party (请客), giving face (面子) to someone, or using ostensibly polite formulas (客套). Inquire into the reasons that prompt their actions and ask if the outcomes generally meet their expectations. Please be respectful of the other person's willingness to respond to your questions and be ready to share your own experiences in your home culture if appropriate. After these interviews, reflect on how the concept of 人情 guides the social relationships and behaviors in Chinese society. Record what you have observed and write down your thoughts in a journal entry. After completion, submit the journal to your teacher.

第十二课　多个朋友多条路

行为聚焦：建立人脉
Behavior highlighted: networking

课文 *Text*

在熟人社会中，人情作用的发挥是和人与人之间的关系紧密相连的。“关系”是中国人的口头禅。在现代汉语里，“关系”有两个方面的含义：一个指的是人与人之间或者事物与事物之间的相互联系，相当于英文的relation；另一个是说人们通过一定的手段，与其他人建立关系或拉近关系，以便获取自己所需要的物质或达到自己所要达到的目的。汉语中的“拉关系”或“搞关系”指的就是这第二种含义，其意思差不多相当于英文里的networking。

台湾大学黄光国教授在其对中国人际关系的研究中，将中国人的人际关系分为三种：第一种是“情感性关系”，也就是家人、爱人、密友等之间的关系；第二种是“工具性关系”，如乘客与司机之间、顾客与售货员之间的关系；第三种是“混合性关系”，是由亲戚、邻居、同学、同事或其他熟人构成的。黄教授指出，中国人采用三种不同的法则跟这三种不同关系里的人打交道。跟情感关系里的人打交道，中国人一般采用“需求法则”，即人们努力提供各种物质或非物质的帮助，以满足对方的需求。跟工具性关系的人打交道，人们使用的是“公平法则”：双方都精打细算，不做让步，自己付出多少，就应得到多少。跟混合性关系里的人打交道，大家则采用的是“人情法则”：人们注重礼尚往来，这一次我帮你一个忙，下次我有需求的时候你也要帮我的忙，否则，欠人情不还，双方的关系就会受到破坏。

前面讨论过的“面子”问题一般发生在混合性关系中，“拉关系”或“搞关系”通常发生在混合性关系与工具性关系中。人情是拉关系的基础，同时也是拉关系的基本内容和手段。如上所述，人情是在不断的“亏欠”和“偿还”中得以加深和延续的。人情的这个潜规则逐渐为人们所利用，成为生活中办事不走程序而“走后门”的便利手段。中国人常说“熟人好办事”，或“多个朋友多条路”。在这些世俗观念的指导下，人们办事先找人，通过请客、送礼等手段拉关系来实现自己的目的。这样，孩子上学通过关系可以去个好学校，老人生病通过关系可以找个好医生。对年轻人找工作来说，找熟人、建立关系就更重要了。目前，“聚餐社交”风行中国的大学校园。根据2016年中国高校传媒联盟的一次调查，在460位受访的大学生中，29.31%的人每周聚会两次以上，其中本科低年级占63.52%。大学生们在学习的同时忙于聚餐或其它社交活动，就是为了结交朋友，建立感情，为毕业后找工作建立人脉关系。

除了个人之间，企业与企业之间也要花大量的时间和精力做“人”的工作。在“做生意就是做关系”的观念影响下，企业老板们为了商业上的成功，在百忙中要抽出大量的时间在包房里应酬。关于中国企业家的生存状态，有人形容说是“脚踏‘两院’”：一方面，老板们在饭桌上谈生意，因常常大吃大喝弄坏了身体要去医院；另一方面，一些老板急于牟利，有时不顾法律，犯了法又要进法院。此外，无论是个人还是企业，用在人情上的花费也日益高涨，以至于因为应酬而产生的焦虑目前在中国已成为一个普遍的社会现象。《重庆晨报》一次对1100名居民进行了调查，95.8%的受访者坦言，当前年轻人的应酬确实太多了。调查还显示，67.9%的受访者为应酬感到“很焦虑”或“非常焦虑”，而只有10.7%的人应酬起来“完全不焦虑”。

生词 New words

简体	繁體	拼音	词性	英文翻译
1. 人脉	人脈	rénmài	n	connections, contacts, network
2. 发挥	發揮	fāhuī	n/v	bringing out implicit or innate qualities; bring into play
3. 紧密	緊密	jǐnmì	adj	inseparably close
4. 相连	相聯	xiānglián	v	be interrelated
5. 口头禅	口頭禪	kǒutóuchán	n	common saying, popular saying
6. 含义	含義	hányì	n	meaning, connotation [a.k.a. 涵(hán)义]
7. 相当于	相當於	xiāngdāngyú	phr	be equivalent to
8. 手段		shǒuduàn	n	means (of doing sth.), stratagem
9. 拉近		lājìn	v	draw close, draw near
10. 以便		yǐbiàn	conj	so as to, so that, with the aim of
11. 获取	獲取	huòqǔ	v	gain, obtain
12. 将	將	jiāng	prep	[introduces the object of the main verb, similar to 把, but more formal than 把]
13. 密友		mìyǒu	n	close friend, buddy
14. 乘客		chéngkè	n	passenger
15. 混合		hùnhé	v	mix, blend
16. 需求		xūqiú	n	demand, request, requirement
17. 满足	滿足	mǎnzú	v	Satisfy

简体	繁體	拼音	词性	英文翻译
18. 精打细算	精打細算	jīngdǎ-xìsuàn	idiom	careful and strict calculation, meticulous planning and careful accounting
19. 让步	讓步	ràng//bù	n/v	yield, concession; yield, compromise, concede, give in
20. 付出		fùchū	v	pay, invest (energy or time in ...)
21. 欠		qiàn	v	owe, lack [亏(kuī)欠: owe, have a deficit]
22. 破坏	破壞	pòhuài	v	destroy, wreck, damage
23. 如上		rúshàng	v	as above [如上所述: as stated above]
24. 偿还	償還	chánghuán	v	repay, pay back
25. 得以		déyǐ	v	be able to
26. 延续	延續	yánxù	v	continue, last
27. 逐渐	逐漸	zhújiàn	adv	gradually
28. 利用		lìyòng	v	use, utilize, take advantage of
29. 程序		chéngxù	n	procedure, protocol [走程序: follow the procedure]
30. 走后门	走後門	zǒu hòumén	phr	get in through the back door, secure sth. through pulling relationships/connections
31. 风行	風行	fēngxíng	v	be popular, be in fashion, spread widely
32. 受访	受訪	shòufǎng	v	be interviewed
33. 本科		běnkē	n	undergraduate
34. 占	佔	zhàn	v	constitute, make up, account for
35. 忙于	忙於	mángyú	v	be busy with [more formal than 忙着]
36. 结交	結交	jiéjiāo	v	befriend, make friends with
37. 精力		jīnglì	n	energy, vigor
38. 抽		chōu	v	draw out, pull out [抽时间: find time to]
39. 包房		bāofáng	n	private room in a restaurant [a.k.a 包间]
40. 应酬	應酬	yìng.chou	v/n	take part in social networking activities; networking activities
41. 生存		shēngcún	v	live, survive, subsist
42. 状态	狀態	zhuàngtài	n	state (of affairs), status, condition
43. 踏		tà	v	step on
44. 弄		nòng	v	make, cause ... to [弄坏: ruin, damage]
45. 急于	急於	jíyú	v	be eager to [more formal than 急着]
46. 牟利		móu//lì	v	seek profit, gain profit
47. 不顾	不顧	búgù	v	ignore, overlook
48. 法院		fǎyuàn	n	(law) court

简体	繁體	拼音	词性	英文翻译
49. 花费	花費	huā.fei	n	expenses, expenditure
50. 日益		rìyì	adv	increasingly, with each passing day
51. 高涨	高漲	gāozhǎng	v	surge up; run high
52. 以至于	以至於	yǐzhìyú	conj	to such an extent as to, so much so that
53. 焦虑	焦慮	jiāolǜ	n/adj	anxiety; anxious
54. 坦言		tǎnyán	v	acknowledge frankly, tell honestly
55. 确实	確實	quèshí	adv	indeed, truly
56. 显示	顯示	xiǎnshì	v	show, demonstrate, manifest

专有名词 Proper nouns

简体	繁體	拼音	英文翻译
1. 黄光国	黃光國	Huáng Guāngguó	Kuang-Kwo Hwang (1945–), professor *emeritus*, Department of Psychology, National Taiwan University
2. 中国高校传媒联盟	中國高校傳媒聯盟	Zhōngguó Gāoxiào Chuánméi Liánméng	China University Media Union, formed by *China Youth Daily* [《中国青年报》] and 63 leading Chinese universities to share university information resources, communicate between university media, and serve the university students [高校: short for 高等院校 (higher-ed institution); 传媒: short for 传播媒体 (传播chuánbō: disseminate, propagate; 媒体méitǐ: media); 联盟: alliance, coalition]
3. 重庆晨报	重慶晨報	Chóngqìng Chén Bào	*Chongqing Morning Post*, a local newspaper in the city of Chongqing [晨 (bf): morning]

词语与句型 Expressions and sentence patterns

1. A 相当于 B　　　A be equivalent to B

课文例句1：在现代汉语里，"关系"有两个方面的含义：一个指的是人与人之间或者事物与事物之间的相互联系，相当于英文的relation。

课文例句2：汉语中的"拉关系"或"搞关系"指的就是这第二种含义，其意思差不多相当于英文里的 networking。

- 中国人受到别人称赞时，经常会说"哪里哪里"，其实就相当于英语里的 thank you。
- 教练告诉我，健身的这段时间不能乱吃东西，比如吃一个冰激凌相当于吃三碗米饭，就白锻炼了。

2. 以便 so as to; so that

课文例句：人们通过一定的手段，与其他人建立关系或拉近关系，以便获取自己所需要的物质或达到自己所要达到的目的。

以便 joins two clauses or a clause and a verb phrase. The clause preceding 以便 introduces a tactic or a process; the second clause or the verb phrase explains the purpose or the goal that the tactic or process is trying to achieve.

❖ S VP1，以便VP2。 S VP1, so as to VP2.
❖ S1 VP1，以便 (S2) VP2。 S1 VP1, so that (S2) VP2.

- 现在大学生都喜欢"聚餐社交"，以便积累毕业以后所需要的人脉。
- 王老师每次下了课都会把PPT放在网站上，以便学生复习课上的学习内容。

3. S VP1，以 VP2 S VP1, so as to VP2

课文例句：跟情感关系里的人打交道，中国人一般采用"需求法则"，即人们努力提供各种物质或非物质的帮助，以满足对方的需求。

The action introduced by 以 states the purpose or goal that the first action is trying to fulfill. This construct is used in formal spoken and written settings.

Unlike 以便, 以 can only be followed by a verbal phrase.

- 这家公司制定了非常详细的广告方案，以满足客户的要求。
- 在人际交往中，中国人经常自贬，以抬高对方。

4. A 为 B 所 VP A be verb-ed by B

课文例句：人情的这个潜规则逐渐为人们所利用，成为生活中办事不走程序而"走后门"的便利手段。

This structure is a formal version of 被-construction. The verb after 所 is more often disyllabic than monosyllabic, and the verb does not need any complement. Some commonly used expressions in this form are listed below:

❖ A为B所利用 A be utilized/taken advantage of by B
❖ A为B所称赞 A be praised by B
❖ A为B所喜爱 A be liked by B
❖ A为B所接受 A be accepted by B

- 小张长期参加志愿活动，他的精神为人们所称赞。
- 中国歌手李健的很多歌都非常美，而且表达了他对生活的理解，因此为歌迷所喜爱。
- 以前电动汽车有各种各样的问题，现在的全电动汽车越来越完善(perfect)，已逐渐为大众所接受。

5. ……，以至于…… to such an extent as to ...; so much so that ...

课文例句：无论是个人还是企业，用在人情上的花费也日益高涨，以至于因为应酬而产生的焦虑目前在中国已成为一个普遍的社会现象。

以至于 highlights the causal relation between the first clause and the second, in which the situation described in the first clause causes the consequence described in the second clause.

❖ S VP1，以至于VP2。 S VP1, so much so that VP2.
❖ S1 VP1，以至于 S2 VP2。 S1 VP1, so much so that S2 VP2.

- 她不知道万一父母问到这件事该怎么回答，以至于好几天没敢跟他们联系。
- 上次考试很难，以至于学生的成绩没有一个上了80分的。

语言练习 To practice and reinforce what you have learned from the Text, New Words, and the section "Expressions and sentence patterns" in this lesson, please visit the companion website to download a PDF version of the exercises.

交际情景 Communication scenarios

Study the following conversations between native speakers on the textbook companion website. Use the plug-in feature to find the definitions of the new words highlighted in orange. Try to visualize the scene as you read and listen to each dialogue. Discuss your reactions to these scenario dialogues with a classmate.

1. Li Aihua complains to Wang Weimin, her husband, about his wasting time and money on treating his colleagues for dinner. In reply, Weimin explains the reason and his purpose for doing so.

王为民：爱华，我今天晚上有应酬，不回来吃饭了。
李爱华：怎么又有应酬？这个星期都三四回了。
王为民：我不是刚换到这个新部门嘛，方方面面的关系都要照顾到，新领导新同事新客户都得搞好关系。你说我刚去，跟谁都不熟，现在不拉拉关系，以后怎么办事儿啊？俗话说"熟人好办事"嘛。
李爱华：这次也是你请客吗？这一个月，咱们已经花了不少冤枉钱了！
王为民：这你就不懂了，怎么是"冤枉钱"？不请客喝酒怎么跟人家搞好关系？你放心吧，这些请客的钱就算是投资了，以后都会有回报的。

思考与讨论：

1) 为什么王为民最近经常应酬，而且每次都是他请客？他为什么不认为这些请客的 钱是"冤枉钱"？
2) 在你的国家，如果新到一个公司或者一个部门，人们会这样做吗？如果不是，他 们会怎么做？为什么？

2. Li Aihua asks Liu Shaohong for a favor because the latter has a friend who works for the private kindergarten that Aihua would like her niece to attend. Pay attention to how Aihua tries to use *guanxi* to help her niece.

李爱华：小刘，我妹妹的孩子前两天报了育英幼儿园,听说报名的人特别多，所以她想托人打听打听，看看有没有办法保证孩子能入园。你有没有熟人在育英啊？
刘少红：我还真有个朋友在育英，而且是个主任。
李爱华：那太好了，你帮我问问她，看她愿不愿意帮个忙。

刘少红：我认识是认识，可这个朋友我好久不联系了，不太好意思直接托她帮忙。
李爱华：朋友不常联系慢慢就疏远了。这样，我做东，回头你请她，咱们一起吃顿饭，聊聊天儿，一回生二回熟嘛。

思考与讨论：

1) 请解释"一回生二回熟"是什么意思。
2) 李爱华为什么要找一个在育英幼儿园工作的人？当她知道刘少红跟育英幼儿园的主任好久没联系的时候，她打算怎么解决这个问题？
3) 在你的国家，如果想让孩子上一个好学校，人们会这么做吗？

3. Jason and Dawei are chatting about the plot twist in *In the Name of the People* (《人民的名义》), a popular TV drama series. Take note of how *guanxi* works within the social clique of the head of the provincial Public Security Department, and the rationale behind such behavior in the drama series.

艾杰森：大伟，你看过《人民的名义》吗？挺有意思的。
王大伟：这么火的电视剧，哪能没看过？
艾杰森：里面那个公安厅长也太腐败了。自从当上厅长以后，他给农村老家的七大姑八大姨都安排了工作。就连一个不识字的农村亲戚，也被他安排了当警察。难道他自己不明白这是腐败吗？
王大伟：他怎么会不知道？但是他自己也说：中国就是这么一个人情社会，他当官了，能不管他老家那些亲戚吗？所以现在政府正在严格管理党员干部，不让人情超越法律。

思考与讨论：

1) 电视剧里的公安厅长有哪些腐败的行为？为什么他明明知道这是腐败还要去做？
2) 在你的国家，人们有这个公安厅长这样的想法吗？为什么？

言语行为例说 Notes on discourse behavior

1. 对话例句：王为民：……新领导新同事新客户都得搞好关系……我刚去，跟谁都不熟，现在不拉拉关系，以后怎么办事儿啊？……
李爱华：这次也是你请客吗？这一个月，咱们已经花了不少冤枉钱了！
王为民：……怎么是"冤枉钱"？不请客喝酒怎么跟人家搞好关系？

关系 has components that are similar, but not identical, to the western idea of networking. In everyday life, behaviors associated with 拉关系 or 搞好关系 include showing respect through flattering (奉承: fèng.cheng), claiming a connection with someone you know (攀关系: pān guān.xi), and initiating socialization activities and exchanging favors, etc. Hosting banquets (请客) and giving gifts (送礼) are the most commonly observed activities when one is trying to cultivate 关系.

- 甲：到了新单位一定要注意跟领导和同事搞好关系。
  乙：妈，我知道了。我带了两盒月饼去单位，到了就给大家分着吃。
- 甲：我工作了几年以后终于明白了，一个人在社会上就得学会拉关系。关系越多，机会就越多。
  乙：一点儿都没错，这就叫人脉。

2. 对话例句：王为民：我刚去，跟谁都不熟，现在不拉拉关系，以后怎么办事儿啊？俗话说"熟人好办事"嘛。
李爱华：这次也是你请客吗？这一个月，咱们已经花了不少冤枉钱了！

Chinese people prefer to work with acquaintances (熟人) rather than with strangers (生人) because it is difficult for 熟人 to refuse to give face (i.e., not to lend help), and because 熟人 can provide introductions to their own network of acquaintances who may have needed skills or connections. Moreover, a person working with 熟人 may be able to access benefits that are not available through official channels because 熟人 may let personal considerations supersede official guidelines. 熟人好办事 or its variant 熟人好说话 (acquaintances are easygoing) are two common sayings that reflect the importance placed on social ties with 熟人 in Chinese culture. By contrast, because 生人 are less likely bounded by 面子 or 情, they are generally more likely to do things in accordance with official guidelines.

- 甲：这次跟我们合作的兴达公司的张经理原来跟我们部门的小王是老同学。
乙：熟人好办事，那这次开会就让小王去跟他谈吧。
- 甲：张姐，你能跟人事部的人说说，把我调到市场部吗？
乙：你自己怎么不去说？
甲：你不是跟人事主管熟嘛，熟人好说话，她肯定给你这个面子。

3. 对话例句1：李爱华：……听说报名的人特别多，所以她想托人打听打听，看看有没有办法保证孩子能入园。
刘少红：我还真有个朋友在育英，而且是个主任。

对话例句2：李爱华：那太好了，你帮我问问她，看她愿不愿意帮个忙。
刘少红：……这个朋友我好久不联系了，不太好意思直接托她帮忙。

托人办事 means to entrust someone to do something, as shown in the first example below. In some cases, 托人办事 implies that the person has asked someone to help by using back channels to accomplish a task that cannot be done by normal means.

- 甲：小李，你的包不错，是名牌吧？
乙：对啊，我是托人从欧洲带回来的，国内买不到。
- 甲：这次去美国访问只有两个名额，靠我自己申请，估计没有什么希望。你能托人帮我搞一个名额吗？
乙：我想想有没有熟人。

4. 对话例句：刘少红：这个朋友好久不联系了，不太好意思托她帮忙。
李爱华：……咱们一起吃顿饭，聊聊天儿，一回生二回熟嘛。

The saying 一回生二回熟 can mean "a stranger the first time, an acquaintance the second," or alternately, "difficult the first time, easy the second." A speaker can use the phrase with its first meaning to encourage the listener to meet with or befriend a stranger. Alternately, the speaker may be urging the listener to continue practicing something unfamiliar until that skill has been mastered.

- 甲：今天晚上聚餐我就不去了，都是你们专业的同学，我也不认识。
乙：没事儿，你来吧，一回生二回熟嘛。

- 甲：我今天第一天上课，紧张死了，也不知道我有没有讲清楚，学生能不能听懂。
  乙：没事，一回生二回熟嘛，你以后多教几次，就不觉得紧张了。

体演情景 Perform the scenario

Select a dialogue from this section and listen to its recording several times. Imitate the speakers in pronunciation, intonation and discourse behavior in terms of both the words they use and the ways in which they carry themselves. Memorize the dialogue for performance in class.

跨文化交际 Cross-cultural communication

一、误解分析 Situation analysis

Break into groups and discuss the misunderstanding in each of the cross-cultural communication incidents below. For each incident, the group should generate an answer that best explains the cultural assumption behind the ways in which the individuals say and do things. In addition, discuss possible strategies to avoid these misunderstandings in similar situations.

（一）Ben刚找到了一份在深圳的工作，没想到干了不到三个月，经理就对他有意见了。原来，Ben的工作经常需要下班后跟客户应酬，一个星期要参加三四个聚会，这让Ben无法适应，所以他就不去了。后来，Ben从一位同事那儿听说经理觉得Ben对工作不热心。Ben有点儿不太高兴，他说："这是我的下班时间，我为什么非要参加这些聚会？"同事安慰他说："上班时间和下班时间哪能分得那么清楚？应酬也是工作的一部分，而且比上班做的那些事还重要呢！"Ben很惊讶同事竟然这么说，难道自己做的工作比不上跟客户吃饭重要吗？

思考与讨论：

1) 为什么经理和同事都把跟客户应酬看得这么重要？
2) 如果你是Ben，你会参加这些应酬吗？

（二）刘英顺的女儿马上就要上小学了，她打算给女儿报一所私立的国际学校。可是这所小学因为竞争激烈，所以入学前需要面试和笔考。刘英顺找到了这所学校的校长，热情地一再邀请对方吃饭，对方却一再拒绝她。刘英顺急了，她给自己的美国朋友Ken打了一个电话："Ken，你女儿不是也上这个学校吗？你有没有熟人可以介绍我认识一下？只要能让我女儿进这个学校，花多少钱我都愿意。"Ken回答说："离考试还有好几个月呢，我帮你女儿练习英文，好好准备一下。"刘英顺听了有点对Ken不满，觉得Ken有认识的人，但却不愿意帮她的忙。

思考与讨论：

1) 是Ken不想帮刘英顺的忙吗？他的想法和刘英顺的想法有什么不同？
2) 如果你是Ken，你觉得最好怎么帮助刘英顺？

（三）十一假期快到了，在中国工作的Andrew最近经常听到同事小马抱怨又收到了“红色炸弹”。Andrew问什么是“红色炸弹”，小马解释说就是结婚请帖。Andrew不解地问：“参加婚礼是高兴的事，怎么是炸弹？”小马回答：“因为参加婚礼就要随份子啊。我好几个朋友、同事都赶在十一假期的时候结婚，如果个个都要给，我这个月就没钱吃饭了。”小马接着说，“我打算告诉他们，我十一不在国内，已经安排好了去泰国旅行。到时候就躲在家里看电影吧。”Andrew以前听说过中国人非常重视人情往来，可是他没想到其实这对中国人也是一种负担。他不明白既然小马不想去，直接说不去就行了，为什么还要撒谎说去泰国呢，这种做法算不算是虚伪呢？

思考与讨论：

1) 小马为什么把红包叫作“红色炸弹”？他不想参加朋友的婚礼而撒谎说他要去泰国，你也跟Andrew一样觉得这种做法虚伪吗？
2) 如果你是小马，遇到这样的情况会怎么做？

（四）Nick和太太李洁结婚后住在上海，Nick在一家贸易公司工作，李洁则是全职太太。上个星期，他们收到Nick的经理的邀请，请他们夫妻这个周末去经理新买的房子聚会，庆祝搬新家。出发前，夫妻两个为了带什么礼物而争吵了起来。李洁坚持应该买比较贵的礼物，因为经理年纪比较大，最好送些补品。而Nick觉得带一束鲜花比较好，再手写一张卡片就足够了。李洁对Nick说：“这次的聚会是个让经理重视你的好机会，送什么礼物太重要了。给经理留下一个好印象，以后对你有好处。”Nick却说：“这是个家庭聚会，你送这么贵的礼物会让经理觉得不安的。你这么做也太功利了吧！”两个人谁都不能说服谁，最后Nick生气地说：“那我们就都不要去了。”李洁觉得很委屈，自己是为Nick好，Nick怎么不理解呢？

思考与讨论：

1) 李洁和Nick在送礼的问题上意见不同的原因是什么？
2) 如果你是Nick，你会听李洁的建议吗？为什么？

二、口语交际练习 Oral communication exercises

1. 角色扮演 Role play

   Pair up with a peer and refer to one of the critical incidents in *Situation analysis* to create a five-minute skit with a similar storyline. Use new vocabulary and speech patterns that you have learned from this lesson in your skit. Perform the dialogue in class and discuss whether each skit properly reflects typical Chinese discourse behavior.

2. 观察与讨论 Observation and discussion

   熟人真的好办事吗？

名校名园
请带户口簿就近入学
熟人
关系
朋友

老王,我女儿入学的事就拜托你啦.
咱们这关系,放心,放心

（1）课前准备

- 请根据这两张图片内容，描述图片里发生的事情。
- 请2–3位中国朋友看看这两张图片和你写的小故事，然后请他们说说他们的想法跟你的有什么一样或不一样的地方。
- 问问他们是否同意“熟人好办事”这种观念？为什么？请他们举例说明。

可能用到的词语：熟人好办事/托sb. + VP/一回生二回熟/人之常情/以便/以至于

（2）课堂活动

上课时跟同学们分组进行下面的活动：

- 互相分享自己写的故事和调查的结果，并讨论以下几个问题。
- 在你们的母语社会中，人们什么时候可能会用“熟人好办事”这种观念请别人帮忙？跟中国的社会情况有什么一样或不一样的地方？
- 课文中提到，中国人采用三种不同的法则跟三种不同关系里的人打交道。你们是否也有这种经验？请举例说明。
- 请每个人都谈谈自己对“熟人好办事” 这种观念的看法。如果你同意这种观念，你会用什么方法达成自己的目的？ 如果你不同意这种观念，你会怎么做？
- 你们认为应该怎么做才能建立一个良好的人脉关系。

三、写作 Composition

1. 作文 (两题选一题)

题目1：谈人脉
提示：

- “人脉”是什么意思，它是怎么形成的？
- 人脉对你重不重要？为什么？
- 你认为建立和维护人脉必须具备那些条件？请举例说明。
- 你的母语文化对建立人脉的概念跟中国人的有什么一样或不一样的地方？
- 你自己或你的亲人、熟人常用什么方式建立人脉？请举例说明。
- 总结人脉的重要性以及你对中国人脉观念的看法。
- 可能用到的词语和句型：紧密/相连/坦言/确实/相当于/以便/……, 以……/以至于/A为B所VP

题目2：期末研究报告 【第一阶段(jiēduàn: stage, phase)】

到目前为止，你学了许多有关中国人行为文化背后的价值观。这些价值观不仅对中国人的日常生活和交际沟通的方式有很大的影响，而且对中国的外交政策(zhèngcè: policy)、国际关系(international relations)、商务往来都有影响。请你从这几个方面中挑选一个你有兴趣的话题，在接下来的4–6周内，完成一个研究课题(yánjiū kètí: research project)。最后用口头报告和书面报告的方式展示你的研究结果。请按照老师的规定准备口头报告的时间长度和书面研究报告的字数。

本周/第一阶段的准备工作:

- 决定你要研究的题目。上网看3–5个相关的文章(wénzhāng: article)或视频(shìpín: video), 其中两个必须是中文的。
- 为三篇文章（其中一个可以是视频）各写80–120字的摘要(zhāiyào: summary)。

- 准备期末研究报告大纲(dàgāng: outline)。大纲的内容必须包括：题目、你研究这个课题的目的、你想要探讨的问题、研究方法等。
- 下周上课时把你所读的文章链接(liànjiē: link)、摘要和大纲交给老师。

2. 文化探索 Cultural exploration: For learners who are currently studying or working in the target culture.

In this lesson, we have learned some common expressions that highlight the importance of building relationships in Chinese society, such as 多个朋友多条路, 熟人好办事, 一回生二回熟, 拉关系, and 走后门. Interview three to six Chinese adults of varying ages and from different socioeconomic backgrounds about the following questions: (1) what notions or values do these sayings endorse? (2) to what extent have these values influenced their own behavior? (3) what are the advantages or disadvantages of these practices? Remember to ask for concrete examples that illustrate the points being discussed. Use a recorder to record what was said. Compare their answers to see whether their respective age, gender, profession, or life experience influenced their respective attitudes and practices. You may make an audio recording or write a journal entry to reflect on their answers. Submit the completed reflection to your instructor.

第六单元 **Unit six**

文化视角：差序格局

Cultural perspective: differentiated mode of association

第十三课　看不懂的中国人？（一）

行为聚焦：亲疏有别

Behavior highlighted: distinguish people based on relationships

课文 *Text*

2016年4月，各大新闻和社交平台报道了一名年轻女子在某酒店遇袭的事件。监控视频显示，这名女子被一个男子强行拖拽着，她大声呼救，并说自己不认识这个男人，然而，几个酒店的员工和客人从二人身边走过，都没有上前施救。虽然女子最后安全脱险，但这一事件还是引发了大量的关注，网上各种言论层出不穷。人们有的批评酒店保安不作为，有的探讨女性在危险时刻应如何自卫，但更多的网友还是对旁人的冷漠甚至社会的无情表达了愤怒。

其实，近些年来，网上关于中国人冷漠的讨论一直没有停止过。例如，"老人街头摔倒没人扶"就是人们热议的另一个现象。但令人困惑的是，中国文化不是一个重情的文化吗？为什么现实中中国人又会显得这样冷漠无情？中国人像这样看起来自相矛盾的行为还有很多。比如，中国人一般都很爱面子，甚至视面子如命，可是我们常常看到人们买东西插队或者开车咄咄逼人连行人都不让的丢面子的行为；中国是个"礼仪之邦"，然而在餐馆或旅馆里常有顾客对服务员大喊大叫，很没有礼貌；中国文化崇尚和谐，但只因为飞机误点，有些旅客竟然大闹机场，甚至闹到后来拒绝登机。诸如此类的矛盾行为还有很多，这些现象令许多人困惑不解，以至于连一些长期研究中国文化的学者都发出"看不懂中国人"的感慨。

有学者认为，中国人很多看似矛盾的行为是由丰富而复杂的中国文化所决定的。中国人处世的哲学观念很多，其中有些就是互相矛盾甚至对立着的。其次，人的行为受到文化和风俗的影响，而文化和风俗还有地域、年龄和教育程度等等之分。更重要的是，面对这些复杂和矛盾的行为，弄清楚事件发生的场合以及当事人双方的关系和身份非常重要。因为交际场合不同，交际对象不同，中国人的行为和说话方式也会不同，甚至完全相反。中国传统社会的"差序格局"使当今的中国人在为人处世时仍下意识地把人分为远近亲疏或上下尊卑。换言之，了解中国人的"亲疏有别""上下有序"等一系列潜意识中的观念对看懂中国人来说非常关键。

"差序格局"一词是社会学家费孝通用来说明传统中国的社会结构和人际关系的。其主要含义有二：一是在中国的传统社会，人们会把有血缘关系的

"自家人"和没有血缘关系的"外人"按亲疏远近分成由近到远不同的圈子；二是人们有意识地把"圈内人"与"圈外人"区别开来，并在与他们的交往中采用不同的"近亲远疏"的行为法则。虽然现代中国的社会结构，特别是家庭结构，已经发生了根本的变化，传统的大家庭已逐渐被现代社会的小家庭所代替，但中国人亲疏有别或内外有别的观念始终没有动摇。源于血缘关系的"自家人"或"自己人"已成为一种心理现象。"圈内人"的概念不再受限于血缘或亲戚关系，即有血缘关系的自家人有可能属于圈内人或自己人，但是没有血缘关系的外人也可以随着地缘、业缘以及其它关系的建立从圈外人变成圈内人。而一旦成为圈内人或自己人，人情、面子等一系列世俗观念便开始支配中国人的行为方式。

由于根深蒂固的亲疏有别观念，中国人的行为似乎因此失去了统一性。中国人虽重"礼"，讲"礼让"和"为他人着想"，但在实际生活中，这些客气和爱面子的行为一般都是发生在自己人和相识的人之间。一旦进入公共场合面对生人，人们心中礼的约束似乎就有所放松。至少，面对发生在陌生人身上的事，很多中国人往往显得比较冷漠，一副"事不关己"的样子。有学者说，中国人总的来说不知道怎样与陌生人打交道。说到底，这也许是因为儒家的伦理道德是建立在传统的宗法社会基础上的，是一套熟人社会的人际关系和交往法则。由此可见，首先观察交际发生的场合以及交际双方的关系，对于理解中国人的行为习惯是何等的重要！

生词 New words

简体	繁體	拼音	词性	英文翻译
1. 差序格局		chāxù géjú	phr	differentiated mode of association, a term coined by Fei Xiaotong in his《乡土中国》 [差: 差别, difference; 序: 顺序, order; 格局: pattern, structure]
2. 亲疏有别	親疏有別	qīnshū yǒu bié	phr	distinguish people based on relationships [亲: 亲近, close; 疏: 疏远, distant; 别(bf): 差别, difference]
3. 平台	平臺	píngtái	n	platform
4. 报道	報道	bàodào	v/n	report; report [same as 报导 (bàodǎo)]
5. 遇袭	遇襲	yùxí	v	suffer attack, be assaulted
6. 监控	監控	jiānkòng	n/v	surveillance; surveil, monitor
7. 视频	視頻	shìpín	n	video
8. 强行	強行	qiángxíng	adv	by force
9. 拖拽		tuōzhuài	v	pull, drag [拖: drag; 拽: pull, tug at (sth.)]
10. 呼救		hūjiù	v	call for help

简体	繁體	拼音	词性	英文翻译
11. 然而		rán'ér	conj	however [more formal than 但是]
12. 施救		shījiù	v	take measures to rescue [施 bestow, carry out; 救(bf): help, relieve]
13. 脱险	脫險	tuō//xiǎn	v	escape danger
14. 引发	引發	yǐnfā	v	trigger, evoke
15. 言论	言論	yánlùn	n	remarks, views, open discussion
16. 层出不穷	層出不窮	céngchū-bùqióng	idiom	emerge one after another, spring up in an endless stream
17. 保安		bǎo'ān	n	security guard, security personnel
18. 不作为	不作為	búzuòwéi	v/n	take no action to fulfill one's duty; negligence of one's duty
19. 探讨	探討	tàntǎo	v	inquire into, discuss
20. 时刻	時刻	shíkè	n	moment, time
21. 如何		rúhé	pron	how [more formal than 怎样 or 怎么]
22. 自卫	自衛	zìwèi	v	defend oneself [卫: 保卫, defend]
23. 冷漠		lěngmò	n/adj	coldness and indifference; cold and indifferent
24. 无情	無情	wúqíng	n/adj	lack of compassion; compassionless, pitiless, heartless
25. 愤怒	憤怒	fènnù	n/adj	indignance; indignant, angry
26. 停止		tíngzhǐ	v	stop, cease
27. 街头	街頭	jiētóu	n	street
28. 摔倒		shuāidǎo	v	fall down
29. 扶		fú	v	help sb. up, support with hand
30. 热议	熱議	rèyì	v	discuss passionately, heatedly debate [热: 热烈(liè), ardent, enthusiastic; 议: 议论, discuss, debate]
31. 现实	現實	xiànshí	n/adj	reality; realistic
32. 自相矛盾		zìxiāng-máodùn	idiom	contradict oneself; self-contradictory
33. 命		mìng	n	(one's) life [命: 生命]
34. 插队	插隊	chā//duì	v	jump a queue, cut in line
35. 咄咄逼人	咄咄逼人	duōduō-bīrén	idiom	overbearing, aggressive
36. 误点	誤點	wù//diǎn	v	[of means of public transportation] be behind schedule, be delayed
37. 竟然		jìngrán	adv	unexpectedly, to one's surprise
38. 闹	鬧	nào	v	run amok, cause havoc
39. 拒绝	拒絕	jùjué	v	refuse, decline, reject
40. 登机	登機	dēng//jī	v	board a plane

简体	繁體	拼音	词性	英文翻译
41. 诸如此类	諸如此類	zhūrú-cǐlèi	idiom	things like this, and so on
42. 发出	發出	fāchū	v	let out, send out, give out
43. 感慨		gǎnkǎi	n/v	lament; sigh with emotion
44. 风俗	風俗	fēngsú	n	social custom
45. 地域		dìyù	n	region, area
46. 程度		chéngdù	n	extent, degree, level
47. 场合	場合	chǎnghé	n	occasion, circumstance
48. 当事人	當事人	dāngshìrén	n	people directly involved or implicated
49. 身份		shēnfèn	n	identity, status
50. 对象	對象	duìxiàng	n	target, object
51. 为人	為人	wéirén	v	conduct oneself
52. 下意识	下意識	xiàyì.shí	adv/n	subconsciously; subconscious mind
53. 尊卑		zūnbēi	n	superiors and inferiors [尊(bf): respect, respectability; 卑(bf): low, inferior]
54. 一系列		yíxìliè	adj	a series of
55. 关键	關鍵	guānjiàn	adj/n	key, critical; crux
56. 区别	區別	qūbié	v/n	distinguish, differentiate; distinction
57. 代替		dàitì	v	replace, substitute
58. 始终	始終	shǐzhōng	adv	from beginning to end, all along
59. 动摇	動搖	dòngyáo	v	waver, destabilize, sway
60. 源于	源於	yuányú	phr	stem from, has (its) origin in
61. 受限于	受限於	shòuxiànyú	phr	be limited to, be constrained by
62. 属于	屬於	shǔyú	v	belong to, be part of
63. 业缘	業緣	yèyuán	n	affinity due to work or line of business
64. 支配		zhīpèi	v	dominate, control, allocate
65. 根深蒂固		gēnshēn-dìgù	idiom	deep-rooted, long-established, inveterate
66. 统一	統一	tǒngyī	adj/v	unified; unify, unite
67. 副		fù	m	[for facial expressions, pairs/sets of things]
68. 事不关己	事不關己	shìbùguānjǐ	idiom	a matter of no concern to oneself
69. 陌生		mòshēng	adj	unfamiliar [陌生人stranger]
70. 说到底	說到底	shuōdàodǐ	phr	in the final analysis, at bottom
71. 宗法		zōngfǎ	n	patriarchal clan system
72. 观察	觀察	guānchá	v	observe, inspect
73. 何等		héděng	adv	how

词语与句型 Expressions and sentence patterns

1. 竟(然) unexpectedly; to one's surprise

课文例句：中国文化崇尚和谐，但只因为飞机误点，有些旅客竟然大闹机场，甚至闹到后来拒绝登机。

竟 is the monosyllabic variation of 竟然.

- 我老家最近几年变化很大，上次我回去，出了火车站竟然不知道回家的公交车要在哪儿坐了。
- 上周五一位老人在这里摔倒，五分钟之内有十多人经过，竟无一人上前帮助老人。

2. 对(于)……而言 with regard to ...; as far as ... is concerned

课文例句：对于学习中国交际文化而言，面对这些复杂和矛盾的行为，弄清楚事件发生的场合以及当事人双方的关系和身份非常重要。

In this pattern, 对于 and 对 can be used interchangeably. 而言 is a more formal replacement for来说.

- 对(于)学习汉语的日本学生而言，汉字不难。
- 多使用公共交通工具对(于)保护环境而言非常重要。

3. ……。换言之，…… ... In other words, ...

课文例句：中国传统社会的"差序格局"使当今的中国人在为人处世时仍下意识地把人分为远近亲疏或上下尊卑。换言之，了解中国人的"亲疏有别""上下有序"等一系列潜意识中的观念对看懂中国人来说非常关键。

换言之 is a formal alternative to 换句话说.

- 钱能买来房子、汽车，却买不来健康、友谊。换言之，不是任何东西都能用钱买到。
- 中国人一般都重视礼尚往来。换言之，与中国人来往，最好不要有来而无往。

4. 说到底 in the final analysis; at the heart of (this matter)

课文例句：有学者说，中国人总的来说不知道怎样与陌生人打交道。说到底，这也许是因为儒家的伦理道德是建立在传统的宗法社会基础上的，是一套熟人社会的人际关系和交往法则。

Depending on the content and length of the preceding clause, a comma or a period can be used before 说到底. Alternately, a comma can be used after 说到底 depending on what follows it.

- 这次考试小王的成绩不够理想，说到底是因为他考前没有好好复习。
- 世界和平是人类的共同愿望。说到底，各国之间要实现和平共处，必须在互相尊重的基础上进行大量的文化交流，加深彼此之间的了解。

> **语言练习** To practice and reinforce what you have learned from the Text, New Words, and the section "Expressions and sentence patterns" in this lesson, please visit the companion website to download a PDF version of the exercises.

交际情景 Communication scenarios

Study the following conversations between native speakers on the textbook companion website. Use the plug-in feature to find the definitions of the new words highlighted in orange. Try to visualize the scene as you read and listen to each dialogue. Discuss your reactions to these scenario dialogues with a classmate.

1. A fellow resident wants to nominate Li Aihua for the position of Resident Representative on their neighborhood committee. However, when her son tells her the news, Aihua immediately opposes the idea. Take note of how she responds and her rationale for doing so.

王大伟：妈，居委会的赵大妈让我告诉你，小区要选居民代表，讨论管理小区的事，她问你愿不愿意当这个代表。
李爱华：我可不想管这些闲事。
王大伟：怎么是闲事？小区的环境卫生要改善，你代表我们这个楼去提提意见，不是挺好吗？
李爱华：我们自己家的事我还管不过来呢。再说了，这种事费力不讨好，我提意见，别人也不会听啊。你就告诉赵大妈，我这两天要出差，没时间。

思考与讨论：

1) "费力不讨好"是什么意思？
2) 李爱华为什么不愿意做居民代表？
3) 在你的国家，在这样的情况下，人们也会像李爱华这么想吗？他们一般会怎么想？

2. Xiao Bai, the new staff in Weiming's office, tried unsuccessfully to book an event in the company auditorium. Take note of why Xiao Bai fails and how Weimin is able to change Secretary Li's mind.

王为民：小白，我让你去订公司的大礼堂，你订好了吗？
小　白：别提了，我去找办公室李秘书，她跟我说大礼堂在维修，这时候不好订。
王为民：你跟李秘书说是我让你去的了吗？
小　白：没说，她说要维修，我也就不好意思再说什么了。

（王为民给李秘书打电话……）

王为民：李秘书，是我，老王啊。有个事求你帮个忙，星期五下午我们能不能用一下公司大礼堂啊？我听说要维修，你看这怎么办？
李秘书：没问题啊。我让维修的人星期四来不就行了。
王为民：那你可帮了我大忙了。
李秘书：我们原来都是一个部门的，您跟我客气什么，咱们谁跟谁啊，有事儿您说话。
王为民：那多谢了，回头请你吃饭。

思考与讨论：

1) 李秘书开始时说大礼堂不好订，但后来主动想办法帮王为民，为什么有这样的转变？
2) 在你的国家，在这样的情况下，人们也会像李秘书这么做吗？他们一般会怎么做？
3) Due to an emergency, Xiao Zhao was forced to ask his neighbor, Wang Weimin, to take care of his daughter Zhao Xiaoming. Pay attention to how Wang Weimin expresses his willingness to do the favor.

小　赵：王哥，我来接孩子了，今天晚上给你们添麻烦了。
王为民：都不是外人，说什么添麻烦啊！小明已经在我家吃过晚饭了，你也在这儿吃点儿吧。
小　赵：不了，不了。小明，有没有谢谢王伯伯啊？
小　明：谢谢伯伯。
王为民：不用不用。小明就像我们自己的孩子一样，吃点儿东西怕什么呀。你太见外了。
小　赵：王哥谢谢了！时间不早了，就不打扰你们了。小明，快跟爸爸回家吧。

思考与讨论：

1) 王为民是怎么表达他愿意照顾小明，并“埋怨”小赵太客气的？请说出两个例子。
2) 在你的国家，在这样的情况下，人们也会像王为民这么说吗？如果不是，他们一般会怎么说？

言语行为例说 Notes on discourse behavior

1. 对话例句：王大伟：妈，居委会的赵大妈让我告诉你，小区要选居民代表，讨论管理小区的事，她问你愿不愿意当这个代表。
　　李爱华：我可不想管这些闲事。

管闲事 means “to meddle in other people’s business”. Being described as 爱管闲事 or 多管闲事 is meant as criticism. On the other hand, being told 你别管闲事 or 你少管闲事 is meant to persuade the listener to meddle less. In colloquial speech, “狗拿耗子，多管闲事” literally translates as “a dog catching mice is meddling in a cat’s business,” meaning that someone is meddling in other people’s business. As a consequence of 爱管/多管闲事, one may find oneself 费力不讨好 (fèilì bù tǎohǎo), or “to waste effort on a thankless task”. For this reason, the Chinese often appear indifferent to the affairs of outsiders (外人) or to public affairs.

- 甲：你这个人怎么这么爱多管闲事？这跟你有什么关系？
  乙：别生气，你误会了，我只是想帮忙。
- 甲：我们公司老张的女儿考大学，想问问我的意见报哪个学校。
  乙：你还是少管闲事。万一她女儿没考上，到时候该埋怨你了。

2. 对话例句：李秘书：我们原来都是一个部门的，您跟我客气什么，咱们谁跟谁啊，有事儿您说话。
　　王为民：那多谢了，回头请你吃饭。

咱们谁跟谁啊 is a colloquial expression used more often in northern China. It means "there is no need to distinguish being yours and mine", and it asks the listener to relax and be less formal. Someone who is granting a favor may say this to casually yet politely inform the beneficiary that no favor is owed, with the intent being to cultivate positive feelings or a closer relationship.

- 甲：今天搬家辛苦你了，回头请你吃饭。
  乙：咱们谁跟谁啊！客气什么！
- 甲：老王，你可帮了我大忙了，我真不知道怎么感谢你。
  乙：咱们认识这么多年了，谁跟谁啊，说这些做什么！

3. 对话例句：小　赵：王哥，我来接孩子了，今天晚上给你们添麻烦了。
   王为民：都不是外人，说什么添麻烦啊！

For historical reasons, the Chinese are accustomed to distinguishing 自己人 from 外人. Expressions like "都不是外人, 都是自己人", or "没把sb当外人" are often used to indicate closeness in a relationship. Regardless the truth, saying this cultivates mutual goodwill and strengthens a social relationship.

- 甲：我有一件事不知道应不应该在这里说。
  乙：这里都不是外人，有什么就说吧。
- 甲：你为什么跟他们说方言？
  乙：他们会把我当自己人，有什么事都会跟我说。要是说普通话，可能他们就把我当外人了。

4. 对话例句：小　赵：不了，不了。小明，有没有谢谢王伯伯啊？
   小　明：谢谢伯伯。
   王为民：不用不用……你太见外了。

见外 literally means "to regard somebody as an outsider." If you feel that the other party is being too formal or too polite with you during an interaction, you may tell them 你/您太见外了 ("You're treating me like an outsider") to encourage them to behave with greater informality. As a host, you may say 不要/别见外 to your guests to encourage them to relax. In English, similar expressions include "be my guest" or "don't be a stranger".

- 甲：你来看我们，我们已经很开心了，还带这么多的礼物就太见外了。
  乙：只是一点儿水果和点心，没什么。
- 甲：小海，看你这么瘦，多吃点儿啊！到这里就跟在自己家一样，别见外。
  乙：谢谢阿姨，这些都是我爱吃的。

体演情景 Perform the scenario

Select a dialogue from this section and listen to its recording several times. Imitate the speakers in pronunciation, intonation and discourse behavior in terms of both the words they use and the ways in which they carry themselves. Memorize the dialogue for performance in class.

跨文化交际 Cross-cultural communication

一、误解分析 Situation analysis

Break into groups and discuss the misunderstanding in each of the cross-cultural communication incidents below. For each incident, the group should generate an answer that best explains the cultural assumptions behind the ways in which the individuals say and do things. In addition, discuss possible strategies to avoid these misunderstandings in similar situations.

（一）Grace在杭州留学时跟一个张姓的中国家庭住在一块儿。张家是三代同堂的大家庭，有爷爷奶奶、爸爸妈妈，还有一个十岁的小孙子张阳。一天晚上，Grace跟这一家人去散步，远远看见前面有一群人围在一起。他们过去看了一下，原来是有一个老人不知道为什么躺在地上，看起来好像很痛苦。张阳想跑进去把老人扶起来，可是妈妈拉住他的手不让他进去，并且跟他和Grace说："别管闲事。"张阳不解地问妈妈："妈，你不是总跟我说要帮助别人吗？这个奶奶躺在地上，我们为什么不帮她？"Grace心里其实也想着一样的问题，平时张家的人都那么友善，为什么面对躺在地上的老人却这么冷漠，而且言行不一呢？

思考与讨论：

1) 你能帮助Grace解除她的疑问吗？
2) 如果你是Grace，你会听中国妈妈的话吗？为什么？

（二）Hannah刚到一家美国公司的上海办事处工作，到了以后她急需办一张中国的电话卡。今天晚上Hannah加班，离开公司的时候已经有点儿晚了。她急急忙忙地跑到电信营业厅，可是工作人员对她说："对不起，我们下班了，明天再来吧。"就在Hannah刚走出门的时候，门外又进来了一个女孩子，也说要办电话卡。营业厅的工作人员笑眯眯地对那个女孩子说："夏红，是你呀！咱们毕业好几年了，你一点儿也没变。快坐，快坐，我马上就给你办好。"Hannah在门口听到这些话非常生气，她心里想：不是已经下班了吗？那你为什么可以给别人办，却不能给我办呢？这不是公私不分吗？

思考与讨论：

1) 这位工作人员为什么对不同的人有不同的处理方式？这算不算公私不分？
2) 如果你是Hannah，在这样的情况下你会怎么做？

（三）May在一家中国公司工作，同事们对她都非常客气，也很照顾。因为上班比较远，她经常搭同事董阳的车。在May的印象里，董阳总是彬彬有礼，有时看见May的东西重，还主动帮她拿东西。但是最近May发现董阳有一个习惯，这个习惯让May很吃惊。董阳非常容易路怒，平时斯斯文文的人，一遇到堵车脾气就变得不好，甚至会骂人，如果有车插在他的前面，他就加速再超过去。可是一到了公司就又变成了那个对领导谦卑有礼，对同事客客气气的董阳。May想不明白，到底哪个才是真正的董阳。

思考与讨论：

1) 董阳的表现为什么差别这么大 ？你觉得哪个是真正的董阳？
2) 如果你是May，你还会继续搭董阳的车并且跟他做朋友吗？

（四）Daniel和他的中国朋友张东明打算合开一个游戏软件公司。大部分技术员都已经招聘好了，还需要一个财务主任。他们两个都觉得这个职位对公司非常重要，一定要选一个合适的人。Daniel想在网站上公开招聘，择优录取，而东明建议请一个他过去的老朋友来做这个职位。东明对Daniel说："财务主任管着全公司的钱，一定要找个知根知底的人。我这个老朋友跟我认识多年，虽然能力一般，但是非常可靠。我们就用他吧。"Daniel非常不理解东明的想法，招聘不就是要择优录取吗，为什么要选能力一般的人？

思考与讨论：

1) 为什么张东明想选这个能力一般的人做公司的财务工作？
2) 如果你是Daniel，在这样的情况下你会同意张东明的做法吗？

二、口语交际练习 Oral communication exercises

1. 角色扮演 Role play

   Pair up with a peer and refer to one of the critical incidents in *Situation analysis* to create a five-minute skit with a similar storyline. Use new vocabulary and speech patterns that you have learned from this lesson in your skit. Perform the dialogue in class and discuss whether each skit properly reflects typical Chinese discourse behavior.

2. 电影欣赏与讨论Film appreciation and discussion

   上YouTube或优酷网站观看电影《不成问题的问题》。看电影的时候，可以注意下列问题；看了电影以后再跟同学们一起讨论。

   1) 这部电影改编(gǎibiān: adapt)自谁的小说(fiction)？
   2) 电影的故事发生在什么时候、什么地方？
   3) 电影的名字是什么意思？跟电影里的哪一个人物(character)有关系？
   4) 丁务源(Dīng Wùyuán)是谁？他为人处世的特点是什么？
   5) 秦妙斋(Qín Miàozhāi)是谁？他有什么特点？
   6) 农场员工对从国外留学回来的博士、新主任尤大兴(Yóu Dàxīng)有什么反应？为什么？
   7) 对丁务源来说，做人重要还是做事重要？他为人处世的方式在今天的中国社会还很普遍吗？
   8) 这个小小的农场怎样反映出整个中国社会的人情世故(shìgù: the ways of the world)？

三、写作 Composition

1. 作文 (两题选一题)

题目1：为《不成问题的问题》写一篇电影评论，至少三段。

- 第一段描述电影的剧情(jùqíng: plot)和主要人物之间的关系。
- 第二段讨论你认为这部电影最有意思的地方是什么，最大的优点(yōudiǎn: merit)和缺点是什么。
- 第三段总结你对这部电影的看法。
- 尽量多用在第十二课和第十三课里学过的词语和句型。

题目2：期末研究报告 【第二阶段】*第一阶段的作业安排，请看第十二课的作文题目2。

- 上周你交了文章摘要和期末研究报告大纲。请根据老师的反馈(fǎnkuì: feedback)和建议，修改题目或要探讨的研究方向。
- 按照老师规定的时间完成第一稿(gǎo: draft)。尽量用本学期学的生词和句型来表达你的想法。
- 继续阅读相关的文章，并开始准备口头报告。口头报告可以采用不同的形式，比方说，PPT、视频、学术(xuéshù: academic)海报(poster presentation)、表演等。请任选一种。
- 收到老师对第一稿的反馈后，开始写第二稿。

2. 文化探索Cultural exploration: For learners who are currently studying or working in the target culture

The idea of building relationships based on 血缘, 地缘, and 业缘 continues to play an important role in the lives of the Chinese. Examples include the Yunnan Association in Beijing (北京云南同乡会), the Wuhan University of Technology Alumni Association in Shanghai (武汉理工大学上海校友会), the Li Clan of Hong Kong Association (香港李氏宗亲会), the Taiwanese Hakka Friendship Association (台湾客家联谊会), the International Chinese Language Teachers Association (国际汉语教师协会), etc.

Use online tools to make a list of social associations near where you live in China. Select one association to study, either by looking at its website (if available) or by directly contacting the organization, and learn about its member services and activities.

As an alternative, interview 2 to 3 Chinese people of different ages and social-economic backgrounds and ask them about organizations in which they hold membership. Ask them about their experiences with these organizations, their participation in these organizations' activities, and the impact that their membership has had on their social and/or professional life.

Write a report to reflect on what you have learned, and submit the report to your instructor. As an alternative, make a 5- to 8-minute audio recording to reflect on your impression of the interviews. Submit the completed recording to your instructor.

第十四课　看不懂的中国人？（二）

行为聚焦：上下有别

Behavior highlighted: distinction between the upper and lower status

课文 *Text*

中国人的人际关系自古以来就存在着一种天然的差等。所谓差序格局，讲的就是传统社会里人与人之间的差等或不平等关系。如果说亲疏远近指的是人际关系横向上的差等，那么长幼尊卑则代表着人与人之间纵向上的区别，即每个人都有各自不同的家庭地位和社会身份。在当今中国，虽然已经过长期的现代化进程，人们仍有意识或无意识地序长幼，定尊卑，在日常生活中遵守着“上下有序”“尊卑有等”的传统观念和行为准则。

华人网络媒体倍可亲上有一篇回国纪实。文中说，中国的经济发展和生活水平的提高并没有带来相应的社会观念的转变。作者尖锐地指出，中国仍是一个没有平等观念的社会。人们彼此之间缺少基本的尊重，更缺少基本的平等相待的行为习惯。她列举了许多亲眼目睹的现象，并总结说，在与别人初次接触时，每个中国人都会先揣摩对方的社会身份和地位，并在心中暗暗地排列自己与对方的上下高低关系。只有在经过这样的揣摩和定位之后，人们才会决定怎样与他人打交道。

中国人根深蒂固的等级观念是在儒家伦理道德长期影响下形成的。儒家强调的是人伦，而“伦”指的就是有差等的次序。儒家最不能容忍的就是对伦的僭越，因为家庭的和睦和社会的稳定是建立在伦的差等和次序之上的。儒家的“五伦”规定了中国传统社会差序格局的根本内容。五伦中的君臣、父子、夫妻、兄弟这四伦，都表现出权力和义务的不对等。即便是朋友之间，当关系发展到结义兄弟时，尊卑有等的观念便会开始支配双方的行为。在中国家文化的社会里，社会关系和组织不过是人伦关系的逐步扩大。当这种严格强调等级的人伦关系扩大到社会，我们便看到了当今仍普遍存在于中国人际关系中的差序性，即上下、长幼，甚至尊卑、贵贱等等。

学者梁漱溟在其《东西文化及其哲学》中指出，强调尊卑和崇尚平等是中西文化不同的精神特质。他说，中国人看见西方人在一起时没有一个人做主，觉得很奇怪。人们平起平坐，似乎完全没有尊卑上下之分。正如中国人看到西方人的行为中常不分谁是领头的、谁是听话的而感到惊讶一样，西方人看到中国上级领导的“一言堂”和下属员工一味的言听计从也感到难以理解。曾在中国华为公司担任管理者的CT Johnson一次告诉媒体，在西方公司工作时，他期待自己的下属以直接但尊重的态度质疑他的提议，希望通过讨论共同改进工作。然而中国的同事们不会这样做，因为对于他们来说，质疑就等同于反对。上级领导“训话”是另一种常使西方人或久居西方的华人感到不可接受的行为。领导开会训话时，不仅自始至终一言堂，而且可以随便训斥人，甚至还会当着众人的面点名批评下属，一点面子也不留。

中国人的等级观念在公共场合生人之间的交往中也明显地反映出来。我们在街头可以看到警察粗鲁地对待一个违反了交规的农民工，而这个农民工始终陪着笑脸不敢回一句话；我们也可以看到一些城管在执法中粗暴无礼，而被驱赶的小商贩在城管所代表的权力面前也不敢做任何的反抗。除了权力以外，金钱也是造成当今中国社会等级分明的主要原因之一。开凯美瑞的人主动让着开奔驰宝马的，低收入阶层的人在高收入者面前也自觉低人一等。在前面提到的华人回国见闻中，作者讲了这样一个故事：一次，她乘飞机从杭州去北京，后面坐着一个看起来像是很有钱的人。从上飞机的那一刻起，他就哇啦哇啦地大声叫个不停，把空中小姐像使唤自己家的保姆一样支来叫去。他并不认为这样做是缺乏教养，相反，像很多的“土豪”一样，他似乎在利用一切机会，向世界申明自己现在是个有钱人了，因此高人一等了。

同样的情景也时常出现在餐馆和宾馆里。一些穿着体面的人对服务员动不动就大呼小叫，就像旧社会官老爷支使自己的佣人一样。但令人惊讶的是，周围的人，包括服务员自己，并不以此为怪，似乎对这些传统的上尊下卑的行为早已司空见惯了。这一切说明了这样一个事实：即一个国家的经济发展与社会观念的转变并不一定是同步的。随着人类的进步，文化传统固然也在发生变化，但在中国的社会环境里，深层文化结构的改变是缓慢的，一些观念甚至在相当长的历史时期内仍不断地延续着。可见，在学习中国人行为习惯的同时，从深层的文化观念上了解他们为什么这样或那样与别人打交道，对看懂“复杂的中国人”十分必要。

生词 New words

简体	繁體	拼音	词性	英文翻译
1. 差等		chāděng	n	subalternation (in status or quality), differentiated ranking, difference
2. 横向		héngxiàng	adj	crosswise, horizontal
3. 长幼	長幼	zhǎngyòu	n	the senior and the young, seniority by age [长 (bf): senior, old; 幼 (bf): young, under age]
4. 纵向	縱向	zòngxiàng	adj	lengthwise, vertical, longitudinal

简体	繁體	拼音	词性	英文翻译
5. 进程	進程	jìnchéng	n	process, course, progress
6. 纪实	紀實	jìshí	n/v	record of actual events; put down in writing
7. 相应	相應	xiāngyìng	v	corresponding; act in response
8. 转变	轉變	zhuǎnbiàn	n/v	transformation; transform
9. 尖锐	尖銳	jiānruì	adj	incisive, penetrating, pointed and sharp
10. 缺少		quēshǎo	v	lack, be short of
11. 列举	列舉	lièjǔ	v	enumerate, list, cite one by one
12. 亲眼	親眼	qīnyǎn	adv	with one's own eyes
13. 目睹		mùdǔ	v	witness, see at first hand [目 (bf): eye; 睹 (bf): see]
14. 初次		chūcì	adv	for the first time
15. 接触	接觸	jiēchù	v	come into contact with
16. 揣摩		chuǎimó	v	try to figure out
17. 暗暗		àn'àn	adv	inwardly, to oneself, secretly
18. 排列		páiliè	v	put in order, arrange
19. 定位		dìng//wèi	v/n	determine the position, characterize (as); positioning
20. 等级	等級	děngjí	n	social status, rank, grade
21. 次序		cìxù	n	sequence, order
22. 僭越		jiànyuè	n/v	overstepping of one's role or authority or ethical relationship with others; overstep one's role or authority or ethical relationship with others
23. 规定	規定	guīdìng	v/n	stipulate; provision, regulation
24. 权力	權力	quánlì	n	power, authority, right
25. 义务	義務	yìwù	n/adj	duty, obligation; mandatory, voluntary
26. 即便		jíbiàn	conj	even if, even though [more formal than 即使]
27. 结义	結義	jiéyì	v	become sworn brothers/sisters
28. 组织	組織	zǔzhī	n/v	organization; organize
29. 逐步		zhúbù	adv	progressively, step by step
30. 严格	嚴格	yán'gé	adj	strict, rigorous
31. 贵贱	貴賤	guìjiàn	n	the noble and the lowly, high versus low social hierarchy
32. 精神		jīngshén	n	spirit, mind, consciousness
33. 特质	特質	tèzhì	n	special quality, characteristic

简体	繁體	拼音	词性	英文翻译
34. 做主		zuò//zhǔ	v	making the decision, be in charge
35. 平起平坐		píngqǐ-píngzuò	idiom	be on an equal footing, be on equal terms
36. 领头	領頭	lǐng//tóu	v	take the lead, be the first to do sth.
37. 惊讶	驚訝	jīngyà	adj	astonished, shocked
38. 上级	上級	shàngjí	n	superior, a higher authority, someone higher in the hierarchy
39. 一言堂		yìyántáng	n	hall of one person's speech [堂(bf): hall], what sb. says goes, deciding everything by one man's say
40. 下属	下屬	xiàshǔ	n	subordinate
41. 一味		yíwèi	adv	blindly, stubbornly
42. 言听计从	言聽計從	yántīng-jìcóng	idiom	always follow sb.'s advice, act upon whatever sb. says
43. 难以	難以	nányǐ	v	be difficult to
44. 担任	擔任	dānrèn	v	hold the post of, serve as
45. 期待		qīdài	v	expect, look forward to
46. 质疑	質疑	zhìyí	v	call into question, question (truth or validity)
47. 提议	提議	tíyì	n/v	proposal, suggestion, propose, suggest
48. 等同	等同	děngtóng	v	equate, be equal
49. 训话	訓話	xùn//huà	v	admonish (subordinates)
50. 自始至终	自始至終	zìshǐ-zhìzhōng	idiom	from start to finish, from beginning to end
51. 训斥	訓斥	xùnchì	v	reprimand, rebuke, berate
52. 点名	點名	diǎn//míng	v	(praise or criticize sb.) by name; call roll
53. 明显	明顯	míngxiǎn	adj	obvious
54. 粗鲁	粗魯	cūlǔ	adj	crude in one's manners, boorish
55. 对待	對待	duìdài	v	treat
56. 交规	交規	jiāoguī	n	traffic regulations, traffic rules [short for 交通规则]
57. 农民工	農民工	nóngmíngōng	n	migrant peasant workers
58. 陪笑脸	陪笑臉	péi xiàoliǎn	phr	put on a smiling face in order to please sb.
59. 城管		chéngguǎn	n	local government law-enforcement officer, city management [short for 城市管理行政执法局 Urban Administrative and Law Enforcement Bureau]
60. 执法	執法	zhífǎ	v	enforce the law

简体	繁體	拼音	词性	英文翻译
61. 粗暴		cūbào	adj	rude and brutal
62. 驱赶	驅趕	qūgǎn	v	drive away, expel
63. 商贩	商販	shāngfàn	n	small retailer, peddler
64. 反抗		fǎnkàng	n/v	resistance; revolt, confront
65. 分明		fēnmíng	adj/adv	clearly demarcated, distinct; evidently
66. 收入		shōurù	n	income
67. 阶层	階層	jiēcéng	n	social stratum
68. 低人一等		dī rén yì děng	idiom	inferior to other people [antonym: 高人一等]
69. 见闻	見聞	jiànwén	n	what one has seen and heard
70. 使唤	使喚	shǐ.huan	v	order sb. around
71. 保姆		bǎomǔ	n	house maid, nanny
72. 缺乏		quēfá	v	lack, be short of
73. 教养	教養	jiàoyǎng	n	upbringing, culture
74. 土豪		tǔháo	n	[slang] uncultured rich people, *nouveau riche*, local tyrant
75. 申明		shēnmíng	n	declare, aver, state formally
76. 穿着	穿著	chuānzhuó	n	apparel, attire
77. 体面	體面	tǐmiàn	adj/n	[of apparel, living, line of work, etc.] decent, honorable; dignity, decency
78. 动不动	動不動	dòng.budòng	adv	apt to happen [usu. of something undesirable], frequently, happening at the slightest provocation
79. 大呼小叫		dàhū-xiǎojiào	idiom	shout and scream, make a big fuss
80. 官老爷	官老爺	guānlǎo.ye	phr	[an honorific for government officials in traditional China, used sarcastically in the text] literal meaning: official master
81. 支使		zhīshǐ	v	order sb. around
82. 佣人	傭人	yōngrén	n	family servant
83. 司空见惯	司空見慣	sīkōng-jiànguàn	idiom	accustomed to seeing sth.
84. 同步		tóngbù	v	synchronize, keep step with
85. 缓慢	緩慢	huǎnmàn	adj	slow, slow-moving
86. 必要		bìyào	adj	necessary, essential, indispensable

专有名词 Proper nouns

简体	繁體	拼音	英文翻译
1. 倍可亲	倍可親	Bèikěqīn	a portal website in Chinese, primarily serving Chinese living in North America [www.backchina.com; 倍: times;]
2. 梁漱溟		Liáng Shùmíng	Liang Shuming (1893–1988), a scholar and philosopher in the neo-Confucian tradition
3. 华为	華為	Huáwéi	Huawei [brand; most famous for mobile phones]
4. 凯美瑞	凱美瑞	Kǎiměiruì	Camry [Toyota automobile model; 凯: victorious; 瑞: auspicious]
5. 奔驰	奔驰	Bēnchí	Benz [brand], gallop
6. 宝马	寶馬	Bǎomǎ	BMW [brand], precious horse
7. 杭州		Hángzhōu	Hangzhou, the capital city of the Zhejiang province in southeast China

词语与句型 Expressions and sentence patterns

1. ……于

课文例句1：当这种严格强调等级的人伦关系扩大到社会，我们便看到了当今仍普遍存在于中国人际关系中的差序性，即上下、长幼，甚至尊卑、贵贱等等。

课文例句2：中国的同事们不会这样做，因为对于他们来说，质疑就等同于反对。

Normally appearing in formal language, 于 can be used after some verbs to mean "in," "to," "from," etc. Here are some examples in this textbook:

- ❖ 存在于 (Lesson fourteen): exist in
- ❖ 等同于 (Lesson fourteen): equal to
- ❖ 源于 (Lesson thirteen): stem from, originate from
- ❖ 受限于 (Lesson thirteen): be limited/restrained to
- ❖ 相当于 (Lesson twelve): be equivalent to
- ❖ 得益于 (Lesson ten): benefit from

于 can also be used after some adjectives. For example:

- ❖ 忙于 (Lesson twelve): be busy with
- ❖ 急于 (Lesson twelve): be eager to

- 面子现象存在于中国人生活的方方面面，人们不仅要考虑怎样使自己有面子，而且还要时常想着怎样给别人留面子。
- 金钱可以买到很多东西，但有钱并不等同于会快乐。
- 西方年轻人习惯于独立生活，因此18岁以后很多会搬离父母家。
- 丽丽小的时候，父母忙于工作，没有照顾好她。
- 刚到一个公司工作的人往往会急于证明自己的能力。

2. V个不停 do something without ever stopping

课文例句：从上飞机的那一刻起，他就哇啦哇啦地大声叫个不停，把空中小姐像使唤自己家的保姆一样支来叫去。

- 刚搬进来的室友太爱聊天了，整天说个不停，大家都觉得有点儿受不了了。
- 邻居家的孩子只要不上课就玩游戏，从早到晚玩个不停。

3. V来V去 do something over and over again

课文例句：从上飞机的那一刻起，他就哇啦哇啦地大声叫个不停，把空中小姐像使唤自己家的保姆一样支来叫去。

This phrase emphasizes the repetition or nonstop occurrence of the action. The phrase can use the same verb, as in 看来看去, 想来想去, 找来找去; or, it can use two different verbs that have similar or identical meanings, as in 支来叫去, 思来想去, 说来道去.

- 小王特别马虎，今天又忘了钱包放在哪儿了。他找来找去，原来忘在车里了。
- 大学快要毕业了，李丽思来想去，还是决定先找一个工作，以后再考虑上不上研究生。
- 妈妈跟姐姐说来道去，就是想让她赶紧找个男朋友。

4. 动不动就VP VP at the slightest provocation; be apt to VP

课文例句：一些穿着体面的人对服务员动不动就大呼小叫，就像旧社会官老爷支使自己的佣人一样。

动不动 calls attention to the fact that the following action, normally undesirable and reproachable, occurs without any clear reason to an observer. It is often followed by 就.

- 王大伟的女朋友最近动不动就生气，弄得王大伟都不知道该怎么跟她相处了。
- 遇到问题，你别动不动就给父母打电话，应该先想想自己能不能解决。

语言练习 To practice and reinforce what you have learned from the Text, New Words, and the section “Expressions and sentence patterns” in this lesson, please visit the companion website to download a PDF version of the exercises.

交际情景 Communication scenarios

Study the following conversations between native speakers on the textbook companion website. Use the plug-in feature to find the definitions of the new words highlighted in orange. Try to visualize the scene as you read and listen to each dialogue. Discuss your reactions to these scenario dialogues with a classmate.

1. While Wang Weimin and his son Dawei are waiting for their orders at a teahouse, they run into Liu Shaohong. Weimin then chats with Shaohong about her daughter Xiao Jing’s plans

after graduating from a high school. Note who is involved in making plans for Xiao Jing and how Wang Weimin responds to his son when Dawei expresses a different opinion.

王为民：小刘，你女儿小静也快考大学了吧。
刘少红：对，明年就要考了。
王为民：那是想出国留学还是申请国内的大学啊？
刘少红：我和她爸都决定让她在国内读大学。现在国内的机会比国外好，她一个人在外面，我们不放心。女孩子嘛，只要稳定就行了，家里也不指望她能多成功。
王大伟：刘阿姨，你们问过小静的意见吗？出不出国得听她的呀。我记得她以前跟我说想出国上学，开阔眼界。
王为民：大伟，大人说话，小孩儿不要插嘴。刘阿姨他们也是为了小静好。
王大伟：你们说是为了她好，可又不尊重她的意见。小静真可怜，一点儿自由也没有。
王为民：大伟，别说了，怎么那么没大没小的。小刘，你别见怪啊，小孩子不懂事。

思考与讨论：

1） 刘少红一家认为他们有没有权利决定女儿的未来？为什么？
2） 当王大伟提出不同意刘阿姨的观点的时候，王为民怎么制止了儿子？为什么要制止他？
3） 在你的国家，家长会不会像刘少红一样决定孩子的未来？如果孩子提出不同意见的时候，父母一般会怎么做？

2. Wang Dawei is an intern at a trading company. Though his team leader asked him to initiate a merchandise return to a partner company via email, Dawei had not done so because he didn't think that the return was a good idea. Pay attention to how the team leader reacts to Dawei's response. After going home, Wang Dawei complains to his father about what happened at work. Take note of Weimin's reasoning in the advice that he gives to Dawei.

组　长：小王，让你发的退货邮件，你发了没有啊？
王大伟：组长，我还没发。我觉得这事儿您还应该再考虑考虑。
组　长：叫你发你就发，哪儿那么多废话？
王大伟：可是这样对方公司会觉得我们不讲诚信的。
组　长：你是组长，还是我是组长？这样的情况我已经处理了很多次了，还用你教我怎么做吗？
王大伟：好吧，那马上照您说的发。

（回到家以后……）

王为民：大伟，怎么了？一回来就拉着脸，看你心情不太好啊。
王大伟：早上被组长训了一顿。她在我们这些实习生面前总是表现得高人一等，其实到了经理面前还不是像老鼠见了猫一样，乖乖听话。
王为民：你刚去实习，不了解情况，应该少说多做。虽说她只是一个组长，但你没听说过官大一级压死人啊？她说什么，你听着就是了。

思考与讨论：

1） 从组长对王大伟说的话里能感觉到"上下尊卑"吗？请举三个例子。
2） 组长对不同的人的态度一样不一样？怎么不一样？

3）王为民为什么叫儿子还是听组长的话？
4）在你的国家，领导会这样随便训斥下属吗？如果你遇到了王大伟这样的问题，你会怎样做，你的家人朋友会有什么意见或建议？

3. On the airplane, a passenger who appears very affluent requests an upgrade to first class. However, this is impossible because the flight attendant says that the plane is full. Observe closely how the passenger expresses his dissatisfaction as well as the reason behind it.

乘务员：先生，真对不起，今天头等舱的客人比较多，没有办法升舱。
乘　客：这么点小事你都解决不了，叫你主管来，我今天非升舱不可。
乘务员：先生，真抱歉，头等舱确实已经满了。我们不能让别的乘客下飞机啊。
乘　客：这我不管。你们不是说"顾客是上帝"嘛！我付了钱就是上帝，你们怎么对待"上帝"的？我是你们公司的VIP，就这么点儿要求你都做不到，那要你有什么用啊？
乘务员：对不起先生，请您尊重我的工作。
乘　客：别跟我说什么尊重不尊重的。你不就是个小小的服务员吗？别废话了，叫你主管来。
乘务员：先生，您消消气，我去叫主管来。

思考与讨论：

1）乘客对工作人员的态度怎么样？请举例子说明。
2）面对这样的乘客，工作人员的态度怎么样？为什么？
3）在你的国家，乘客会不会对工作人员有这样的态度？遇到这样的乘客，工作人员会怎么处理？

言语行为例说 Notes on discourse behavior

1. 对话例句：王大伟：刘阿姨，你们问过小静的意见吗？出不出国得听她的呀。我记得她以前跟我说想出国上学，开阔眼界。
王为民：大伟，大人说话，小孩儿不要插嘴。刘阿姨他们也是为了小静好。

插嘴 (chāzuǐ literally "to insert one's mouth") means to cut into a conversation or to interrupt someone. This behavior is judged to be very impolite, particularly if it is a child or a subordinate doing the interrupting, regardless of whether a valid point was made.

Traditionally, children and subordinates are expected to remain silent. When a child offers an opinion that contradicts that of the parent's, the parent may often scold the child by saying "大人说话，小孩子不要插嘴 (When adults are talking, children should remain quiet.)." When the person being interrupted is a superior at work, that person may reprimand the subordinate by saying "不要/别插嘴." The seriousness of the tone and body language all convey the message that speaker is in charge (做主).

- 甲：爷爷，您刚才说要跟李爷爷去旅游？我看你们都别去了，不适合你们。
乙：大人说话，小孩儿别插嘴。
- 甲：张总，我有两句话要说。
乙：小刘，你别插嘴。张总，您继续说。

2. 对话例句：王大伟：你们说是为了她好，可又不尊重她的意见……
王为民：大伟，别说了，怎么那么没大没小的。

没大没小 is used to reproach someone who displays no understanding of the social order. In other words, that person cannot distinguish between who is "bigger" or higher in the hierarchy versus those who are "smaller" or lower. This person is judged to have not shown proper respect for his social superior, whether it's an elder or a supervisor at work. In addition to demonstrating authority, adults also often repeat this saying when lecturing young people on proper social behavior.

- 甲：怎么跟爷爷说话的！这么没大没小的。快跟爷爷道歉。
  乙：爸爸、爷爷，我错了。
- 甲：小张，这里没有你说话的地方，不许没大没小的。
  乙：对不起经理，我多嘴了。

3. 对话例句：组 长：叫你发你就发，哪儿那么多废话？
   ……
   组 长：你是组长，还是我是组长？这样的情况我已经处理了很多次了，还用你教我怎么做吗？

In traditional Chinese culture, those higher in the social hierarchy, such as elders or leaders, have absolute authority over their subordinates. The phrase 一言堂, literally meaning "the hall of one person's speech" reflects this social mentality, because it conveys the sentiment that only one person has the final word. Expressions such as "别插嘴," "少多嘴," "少废话," "你是老板还是我是老板?" all reveal the mental conception of a Confucian hierarchy of social relations at work. Despite the fact that this 礼-based assumption is showing signs of change in contemporary China, the concept of hierarchy is deeply entrenched in Chinese society and reflected in its social behavior.

- 甲：爸，您这么做不对，这样根本不能解决问题。
  乙：少多嘴。还用你教我怎么做吗？
- 甲：老板，你能听我说几句吗？
  乙：你是老板，还是我是老板？少说废话，照我说的做。

4. 对话例句：王大伟：早上被组长训了一顿。她在我们这些实习生面前总是表现得高人一等，其实到了经理面前还不是像老鼠见了猫一样，乖乖听话。
   王为民：……虽说她只是一个组长，但你没听说过官大一级压死人啊？她说什么，你听着就是了。

In Chinese social hierarchy, one's social status and rights are determined by his or her job title. In other words, job title defines who gives orders and who must obey them. The proverb 官大一级压死人 implies that even if a person's job title is only one level higher, that person holds absolute power over his subordinates. The speaker is usually trying to convey a feeling of helplessness when using this expression.

- 甲：不管领导说得对不对，都得听他的。
  乙：没办法，官大一级压死人。
- 甲：今天太委屈了，被领导给骂了。
  乙：你就忍着吧，你没听说过官大一级压死人吗？

体演情景 Perform the scenario

Select a dialogue from this section and listen to its recording several times. Imitate the speakers in pronunciation, intonation and discourse behavior in terms of both the words they use and the ways in which they carry themselves. Memorize the dialogue for performance in class.

跨文化交际 Cross-cultural communication

一、误解分析 Situation analysis

Break into groups and discuss the misunderstanding in each of the cross-cultural communication incidents below. For each incident, the group should generate an answer that best explains the cultural assumptions behind the ways in which the individuals say and do things. In addition, discuss possible strategies to avoid these misunderstandings in similar situations.

（一）Charlotte在一家中国公司给总经理做翻译，所以常常跟总经理和他的秘书小张一起出差开会。在Charlotte的印象里，小张是一个非常注重礼貌的人，对总经理特别恭敬，也经常关心和帮助Charlotte。但是有一件事改变了Charlotte的想法。有一次，他们开会以后一起吃饭，一个服务员不小心把茶水洒了，弄脏了小张的衣服。服务员不停地道歉，可小张跳起来大声地骂服务员说："你怎么回事？没长眼睛啊？知道我这件衣服有多贵吗？你根本就赔不起。"Charlotte听了以后非常惊讶，她完全没想到小张好像变成了另一个人，那么咄咄逼人。

思考与讨论：

1) Charlotte 为什么惊讶？为什么小张对人的态度这么不同？
2) 如果你是 Charlotte，以后你还会跟小张交朋友吗？

（二）Nora和先生王平在南京工作。有一天，王平下班回来对Nora说，明天上班，咱们俩换一下车吧。Nora觉得很奇怪，因为王平开的是新买的宝马，而她的车则是一辆普通的国产车。王平解释说："我发现我们老板开的是一辆很旧的日系车，最近这几个月，我都要跟着老板出去开会。我开新宝马而他开普通的车去见客户，我觉得不太合适。每次到了那儿，对方都以为我是老板，他是员工呢。"Nora虽然同意了换车开，但她想，买什么车开什么车这不是老板自己的选择吗，王平是不是想得太多了？

思考与讨论：

1) 王平跟Nora换车开的原因是什么？他的担心有道理吗？
2) 如果你是王平，你会不会也选择换一辆普通的车去上班？

（三）Katie刚刚被一家美国公司录取了，可是她的中国同屋杨易发现Katie好像并没有那么兴奋。杨易好奇地问Katie怎么了。Katie回答说："这份工作挺辛苦的，收入却不公平。"杨易问："怎么不公平？"Katie说："我有一个同专业的男同学跟我一起申请了这家公司，我们都被录取了。可我发现他的工资比我高不少。"杨易听了有些惊讶，她想，西方国家不是主张平等吗，为什么也会有这种事？不过，她劝Katie说，"工资少一点就少一点呗，也没什么了不起的，有工作就很好了。"

思考与讨论：

1) 杨易为什么感到惊讶？Katie和男同学工资不同的原因有可能是什么？
2) 如果你是Katie，你能不能接受这样的情况？

（四）艾杰森最近听到他的同学都在讨论某大学一名研究生自杀的新闻。在新闻里，这个研究生不仅帮导师工作，甚至还要去导师家里做饭、洗车、打扫卫生。艾杰森听了以后非常吃惊，他没想到在中国会有导师让学生当保姆，更没想到会有这样软弱的学生。最令艾杰森不解的是为什么那个学生要通过自杀来解决问题，他不能拒绝导师的要求吗？或者把导师的行为告诉学校不就行了嘛，如果再不行，还可以上法庭嘛。

思考与讨论：

1) 你能向艾杰森解释清楚为什么那个研究生不反抗而选择自杀吗？
2) 如果你在中国学习遇到类似的问题，你会用什么方式解决？

二、口语交际练习 Oral communication exercises

1. 角色扮演 Role play

   Pair up with a peer and refer to one of the critical incidents in *Situation analysis* to create a five-minute skit with a similar storyline. Use new vocabulary and speech patterns that you have learned from this lesson in your skit. Perform the dialogue in class and discuss whether each skit properly reflects typical Chinese discourse behavior.

2. 社会调查与报告 Survey and report

   题目："尊卑有等与人人平等"

   1) 活动目的：跟一位同班同学一起设计一份中英文双语问卷(wènjuàn: questionnaire)，调查人们对"尊卑有等"和"人人平等"这两个观念的看法和态度，以及这些观念对社会的影响。
   2) 调查对象：最少10个中国人和10个其他国家的人。
   3) 设计(shèjì: design)一份12–15个问题的问卷，其中必须包括下面几个问题：

      - 个人信息：国籍、年龄、职业、性别等。
      - 什么是"尊卑有等"、 什么是"人人平等"？
      - 你的母语文化更重视"尊卑有等"还是更崇尚"人人平等"？
      - 尊卑有等的观念可能会有什么正面和负面的影响？（可以从家庭关系、学校、工作、社会等方面来考虑。设计两个正面的问题，两个负面的问题）

- 人人平等的观念可能会有什么正面和负面的影响？（同上。）
- 网络科技和全球化的发展对这两种观念可能会带来什么影响？

4) 请在问卷开头简单地介绍一下你自己、这个问卷的题目和目的、你的联系方式(liánxì fāngshì: contact details)等。
5) 把问卷用手机或者电子邮件寄给你们的调查对象，并在三天之内收回。
6) 分析问卷调查的结果，并向全班做作报告。

三、写作 Composition

1. 作文 (两题选一题)

题目1：尊卑有等与人人平等

- 做了上面的社会调查以后，请把问卷结果写成一篇期末报告，最少分成四段。
- 写作时请尽量使用这个学期学过的生词和句型。

题目2：期末研究报告 【第三/最后一个阶段】*第二阶段的作业，请看第十三课的作文题目2。

- 收到老师对上一稿的反馈后，请在规定的时间内完成最后一稿。
- 最后一稿必须包括100–150字的摘要(zhāiyào: abstract)和参考文献(cānkǎo wénxiàn: cited material, reference)。这两个部分的字数不包括在老师规定的书面报告字数之内。
- 请每位同学做口头报告，并让同学们提问和讨论。做口头报告时，请注意说话的礼节，并尽量使用本学期所学的生词和句型。
- 在老师规定的时间内，把最后一稿的书面报告交给老师。

2. 文化探索 Cultural exploration: For learners who are currently studying or working in the target culture.

Though Chinese society has liberalized considerably, the traditional concepts of social hierarchy (尊卑有等) and generational hierarchy (长幼有序) continue to influence how Chinese people build relationships with each other. These values manifest themselves in the ways that the Chinese talk to each other, such as in the words they use, their body language, or their tone of voice.

Observe how your Chinese friends interact with their family members, work colleagues, social acquaintances, and strangers. Take notes on occasions in which their behaviors respect the principles of 尊卑有等 and 长幼有序. Fill out the table in *Appendix I: cultural exploration* with the information that you gather and write a paragraph reflecting on what you have observed. Submit the table and the paragraph to your teacher.

Appendix: reflection worksheet for cultural exploration 文化探索

Now that you are living in Chinese society, you have plentiful opportunities to explore Chinese interpersonal and social communication, regardless of the length of your stay. Please prepare a pocket notebook and use the table below as a guide when you observe, record, or reflect events that interest you or that may be used as training opportunities to raise your cultural awareness. Note the ways in which native speakers use language in various interpersonal or social contexts. Do not worry if you do not understand or remember every detail. The key is to raise your sensitivity to Chinese communication in a way that is most conducive to learning.

观察事项 *(guānchá shìxiàng: component)*	解释/说明 *Explanation/Description*
时间	
地点 (scene or location)	
参加者 (the roles involved, including yourself as audience)	
目的 (mùdì: purpose)	事件原因/活动目的:
	说话人的目的:
对话的内容 (conversations of the interaction)	他们说什么 (recall as much information as you can):
	语气 (mood/ tone):
	身体语言 (body language):
心得 (xīndé: What did you learn from this event? Reflect on this experience.)	

Source: Adapted from Meechan & Rees-Miller, 2001[1]

Note

1 Meechan, M., and Rees-Miller, J. (2001). Language in social contexts. In W. O'Grady, J. Archibald, M. Aronoff, and J. Rees-Miller (Eds.), *Contemporary linguistics: An introduction* (4th ed., pp. 537–590). New York: Bedford/St. Martin's.

課文繁體字版

第一課　一起吃飯是緣分

行為聚焦：愛湊熱鬧

Behavior highlighted: love to be part of the fun

課文 *Text*

廈門大學易中天教授在他的《閒話中國人》一書中，詳細地介紹了他多年來對中國文化的思考。他認為，中國文化最根本的特點就是“群體意識”；與之相反，西方文化最根本的特點是“個體意識”。易教授以吃飯為例來說明他這個觀點。他說，中國人吃飯，所有的筷子都伸向同一個菜盤，所有的勺子都伸向同一個湯碗，不管什麼菜，大家都一起吃。而在西方國家，人們各點各的菜，各吃各的飯。在中國人看來，一起吃飯是“緣分”，也是為了享受在一起的感覺。如果大家還是各點各的，各吃各的，那又何必聚餐呢？

易教授還講了一個笑話：一次，一個中國人請他的幾個朋友和兩位“老外”一起到餐館吃飯。出於禮貌，主人請每個人都點一道菜。兩位外國朋友一個點了芙蓉雞片，另一個在猶豫，不知點什麼菜好。主人發現還少了一個湯，就建議他點一個榨菜肉絲湯，反正大家一起吃飯嘛。服務員上的第一道菜就是芙蓉雞片。點這個菜的“老外”得知這是自己要的菜以後，就接過盤子放到自己的面前。過了一會兒，榨菜肉絲湯也上來了，點這個湯的外國朋友也把湯碗接過來放在自己的面前。菜上齊了以後，大家就開始吃了起來。兩位“老外”自己吃自己點的菜，完全沒有要跟別人分享的意思。幾個中國人只好“主隨客便”，按照西方人的習慣各吃各的菜。當然，點湯的那位外國朋友那頓飯也只喝下了一大碗榨菜肉絲湯。

易教授用這個有趣的故事說明中國人的群體意識和西方人的個體意識。簡單地說，群體意識就是認為每個人都是群體中的一員，群體的利益就是個人的利益，群體的利益比個體的利益更重要。而西方人重視個人的獨立和自由，你是你，我是我，他是他。每個人都有選擇的自由，每個人的行為，他人也都不能干涉，除非是危害了公眾的利益。很多西方人喜歡獨自活動，他們常常一個人散步，一個人鍛煉身體；年輕人一個人背著個大包在國外旅遊也很常見。中國人一般愛湊熱鬧，喜歡大家一起活動。比方說打麻將、下象棋、坐在一起拉家常等等，這些都是中國人喜歡的群體活動。現在中國人有錢了，出去旅遊的人也多了，也經常是大家約好報個旅遊團一起去。

第二課 人多力量大

行為聚焦：從眾行為

Behavior highlighted: follow the pack

課文 *Text*

中國文化的特點是群體意識，這可能是因為在中國人看來，先有群體，然後才有個體。個體是群體的一員，個體不能離開群體而單獨地存在。最近幾年，漢語裡又出現了一個新的詞語“從眾”，用來描述中國人愛跟風的現象。什麼是“從眾”？“從”字裡有兩個“人”字，表示一個人跟著另外一個人。“眾”字表示三人站立，“三”代表很多，所以“三人”也就是很多人或者群體。“從眾”指的就是個人跟著群體，別人做什麼，自己也做什麼，表示個人追求大家的認同，希望得到大家的認可。

“從眾消費”一詞指的是跟著別人買一樣的東西；“從眾行為”這個詞說的是別人怎麼做，我也怎麼做。聽說過“中國式過馬路”嗎？這曾經是微博上一個流行的說法，說的是現在仍然經常可以見到的中國人過馬路的方式。在中國，不少人認為是不是路口，甚至是不是綠燈都無所謂，只要聚起了一些人就可以一起過馬路了。這個說法一在網上發表就引起很多網民的共鳴，一天之內被轉發了近10萬次。許多網友評論說，這描述得太形象了！我們這裡就是這樣！不少網友還表示，自己也經常是“闖燈大軍”中的一員。

重慶的一名網友說，“中國式過馬路”反映了中國人的從眾行為，同時也反映了中國人特有的一種心理，即“法不責眾”。國家是有法律的，但是很多中國人認為，如果某種行為具有一定的群體性，即使不合法，也不一定會受到法律的懲罰。有人批評說，“中國式過馬路”反映了中國人的規則意識淡薄，但也有人認為，這種現象的產生有它的社會原因。中國人多、車多，為了不造成交通堵塞，紅綠燈給車輛通過的時間有兩三分鐘，而給行人過馬路的時間只有幾十甚至十幾秒，有時行人過馬路得小跑才來得及。

現在很多中國人喜歡跳的“廣場舞”是另外一種引起許多爭議的從眾行為。中老年人，其中大多數是退了休的婦女，出來和鄰居們一起跳跳舞、鍛煉鍛煉身體是一件好事，可是她們大聲播放的音樂卻影響了周圍居民的休息。廣場、街道、公園等是公共空間，“大媽”們跳廣場舞的時候，同時也影響了他人享受這些公共的空間。有的居民也抱怨，可是拿跳舞的人沒辦法，因為她們是“群體”，人多力量大啊！

第三課　人人都是一個"角色"

行為聚焦：關係本位

Behavior highlighted: relation-based conduct

課文 *Text*

在中國人的意識中，人不是一個個獨立的個體，而是通過各種家庭關係和社會關係聯繫在一起的。中國人在稱呼他人的時候，首先要確定自己和那個人之間的相互關係。中國人的家庭關係很明確，除了父母和兄弟姐妹以外，對親戚的稱呼也分得清清楚楚。在社會上也是一樣，除了稱呼要加職業或職位（如張老師、王校長、李局長等等），對鄰居、同事和朋友，大一輩的一般要叫大伯、大媽、叔叔、阿姨，同輩但年長一點的要叫大哥、大姐。對同輩但比自己年少的人，稱呼對方小弟或小妹也很常見。總之，我不是“我”，你也不是“你”，大家都是人際關係裡的一個“角色”。

社會關係的家庭化反映了中國文化中的“家本位”思想，而這種思想又是跟中國傳統社會的特點分不開的。中國古代的農業生活決定了社會是由家庭組成的，不像古希臘的商業社會，是由單獨的、具有獨立思想的個人組成的。有人說，中國的社會就像一個大家庭，裡面套著無數的小家庭。漢語中的“國家”這個詞，說明了中國人的“家國”觀念，即“家”就是“國”，“國”就是“家”。電影演員成龍唱過一首名叫《國家》的歌，裡面有一句歌詞就是：“家是最小國，國是千萬家”。在這樣的社會裡，完全獨立的“我”是不存在的，或者說有一個“小我”，上面還有一個或幾個“大我”。如果離開了“大我”，“小我”就無法實現自己的價值。

由於受到家本位思想的影響，中國人有著自己獨特的人際關係和交往方式。大多數中國人的社交生活，都是由無數個“圈子”組成的。這從目前中國人普遍使用的微信就可以看出。一個人的朋友圈或微信群裡，有家人圈、鄰居圈、同學圈、同事圈、戰友圈，等等。每個圈子裡又可分出更多的小圈子，比如同學圈又可分成小學同學圈、中學同學圈等。微信能在很短的時間內成為中國人網絡社交的主要工具，就是因為它在手機上成功地搭起了中國人熟悉的人際交往圈子。

有些學者認為，中國文化的根本特點不是群體意識，而是“關係本位”。其實，關係本位也是群體意識的一種表現，只是中國人意識中的群體不一定總是一個大的整體，而是經常表現為小群。有人問過這樣一個問題：中國人崇尚集體主義，可是有的時候合作意識卻不強，那應該怎樣解釋這個現象呢？這個問題的答案也許就在中國人的“小群意識”中吧。

第四課　禮多人不怪

行為聚焦：禮俗客套

Behavior highlighted: li-based civilities

課文 *Text*

在西方社會，人與人、個體與群體之間遵循的主要是一種契約關係，維護這樣的關係靠的是法律。而在中國文化裡，由於家本位思想的影響，人與人、個體與群體的關係常常被視為先天的或天然的，維護這些關係主要不是靠法律，而是靠在今天仍然有著廣泛影響的儒家思想和道德觀念。

歷史上儒家思想統治中國社會長達兩千多年。儒家思想的核心是“禮”。“禮”也可叫作“禮儀”或“禮節”。中國人常把自己的國家稱為“禮儀之邦”，其禮儀傳統可追溯到古代的西周社會（公元前1046年－公元前771年）。到了春秋戰國時期（公元前770年－公元前221年），孔子提倡“禮治”，把恢復周禮當做提高個人修養和治理國家的重要方法。孔子說：“不學禮，無以立”。可見，禮對中國人和中國社會是多麼重要。

隨著中國社會的長期發展，禮的內容發生了很大的變化。但是，當代的中國人在人際交往中仍然“好禮”，講究客氣。“客氣”一詞英文常常翻譯成polite，但它與“禮貌”（也英譯為polite）並不完全一樣。“客氣”主要的意思是“懂禮”，指的是按照約定俗成的禮節說話做事。“禮”的基本內容是對他人的尊敬和體貼，所以客氣在行為上往往表現為“禮讓”或“辭讓”。以兩個人一起去餐館吃飯為例，從進門到坐下，從吃飯到離開，我們常常可以看到禮讓式的客氣。首先是“讓門”：兩個人同進一個門，出於客氣，一個人常常停下來讓另一個人先進；其次是“讓座”：雙方都要把好的座位讓給對方，不這樣做，就會被認為不客氣；最後吃飯時，兩人也要“讓菜”：對於好吃的菜，自己少吃一點，讓對方多吃一點，要不然就顯得不夠體貼。

有外國朋友說，在中國人家裡做客，吃點什麼或喝點什麼，主人一定要讓幾次，客人也一定要推辭幾次，這樣你讓我辭，大家看起來才有禮貌。其實，這是中國人典型的客氣行為，是與中國人禮的文化傳統分不開的。此外，這種禮讓或辭讓式的客氣也表現在中國人日常生活的許多其它方面，比如贈送禮物、接受禮物、誇獎別人以及接受別人的誇獎等等。當然，在非常熟悉的朋友之間，特別是在現在的年輕人之間，情況會有些不同。中國人有句俗話說，“禮多人不怪”，意思是說，一個人越懂禮、越按照禮節做事，別人就越喜歡他。如果一個人不懂禮，他就不知道怎樣“做人”，而在中國文化裡沒有人願意跟一個不知道怎樣做人的人交朋友。

第五課　中國人到底有沒有禮貌？

行為聚焦：自謙敬人

Behavior highlighted: humble oneself and exalt others

課文 *Text*

在日常生活中，中國人常常把“客氣”說成“禮貌”，把“禮貌”說成“客氣”，這很容易讓學習漢語的外國學生產生困惑。網上曾經有一篇博文，作者是一名剛從中國回來的美國學生，題目是《中國人到底有沒有禮貌？》。他說，在沒去中國以前，他經常在漢語課上聽老師們說中國人很客氣、很有禮貌，所學的漢語課本也都是這麼說的。可是到了中國以後，他感到很困惑，因為他常常看到中國人沒有禮貌的行為。他舉例說，在飯館，服務員端來飯菜以後，顧客很少說“謝謝”；超市里，收銀員收了顧客的錢以後，也從來不說“謝謝”“再見”什麼的。還有，有些人從你的旁邊走過時，即使空間很小，也不會說“借過”或“麻煩讓一下”，而往往是什麼都不說，側著身子就從你的身旁“擠”過去了。可是，中國人又是非常禮貌的。比如，你剛用漢語說了一個“你好”，他們就會熱情地誇獎，說你的中文很棒。他們也會當著你的面誇你長得漂亮，叫你“帥哥”或“美女”，不管實際情況是不是這樣。這位美國學生最後不解地問道，“中國人到底是有禮貌還是沒有禮貌？”

其實，這個問題不是一個簡單的“有”或者“沒有”可以回答的，因為不同文化之間的禮節不同，人們對禮貌的理解也不同。此外，“禮貌”與“客氣”兩個詞的混用也容易讓人們產生誤解。“禮貌”其實不等於“客氣”，“客氣”也不等於“禮貌”。“客氣”一定是“有禮貌”的，可是“有禮貌”並不一定就是“客氣”。前面說過，客氣是中國禮文化的一部分，它的內容比禮貌豐富多了。除了“尊敬”“體貼”和“禮讓”以外，“客氣”還包含“謙虛”“熱情”“慷慨”“為別人著想”等意思。就拿“為別人著想”這個意思來說，中國人在跟別人打交道時，為了讓對方高興，經常刻意地“抬高”對方。他們不但喜歡誇獎別人，而且還常常“貶低”自己，用降低自己的方式來抬高別人。

漢語裡有很多的說法都是“謙辭”或“敬辭”。前者可以用來貶低自己，後者可以用來抬高別人。這樣說來，很多中國人的客氣行為和說法都是客套或客套話。比如，聽到別人誇獎自己時，中國人會馬上說“哪裡，哪裡”，或者“過獎了，跟你比還差得遠呢。”不過，許多這樣的客套或客套話一般都是發生在雙方相識的人之間，而生人之間，中國人一般顯得比較冷淡。前面講到的美國學生的困惑，也許就是這個原因吧。有位美籍華人學者曾提出，美國人講禮貌，不懂客氣；中國人講客氣，不懂禮貌。一些中國人聽了以後感到非常吃驚，認為這樣說不符合事實。其實，從“禮貌”和“客氣”這兩個詞的意思來看，這位華人學者的說法也有一些道理呢。

第六課　禮之用，和為貴

行為聚焦：以和為貴

Behavior highlighted: harmony as priority

課文 *Text*

《論語》裡說："禮之用，和為貴。"意思是說，禮的作用在於它能調節人與人之間的關係，使人們和睦相處，使社會和諧發展。中國文化自古以來就崇尚和諧。不僅儒家思想以和為貴，道家和其他的哲學思想也是這樣。如果說儒家重視的是人與人、人與社會之間的和諧，那麼道家更多關心的是人與自然的和諧共處。

和諧是中國人的世界觀和最重要的價值觀，也是中國人做人做事所遵守的基本原則。2008年北京奧運會開幕式上有這樣一幕，令許多人至今難忘：扮演孔子三千弟子的演員們，用5897塊字盤變換著不同字體的"和"字。他們通過這個漢字的歷史演變，向全世界觀眾展示了中國文化傳統中源遠流長的和諧思想。

中國人有很多關於和諧的觀念和說法：家庭方面的有"家和萬事興"；外交方面的有"和平共處"；經濟方面的有"和氣生財"；軍事方面的有"天時地利人和"。"和"字的使用非常廣泛，包括和氣、和睦、和平、和好等。漢語裡含有"和"字的成語也很多，比如和藹可親、心平氣和，等等。這些都體現了中國人對和諧的追求，也反映了中國人的行為往往會受到以和為貴思想的影響。

中國土地面積廣大，但是人口眾多，生活資源相對有限。此外，中國人的人際關係主要是一種熟人關係，禮讓和客氣也主要發生在雙方相識的人之間。由於這些原因，人們在中國常常可以看到有些人買東西時不排隊，公共汽車上搶座位，公共場所抽煙和大聲講話等。在西方社會，這些行為都會被認為侵犯了他人的利益或空間，因此會引起他人的反感和批評。而在中國，人們對這些行為卻表現出了極大的寬容和忍讓。研究跨文化教育的Caryn Voskuil教授在她的《水與木：中國人的社會行為》一文中，用"木頭"比喻西方人不忍讓的行為，用"水"比喻中國人的妥協態度。Voskuil教授也許不知道，"水"正是中國和諧文化的高度象徵。老子說："上善若水"。他還說，水造福萬物而不與它們相爭。中國人崇尚水的態度，主張遇到不順心的事時要忍讓。不過，令人遺憾的是，在經濟發展越來越快、社會發展越來越不平衡的今天，人與人之間、特別是生人之間的矛盾和衝突也經常發生。

第七課　忍字頭上一把刀

行為聚焦：忍字當頭

Behavior highlighted: forbear and forgive

課文 *Text*

來自不同文化的人們發生衝突時，很可能常常分不清到底是誰對誰錯。在全球化背景下，管理學學者越來越清楚地認識到，文化不同，其企業管理的方式也有所不同。因中西文化差別而引起的衝突，可能是外籍高管在與中國同事溝通時遇到的最大問題。

德勤亞太及中國區一位負責人認為，中西企業管理的差別主要是因為不同的思維方式和溝通方式。他說，中國人常常從整體上思考問題，在與別人說話時也比較含蓄。他們更關心的是交談後雙方是否和諧，所以說話時特別關注對方的反應和感受。西方人的思維比較具體，而且，他們習慣明確地表達自己的觀點，一般不會像中國人一樣總是考慮我這樣說，對方會怎麼想。

為了避免衝突，保持人際關係的和諧，中國人對自己認識的人常常採取忍讓的態度，即使這個人說了不合適的話、做了讓自己不高興的事也是一樣。因為不忍讓就會引起面對面的爭吵，而一旦發生爭吵，傷了和氣，兩個人以後就很難繼續做朋友，甚至很難繼續說話或打交道了。交一個朋友很難，而失去一個朋友很容易，所以中國人常常提醒自己說“忍一時風平浪靜”，或“忍字頭上一把刀”。另外，為了保持熟人之間的和氣，中國人在與朋友交往時，還常常喜歡將心比心。他們認為只有遇到問題時先為他人著想，朋友之間才能和睦相處。可是，這個“以己度人”的習慣到了注重個人自由的西方文化裡，卻可能容易引起他人的誤會。下面的故事就是一個很好的例子。

這是一個真實的故事，發表在英國《金融時報》的中文網上。文章講的是作者剛到美國讀博士時與美國室友發生的文化衝突。在美國室友搬進來的第一天，兩人之間就發生了一件不愉快的事情。那天，室友在往屋子裡搬東西，她的東西特別多。作者想，從今天起她們就要成為室友了，不幫忙搬東西不好意思，所以她對室友說：“讓我幫你吧。”對方回答說：“不用了，不過真的很謝謝你。”作者覺得她只是在客氣，所以就一邊跟著她下樓一邊說：“沒關係，我反正也沒什麼事。”美國室友突然不高興了，回過頭來嚴肅地對她說：“我說了不用就是不用。你難道不知道‘不’的意思嗎？”作者一下子愣住了，她完全沒有想到自己的一片好心會引來室友這樣的反應。後來，美國室友送給她一本書，並且向她道了歉，可是在很長的時間裡，作者心裡還在想著室友生氣時喊出來的“No means No!”

第八課　保持中道

行為聚焦：中庸之道

Behavior highlighted: (take) the middle road

課文 *Text*

中國文化中以和為貴的思想，是與中國人的“中庸”觀念聯繫在一起的。儒家經典《中庸》說：“中也者，天下之大本也；和也者，天下之達道也。致中和，天地位焉，萬物育焉。”[1] 這段話的意思是說，“中”是天下萬事萬物的根本，“和”是天下萬事萬物所共同遵守的規則。只有保持“中和”，天與地才能各得其位，天地之間的萬物才能蓬勃生長。

20世紀初，《中庸》被儒家學者辜鴻銘翻譯成了英文，傳到西方後引起了不小的轟動。人們是看了標題去讀這篇文章的，因為辜先生把《中庸》的標題翻譯成了“普遍秩序或人生準則”。一篇幾千字的文章為什麼採用這樣高深的題目呢？這是因為中庸之道在儒家思想中代表著最高的智慧和真理，被認為是解決一切問題的最好方法。中庸之道的核心是“中”。“中”有兩個基本意思：一是保持中道，二是調和兩端。前者講的是做任何事情都應該做到正好，既不應該做過了頭，也不應該做得不夠；後者講的是不同事物之間，應該追求大方面的相同，忽略小方面的不同，做到“和而不同”。

儒家的中庸思想其實與古希臘哲學中mean（常譯為“中道”或“適度”）的意思差不多相同。但與後者不同的是，幾千年以後，中庸之道並沒有隨著時間的過去成為歷史，而是作為一種高級智慧深深地滲入了中國人的血液中，已成為中國人做人做事的普遍規則。中國人崇尚中庸，對“中”有著特殊的喜好。有人開玩笑說，中國人坐位子喜歡坐中間，住房子喜歡住中層，就連吃東西，很多人也是喜歡吃中間的部分。中國人說話常常喜歡說“適中”的話，朋友之間遇到問題發生矛盾，也常會找個“中間人”幫助解決。一般來說，中國人不喜歡出風頭，認為“槍打出頭鳥”；很多人更不喜歡發了財以後炫富，因為“樹大招風”。

中庸之道這一古老智慧，既可以用於做人做事，也可以用於治理國家。它既是人與人之間的求和之道，也是國與國之間和平相處的法則。有人認為，中國“和平共處、互不干涉”的外交理念就體現了中國人的中庸思想。還有人把中國在聯合國安理會投票的規律也解釋為中庸思想的表現。對於沒有什麼爭議

1 Zhōng yě zhě, tiān xià zhī dà běn yě; hé yě zhě, tiān xià zhī dá dào yě. Zhì zhōng hé, tiān dì wèi yān, wàn wù yù yān. This Equilibrium is the great root from which grow all the human actings in the world, and this Harmony is the universal path which they all should pursue. Let the states of equilibrium and harmony exist in perfection, and a happy order will prevail throughout heaven and earth, and all things will be nourished and flourish. (*Trans*. James Legge)

的問題，中國基本上投贊同票，涉及自己利益的問題，中國會投反對票，其它的一律投棄權票。在2014年發生的有關烏克蘭問題的重大事件上，中國又投了棄權票。因為對立的兩端一方是美國，一方是俄羅斯，作為三個大國之一，中國似乎只有保持中道，投個棄權票。

第九課　面子—打開中國人性格之鎖

行為聚焦：保全面子

Behavior highlighted: saving face

課文 *Text*

一個文化的深層結構往往是通過一些世俗觀念對人們產生影響的。這些世俗觀念並不一定在哲學經典裡找得到，但它們的意義更實際、更具體，因此對人們的影響也更直接。中國文化裡的“面子”“人情”“關係”等，就是這樣一些既實際又具體的世俗化觀念。

眾所周知，中國人“愛面子”。事實上，許多中國人不僅是“愛面子”或“要面子”，而且是“死要面子”。所謂“死要面子”，就是說一個人寧可委屈自己，甚至寧可受罪也要保全自己的面子。最早發現中國人這個特點的西方人，是一百多年前到中國傳教的美國人亞瑟·史密斯。他在中國生活了二十二年，並根據自己的生活經歷寫了一本書，叫《中國人的性格》。在這本書裡，史密斯總結了中國人的二十多種性格特點，其中第一種就是“保全面子”。他說，面子好像是一把鑰匙，如果掌握了中國人面子的秘密，你就能夠打開中國人性格的這把鎖。

中國人的面子是什麼？它跟西方人的面子觀念又有什麼不同？一般來說，面子指的是一個人在別人眼中的形象或尊榮。可是，中國人的面子有些複雜，一個主要的原因在於它是由“臉”和“面”兩個部分組成的。從這兩個詞的基本意義來看，“臉”指的是頭的前面，即面孔；“面”說的是一個物體的表面。兩者指的都是表面，所以中國人用這兩個詞來形容面子心理時常常混用。很多情況下，“有面子”也可以說是“有臉”，“丟面子”也可以說是“丟臉”。可是，“臉”和“面子”的意思又不完全相同。人類學家胡先縉女士早在上世紀四十年代就指出，“臉”含有很強的道德意義，而“面子”主要指的是一個人在他人眼裡的地位和尊榮。所以，“不要面子”也許是說一個人對自己在別人眼裡的形象不那麼在乎，而“不要臉”則有可能說一個人做了什麼不光彩的事，是一個道德問題了。

“臉”和“面”不僅常常混用，而且還可以連用（如“要臉面”“丟臉面”等），這使得中國人的面子在很多情況下帶有道德的色彩。所謂中國人愛面子，其實主要是說中國人在做人做事時努力保全自己的形象，不讓自己丟臉。此外，由於中國人的群體意識，生活在這種環境裡的人必須時時面對他人，並通過他人來評價自己，中國人面子裡的他人因素也非常的強。如果說在西方，一個人的面子是通過積極地表現自己而贏得的，那麼在中國文化裡，一個人的面子則常常是由他人給的、傷害的，甚至拿去的。最後，也是由於群體意識的文化原因，中國人的面子不僅包括“我的面子”“你的面子”，而且還包括“我們大家的面子”。

中華民族自古以來就是一個愛面子的民族。到了今天，中國人還是一樣地愛面子，要面子，甚至想方設法爭面子。多年前，央視春晚有個小品叫《有事您說話》。小品裡的主人公為了有個好人緣，寧可夜裡不睡覺在火車站排隊幫人買車票。他不想讓人知道這個秘密，所以回來後跟別人說票都是自己通過關係拿到的。這個小品雖然是為了搞笑，可是它傳遞的信息，即面子問題的嚴重性，卻值得廣大觀眾思考。有人說，隨著中國商品經濟的進一步發展，中國人的面子問題現在變得越來越嚴重、越來越不正常了。“美女經濟”“面子消費”“形象工程”等等，這些都是面子心理在當今物質化社會的表現。難怪網上有人把目前中國所處的時代叫做“眼球時代”！

第十課　傷什麼也不能傷面子

行為聚焦：面子運作

Behavior highlighted: face work

課文 *Text*

簡單地說，“有面子”其實就是受他人的尊重。人們都希望別人尊重自己，不分種族和國籍。可是在中國，由於儒家的道德觀念和“恥感文化”的影響，人們特別在乎自己的公眾形象，也十分期望得到周圍人的尊重。中國有句俗話說，“人活一張臉，樹活一張皮”，面子被看得跟生命一樣重要。正因如此，中國人認為，在與自己相識的人交往中，傷什麼也不能傷面子。特別是當對方是自己的領導時，說話做事更要小心。因為地位越高，面子也越大，如果領導的面子傷了，有時後果會很嚴重。

端傳媒網站上有一篇文章，講的是加拿大人John在中國成功創業的經歷。John在中國生活了很多年，現在已是兩個公司的老闆。他對記者說，他的成功得益於自己對中國面子文化的深入瞭解(或:了解)。他還清楚地記得自己過去由於無知犯的一個錯誤。1998年，John辭去外教工作，到青島的一家五星級酒店負責開發國際業務。他工作得很認真，又做市場調查，又找員工談話，對酒店在運營和管理方面的問題進行了深入的研究。他花了很長時間向董事會彙報了他的研究結果，並把自己的改進意見詳詳細細地講了一遍。聽完他的報告，董事們無不稱讚，並說可以馬上開始行動。

可是散會以後，什麼也沒有發生。不僅John的計劃一個都沒有得到實施，而且更糟糕的是，他被告知以後不要再做相關的工作了。後來John明白了，自己犯了一個“嚴重”的錯誤。他對記者說，董事們都是五六十歲的領導，有二三十年酒店工作的經歷，而他那時35歲，並且沒有在酒店工作過。可是他的做法似乎是在告訴領導，他們做錯了，現在應該按照他的建議重新開始。這對於中國領導來說是不可接受的。如果他的方案被採用，問題得到解決，別人就會認為那是John的功勞而不是領導們的，這會讓領導很沒有面子。如果領導不採用John的方案，即使工作沒有得到改善，他們也不會丟面子。John強調說，“在中國面子比成功重要。”

半年以後，John去了上海一家五星級酒店工作，還是負責國際業務的開發。但這一次，John 沒有把自己發現的問題直接向董事會匯報，而是先私下找到了董事會主席，提出自己的想法並徵求他的意見。主席同意的方案就留下，不同意的就放到了一邊。這些主席同意了的方案最後再由主席自己向董事會匯報。這一次，董事會採納了John的建議，他成功了。

John的故事是一個很好的案例，它告訴我們，在中國面子不僅僅是一個心理現象，而且還代表著一套重要的行為規則。這個案例還告訴我們，跟中國人打交道，考慮怎樣保全自己的面子固然很重要，但考慮怎樣保全對方的面子更重要。知道怎樣給別人留面子，甚至知道怎樣幫別人挽回面子，其實是中國面子文化最重要的內容。

那麼，怎麼給別人留面子呢？首先不要當著眾人的面批評一個人，這會讓人感到下不來台。其次，千萬不要證明別人錯了。如果需要表達自己的看法，話要講得委婉、含蓄。此外，如果對方做了什麼丟面子的事，比如說借了你的錢忘了還，最好不要當面提醒他，發個委婉的短信或請個中間人幫幫忙都是不錯的辦法。最後，如果一個人遇到了尷尬的情況，比如當眾說錯了話，如果你能說點什麼幫他解圍，在很長的時間裡，這個人都會對你非常感激。

總之，按照面子規則做事是中國人的做人之道和處世之道。這不僅在人際交往中，而且在企業的商務來往中，甚至在國家之間的政治談判中都非常重要。面子是一門深奧的學問，雖然在學校裡學不到，但卻是中國人在一生中都必須努力掌握的。

第十一課　來而不往非禮也

行為聚焦：禮尚往來

Behavior highlighted: reciprocation

課文 *Text*

除了面子以外，“人情”和“關係”是另外兩個對中國人的行為方式有著直接影響的世俗化觀念。

中國社會是一個人情社會，講人情、重關係是中國文化的一個重要特徵。中國的人情社會是建立在傳統的熟人社會基礎上的。最早提出“熟人社會”這個概念的是著名社會學家費孝通。在其《鄉土中國》一書中，費先生講述了中國傳統鄉土社會的種種特點，其中最主要的是人與人之間的關係網：人們通過血緣和地緣，把各種人際關係像網一樣聯繫起來。關係網不斷擴大，就形成了帶有中國特色的熟人社會。

中國傳統農業是熟人社會形成的最根本原因。在傳統農業社會中，商品經濟不發達，人口流動較少。人們受到土地的束縛，長期生活在某個固定的地方，過著自給自足、封閉保守的農耕生活。家是人們生活的最小單位，其次是家族和鄰里。在這樣的生活環境裡，人們相互熟悉並且關係穩定，人與人交往或處理問題時，親緣或情感的作用很大。

儒家思想也促進了中國人情社會的形成和發展。儒家把社會中人與人的關係視為人倫關係，把夫婦、父子、兄弟、君臣、朋友這五種最基本的人際關係稱為“五倫[2]”。儒家思想提倡“君義、臣行、父慈、子孝、兄愛、弟敬”。這些人倫關係不僅井然有序，而且也充滿了濃厚的人情味，因為維護這些關係的不是法律，而是倫理和情感。

2 五倫 refers to the five cardinal Confucian relationships, i.e. 夫婦(fūfù: husband-wife), 父子, 兄弟, 君臣(jūnchén: ruler-subject), and 朋友. 君義: righteousness on the part of the ruler; 臣行: loyalty on the part of the minister; 父慈(cí): kindness on the part of the father; 子孝: filial piety on the part of the son; 兄愛: gentleness on the part of the elder brother; 弟敬: respect on the part of the younger brother.

作為一個詞語，“人情”首先指的是人的感情。中國人十分看重人與人之間的感情，所以有著愛情、親情、父母情、兒女情、兄弟情、姐妹情、鄰里情、鄉情、同學情、戰友情等等許多說法。但在實際生活中，人與人之間的情感常常表現為各種各樣的互助或互惠活動，因此，“人情”一詞在實際使用中更多指的是這些互助互惠活動。這些活動可以是物質的（如給他人金錢和禮品），也可以是非物質的（如給他人提供一次方便的機會）。同時，這些活動又遵循著一套約定俗成的規則，人們是根據這些規則做人做事並把握關係和交往的。

“知恩圖報”和“禮尚往來”是人情的兩個基本法則。“報”即“報恩”，指的是報答別人對自己的恩情，比如父母的養育之恩、學校老師的培育之恩、朋友的知遇之恩，等等。知恩圖報是儒家“禮”的重要內容，而禮注重有來有往，即所謂“禮尚往來”。所以，知恩而不報，就如有來而無往，這樣做不僅違反了禮的規範，而且也會傷害人與人之間的感情。人們有來有往，而且常來常往，這樣既可以加深彼此之間的感情和友誼，同時也反映了人情的道德約束及其背後的公平法則。

《新京報》有一篇文章，作者談到他與其它國家的人打交道時所遇到的相互不理解。有一次，他的一位歐洲朋友問他，中國人忌諱當面談錢的問題，認為談錢傷感情，可是為什麼春節時長輩要給晚輩錢，為什麼親人和朋友結婚時，人們也要送錢呢？作者解釋說：春節發紅包和婚禮隨份子錢背後其實存在著一個公平系統。你的小孩收了人家多少壓歲錢，你以後也要把這些錢以壓歲錢或其它的方式還給人家；別人的婚禮你隨了多少份子錢，你結婚的時候人家也會還回來。這樣，彼此之間既沒有經濟損失，還在這一來一往的過程中體現了人情並加深了雙方的感情。作者的解釋讓他的外國朋友更糊塗了。對方問，人們非要這樣做嗎？難道他們沒有選擇的自由嗎？作者愣了一下，最後只好說，在大多數情況下是沒有的。

第十二課　多個朋友多條路

行為聚焦：建立人脈

Behavior highlighted: networking

課文 *Text*

在熟人社會中，人情作用的發揮是和人與人之間的關係緊密相連的。“關係”是中國人的口頭禪。在現代漢語裡，“關係”有兩個方面的含義：一個指的是人與人之間或者事物與事物之間的相互聯繫，相當於英文的relation；另一個是說人們通過一定的手段，與其他人建立關係或拉近關係，以便獲取自己所需要的物質或達到自己所要達到的目的。漢語中的"拉關係"或"搞關係"指的就是這第二種含義，其意思差不多相當於英文裡的networking。

臺灣大學黃光國教授在其對中國人際關係的研究中，將中國人的人際關係分為三種：第一種是"情感性關係"，也就是家人、愛人、密友等之間的關係；第二種是"工具性關係"，如乘客與司機之間、顧客與售貨員之間的關係；第三種是"混合性關係"，是由親戚、鄰居、同學、同事或其他熟人構成的。黃教授指出，中國人採用三種不同的法則跟這三種不同關係裡的人打交道。跟情感關係裡的人打交道，中國人一般採用"需求法則"，即人們努力提供各種物質或非物質的幫助，以滿足對方的需求。跟工具性關係的人打交道，人們使用的是"公平法則"：雙方都精打細算，不做讓步，自己付出多少，就應得到多少。跟混合性關係裡的人打交道，大家則採用的是"人情法則"：人們注重禮尚往來，這一次我幫你一個忙，下次我有需求的時候你也要幫我的忙，否則，欠人情不還，雙方的關係就會受到破壞 。

前面討論過的"面子"問題一般發生在混合性關係中，"拉關係"或"搞關係"通常發生在混合性關係與工具性關係中。人情是拉關係的基礎，同時也是拉關係的基本內容和手段。如上所述，人情是在不斷的"虧欠"和"償還"中得以加深和延續的。人情的這個潛規則逐漸為人們所利用，成為生活中辦事不走程序而"走後門"的便利手段。中國人常說"熟人好辦事"，或"多個朋友多條路"。在這些世俗觀念的指導下，人們辦事先找人，通過請客、送禮等手段拉關係來實現自己的目的。這樣，孩子上學通過關係可以去個好學校，老人生病通過關係可以找個好醫生。對年輕人找工作來說，找熟人、建立關係就更重要了。目前，"聚餐社交"風行中國的大學校園。根據2016年中國高校傳媒聯盟的一次調查，在460位受訪的大學生中，29.31%的人每週聚會兩次以上，其中本科低年級占63.52%。大學生們在學習的同時忙於聚餐或其它社交活動，就是為了結交朋友，建立感情，為畢業後找工作建立人脈關係。

除了個人之間，企業與企業之間也要花大量的時間和精力做"人"的工作。在"做生意就是做關係"的觀念影響下，企業老闆們為了商業上的成功，在百忙中要抽出大量的時間在包房裡應酬。關於中國企業家的生存狀態，有人形容說是"腳踏'兩院'"：一方面，老闆們在飯桌上談生意，因常常大吃大喝弄壞了身體要去醫院；另一方面，一些老闆急於牟利，有時不顧法律，犯了法又要進法院。此外，無論是個人還是企業，用在人情上的花費也日益高漲，以至於因為應酬而產生的焦慮目前在中國已成為一個普遍的社會現象。《重慶晨報》一次對1100名居民進行了調查，95.8%的受訪者坦言，當前年輕人的應酬確實太多了。調查還顯示，67.9%的受訪者為應酬感到"很焦慮"或"非常焦慮"，而只有10.7%的人應酬起來"完全不焦慮"。

第十三課　看不懂的中國人？（一）

行為聚焦：親疏有別

Behavior highlighted: distinguish people based on relationships

課文 *Text*

2016年4月，各大新聞和社交平臺報導了一名年輕女子在某酒店遇襲的事件。監控視頻顯示，這名女子被一個男子強行拖拽著，她大聲呼救，並說自己不認識這個男人，然而，幾個酒店的員工和客人從二人身邊走過，都沒有上前施救。雖然女子最後安全脫險，但這一事件還是引發了大量的關注，網上各種言論層出不窮。人們有的批評酒店保安不作為，有的探討女性在危險時刻應如何自衛，但更多的網友還是對旁人的冷漠甚至社會的無情表達了憤怒。

其實，近些年來，網上關於中國人冷漠的討論一直沒有停止過。例如，“老人街頭摔倒沒人扶”就是人們熱議的另一個現象。但令人困惑的是，中國文化不是一個重情的文化嗎？為什麼現實中中國人又會顯得這樣冷漠無情？中國人像這樣看起來自相矛盾的行為還有很多。比如，中國人一般都很愛面子，甚至視面子如命，可是我們常常看到人們買東西插隊或者開車咄咄逼人連行人都不讓的丟面子的行為；中國是個“禮儀之邦”，然而在餐館或旅館裡常有顧客對服務員大喊大叫，很沒有禮貌；中國文化崇尚和諧，但只因為飛機誤點，有些旅客竟然大鬧機場，甚至鬧到後來拒絕登機。諸如此類的矛盾行為還有很多，這些現象令許多人困惑不解，以至於連一些長期研究中國文化的學者都發出“看不懂中國人”的感慨。

有學者認為，中國人很多看似矛盾的行為是由豐富而複雜的中國文化所決定的。中國人處世的哲學觀念很多，其中有些就是互相矛盾甚至對立著的。其次，人的行為受到文化和風俗的影響，而文化和風俗還有地域、年齡和教育程度等等之分。更重要的是，面對這些複雜和矛盾的行為，弄清楚事件發生的場合以及當事人雙方的關係和身份非常重要。因為交際場合不同，交際對象不同，中國人的行為和說話方式也會不同，甚至完全相反。中國傳統社會的“差序格局”使當今的中國人在為人處世時仍下意識地把人分為遠近親疏或上下尊卑。換言之，了解中國人的“親疏有別”“上下有序”等一系列潛意識中的觀念對看懂中國人來說非常關鍵。

“差序格局”一詞是社會學家費孝通用來說明傳統中國的社會結構和人際關係的。其主要含義有二：一是在中國的傳統社會，人們會把有血緣關係的“自家人”和沒有血緣關係的“外人”按親疏遠近分成由近到遠不同的圈子；二是人們有意識地把“圈內人”與“圈外人”區別開來，並在與他們的交往中採用不同的"近親遠疏"的行為法則。雖然現代中國的社會結構，特別是家庭結構，已經發生了根本的變化，傳統的大家庭已逐漸被現代社會的小家庭所代替，但中國人親疏有別或內外有別的觀念始終沒有動搖。源於血緣關係的"自家人"或"自己人"已成為一種心理現象。"圈內人"的概念不再受限於血緣或親戚關係，即有血緣關係的自家人有可能屬於圈內人或自己人，但是沒有血緣關係的外人也可以隨著地緣、業緣以及其他關係的建立從圈外人變成圈內人。而一旦成為圈內人或自己人，人情、面子等一系列世俗觀念便開始支配中國人的行為方式。

由於根深蒂固的親疏有別觀念，中國人的行為似乎因此失去了統一性。中國人雖重"禮"，講"禮讓"和"為他人著想"，但在實際生活中，這些客氣和愛面子的行為一般都是發生在自己人和相識的人之間。一旦進入公共場合面對生人，人們心中禮的約束似乎就有所放鬆。至少，面對發生在陌生人身上的事，很多中國人往往顯得比較冷漠，一副"事不關己"的樣子。有學者說，中國人總的來說不知道怎樣與陌生人打交道。說到底，這也許是因為儒家的倫理道德是建立在傳統的宗法社會基礎上的，是一套熟人社會的人際關係和交往法則。由此可見，首先觀察交際發生的場合以及交際雙方的關係，對於理解中國人的行為習慣是何等的重要！

第十四課　看不懂的中國人？（二）

行為聚焦：上下有別

Behavior highlighted: distinction between the upper and lower status

課文 *Text*

中國人的人際關係自古以來就存在著一種天然的差等。所謂差序格局，講的就是傳統社會裡人與人之間的差等或不平等關係。如果說親疏遠近指的是人際關係橫向上的差等，那麼長幼尊卑則代表著人與人之間縱向上的區別，即每個人都有各自不同的家庭地位和社會身份。在當今中國，雖然已經過長期的現代化進程，人們仍有意識或無意識地序長幼，定尊卑，在日常生活中遵守著"上下有序""尊卑有等"的傳統觀念和行為準則。

華人網路媒體倍可親上有一篇回國紀實。文中說，中國的經濟發展和生活水平的提高並沒有帶來相應的社會觀念的轉變。作者尖銳地指出，中國仍是一個沒有平等觀念的社會。人們彼此之間缺少基本的尊重，更缺少基本的平等相待的行為習慣。她列舉了許多親眼目睹的現象，並總結說，在與別人初次接觸時，每個中國人都會先揣摩對方的社會身份和地位，並在心中暗暗地排列自己與對方的上下高低關係。只有在經過這樣的揣摩和定位之後，人們才會決定怎樣與他人打交道。

中國人根深蒂固的等級觀念是在儒家倫理道德長期影響下形成的。儒家強調的是人倫，而"倫"指的就是有差等的次序。儒家最不能容忍的就是對倫的僭越，因為家庭的和睦和社會的穩定是建立在倫的差等和次序之上的。儒家的"五倫"規定了中國傳統社會差序格局的根本內容。五倫中的君臣、父子、夫妻、兄弟這四倫，都表現出權力和義務的不對等。即便是朋友之間，當關係發展到結義兄弟時，尊卑有等的觀念便會開始支配雙方的行為。在中國家文化的社會裡，社會關係和組織不過是人倫關係的逐步擴大。當這種嚴格強調等級的人倫關係擴大到社會，我們便看到了當今仍普遍存在於中國人際關係中的差序性，即上下、長幼，甚至尊卑、貴賤等等。

學者梁漱溟在其《東西文化及其哲學》中指出，強調尊卑和崇尚平等是中西文化不同的精神特質。他說，中國人看見西方人在一起時沒有一個人做主，覺得很奇怪。人們平起平坐，似乎完全沒有尊卑上下之分。正如中國人看到西方人的行為中常不分誰是領頭的、誰是聽話的而感到驚訝一樣，西方人看到中國上級領導的"一言堂"和下屬員工一味的言聽計從也感到難以理解。曾在中國華為公司擔任管理者的CT Johnson一次告訴媒體，在西方公司工作時，他期待自己的下屬以直接但尊重的態度質疑他的提議，希望通過討論共同改進工作。然而中國的同事們不會這樣做，因為對於他們來說，質疑就等同於反對。上級領導"訓話"是另一種常使西方人或久居西方的華人感到不可接受的行為。領導開會訓話時，不僅自始至終一言堂，而且可以隨便訓斥人，甚至還會當著眾人的面點名批評下屬，一點面子也不留。

中國人的等級觀念在公共場合生人之間的交往中也明顯地反映出來。我們在街頭可以看到員警粗魯地對待一個違反了交規的農民工，而這個農民工始終陪著笑臉不敢回一句話；我們也可以看到一些城管在執法中粗暴無禮，而被驅趕的小商販在城管所代表的權力面前也不敢做任何的反抗。除了權力以外，金錢也是造成當今中國社會等級分明的主要原因之一。開凱美瑞的人主動讓著開奔馳寶馬的，低收入階層的人在高收入者面前也自覺低人一等。在前面提到的華人回國見聞中，作者講了這樣一個故事：一次，她乘飛機從杭州去北京，後面坐著一個看起來像是很有錢的人。從上飛機的那一刻起，他就哇啦哇啦地大聲叫個不停，把空中小姐像使喚自己家的保姆一樣支來叫去。他並不認為這樣做是缺乏教養，相反，像很多的"土豪"一樣，他似乎在利用一切機會，向世界申明自己現在是個有錢人了，因此高人一等了。

同樣的情景也時常出現在餐館和賓館裡。一些穿著體面的人對服務員動不動就大呼小叫，就像舊社會官老爺支使自己的傭人一樣。但令人驚訝的是，周圍的人，包括服務員自己，並不以此為怪，似乎對這些傳統的上尊下卑的行為早已司空見慣了。這一切說明了這樣一個事實：即一個國家的經濟發展與社會觀念的轉變並不一定是同步的。隨著人類的進步，文化傳統固然也在發生變化，但在中國的社會環境裡，深層文化結構的改變是緩慢的，一些觀念甚至在相當長的歷史時期內仍不斷地延續著。可見，在學習中國人行為習慣的同時，從深層的文化觀念上瞭解他們為什麼這樣或那樣與別人打交道，對看懂“複雜的中國人”十分必要。

Pinyin-English vocabulary

拼音 A	*简体*	*繁體*	*词性*	*英文翻译*	
àn'àn	暗暗		adv	inwardly, to oneself, secretly	Lesson fourteen
Ān Lǐ Huì	安理会	安理會		UNSC [short form of 联合国安全理事会, United Nations Security Council]	Lesson eight
ànlì	案例		n	case for study	Lesson ten
ànzhào	按照		prep	according to, in accordance with	Lesson one
Àoyùnhuì	奥运会	奥運會		Olympics [short for 奥林匹克运动会: Àolínpǐkè Yùndònghuì, Olympic Games]	Lesson six

拼音 B	*简体*	*繁體*	*词性*	*英文翻译*	
bàng	棒		adj	[colloquial] good, fine, strong	Lesson five
bànyǎn	扮演		v	play part of	Lesson six
bào	报	報	v	sign up [as in 报名]	Lesson one
bào.yuàn	抱怨		v	complain, grumble	Lesson two
bǎo'ān	保安		n	security guard, security personnel	Lesson thirteen
bǎochí	保持		v	maintain, keep, preserve	Lesson seven
bàodào	报道	報道	v/n	report; report [same as 报导 (bàodǎo)]	Lesson thirteen

拼音 B	*简体*	*繁體*	*词性*	*英文翻译*	
bāofáng	包房		n	private room in a restaurant [a.k.a 包间]	Lesson twelve
bāohán	包含		v	contain, include	Lesson five
bāokuò	包括		v	include	Lesson six
Bǎomǎ	宝马	寶馬		BMW [brand], precious horse	Lesson fourteen
bǎomǔ	保姆		n	house maid, nanny	Lesson fourteen
bǎoquán	保全		v	keep ... intact, safeguard	Lesson nine
bǎoshǒu	保守		adj	conservative	Lesson eleven
bǎwò	把握		v/n	grasp firmly, command; assurance, certainty	Lesson eleven
bèi	辈	輩	n	generation, lifetime [同辈: the same generation; 大一辈: one generation older]	Lesson three
bēi	背		v	carry on one's back or shoulder(s)	Lesson one
bèihòu	背后	背後	n	back, rear	Lesson eleven
bèijǐng	背景		n	background, backdrop	Lesson seven
Bèikěqīn	倍可亲	倍可親		a portal website in Chinese, primarily serving Chinese living in North America [https://www.backchina.com; 倍: times;]	Lesson fourteen
Bēnchí	奔驰	奔驰		Benz [brand], gallop	Lesson fourteen
běnkē	本科		n	undergraduate	Lesson twelve
běnwèi	本位		n	one's own position (seen as being central) [关系本位: relation-based; 家本位: family-based, family-oriented]	Lesson three
biǎndī	贬低	貶低	v	belittle, disparage, play down	Lesson five

拼音 B	*简体*	*繁體*	*词性*	*英文翻译*	
biànhuàn	变换	變換	v	vary, alternate	Lesson six
biǎodá	表达	表達	v	voice (opinion, feelings), express, convey	Lesson seven
biǎomiàn	表面		n	surface	Lesson nine
biǎoshì	表示		v	indicate, show, express	Lesson two
biāotí	标题	標題	n	(book, article) title, (news) headline	Lesson eight
biǎoxiàn	表现	表現	n/v	display, manifestation; show, display	Lesson three
bǐcǐ	彼此		pron	each other, one another	Lesson eleven
bìmiǎn	避免		v	avoid, avert, refrain from	Lesson seven
bìngqiě	并且	並且	conj	and, besides, moreover	Lesson seven
bìyào	必要		adj	necessary, essential, indispensable	Lesson fourteen
bǐyù	比喻		v/n	draw analogy; metaphor, analogy	Lesson six
bōfàng	播放		v	broadcast, transmit	Lesson two
bóshì	博士		n	Ph.D.	Lesson seven
bówén	博文		n	blog post	Lesson five
bù xué lǐ, wú yǐ lì	不学礼，无以立	不學禮，無以立		If you do not learn the rules of Propriety, your character cannot be established. [from *The Analects* of Confucius; trans. by James Legge]	Lesson four
búduàn	不断	不斷	adv	unceasingly, continuously	Lesson eleven
búgù	不顾	不顧	v	ignore, overlook	Lesson twelve
bùjiě	不解		adj/v	puzzled; not understand	Lesson five
búzuòwéi	不作为	不作為	v/n	take no action to fulfill one's duty; negligence of one's duty	Lesson thirteen

拼音 C	*简体*	*繁體*	*词性*	*英文翻译*	
cǎinà	采纳	採納	v	adopt	Lesson ten
cǎiqǔ	采取	採取	v	adopt	Lesson seven
cǎiyòng	采用	採用	v	select, employ, adopt	Lesson eight
cè	侧	側	v	lean on one side, turn . . . sideways	Lesson five
céngchū-bùqióng	层出不穷	層出不窮	idiom	emerge one after another, spring up in an endless stream	Lesson thirteen
céngjīng	曾经	曾經	adv	once, ever	Lesson two
chā//duì	插队	插隊	v	jump a queue, cut in line	Lesson thirteen
chāděng	差等		n	subalternation (in status or quality), differentiated ranking, difference	Lesson fourteen
chángdá	长达	長達	phr	lengthen out to, extend as long as [长达两千年: extend as long as 2000 years]	Lesson four
chǎnghé	场合	場合	n	occasion, circumstance	Lesson thirteen
chánghuán	偿还	償還	v	repay, pay back	Lesson twelve
chǎngsuǒ	场所	場所	n	venue, place	Lesson six
chǎnshēng	产生	產生	v	arise, come in being	Lesson two
chāxù géjú	差序格局		phr	differentiated mode of association, a term coined by Fei Xiaotong in his《乡土中国》[差: 差别, difference; 序: 顺序, order; 格局: pattern, structure]	Lesson thirteen
chēliàng	车辆	車輛	n	[collective] vehicles, cars	Lesson two
chēng	称	稱	v	address, call	Lesson four
Chéng Lóng	成龙	成龍		Jackie Chan (1954–), Hong Kong martial artist, actor, film director, producer, stuntman, and singer	Lesson three
chēng.hu	称呼	稱呼	v/n	address, call; form of address, appellation	Lesson three
chéngdù	程度		n	extent, degree, level	Lesson thirteen
chéngfá	惩罚	懲罰	n/v	punishment; punish	Lesson two

拼音 C	*简体*	*繁體*	*词性*	*英文翻译*	
chéngguǎn	城管		n	local government law-enforcement officer, city management [short for 城市管理行政执法局 Urban Administrative and Law Enforcement Bureau]	Lesson fourteen
chéngkè	乘客		n	passenger	Lesson twelve
chéngxù	程序		n	procedure, protocol [走程序: follow the procedure]	Lesson twelve
chēngzàn	称赞	稱讚	v	praise, acclaim, commend, compliment	Lesson ten
chǐ gǎn wénhuà	耻感文化	恥感文化	phr	shame-based culture [耻 (bf): shame, disgrace]	Lesson ten
chī//jīng	吃惊	吃驚	v	be surprised, be shocked	Lesson five
chōngmǎn	充满	充滿	v	be brimming/permeated with	Lesson eleven
Chóngqìng	重庆	重慶		Chongqing or Chungking, a direct-controlled municipality under China's central government	Lesson two
Chóngqìng Chén Bào	重庆晨报	重慶晨報		*Chongqing Morning Post*, a local newspaper in the city of Chongqing [晨 (bf): morning]	Lesson twelve
chóngshàng	崇尚		v	hold up (as a model), hold in esteem	Lesson three
chōngtū	冲突	衝突	n/v	clash; conflict	Lesson six
chóngxīn	重新		adv	once more	Lesson ten
chōu	抽		v	draw out, pull out [抽时间: find time to]	Lesson twelve
chǔ	处	處	v	be situated at, be in a position of [所处的时代: the era that people live in]	Lesson nine
chū	初		n	the beginning of (a period of time)	Lesson eight
chū fēng.tou	出风头	出風頭	phr	seek the limelight	Lesson eight

拼音 C	*简体*	*繁體*	*词性*	*英文翻译*	
chuǎimó	揣摩		v	try to figure out	Lesson fourteen
chuán	传	傳	v	spread, pass on, circulate	Lesson eight
chuán//jiào	传教	傳教	v	spread a religion, preach	Lesson nine
chuándì	传递	傳遞	v	transmit, pass on	Lesson nine
chuǎng	闯	闖	v	rush, dash [闯红灯: run a red light]	Lesson two
chuàngyè	创业	創業	v	begin an undertaking, start a venture	Lesson ten
chuántǒng	传统	傳統	adj/n	traditional; tradition	Lesson three
chuānzhuó	穿着	穿著	n	apparel, attire	Lesson fourteen
chūcì	初次		adv	for the first time	Lesson fourteen
chúfēi	除非		conj	unless	Lesson one
chǔlǐ	处理	處理	v	handle, deal with, process	Lesson eleven
Chūnqiū	春秋			Spring and Autumn Period (771–476 BC)	Lesson four
chūnwǎn	春晚		n	Chinese New Year's eve gala [short for 春节联欢晚会]	Lesson nine
chǔshì	处世	處世	v	conduct oneself in society	Lesson ten
chūxiàn	出现	出現	v	appear, emerge	Lesson two
chūyú	出于	出於	v	(do sth.) out of (politeness, curiosity, compassion, etc.), due to	Lesson one
cí	辞	辭	v	resign (from a job), quit (a job) [辞去工作 or 辞职 (cí//zhí): resign from a job]	Lesson ten
círàng	辞让	辭讓	v	decline and yield [辞: decline, resign, dismiss; 让: yield]	Lesson four
cìxù	次序		n	sequence, order	Lesson fourteen
cóngzhòng	从众	從眾	v	follow the crowd, conform	Lesson two
còu	凑	湊	v	gather together, pool, collect [凑热闹còu rè.nao: join in the fun]	Lesson one
cūbào	粗暴		adj	rude and brutal	Lesson fourteen
cùjìn	促进	促進	v	accelerate, promote	Lesson eleven

拼音 C	*简体*	*繁體*	*词性*	*英文翻译*	
cūlǔ	粗鲁	粗魯	adj	crude in one's manners, boorish	Lesson fourteen
cúnzài	存在		v/n	exist; existence	Lesson two
cuòwù	错误	錯誤	n/adj	mistake, error; erroneous, incorrect	Lesson ten

拼音 D	*简体*	*繁體*	*词性*	*英文翻译*	
dā	搭		v	put up, construct (platform, shed, rack, etc.)	Lesson three
dǎ jiāo.dao	打交道		phr	interact with, have dealings with	Lesson five
dǎ májiàng	打麻将	打麻將	phr	play *mahjong*	Lesson one
dàbó	大伯		n	[address for father's eldest brother] [polite address for an elderly man]	Lesson three
dàduōshù	大多数	大多數	n	the majority	Lesson two
dàhū-xiǎojiào	大呼小叫		idiom	shout and scream, make a big fuss	Lesson fourteen
dàibiǎo	代表		v/n	represent; representative, representation	Lesson two
dàitì	代替		v	replace, substitute	Lesson thirteen
dànbó	淡薄		adj	weak (sense of . . .), thin, light	Lesson two
dāndú	单独	單獨	adv	individually, on one's own	Lesson two
dāngdài	当代	當代	n	the present day, contemporary	Lesson four
dāngjīn	当今	當今	n	present time	Lesson nine
dāngshìrén	当事人	當事人	n	people directly involved or implicated	Lesson thirteen
dàngzuò	当做	當做	v	treat as, regard as, look upon as	Lesson four
dānrèn	担任	擔任	v	hold the post of, serve as	Lesson fourteen
dānwèi	单位	單位	n	unit (in measurement or organization)	Lesson eleven
dào	道		v	say [usu. used with direct quotations in literary or formal narratives, as in 问道: asked, 说道: said, 解释道: explained]	Lesson five

拼音 D	*简体*	*繁體*	*词性*	*英文翻译*	
dào.lǐ	道理		n	reason, rationality [有道理: be reasonable, be convincing]	Lesson five
dào//qiàn	道歉		v	apologize	Lesson seven
dàodé	道德		n	morals, morality	Lesson four
dàodǐ	到底		adv	(who, when, what, why, how) on earth	Lesson five
Dàojiā	道家			Daoist School of the Warring States Period (475–221 BC) based on the teachings of Laozi or Lao Tze [老子, c. 6th century BC] and Zhuangzi or Chuang Tzu [庄子, 369–286 BC]	Lesson six
dēng//jī	登机	登機	v	board a plane	Lesson thirteen
děngjí	等级	等級	n	social status, rank, grade	Lesson fourteen
děngtóng	等同	等同	v	equate, be equal	Lesson fourteen
děngyú	等于	等於	v	equal to, tantamount to	Lesson five
Déqín	德勤			Chinese translation of Deloitte, a company that provides accounting and consulting services [德: virtue; 勤: diligence]	Lesson seven
déyǐ	得以		v	be able to	Lesson twelve
déyìyú	得益于	得益於	phr	benefit from, be the beneficial result of	Lesson ten
dézhī	得知		v	learn of	Lesson one
dī rén yì děng	低人一等		idiom	inferior to other people [antonym: 高人一等]	Lesson fourteen
diǎn//míng	点名	點名	v	(praise or criticize sb.) by name; call roll	Lesson fourteen
diǎnxíng	典型		adj/n	typical, representative; typical case	Lesson four
diàochá	调查	調查	n/v	investigation; investigate [市场调查: market research]	Lesson ten
dìng//wèi	定位		v/n	determine the position, characterize (as); positioning	Lesson fourteen

拼音 D	*简体*	*繁體*	*词性*	*英文翻译*	
dìwèi	地位		n	rank, social status	Lesson nine
dìyù	地域		n	region, area	Lesson thirteen
dìyuán	地缘	地緣	n	regional ties	Lesson eleven
dìzǐ	弟子		n	disciple	Lesson six
dòng.budòng	动不动	動不動	adv	apt to happen [usu. of something undesirable], frequently, happening at the slightest provocation	Lesson fourteen
dǒngshìhuì	董事会	董事會	n	board of directors [董事: board member] [董事长: chairman of board]	Lesson ten
dòngyáo	动摇	動搖	v	waver, destabilize, sway	Lesson thirteen
duān	端		v	hold sth level with palm(s) facing upward	Lesson five
duān	端		bf	end, extremity [两端: two ends]	Lesson eight
Duān Chuánméi	端传媒	端傳媒		Initium Media (https://theinitium.com), Hong Kong-based digital media outlet launched in August, 2015 [端: beginning, initium; 传媒: media]	Lesson ten
duànliàn	锻炼	鍛鍊	v	do physical exercise, work out	Lesson one
duìdài	对待	對待	v	treat	Lesson fourteen
duìfāng	对方	對方	n	the other party (of two)	Lesson three
duìlì	对立	對立	v/n	oppose, be antagonistic to; opposition	Lesson eight
duìxiàng	对象	對象	n	target, object	Lesson thirteen
duìyú	对于	對於	prep	regarding, with regards to	Lesson four
dúlì	独立	獨立	n/adj	independence; independent	Lesson one
duōduō-bīrén	咄咄逼人	咄咄逼人	idiom	overbearing, aggressive	Lesson thirteen
dǔsè	堵塞		n/v	(traffic) jam, congestion; jam, congest	Lesson two
dútè	独特	獨特	adj	unique, distinctive	Lesson three
dúzì	独自	獨自	adv	by oneself	Lesson one

拼音 E	*简体*	*繁體*	*词性*	*英文翻译*	*E*
Éluósī	俄罗斯	俄羅斯		Russia [short form of 俄罗斯联邦: Éluósī Liánbāng; the Russian Federation]	Lesson eight

拼音 F	*简体*	*繁體*	*词性*	*英文翻译*	
fā//cái	发财	發財	v	make a fortune	Lesson eight
fābiǎo	发表	發表	v	publish (article, opinion, viewpoint, etc.)	Lesson two
fǎbùzézhòng	法不责众	法不責眾	idiom	The law does not punish numerous offenders./The law fails where violators are legion.	Lesson two
fāchū	发出	發出	v	let out, send out, give out	Lesson thirteen
fādá	发达	發達	adj	developed	Lesson eleven
fāhuī	发挥	發揮	n/v	bringing out implicit or innate qualities; bring into play	Lesson twelve
fǎlǜ	法律		n	law	Lesson two
fàn	犯		v	commit [犯错误: commit an error, make a mistake, 犯罪 (zuì): commit a crime, 犯法: break the law]	Lesson ten
fǎn.zhèng	反正		adv	anyway, anyhow, in any case, under whatever circumstances	Lesson one
fǎn'gǎn	反感		n/adj	dislike, antipathy; disgusted with	Lesson six
fǎnduì	反对	反對	v/n	oppose, disagree; disagreement	Lesson eight
fāng'àn	方案		n	plan, proposal	Lesson ten
fāngfǎ	方法		n	method, way, means	Lesson four
fāngshì	方式		n	way, style, pattern	Lesson two
fǎnkàng	反抗		n/v	resistance; revolt, confront	Lesson fourteen
fānyì	翻译	翻譯	v/n	translate; translator, translation	Lesson eight
fǎnyìng	反映		v	reflect	Lesson two
fǎnyìng	反应	反應	n/v	reaction; react	Lesson seven
fāxiàn	发现	發現	v/n	discover, find; discovery, findings	Lesson one

拼音 F	*简体*	*繁體*	*词性*	*英文翻译*	
fǎyuàn	法院		n	(law) court	Lesson twelve
fǎzé	法则	法則	n	law, rule, principle	Lesson eight
fēi	非		bf/adv	non- [非物质: non-material, intangible]; have got to, simply must	Lesson eleven
Fèi Xiàotōng	费孝通	費孝通		Fei Xiaotong or Fei Hsiao-Tung (1910–2005), a renowned scholar and professor of sociology and anthropology. His famous work 《乡土中国》, translated as *From the Soil: The Foundations of Chinese Society*, was first published in 1948 and widely referenced by Chinese sociologists and anthropologists.	Lesson eleven
fèn.ziqián	份子钱	份子錢	n	share for a joint undertaking [as in buying a gift; a.k.a. 份子]	Lesson eleven
fēn//qīng	分清		v	distinguish; draw a clear distinction between	Lesson seven
fēngbì	封闭	封閉	adj/v	enclosed, confined; seal off, close down	Lesson eleven
fēngfù	丰富	豐富	adj/v	rich, plentiful, abundant; enrich	Lesson five
fēngsú	风俗	風俗	n	social custom	Lesson thirteen
fēngxíng	风行	風行	v	be popular, be in fashion, spread widely	Lesson twelve
fēnmíng	分明		adj/adv	clearly demarcated, distinct; evidently	Lesson fourteen
fènnù	愤怒	憤怒	n/adj	indignance; indignant, angry	Lesson thirteen
fēnxiǎng	分享		v	share (food, happiness, rights, etc.)	Lesson one
fú	扶		v	help sb. up, support with hand	Lesson thirteen
fù	副		m	[for facial expressions, pairs/sets of things]	Lesson thirteen
fùchū	付出		v	pay, invest (energy or time in . . .)	Lesson twelve
fúhé	符合		v	conform to, tally with	Lesson five

拼音 F	*简体*	*繁體*	*词性*	*英文翻译*	
fúróng jī piàn	芙蓉鸡片	芙蓉雞片		chicken egg *foo young* [芙蓉: hibiscus]	Lesson one
fùzá	复杂	複雜	adj	complicated, complex	Lesson nine
fùzé	负责	負責	v	be in charge of, take responsibility for; [负责人: person in charge]	Lesson seven

拼音 G	*简体*	*繁體*	*词性*	*英文翻译*	
gǎijìn	改进	改進	v	improve	Lesson ten
gàiniàn	概念		n	concept, notion	Lesson eleven
gǎishàn	改善		v	make better, improve	Lesson ten
gān'gà	尴尬	尷尬	adj	embarrassed, awkward	Lesson ten
gǎndào	感到		v	feel, sense	Lesson five
gǎnjī	感激		v	be grateful, appreciate	Lesson ten
gǎnjué	感觉	感覺	n/v	feeling; feel	Lesson one
gǎnkǎi	感慨		n/v	lament; sigh with emotion	Lesson thirteen
gǎnqíng	感情		n	feeling [爱情: romantic love; 亲情: family love; 乡情: affection for native place; 战友情: friendship between or among fellow soldiers]	Lesson eleven
gānshè	干涉		v	interfere	Lesson one
gǎnshòu	感受		n/v	a feeling; experience, feel	Lesson seven
gǎo//xiào	搞笑		v/adj	make people laugh, entertain; hilarious	Lesson nine
gāodù	高度		adj/n	high-degree; height	Lesson six
gāoguǎn	高管		n	high-rank managerial personnel, senior executive [short for 高级管理人员]	Lesson seven
gāojí	高级	高級	adj	supreme, advanced	Lesson eight
gāoshēn	高深		adj	profound [深: deep]	Lesson eight
gāozhǎng	高涨	高漲	v	surge up; run high	Lesson twelve

拼音 G	*简体*	*繁體*	*词性*	*英文翻译*	
gàozhī	告知		v	inform	Lesson ten
gèdé-qíwèi	各得其位		phr	Each is in its proper place./ Each has a role to play.	Lesson eight
gēnběn	根本		adj	fundamental, basic	Lesson one
gēnfēng	跟风	跟風	v	follow the trend	Lesson two
gēnjù	根据	根據	prep/v/n	based on; base . . . on; basis	Lesson nine
gēnshēn-dìgù	根深蒂固		idiom	deep-rooted, long-established, inveterate	Lesson thirteen
gèrén	个人	個人	n	individual [person]	Lesson one
gètǐ	个体	個體	n	individual (person or entity) [个体意识: individual-oriented consciousness]	Lesson one
gōngchéng	工程		n	project, engineering [形象工程: vanity project]	Lesson nine
gōngjù	工具		n	tool, instrument	Lesson three
gōngláo	功劳	功勞	n	meritorious service, achievement, credit	Lesson ten
gòngmíng	共鸣	共鳴	n	resonance, sympathetic response	Lesson two
gōngpíng	公平		adj/n	fair, just, impartial; fairness	Lesson eleven
gòngtóng	共同		adv/adj	jointly, together; common, mutual	Lesson eight
gōngyuán qián	公元前		n	B.C. [公元: A.D.]	Lesson four
gōngzhòng	公众	公眾	n	the public	Lesson one
gōutōng	沟通	溝通	v	communicate	Lesson seven
Gū Hóngmíng	辜鸿铭	辜鴻銘		Hung-ming Ku or Hongming Gu (1857–1928), a Malaysian Chinese man of letters known for his monarchist views and highly regarded for his works in English.	Lesson eight
gù.shi	故事		n	story	Lesson one
guān	观	觀	bf	outlook [世界观: worldview; 价值观: values]	Lesson six
guānchá	观察	觀察	v	observe, inspect	Lesson thirteen

拼音 G	*简体*	*繁體*	*词性*	*英文翻译*	
guāndiǎn	观点	觀點	n	point of view, viewpoint	Lesson one
guāngcǎi	光彩		adj/n	glorious, honorable; glory, luster, splendor	Lesson nine
guǎngchǎng	广场	廣場	n	public square, plaza [广场舞: square dancing, plaza dancing]	Lesson two
guǎngfàn	广泛	廣泛	adj	wide-ranging, widespread	Lesson four
guānjiàn	关键	關鍵	adj/n	key, critical; crux	Lesson thirteen
guānlǎo.ye	官老爷	官老爺	phr	[an honorific for government officials in traditional China, used sarcastically in the text] literal meaning: official master	Lesson fourteen
guǎnlǐ	管理		v	manage [管理学: management science]	Lesson seven
guānniàn	观念	觀念	n	sense, conception, notion, idea	Lesson three
guānzhòng	观众	觀眾	n	audience, spectators	Lesson six
guānzhù	关注	關注	v	pay close attention to, follow with interest	Lesson seven
gǔdài	古代		n	ancient times, antiquity	Lesson three
gùdìng	固定		adj/v	fixed, regular; fasten, set rigidly in place	Lesson eleven
guīdìng	规定	規定	v/n	stipulate; provision, regulation	Lesson fourteen
guīfàn	规范	規範	n/adj/v	norm; standard; regulate, standardize	Lesson eleven
guìjiàn	贵贱	貴賤	n	the noble and the lowly, high versus low social hierarchy	Lesson fourteen
guīlǜ	规律	規律	n/adj	pattern; regular	Lesson eight
guīzé	规则	規則	n	rule, regulation	Lesson two
gùkè	顾客	顧客	n	customer	Lesson five
guò//tóu	过头	過頭	adj	going too far	Lesson eight
guòchéng	过程	過程	n	course of events, process, procedure	Lesson eleven
guòjiǎng	过奖	過獎	v	overpraise [您过奖了: You flattered me.]	Lesson five
gùrán	固然		conj	admittedly, it's true that	Lesson ten

拼音 H	*简体*	*繁體*	*词性*	*英文翻译*	
hǎn	喊		v	cry out, yell	Lesson seven
Hángzhōu	杭州			Hangzhou, the capital city of the Zhejiang province in southeast China	Lesson fourteen
hánxù	含蓄		adj	implicit, reserved, veiled	Lesson seven
hányì	含义	含義	n	meaning, connotation [a.k.a. 涵(hán)义]	Lesson twelve
hào	好		v	like, be fond of [好礼: be fond of the rites and etiquettes]	Lesson four
hǎoxīn	好心		n	good intention, kind heart [一片好心: the best of intentions]	Lesson seven
hé ér bùtóng	和而不同		idiom	harmony without uniformity	Lesson eight
hé.qi shēngcái	和气生财	和氣生財	idiom	Geniality brings wealth. [和气: geniality; 生: generate; 财 (bf): wealth]	Lesson six
hé'ǎi kěqīn	和蔼可亲	和藹可親	idiom	affable, genial	Lesson six
hébì	何必		adv	why should, there is no need [何: what; 必: must]	Lesson one
héděng	何等		adv	how	Lesson thirteen
héfǎ	合法		adj	lawful, legitimate, rightful	Lesson two
héhǎo	和好		v	restore good relations, become reconciled	Lesson six
hémù	和睦		adj	harmonious [often interpersonal or familial]	Lesson six
héngxiàng	横向		adj	crosswise, horizontal	Lesson fourteen
hépíng	和平	和平	n	peace	Lesson six

拼音 H	*简体*	*繁體*	*词性*	*英文翻译*	
héxié	和谐	和諧	adj/n	harmonious [often international or societal]; harmony	Lesson six
héxīn	核心		n	core, the heart of the matter	Lesson four
hézuò	合作		n/v	collaboration; collaborate, cooperate	Lesson three
hōngdòng	轰动	轟動	v	cause a great sensation	Lesson eight
hòuguǒ	后果	後果	n	consequence, aftermath	Lesson ten
Hú Xiānjìn	胡先缙	胡先縉		Hsien Chin Hu, a pioneering Chinese anthropologist	Lesson nine
hú.tu	糊涂	糊塗	adj	muddled, confused	Lesson eleven
huà	化		bf	-ize, -ify [added to a noun or an adjective to form a verb, as in 家庭化: familize, 现代化: modernize, etc.]	Lesson three
huā.fei	花费	花費	n	expenses, expenditure	Lesson twelve
Huáng Guāngguó	黄光国	黃光國		Kuang-Kwo Hwang (1945–), professor emeritus, Department of Psychology, National Taiwan University	Lesson twelve
huǎnmàn	缓慢	緩慢	adj	slow, slow-moving	Lesson fourteen
huárén	华人	華人	n	people of Chinese descent	Lesson five
Huáwéi	华为	華為		Huawei [brand; most famous for mobile phones]	Lesson fourteen
hùhuì	互惠		v	mutually benefit	Lesson eleven

拼音 H	*简体*	*繁體*	*词性*	*英文翻译*	
huìbào	汇报	匯報	v	collect information and report (to an authoritarian figure)	Lesson ten
huīfù	恢复	恢復	v	restore, recover	Lesson four
hūjiù	呼救		v	call for help	Lesson thirteen
hūlüè	忽略		v	ignore, overlook	Lesson eight
hùn	混		v	mix, confuse	Lesson five
hùnhé	混合		v	mix, blend	Lesson twelve
hūnlǐ	婚礼	婚禮	n	wedding ceremony	Lesson eleven
huódòng	活动	活動	v/n	engage in various activities; activity	Lesson one
huòqǔ	获取	獲取	v	gain, obtain	Lesson twelve

拼音 J	*简体*	*繁體*	*词性*	*英文翻译*	
jí	即		v/adv	be the same as, be precisely [more formal than 就是]; namely	Lesson two
jí	籍		bf	native place, membership [as in 国籍 (nationality, citizenship), 美籍, 外籍]	Lesson five
jǐ	挤	擠	v	force others aside, squeeze	Lesson five
jià hé wànshì xīng	家和万事兴	家和萬事興	idiom	Harmony in the family leads to prosperity in all undertakings. [万事: all things; 兴: prosper]	Lesson six
jiǎng	讲	講	v	stress, pay attention to	Lesson five
jiāng	将	將	prep	[introduces the object of the main verb, similar to 把, but more formal than 把]	Lesson twelve
jiǎng.jiu	讲究	講究	v/adj	be particular about, pay special attention to; exquisite, tasteful	Lesson four
jiàngdī	降低		v	lower, cut down, drop, reduce	Lesson five

拼音 J	*简体*	*繁體*	*词性*	*英文翻译*	
jiǎngshù	讲述	講述	v	narrate, tell about, describe	Lesson eleven
jiāngxīn-bǐxīn	将心比心	將心比心	idiom	judge another's feelings by one's own, put oneself in somebody else's shoes	Lesson seven
jiānkòng	监控	監控	n/v	surveillance; surveil, monitor	Lesson thirteen
jiànlì	建立		v	found, establish	Lesson eleven
jiānruì	尖锐	尖銳	adj	incisive, penetrating, pointed and sharp	Lesson fourteen
jiànwén	见闻	見聞	n	what one has seen and heard	Lesson fourteen
jiànyì	建议	建議	v/n	suggest, advise; suggestion, advice	Lesson one
jiànyuè	僭越		n/v	overstepping of one's role or authority or ethical relationship with others; overstep one's role or authority or ethical relationship with others	Lesson fourteen
jiāoguī	交规	交規	n	traffic regulations, traffic rules [short for 交通规则]	Lesson fourteen
jiāolǜ	焦虑	焦慮	n/adj	anxiety; anxious	Lesson twelve
jiāotán	交谈	交談	v	converse	Lesson seven
jiāotōng	交通		n	traffic	Lesson two
jiāowǎng	交往		v	associate (with), have dealings (with)	Lesson three
jiàoyǎng	教养	教養	n	upbringing, culture	Lesson fourteen
jiāshēn	加深		v	deepen	Lesson eleven
jiàzhí	价值	價值	n	value, worth	Lesson three
jiāzú	家族		n	clan, family	Lesson eleven
jīběn.shàng	基本上		adv	basically, primarily	Lesson eight
jíbiàn	即便		conj	even if, even though [more formal than 即使]	Lesson fourteen
jiē	接		v	take over (something handed to oneself)	Lesson one
jiě//wéi	解围	解圍	v	help someone out of embarrassment, lift a siege	Lesson ten
jiēcéng	阶层	階層	n	social stratum	Lesson fourteen

拼音 J	*简体*	*繁體*	*词性*	*英文翻译*	
jiēchù	接触	接觸	v	come into contact with	Lesson fourteen
jiégòu	结构	結構	n	structure, construction	Lesson nine
jièguò	借过	借過	phr	excuse me [used when one tries to pass someone in a crowd]	Lesson five
jiéjiāo	结交	結交	v	befriend, make friends with	Lesson twelve
jiějué	解决	解決	v	solve, resolve	Lesson eight
jiěshì	解释	解釋	v	explain	Lesson three
jiēshòu	接受		v	accept, receive	Lesson four
jiētóu	街头	街頭	n	street	Lesson thirteen
jiéyì	结义	結義	v	become sworn brothers/ sisters	Lesson fourteen
jìhuì	忌讳	忌諱	v/n	avoid as a taboo, abstain from; taboo	Lesson eleven
jījí	积极	積極	adj	positive, proactive	Lesson nine
jìnchéng	进程	進程	n	process, course, progress	Lesson fourteen
jìngcí	敬辞	敬辭	n	respectful language [a rhetoric device, and a type of Chinese honorifics]	Lesson five
jīngdǎ-xìsuàn	精打细算	精打細算	idiom	careful and strict calculation, meticulous planning and careful accounting	Lesson twelve
jīngdiǎn	经典	經典	n/adj	classics, canons; classical	Lesson eight
jīnglì	经历	經歷	n/v	experience; go through (event, era)	Lesson nine
jīnglì	精力		n	energy, vigor	Lesson twelve
jìngrán	竟然		adv	unexpectedly, to one's surprise	Lesson thirteen
jǐngrán-yǒuxù	井然有序		idiom	in order, orderly	Lesson eleven
jīngshén	精神		n	spirit, mind, consciousness	Lesson fourteen
jīngyà	惊讶	驚訝	adj	astonished, shocked	Lesson fourteen
jǐnmì	紧密	緊密	adj	inseparably close	Lesson twelve
jīnqián	金钱	金錢	n	money, wealth	Lesson eleven
Jīnróng Shíbào	金融时报	金融時報		*Financial Times*, a British newspaper	Lesson seven

拼音 J	*简体*	*繁體*	*词性*	*英文翻译*	
jìnxíng	进行	進行	v	carry out, execute	Lesson ten
jìnyíbù	进一步	進一步	adv	one step further, further onward	Lesson nine
jìshí	纪实	紀實	n/v	record of actual events; put down in writing	Lesson fourteen
jìxù	继续	繼續	v	continue	Lesson seven
jíyú	急于	急於	v	be eager to [more formal than 急着]	Lesson twelve
jìzhě	记者	記者	n	reporter, journalist	Lesson ten
jù//cān	聚餐		v	get together and have a meal together	Lesson one
jǔ//lì	举例	舉例	v	give an example	Lesson five
juésè	角色		n	role, part	Lesson three
jùjiāo	聚焦		v	focalize, focus	Lesson one
jùjué	拒绝	拒絕	v	refuse, decline, reject	Lesson thirteen
jūmín	居民		n	resident, inhabitant	Lesson two
jūn	军	軍	n	troops, armed forces	Lesson two
jūnshì	军事	軍事	n	military affairs	Lesson six
jùtǐ	具体	具體	adj	concrete, specific	Lesson seven
jùyǒu	具有		v	possess (characteristics, functionalities, etc.)	Lesson two

拼音 K	*简体*	*繁體*	*词性*	*英文翻译*	
kāifā	开发	開發	v	develop, exploit (a resource)	Lesson ten
Kǎiměiruì	凯美瑞	凱美瑞		Camry [Toyota automobile model; 凯: victorious; 瑞: auspicious]	Lesson fourteen
kāimùshì	开幕式	開幕式	n	opening ceremony [幕: curtain, screen]	Lesson six
kāngkǎi	慷慨		adj	generous	Lesson five
kànzhòng	看重		v	value	Lesson eleven
kètào	客套		n	civilities, polite formula	Lesson four
kèyì	刻意		adv	deliberately, purposefully	Lesson five
kōngjiān	空间	空間	n	space, room	Lesson two

拼音 K	*简体*	*繁體*	*词性*	*英文翻译*	
Kǒngzǐ	孔子			Confucius, Chinese social philosopher and educator	Lesson four
kǒutóuchán	口头禅	口頭禪	n	common saying, popular saying	Lesson twelve
kuājiǎng	夸奖	誇獎	v/n	praise; compliment	Lesson four
kuānróng	宽容	寬容	v	tolerate, pardon	Lesson six
kùnhuò	困惑		n/adj	perplexity; perplexed, puzzled	Lesson five
kuòdà	扩大	擴大	v	expand, enlarge, broaden, extend	Lesson eleven

拼音 L	*简体*	*繁體*	*词性*	*英文翻译*	
lā jiācháng	拉家常		phr	chat about domestic trivia	Lesson one
lái ér bù wǎng fēi lǐ yě	来而不往非礼也	來而不往非禮也		Courtesy demands reciprocity./Respond in kind. [This expression has its origin in The Book of Rites.]	Lesson eleven
lái.dejí	来得及	來得及	v	able to do sth. in time [来不及: unable to do sth. in time]	Lesson two
lājìn	拉近		v	draw close, draw near	Lesson twelve
lèng	愣		v	be stupefied, be distracted	Lesson seven
lěngdàn	冷淡		adj	cold, indifferent	Lesson five
lěngmò	冷漠		n/adj	coldness and indifference; cold and indifferent	Lesson thirteen
lì	例		n	example [as in 以······为例, 例子, etc.]	Lesson one
lǐ duō rén bú guài	礼多人不怪	禮多人不怪	idiom	One won't be blamed for being extra- polite. [怪: blame]	Lesson four
lǐ zhī yòng, hé wéi guì	礼之用，和为贵	禮之用，和為貴		In practicing the rules of propriety, a natural ease is to be prized. [from Analects of Confucius; trans. James Legge]	Lesson six
lì.liàng	力量		n	power, force, physical strength [人多力量大 (proverb): There is strength in numbers.]	Lesson two

拼音 L	*简体*	*繁體*	*词性*	*英文翻译*	
Liáng Shùmíng	梁漱溟			Liang Shuming (1893–1988), a scholar and philosopher in the neo-Confucian tradition	Lesson fourteen
Liánhéguó	联合国	聯合國		United Nations	Lesson eight
liǎojiě	了解		n/v	understanding, comprehension; understand	Lesson ten
lièjǔ	列举	列舉	v	enumerate, list, cite one by one	Lesson fourteen
lǐjiě	理解		n/v	interpretation; interpret, understand	Lesson five
lǐmào	礼貌	禮貌	n/adj	courtesy, politeness, manners; polite	Lesson one
lìng	令		v	cause, make (something to happen) [more formal than 让 and 使]	Lesson six
lǐng//tóu	领头	領頭	v	take the lead, be the first to do sth.	Lesson fourteen
lǐngdǎo	领导	領導	n/v	leader, leadership; lead	Lesson ten
lǐniàn	理念		n	concept, notion, idea	Lesson eight
línlǐ	邻里	鄰里	n	neighbors, neighborhood	Lesson eleven
lǐpǐn	礼品	禮品	n	gift, present	Lesson eleven
lǐshàngwǎnglái	礼尚往来	禮尚往來	idiom	What the rules of propriety value is reciprocity. [trans. by James Legge]	Lesson eleven
lǐsú	礼俗	禮俗	n	etiquette and custom	Lesson four
liúdòng	流动	流動	v	flow	Lesson eleven
lìyì	利益		n	benefit, (someone's) interest	Lesson one
lǐyí	礼仪	禮儀	n	rite, etiquette and ritual [礼仪之邦: state of ceremonies, state exemplary in observation of etiquette and rituals; 邦bāng (bf): state] [礼节: etiquette]	Lesson four
lìyòng	利用		v	use, utilize, take advantage of	Lesson twelve
Lúnyǔ	论语	論語		*The Analects* ["edited conversations" literally], a collection of sayings and ideas attributed to Confucius and his contemporaries, including his disciples.	Lesson six

拼音 M	*简体*	*繁體*	*词性*	*英文翻译*	
mángyú	忙于	忙於	v	be busy with [more formal than 忙着]	Lesson twelve
mǎnzú	满足	滿足	v	satisfy	Lesson twelve
máodùn	矛盾		n/adj	contradiction; contradictory	Lesson six
miànduì	面对	面對	v	face, confront	Lesson nine
miànduìmiàn	面对面	面對面	phr	face-to-face	Lesson seven
miànjī	面积	面積	n	surface area	Lesson six
miànkǒng	面孔		n	face	Lesson nine
miǎo	秒		n	second	Lesson two
miáoshù	描述		v	describe	Lesson two
mìmì	秘密		n/adj	secret, secrecy; secret	Lesson nine
míng	名		m	[used with multisyllabic nouns for people, such as 网友, 学生; more formal than 个]	Lesson two
mìng	命		n	(one's) life [命: 生命]	Lesson thirteen
míng.bai	明白		v/adj	realize, understand; clear, obvious	Lesson ten
míngquè	明确	明確	adj/v	unequivocal, clear-cut; make definite	Lesson three
míngxiǎn	明显	明顯	adj	obvious	Lesson fourteen
mínzú	民族		n	nation-state, ethnic group	Lesson nine
mìyǒu	密友		n	close friend, buddy	Lesson twelve
mòshēng	陌生		adj	unfamiliar [陌生人stranger]	Lesson thirteen
mǒu	某		pron	some (kind of)	Lesson two
móu//lì	牟利		v	seek profit, gain profit	Lesson twelve
mù.tou	木头	木頭	n	wood, log, timber	Lesson six
mùdǔ	目睹		v	witness, see at first hand [目 (bf): eye; 睹 (bf): see]	Lesson fourteen
mùqián	目前		n	at present	Lesson three

拼音 N	*简体*	*繁體*	*词性*	*英文翻译*	
nándào	难道	難道	adv	do you really mean to say that . . . ; could it be that . . .	Lesson seven
nánguài	难怪	難怪	adv	no wonder	Lesson nine
nányǐ	难以	難以	v	be difficult to	Lesson fourteen
nào	闹	鬧	v	run amok, cause havoc	Lesson thirteen
nèiróng	内容	內容	n	content	Lesson four
niánshào	年少		adj	young of age	Lesson three
niánzhǎng	年长	年長	adj	senior, elderly, older in age	Lesson three
nìngkě	宁可	寧可	adv	would rather	Lesson nine
nòng	弄		v	make, cause . . . to [弄坏: ruin, damage]	Lesson twelve
nónggēng	农耕	農耕	n/v	farming; practice farming [耕: till (fields)]	Lesson eleven
nónghòu	浓厚	濃厚	adj	strong, deep, dense, pronounced	Lesson eleven
nóngmíngōng	农民工	農民工	n	migrant peasant workers	Lesson fourteen
nóngyè	农业	農業	n	agriculture, farming	Lesson three

拼音 O	*简体*	*繁體*	*词性*	*英文翻译*	*O*
Ōuzhōu	欧洲	歐洲		Europe	Lesson eleven

拼音 P	*简体*	*繁體*	*词性*	*英文翻译*	
páiliè	排列		v	put in order, arrange	Lesson fourteen
péi xiàoliǎn	陪笑脸	陪笑臉	phr	put on a smiling face in order to please sb.	Lesson fourteen
péiyù	培育		v	cultivate, foster, breed	Lesson eleven
Péng.yǒuquān	朋友圈			Moments [WeChat's brand name for its social feed of friends' updates]	Lesson three
péngbó	蓬勃		adj	vigorous, full of vitality	Lesson eight
pínghéng	平衡		adj/n/v	balanced; equilibrium, balance; balance	Lesson six

拼音 P	*简体*	*繁體*	*词性*	*英文翻译*	
píngjià	评价	評價	v/n	appraise, evaluate; evaluation	Lesson nine
pínglùn	评论	評論	v/n	comment on; comments	Lesson two
píngqǐ-píngzuò	平起平坐		idiom	be on an equal footing, be on equal terms	Lesson fourteen
píngtái	平台	平臺	n	platform	Lesson thirteen
pīpíng	批评	批評	v	criticize	Lesson two
pòhuài	破坏	破壞	v	destroy, wreck, damage	Lesson twelve
pǔbiàn	普遍		adj	universal, prevalent, common, widespread	Lesson three

拼音 Q	*简体*	*繁體*	*词性*	*英文翻译*	*Q*
qí	齐	齊	adj	complete, all present	Lesson one
qí	其		pron	its, their, his, her [more formal than他的, 她的, 它的, 他们的]	Lesson four
qì//quán	弃权	棄權	v/n	abstain from voting; abstention	Lesson eight
qiàn	欠		v	owe, lack [亏(kuī)欠: owe, have a deficit]	Lesson twelve
qiāncí	谦辞	謙辭	n	humble language [a rhetoric device, and a type of Chinese honorifics]	Lesson five
qiáng	强	強	adj	strong, powerful, vigorous	Lesson three
qiǎng	抢	搶	v	fight over, snatch, loot	Lesson six
qiāng dǎ chūtóuniǎo	枪打出头鸟	槍打出頭鳥	idiom	The shot hits the bird that pokes its head out./ Nonconformity gets punished.	Lesson eight
qiángdiào	强调	強調	v	emphasize, stress	Lesson ten
qiángxíng	强行	強行	adv	by force	Lesson thirteen
qiānwàn	千万	千萬	adv	by all means	Lesson ten
qiānxū	谦虚	謙虛	adj/v	modest; make modest remarks	Lesson five
qiánzhě	前者		n	the former [后者: the latter]	Lesson five
qícì	其次		conj	secondly, next	Lesson four

拼音 Q	*简体*	*繁體*	*词性*	*英文翻译*	*Q*
qīdài	期待		v	expect, look forward to	Lesson fourteen
qīn.qi	亲戚		n	relatives	Lesson three
Qīngdǎo	青岛	青島		Qingdao, sub-provincial city in Shandong Province [a.k.a. Tsingtao]	Lesson ten
qínggǎn	情感		n	feeling [same as 感情], emotion	Lesson eleven
qīnshū yǒu bié	亲疏有别	親疏有別	phr	distinguish people based on relationships [亲: 亲近, close; 疏: 疏远, distant; 别(bf): 差别, difference]	Lesson thirteen
qīnyǎn	亲眼	親眼	adv	with one's own eyes	Lesson fourteen
qīnyuán	亲缘	親緣	n	family ties	Lesson eleven
qīwàng	期望		v	expect, earnestly hope	Lesson ten
qǐyè	企业	企業	n	enterprise, corporation	Lesson seven
qìyuē	契约	契約	n	contract, deed	Lesson four
qū	区	區	n	region, district	Lesson seven
quán	全		adj/adv	entire, complete; entirely, completely [全世界: the whole world]	Lesson six
quān.zi	圈子		n	circle	Lesson three
quánlì	权力	權力	n	power, authority, right	Lesson fourteen
quánqiú	全球		n	whole world [全球化: globalize; 地球: the Earth]	Lesson seven
qūbié	区别	區別	v/n	distinguish, differentiate; distinction	Lesson thirteen
quèdìng	确定	確定	v/adj	determine, decide firmly; definite	Lesson three
quēfá	缺乏		v	lack, be short of	Lesson fourteen
quēshǎo	缺少		v	lack, be short of	Lesson fourteen
quèshí	确实	確實	adv	indeed, truly	Lesson twelve
qūgǎn	驱赶	驅趕	v	drive away, expel	Lesson fourteen
qúntǐ	群体	群體	n	group	Lesson one

拼音 R	*简体*	*繁體*	*词性*	*英文翻译*	
rán'ér	然而		conj	however [more formal than 但是]	Lesson thirteen
ràng//bù	让步	讓步	n/v	yield, concession; yield, compromise, concede, give in	Lesson twelve
rén huó yì zhāng liǎn, shù huó yì zhāng pí	人活一张脸，树活一张皮	人活一張臉，樹活一張皮	proverb	Humans depend on their face just as trees depend on their bark for life. [皮: (tree) bark, skin]	Lesson ten
rěn yìshí fēngpíng-làngjìng	忍一时风平浪静	忍一時風平浪靜	proverb	"Practice forbearance for a short while, and the winds and waves will subside."/ Practicing forbearance for a short while will bring about tranquility.	Lesson seven
rěn zì dāngtóu	忍字当头	忍字當頭	phr	Forbearance is the most important principle. [当头: put ahead of everything else]	Lesson seven
rěn zì tóu .shang yì bǎ dāo	忍字头上一把刀	忍字頭上一把刀	proverb	"The top portion of the character ren is a knife."/ Practice forbearance as if there were a knife hanging above the head.	Lesson seven
réngrán	仍然		adv	still, yet	Lesson two
rènhé	任何		pron	any	Lesson eight
rénjì	人际	人際	adj	interpersonal [人际关系: interpersonal relationship]	Lesson three
rènkě	认可	認可	v	approve of	Lesson two
rénlèixué	人类学	人類學	n	anthropology [人类: mankind; 人类学家: anthropologist]	Lesson nine
rénlún	人伦	人倫	n	ethical relations, human relationship according to the Confucian ethics [伦理: ethics]	Lesson eleven
rénmài	人脉	人脈	n	connections, contacts, network	Lesson twelve
rénqíng	人情		n	human feelings, favor	Lesson nine
rěnràng	忍让	忍讓	v	be conciliatory, exercise forbearance	Lesson six
rénshēng	人生		n	human life, one's lifetime	Lesson eight
rèntóng	认同	認同	v	identify oneself with	Lesson two
rényuán	人缘	人緣	n	relations with other people, popularity among people	Lesson nine

拼音 R	*简体*	*繁體*	*词性*	*英文翻译*	
rèqíng	热情	熱情	adj/n	cordial, enthusiastic, passionate; cordialness, enthusiasm, passion	Lesson five
rèyì	热议	熱議	v	discuss passionately, heatedly debate [热: 热烈(liè), ardent, enthusiastic; 议: 议论, discuss, debate]	Lesson thirteen
rìcháng	日常		adj	day-to-day, everyday	Lesson four
rìyì	日益		adv	increasingly, with each passing day	Lesson twelve
rúhé	如何		pron	how [more formal than 怎样 or 怎么]	Lesson thirteen
Rújiā	儒家			Confucian Philosophical School, initiated by Confucius (551–479 BC) and developed by Mencius (c. 372 – c. 289 BC)	Lesson four
rúshàng	如上		v	as above [如上所述: as stated above]	Lesson twelve

拼音 S	*简体*	*繁體*	*词性*	*英文翻译*	
sàn//bù	散步		v	take a walk, go for a stroll	Lesson one
sàn//huì	散会	散會	v	disperse a meeting	Lesson ten
sècǎi	色彩		n	color, hue	Lesson nine
shāng	伤	傷	v	hurt, do harm to, injure, wound	Lesson seven
shàng shàn ruò shuǐ	上善若水			The highest excellence is like (that of) water. [from *Tao Te Ching*; trans. by James Legge]	Lesson six
shāngfàn	商贩	商販	n	small retailer, peddler	Lesson fourteen
shānghài	伤害	傷害	v	harm, hurt	Lesson nine
shàngjí	上级	上級	n	superior, a higher authority, someone higher in the hierarchy	Lesson fourteen
shāngwù	商务	商務	n	business affairs	Lesson ten
shāngyè	商业	商業	n	commerce, trade, business	Lesson three
sháozi	勺子		n	spoon	Lesson one

拼音 S	*简体*	*繁體*	*词性*	*英文翻译*	
shèhuì	社会	社會	n	society	Lesson two
shèjí	涉及		v	involve, relate to	Lesson eight
shèjiāo	社交		n	social contact/interaction	Lesson three
shēn	伸		v	extend, stretch	Lesson one
shēn'ào	深奥	深奧	adj	profound, abstruse	Lesson ten
shēncéng	深层	深層	adj/n	deep, deep-seated; deep layer	Lesson nine
shēnfèn	身份		n	identity, status	Lesson thirteen
shēngcún	生存		v	live, survive, subsist	Lesson twelve
shēngmìng	生命		n	life	Lesson ten
shēngzhǎng	生长	生長	v	grow, develop	Lesson eight
shēnmíng	申明		n	declare, aver, state formally	Lesson fourteen
shènrù	渗入	滲入	v	enter, penetrate	Lesson eight
shēnrù	深入		adj/v	thorough; go deep into	Lesson ten
shènzhì	甚至		conj	even	Lesson two
shǐ.de	使得		v	(intentions, plans, things) cause (a result) [more formal than 让]	Lesson nine
shǐ.huan	使唤	使喚	v	order sb. around	Lesson fourteen
shìbùguānjǐ	事不关己	事不關己	idiom	a matter of no concern to oneself	Lesson thirteen
shídài	时代	時代	n	times, age, epoch, era	Lesson nine
shìdù	适度	適度	adj	moderate, appropriate	Lesson eight
shífēn	十分		adv	very, extremely	Lesson eleven
shìfǒu	是否		adv	whether or not [more formal than 是不是; 能否: 能不能; 可否: 可不可以]	Lesson seven
shìjì	世纪	世紀	n	century	Lesson eight
shìjiàn	事件		n	event, incident	Lesson eight
shījiù	施救		v	take measures to rescue [施 bestow, carry out; 救 (bf): help, relieve]	Lesson thirteen
shíkè	时刻	時刻	n	moment, time	Lesson thirteen
shìpín	视频	視頻	n	video	Lesson thirteen

拼音 S	*简体*	*繁體*	*词性*	*英文翻译*	
shíqī	时期	時期	n	period, phase	Lesson four
shīqù	失去		v	lose	Lesson seven
shíshí	时时	時時	adv	frequently, constantly	Lesson nine
shíshī	实施	實施	v	implement	Lesson ten
shìshí	事实	事實	n	fact	Lesson five
shìshí.shàng	事实上	事實上	adv	in reality, in fact	Lesson nine
shìsú	世俗		adj/n	earthly, secular; the worldly [世俗观念: worldly views, common views]	Lesson nine
shíxiàn	实现	實現	v	realize, achieve, (dream) come true	Lesson three
shǐyòng	使用		v	use (something to serve a purpose)	Lesson three
shìzhōng	适中	適中	adj	appropriate, moderate	Lesson eight
shǐzhōng	始终	始終	adv	from beginning to end, all along	Lesson thirteen
shòu//zuì	受罪		v	endure hardship, suffer	Lesson nine
shǒuduàn	手段		n	means (of doing sth.), stratagem	Lesson twelve
shòufǎng	受访	受訪	v	be interviewed	Lesson twelve
shōurù	收入		n	income	Lesson fourteen
shǒuxiān	首先		adv/pron	first; first of all, in the first place	Lesson three
shòuxiànyú	受限于	受限於	phr	be limited to, be constrained by	Lesson thirteen
shōuyínyuán	收银员	收銀員	n	cashier [收: collect, receive; 银 (bf): silver (referring to money here)]	Lesson five
shú.xi	熟悉		v	know . . . well, familiarize	Lesson three
shuāidǎo	摔倒		v	fall down	Lesson thirteen
shuāngfāng	双方	雙方	n	both sides, the two parties [对方: other side, opposite side, counterpart]	Lesson four
shùdà-zhāofēng	树大招风	樹大招風	idiom	A tall tree catches the wind./A prominent person attracts attention [i.e., criticism].	Lesson eight

拼音 S	*简体*	*繁體*	*词性*	*英文翻译*	
shùfù	束缚	束縛	n/v	restriction, fetters; tie up, fetter, restrict	Lesson eleven
shùn//xīn	顺心	順心	adj	things going as one hopes, satisfactory	Lesson six
shuōdàodǐ	说到底	說到底	phr	in the final analysis, at bottom	Lesson thirteen
shuōmíng	说明	說明	v/n	illustrate, show, explain; explanation	Lesson one
shúrén	熟人		n	acquaintance [生人: stranger]	Lesson six
shǔyú	属于	屬於	v	belong to, be part of	Lesson thirteen
sìhū	似乎		adv	seemingly	Lesson eight
sīkǎo	思考		n/v	reflection; reflect on, ponder over	Lesson one
sīkōng-jiànguàn	司空见惯	司空見慣	idiom	accustomed to seeing sth.	Lesson fourteen
sīwéi	思维	思維	n/v	thinking, thought; think	Lesson seven
sīxià	私下		adv	in private, privately	Lesson ten
sīxiǎng	思想		n	thought, thinking, idea, ideology	Lesson three
súhuà	俗话	俗話	n	common saying, proverb	Lesson four
suí	随	隨	v	go along with (some action)	Lesson eleven
suí.zhe	随着	隨著	prep	along with, in pace with, following	Lesson four
sǔnshī	损失	損失	n/v	loss, damage; lose	Lesson eleven
suǒ	锁	鎖	n/v	lock; lock	Lesson nine

拼音 T	*简体*	*繁體*	*词性*	*英文翻译*	
tà	踏		v	step on	Lesson twelve
tài.dù	态度	態度	n	attitude	Lesson six
tái//gāo	抬高		v	raise, exalt	Lesson five
tánpàn	谈判	談判	n/v	negotiation; negotiate	Lesson ten
tàntǎo	探讨	探討	v	inquire into, discuss	Lesson thirteen
tǎnyán	坦言		v	acknowledge frankly, tell honestly	Lesson twelve
tào	套		v/n/m	encase; cover, sheath; set (of . . .)	Lesson three

拼音 T	*简体*	*繁體*	*词性*	*英文翻译*	
tārén	他人		pron	other people [more formal than 别人]	Lesson one
tèdiǎn	特点	特點	n	characteristic	Lesson one
tèsè	特色		n	unique feature, distinguishing quality	Lesson eleven
tèshū	特殊		adj	special, unusual	Lesson eight
tèyǒu	特有		adj	specific to, characteristic of	Lesson two
tèzhēng	特征	特徵	n	distinctive feature, trait	Lesson eleven
tèzhì	特质	特質	n	special quality, characteristic	Lesson fourteen
tiānrán	天然		adj	natural	Lesson four
tiānshí dìlì rénhé	天时地利人和	天時地利人和	idiom	opportune time, advantageous terrain, popular support [origin: *Mencius*]	Lesson six
tiānxià	天下		n	everywhere under heaven, world, China	Lesson eight
tiáohé	调和	調和	v	mediate, reconcile	Lesson eight
tiáojié	调节	調節	v	adjust, regulate	Lesson six
tíchàng	提倡		v	advocate, promote	Lesson four
tíchū	提出		v	put forward, raise (an issue)	Lesson five
tígōng	提供		v	supply, provide, furnish	Lesson eleven
tǐmiàn	体面	體面	adj/n	[of apparel, living, line of work, etc.] decent, honorable; dignity, decency	Lesson fourteen
tímù	题目	題目	n	title, topic	Lesson five
tíngzhǐ	停止		v	stop, cease	Lesson thirteen
tǐtiē	体贴	體貼	n/v	showing consideration; be considerate	Lesson four
tǐxiàn	体现	體現	v	embody, give expression to	Lesson six
tíxǐng	提醒	提醒	v	remind, call attention to	Lesson seven
tíyì	提议	提議	n/v	proposal, suggestion, propose, suggest	Lesson fourteen
tóngbù	同步		v	synchronize, keep step with	Lesson fourteen
tōngguò	通过	通過	v/prep	pass through, get through; by means of, through	Lesson two
tǒngyī	统一	統一	adj/v	unified; unify, unite	Lesson thirteen
tǒngzhì	统治	統治	v	rule (a country), govern	Lesson four
tóu//piào	投票		v	cast vote	Lesson eight

拼音 T	*简体*	*繁體*	*词性*	*英文翻译*	
tuán	团	團	n	team, group [as in报(旅游)团]	Lesson one
tǔdì	土地		n	land, soil, territory	Lesson six
tǔháo	土豪		n	[slang] uncultured rich people, nouveau riche, local tyrant	Lesson fourteen
tuīcí	推辞	推辭	v	decline (an offer, invitation, etc.)	Lesson four
tuìxiū	退休		v	retire	Lesson two
tuō//xiǎn	脱险	脫險	v	escape danger	Lesson thirteen
tuǒxié	妥协	妥協	v	compromise, come to terms	Lesson six
tuōzhuài	拖拽		v	pull, drag [拖: drag; 拽: pull, tug at (sth.)]	Lesson thirteen
tūrán	突然		adj	sudden, abrupt, unexpected	Lesson seven

拼音 W	*简体*	*繁體*	*词性*	*英文翻译*	
wàijiào	外教		n	foreign teacher [abbr. for 外国教师]	Lesson ten
wàijiāo	外交		n	diplomacy, foreign affairs	Lesson six
wǎngmín	网民	網民	n	netizen, Internet users [网友: Internet user, cyber acquaintance]	Lesson two
wǎnhuí	挽回		v	redeem, retrieve	Lesson ten
wànwù	万物	萬物	n	all things in the universe	Lesson six
wěi.qu	委屈		v/adj	resign oneself to; feeling wronged	Lesson nine
wēibó	微博		n	micro-blog, micro-blog post [usu. refers to the Sina (新浪: Xīnlàng) micro-blog platform, http://www.weibo.com]	Lesson two
wéifǎn	违反	違反	v	violate (law, regulation, principle, etc.)	Lesson eleven
wēihài	危害		v	jeopardize, harm, endanger	Lesson one
wéihù	维护	維護	v	safeguard, defend, uphold	Lesson four
wéirén	为人	為人	v	conduct oneself	Lesson thirteen

拼音 W	*简体*	*繁體*	*词性*	*英文翻译*	
wěiwǎn	委婉		adj	tactful, indirect, euphemistic	Lesson ten
Wēixìn	微信			WeChat, Chinese multi-purpose messaging, social media and mobile payment APP developed and first released in 2011 by Tencent [腾讯: Téngxùn] [http://www.wechat.com] [微信群: WeChat group]	Lesson three
wěndìng	稳定	穩定	adj/v	stable, steady; stabilize	Lesson eleven
wù//diǎn	误点	誤點	v	[of means of public transportation] be behind schedule, be delayed	Lesson thirteen
wúbù	无不	無不	adv	without exception, invariably	Lesson ten
wúfǎ	无法	無法	v	unable to, cannot	Lesson three
wùhuì	误会	誤會	n/v	misunderstanding; misunderstand	Lesson seven
wùjiě	误解	誤解	n/v	misunderstanding; misunderstand	Lesson five
Wūkèlán	乌克兰	烏克蘭		Ukraine	Lesson eight
wúqíng	无情	無情	n/adj	lack of compassion; compassionless, pitiless, heartless	Lesson thirteen
wúshù	无数	無數	adj	innumerable, countless	Lesson three
wúsuǒwèi	无所谓	無所謂	v	not to matter, be indifferent	Lesson two
wùtǐ	物体	物體	n	object	Lesson nine
wúzhī	无知	無知	n/adj	ignorance; ignorant	Lesson ten
wùzhì	物质	物質	adj/n	materialistic; material, matter	Lesson nine

拼音 X	*简体*	*繁體*	*词性*	*英文翻译*	
Xī Zhōu	西周			Western Zhou Dynasty (1046–771 BC)	Lesson four
xià .bu lái tái	下不来台	下不來臺	phr	in an awkward situation that is hard to escape from [下台: get off the stage]	Lesson ten
xià xiàngqí	下象棋		phr	play Chinese chess	Lesson one

拼音 X	*简体*	*繁體*	*词性*	*英文翻译*	
Xiàmén	厦门	廈門		sub-provincial city in Fujian, a.k.a. Amoy	Lesson one
xiǎn.de	显得	顯得	v	seem, look, appear	Lesson four
xiàng	向		prep	to, towards	Lesson one
xiāngchǔ	相处	相處	v	get along [共处: co-exist]	Lesson six
xiāngdāngyú	相当于	相當於	phr	be equivalent to	Lesson twelve
xiāngduì	相对	相對	adj	relative [绝(jué)对: absolute]	Lesson six
xiāngfǎn	相反		adj	contrary, opposite	Lesson one
xiǎngfāng-shèfǎ	想方设法	想方設法	idiom	try every means, leave no stone unturned	Lesson nine
xiāngguān	相关	相關	adj/v	related, relevant; be interrelated	Lesson ten
xiānghù	相互		adj/adv	mutual; mutually, reciprocally	Lesson three
xiānglián	相连	相聯	v	be interrelated	Lesson twelve
xiǎngshòu	享受		v	enjoy	Lesson one
xiángxì	详细	詳細	adj	detailed, in detail	Lesson one
xiāngyìng	相应	相應	v	corresponding; act in response	Lesson fourteen
xiàngzhēng	象征	象徵	n/v	symbol, emblem; symbolize	Lesson six
xiànshí	现实	現實	n/adj	reality; realistic	Lesson thirteen
xiǎnshì	显示	顯示	v	show, demonstrate, manifest	Lesson twelve
xiāntiān	先天		adj/n	inborn, innate; being inborn, innateness	Lesson four
xiànxiàng	现象	現象	n	phenomenon	Lesson two
xiāofèi	消费	消費	v	consume	Lesson two
xiàohua	笑话	笑話	n/v	joke; laugh at	Lesson one
xiǎopǐn	小品		n	skit, short act	Lesson nine
xiàshǔ	下属	下屬	n	subordinate	Lesson fourteen
xiàyì.shí	下意识	下意識	adv/n	subconsciously; subconscious mind	Lesson thirteen
xǐhào	喜好		n/v	preference, fondness; love, like, be fond of	Lesson eight

拼音 X	*简体*	*繁體*	*词性*	*英文翻译*	
Xīlà	希腊	希臘		Greece	Lesson three
Xīn Jīng Bào	新京报	新京報		*The Beijing News* [http://www.bjnews.com.cn/]	Lesson eleven
xìng	性		bf	nature, property, attribute [can be used as a suffix, corresponding to -ness or -ity to form a noun, as in 合法性, 准确性, etc.]	Lesson two
xíngchéng	形成		v	form, develop into, take shape	Lesson eleven
xìnggé	性格		n	character, temperament	Lesson nine
xíngrén	行人		n	pedestrian	Lesson two
xíngróng	形容		v	describe	Lesson nine
xíngwéi	行为	行為	n	behavior, conduct, action	Lesson one
xíngxiàng	形象		adj/n	(description or portrayal) true to life; image	Lesson two
xīnlǐ	心理		n	mentality, psychology	Lesson two
xīnpíng-qìhé	心平气和	心平氣和	idiom	even-tempered and good-humored	Lesson six
xìnxī	信息		n	information, message	Lesson nine
xìtǒng	系统	系統	n/adj	system; systematic	Lesson eleven
xiūyǎng	修养	修養	n	self-cultivation	Lesson four
xuàn//fù	炫富		v	flaunt wealth	Lesson eight
xuǎnzé	选择	選擇	n/v	choice, option; choose, select	Lesson one
xǔduō	许多	許多	adj	many, a lot of	Lesson two
xué.wen	学问	學問	n	learning, knowledge, scholarship [classifier: 门]	Lesson ten
xuèyè	血液		n	blood	Lesson eight
xuèyuán	血缘	血緣	n	consanguinity, ties of blood	Lesson eleven
xuézhě	学者	學者	n	scholar, learned person	Lesson three
xùn//huà	训话	訓話	v	admonish (subordinates)	Lesson fourteen
xùnchì	训斥	訓斥	v	reprimand, rebuke, berate	Lesson fourteen
xūqiú	需求		n	demand, request, requirement	Lesson twelve

拼音 Y	*简体*	*繁體*	*词性*	*英文翻译*	*Y*
Yà Tài	亚太	亞太		Asia-Pacific [亚洲: Asia; 太平洋: Pacific Ocean]	Lesson seven
yán'gé	严格	嚴格	adj	strict, rigorous	Lesson fourteen
yǎnbiàn	演变	演變	v	evolve, develop	Lesson six
Yāngshì	央视	央視		CCTV [short for 中国中央电视台, China Central Television]	Lesson nine
yǎngyù	养育	養育	v	rear (child), bring up	Lesson eleven
yánlùn	言论	言論	n	remarks, views, open discussion	Lesson thirteen
yǎnqiú	眼球		n	eyeball, [fig.] attention	Lesson nine
yánsù	严肃	嚴肅	adj	serious, solemn	Lesson seven
yántīng-jìcóng	言听计从	言聽計從	idiom	always follow sb.'s advice, act upon whatever sb. says	Lesson fourteen
yánxù	延续	延續	v	continue, last	Lesson twelve
yǎnyuán	演员	演員	n	actor	Lesson three
yào.shi	钥匙	鑰匙	n	key [classifier: 把]	Lesson nine
Yàsè Shǐmìsī	亚瑟•史密斯	亞瑟•史密斯		Arthur Henderson Smith (1845–1932), Chinese name 明恩溥 (Míng Ēnpǔ), a missionary of the American Board of Commissioners for Foreign Missions. His *Chinese Characteristics* (1894) was the most widely read book on China by foreigners living in the country through the 1920s.	Lesson nine
yāsuìqián	压岁钱	壓歲錢	n	lunar New Year gift money given to children for luck and good health	Lesson eleven
yèwù	业务	業務	n	business, service	Lesson ten
yèyuán	业缘	業緣	n	affinity due to work or line of business	Lesson thirteen
Yì Zhōngtiān	易中天			a Chinese historian, scholar and TV personality, author of 《闲话中国人》 [闲话 xiánhuà: talk casually about]	Lesson one
yì.shí	意识	意識	n	consciousness [群体意识: group-oriented consciousness]	Lesson one

拼音 Y	*简体*	*繁體*	*词性*	*英文翻译*	*Y*
yǐbiàn	以便		conj	so as to, so that, with the aim of	Lesson twelve
yídàn	一旦		adv	if one day (something happens)	Lesson seven
yídìng	一定		adj/adv	a certain (extent), given; definitely, surely	Lesson two
yíhàn	遗憾	遺憾	adj/n	regretful; regret, pity	Lesson six
yǐhé-wéiguì	以和为贵	以和為貴	idiom	regard harmony as the most important [和 (n): harmony; 贵 (bf): highly valued]	Lesson six
yǐjí	以及		conj	as well as, and [more formal than 还有]	Lesson four
yǐjǐ-duórén	以己度人		idiom	place oneself in another's position, judge others by oneself	Lesson seven
yìjiàn	意见	意見	n	opinion, suggestion, complaint	Lesson ten
yílǜ	一律		adv	without exception	Lesson eight
yǐnfā	引发	引發	v	trigger, evoke	Lesson thirteen
yìng.chou	应酬	應酬	v/n	take part in social networking activities; networking activities	Lesson twelve
yíngdé	赢得		v	win	Lesson nine
yǐnqǐ	引起		v	give rise to, lead to	Lesson two
yīnsù	因素		n	factor, element	Lesson nine
yíqiè	一切		pron	all, everything	Lesson eight
yíwèi	一味		adv	blindly, stubbornly	Lesson fourteen
yìwù	义务	義務	n/adj	duty, obligation; mandatory, voluntary	Lesson fourteen
yíxià.zi	一下子		n	a short while	Lesson seven
yíxìliè	一系列		adj	a series of	Lesson thirteen
yìyántáng	一言堂		n	hall of one person's speech [堂(bf): hall], what sb. says goes, deciding everything by one man's say	Lesson fourteen
yìyì	意义	意義	n	meaning, significance	Lesson nine
yǐzhìyú	以至于	以至於	conj	to such an extent as to, so much so that	Lesson twelve

拼音 Y	*简体*	*繁體*	*词性*	*英文翻译*	*Y*
yōngrén	佣人	傭人	n	family servant	Lesson fourteen
yòngyú	用于	用於	v	use in/on [于: more formal than "在……上/中"]	Lesson eight
yóu	由		prep	by, from	Lesson three
yǒuqù	有趣		adj	intriguing	Lesson one
yǒuxiàn	有限		adj	limited, finite [无(wú)限: unlimited, infinite]	Lesson six
yǒuyì	友谊	友誼	n	friendship	Lesson eleven
yóuyú	由于	由於	conj/prep	due to, thanks to, owing to, as a result of	Lesson three
yóuyù	犹豫	猶豫	adj	hesitant	Lesson one
yǔ	与	與	conj	and [more formal than 和 and 跟]	Lesson one
yuán	员	員	bf	member [as in 一员, a member]	Lesson one
yuán.fèn	缘分	緣分	n	predestined affinity or relationship, fateful coincidence	Lesson one
yuángōng	员工	員工	n	employee, staff	Lesson ten
yuányú	源于	源於	phr	stem from, has (its) origin in	Lesson thirteen
yuányuǎn-liúcháng	源远流长	源遠流長	idiom	[of tradition, history, etc.] go back to the distant past, long-standing and well-established	Lesson six
yuánzé	原则	原則	n	principle	Lesson six
yuē	约	約	v	make an appointment (with someone)	Lesson one
yuēdìng-súchéng	约定俗成	約定俗成	idiom	established by popular usage, customary convention	Lesson four
yuēshù	约束	約束	n/v	restriction; restrain, bind	Lesson eleven
yúkuài	愉快		adj	pleasant, joyful	Lesson seven
yùnyíng	运营	運營	n/v	operation; operate	Lesson ten
yùnzuò	运作	運作	n/v	operation [面子运作: face operation, face work]; operate	Lesson ten
yùxí	遇袭	遇襲	v	suffer attack, be assaulted	Lesson thirteen

拼音 Z	*简体*	*繁體*	*词性*	*英文翻译*	
zàiyú	在于	在於	v	lie in, rest with, depend on	Lesson six
zàntóng	赞同	贊同	v/n	approve of, agree with, endorse; approval, endorsement	Lesson eight
zàochéng	造成		v	bring about, cause	Lesson two
zàofú	造福		v	bring benefit to (society, people, things, etc.)	Lesson six
zèngsòng	赠送	贈送	v	present as a gift	Lesson four
zhàcài ròusī tāng	榨菜肉丝汤	榨菜肉絲湯		pickled mustard tuber and shredded pork soup	Lesson one
zhàn	占	佔	v	constitute, make up, account for	Lesson twelve
zhǎng	长	長	bf	chief, head [校长: headmaster, (university) president; 局长júzhǎng: bureau chief]	Lesson three
Zhànguó	战国	戰國		Warring States Period (475–221 BC)	Lesson four
zhǎngwò	掌握		v	master	Lesson nine
zhǎngyòu	长幼	長幼	n	the senior and the young, seniority by age [长 (bf): senior, old; 幼 (bf): young, under age]	Lesson fourteen
zhǎnshì	展示		v	reveal, display, show, exhibit	Lesson six
zhànyǒu	战友	戰友	n	comrade-in-arms	Lesson three
zhèng	正		adv	precisely	Lesson six
zhēng	争		v	contend, vie for, strive for [与…… 相争: contend with ...]	Lesson six
zhèngcháng	正常		adj	normal	Lesson nine
zhēngchǎo	争吵	爭吵	v	quarrel, dispute, argue	Lesson seven
zhènghǎo	正好		adj/adv	just right; precisely	Lesson eight
zhèngmíng	证明	證明	v/n	prove; proof	Lesson ten
zhēngqiú	征求	徵求	v	seek (opinions, feedback, etc.)	Lesson ten
zhěngtǐ	整体	整體	n	entirety, whole entity, synthesis	Lesson three

拼音 Z	*简体*	*繁體*	*词性*	*英文翻译*	
zhēngyì	争议	爭議	n/v	controversy; dispute	Lesson two
zhèngzhì	政治		n	politics, political affairs	Lesson ten
zhēnlǐ	真理		n	truth	Lesson eight
zhēnshí	真实	真實	adj	true, real	Lesson seven
zhéxué	哲学	哲學	n	philosophy	Lesson six
zhèyàng shuōlái	这样说来	這樣說來	phr	putting it this way, if so	Lesson five
zhì	治		v	rule, govern [礼治: rule of the rites; 法治: rule of law; 治理: govern, administer]	Lesson four
zhǐ	指		v	refer to, point at; finger	Lesson two
zhī	之		pron	[only in object position; formal] it, him, her, this	Lesson one
zhí//.dé	值得		v	merit, be worthy of	Lesson nine
zhīēn-túbào	知恩图报	知恩圖報	idiom	be grateful for a kind act and seek ways to repay it [恩 or恩情: favor, kindness] [图: seek] [报 or 报答: repay]	Lesson eleven
zhífǎ	执法	執法	v	enforce the law	Lesson fourteen
zhìhuì	智慧		n	wisdom	Lesson eight
zhíjiē	直接		adj	direct [间接 (jiànjiē): indirect]	Lesson nine
zhìjīn	至今		adv	to this day, up until now, as yet	Lesson six
zhīpèi	支配		v	dominate, control, allocate	Lesson thirteen
zhīshǐ	支使		v	order sb. around	Lesson fourteen
zhíwèi	职位	職位	n	position, post	Lesson three
zhìxù	秩序		n	order, sequence	Lesson eight
zhíyè	职业	職業	n	profession, occupation, vocation	Lesson three
zhìyí	质疑	質疑	v	call into question, question (truth or validity)	Lesson fourteen
zhīyù	知遇		v	recognize someone's worth	Lesson eleven

拼音 Z	*简体*	*繁體*	*词性*	*英文翻译*	
Zhōngguó Gāoxiào Chuánméi Liánméng	中国高校传媒联盟	中國高校傳媒聯盟		China University Media Union, formed by *China Youth Daily* [《中国青年报》] and 63 leading Chinese universities to share university information resources, communicate between university media, and serve the university students [高校: short for高等院校 (higher-ed institution); 传媒: short for 传播媒体 (传播chuánbō: disseminate, propagate; 媒体méitǐ: media); 联盟: alliance, coalition]	Lesson twelve
zhōngjiānrén	中间人	中間人	n	mediator, middleman	Lesson eight
zhòngshì	重视	重視	v	attach importance to, take . . . seriously	Lesson one
zhòngsuǒzhōuzhī	众所周知	眾所周知	idiom	as everybody knows, as it is known	Lesson nine
Zhōngyōng	《中庸》			*The Doctrine of the Mean*, one of the Four Books of the Confucian philosophy. Originally published as a chapter in the *Classic of Rites*, the text is attributed to Zisi or Kong Ji, the grandson of Confucius.	Lesson eight
zhōngyōng zhī dào	中庸之道		idiom	the golden mean (of the Confucian school) [中庸: Mean; 道: the Way]	Lesson eight
zhǒngzú	种族	種族	n	race	Lesson ten
zhōulǐ	周礼	周禮	n	the rites of Western Zhou Dynasty	Lesson four
zhōuwéi	周围	周圍	n	vicinity, surroundings	Lesson two
zhǔ suí kè biàn	主随客便	主隨客便	phr	As a host, one does as the guest thinks fit. [主随客便 is a spinoff of the idiom 客随主便 (As a guest, one should do as the host thinks fit.)]	Lesson one

拼音 Z	*简体*	*繁體*	*词性*	*英文翻译*	
zhuǎnbiàn	转变	轉變	n/v	transformation; transform	Lesson fourteen
zhuǎnfā	转发	轉發	v	forward (mail, SMS, etc.), repost (tweet, online post, etc.)	Lesson two
zhuàngtài	状态	狀態	n	state (of affairs), status, condition	Lesson twelve
zhúbù	逐步		adv	progressively, step by step	Lesson fourteen
zhuīqiú	追求		v	pursue, seek after	Lesson two
zhuīsù	追溯		v	be traced back to, date back to	Lesson four
zhújiàn	逐渐	逐漸	adv	gradually	Lesson twelve
zhùmíng	著名		adj	renowned, celebrated	Lesson eleven
zhuóxiǎng	着想	著想	v	consider, give thought (to . . .) [为……着想: be considerate towards . . .]	Lesson five
zhǔréngōng	主人公		n	protagonist	Lesson nine
zhūrú-cǐlèi	诸如此类	諸如此類	idiom	things like this, and so on	Lesson thirteen
zhǔxí	主席		n	chairperson	Lesson ten
zhǔyào	主要		adj	main, principal, chief, major	Lesson three
zhǔyì	主义	主義	n	-ism [as in 集体主义: collectivism; 个人主义: individualism; 社会主义: socialism]	Lesson three
zhǔzhāng	主张	主張	v/n	advocate, maintain; proposition, position	Lesson six
zhùzhòng	注重		v	emphasize, lay stress on	Lesson seven
zìgǔ	自古		adv	since ancient times	Lesson six
zìjǐ-zìzú	自给自足	自給自足	idiom	self-sufficient; maintain self-sufficiency	Lesson eleven
zìpán	字盘	字盤	n	type case	Lesson six
zìqiān	自谦	自謙	v/adj	humble oneself; self-effacing, self-deprecating	Lesson five
zìrán	自然		n/adj	nature, natural world; natural	Lesson six
zìshǐ-zhìzhōng	自始至终	自始至終	idiom	from start to finish, from beginning to end	Lesson fourteen

拼音 Z	简体	繁體	词性	英文翻译	
zìtǐ	字体	字體	n	calligraphic style, typeface, font	Lesson six
zìwèi	自卫	自衛	v	defend oneself [卫: 保卫, defend]	Lesson thirteen
zìxiāng-máodùn	自相矛盾		idiom	contradict oneself; self-contradictory	Lesson thirteen
zìyóu	自由		n/adj	freedom, liberty; free, unrestrained	Lesson one
zīyuán	资源	資源	n	resources	Lesson six
zōngfǎ	宗法		n	patriarchal clan system	Lesson thirteen
zǒngjié	总结	總結	v/n	summarize, sum up; summary	Lesson nine
zòngxiàng	纵向	縱向	adj	lengthwise, vertical, longitudinal	Lesson fourteen
zǒngzhī	总之	總之	conj	in a word; in short	Lesson three
zǒu hòumén	走后门	走後門	phr	get in the rear door, secure sth. through pulling relationships/ connections	Lesson twelve
zǔchéng	组成	組成	v	form, make up, constitute	Lesson three
zūnbēi	尊卑		n	superiors and inferiors [尊(bf): respect, respectability; 卑(bf): low, inferior]	Lesson thirteen
zūnjìng	尊敬		n/v	respect; respect, revere	Lesson four
zūnróng	尊荣	尊榮	n	dignity and honor	Lesson nine
zūnshǒu	遵守		v	abide by, observe	Lesson six
zūnxún	遵循		v	follow, abide by, comply with	Lesson four
zūnzhòng	尊重		v/n	respect; respect, esteem, honor	Lesson ten
zuò//kè	做客		v	be a guest	Lesson four
zuò//zhǔ	做主		v	making the decision, be in charge	Lesson fourteen
zuòrén	做人		v	conduct oneself (according to li), behave with integrity	Lesson four
zuòwéi	作为	作為	prep/v	as; regard as, take for	Lesson eight
zuòyòng	作用		n	function, effect	Lesson six
zǔzhī	组织	組織	n/v	organization; organize	Lesson fourteen

English-Chinese vocabulary

英文翻译 A	*简体*	*繁體*	*拼音*	*词性*	
a certain (extent), given; definitely, surely	一定		yídìng	adj/adv	Lesson two
a Chinese historian, scholar and TV personality, author of 《闲话中国人》 [闲话 xiánhuà: talk casually about]	易中天		Yì Zhōngtiān		Lesson one
a feeling; experience, feel	感受		gǎnshòu	n/v	Lesson seven
a matter of no concern to oneself	事不关己	事不關己	shìbùguānjǐ	idiom	Lesson thirteen
a portal website in Chinese, primarily serving Chinese living in North America [https://www.backchina.com; 倍: times;]	倍可亲	倍可親	Bèikěqīn		Lesson fourteen
a series of	一系列		yíxìliè	adj	Lesson thirteen
a short while	一下子		yíxià.zi	n	Lesson seven
A tall tree catches the wind. / A prominent person attracts attention [i.e., criticism].	树大招风	樹大招風	shùdà-zhāofēng	idiom	Lesson eight
abide by, observe	遵守		zūnshǒu	v	Lesson six
able to do sth. in time [来不及: unable to do sth. in time]	来得及	來得及	lái.dejí	v	Lesson two
abstain from voting; abstention	弃权	棄權	qì//quán	v/n	Lesson eight
accelerate, promote	促进	促進	cùjìn	v	Lesson eleven
accept, receive	接受		jiēshòu	v	Lesson four
according to, in accordance with	按照		ànzhào	prep	Lesson one

英文翻译 A	*简体*	*繁體*	*拼音*	*词性*	
accustomed to seeing sth.	司空见惯	司空見慣	sīkōng-jiànguàn	idiom	Lesson fourteen
acknowledge frankly, tell honestly	坦言		tǎnyán	v	Lesson twelve
acquaintance [生人: stranger]	熟人		shúrén	n	Lesson six
actor	演员	演員	yǎnyuán	n	Lesson three
address, call	称	稱	chēng	v	Lesson four
address, call; form of address, appellation	称呼	稱呼	chēng.hu	v/n	Lesson three
[address for father's eldest brother] [polite address for an elderly man]	大伯		dàbó	n	Lesson three
adjust, regulate	调节	調節	tiáojié	v	Lesson six
admittedly, it's true that	固然		gùrán	conj	Lesson ten
admonish (subordinates)	训话	訓話	xùn//huà	v	Lesson fourteen
adopt	采纳	採納	cǎinà	v	Lesson ten
adopt	采取	採取	cǎiqǔ	v	Lesson seven
advocate, maintain; proposition, position	主张	主張	zhǔzhāng	v/n	Lesson six
advocate, promote	提倡		tíchàng	v	Lesson four
affable, genial	和蔼可亲	和藹可親	hé'ǎi kěqīn	idiom	Lesson six
affinity due to work or line of business	业缘	業緣	yèyuán	n	Lesson thirteen
agriculture, farming	农业	農業	nóngyè	n	Lesson three
all things in the universe	万物	萬物	wànwù	n	Lesson six
all, everything	一切		yíqiè	pron	Lesson eight
along with, in pace with, following	随着	隨著	suí.zhe	prep	Lesson four
always follow sb.'s advice, act upon whatever sb. says	言听计从	言聽計從	yántīng-jìcóng	idiom	Lesson fourteen
ancient times, antiquity	古代		gǔdài	n	Lesson three
and [more formal than 和 and 跟]	与	與	yǔ	conj	Lesson one
and, besides, moreover	并且	並且	bìngqiě	conj	Lesson seven
anthropology [人类: mankind; 人类学家: anthropologist]	人类学	人類學	rénlèixué	n	Lesson nine

英文翻译 A	*简体*	*繁體*	*拼音*	*词性*	
anxiety; anxious	焦虑	焦慮	jiāolǜ	n/adj	Lesson twelve
any	任何		rènhé	pron	Lesson eight
anyway, anyhow, in any case, under whatever circumstances	反正		fǎn.zhèng	adv	Lesson one
apologize	道歉		dào//qiàn	v	Lesson seven
apparel, attire	穿着	穿著	chuānzhuó	n	Lesson fourteen
appear, emerge	出现	出現	chūxiàn	v	Lesson two
appraise, evaluate; evaluation	评价	評價	píngjià	v/n	Lesson nine
appropriate, moderate	适中	適中	shìzhōng	adj	Lesson eight
approve of	认可	認可	rènkě	v	Lesson two
approve of, agree with, endorse; approval, endorsement	赞同	贊同	zàntóng	v/n	Lesson eight
apt to happen [usu. of something undesirable], frequently, happening at the slightest provocation	动不动	動不動	dòng.budòng	adv	Lesson fourteen
arise, come in being	产生	產生	chǎnshēng	v	Lesson two
Arthur Henderson Smith (1845-1932), Chinese name 明恩溥 (Míng Ēnpǔ), a missionary of the American Board of Commissioners for Foreign Missions. His *Chinese Characteristics* (1894) was the most widely read book on China by foreigners living in the country through the 1920s.	亚瑟•史密斯	亞瑟•史密斯	Yàsè Shǐmìsī		Lesson nine
As a host, one does as the guest thinks fit. [主随客便 is a spinoff of the idiom 客随主便 (As a guest, one should do as the host thinks fit.)]	主随客便	主隨客便	zhǔ suí kè biàn	phr	Lesson one
as above [如上所述: as stated above]	如上		rúshàng	v	Lesson twelve

英文翻译 A	简体	繁體	拼音	词性	
as everybody knows, as it is known	众所周知	眾所周知	zhòngsuǒzhōuzhī	idiom	Lesson nine
as well as, and [more formal than 还有]	以及		yǐjí	conj	Lesson four
as; regard as, take for	作为	作為	zuòwéi	prep/v	Lesson eight
Asia-Pacific [亚洲: Asia; 太平洋: Pacific Ocean]	亚太	亞太	Yà Tài		Lesson seven
associate (with), have dealings (with)	交往		jiāowǎng	v	Lesson three
astonished, shocked	惊讶	驚訝	jīngyà	adj	Lesson fourteen
at present	目前		mùqián	n	Lesson three
attach importance to, take . . . seriously	重视	重視	zhòngshì	v	Lesson one
attitude	态度	態度	tài.dù	n	Lesson six
audience, spectators	观众	觀眾	guānzhòng	n	Lesson six
avoid as a taboo, abstain from; taboo	忌讳	忌諱	jìhuì	v/n	Lesson eleven
avoid, avert, refrain from	避免		bìmiǎn	v	Lesson seven

英文翻译 B	简体	繁體	拼音	词性	
B.C. [公元: A.D.]	公元前		gōngyuán qián	n	Lesson four
back, rear	背后	背後	bèihòu	n	Lesson eleven
background, backdrop	背景		bèijǐng	n	Lesson seven
balanced; equilibrium, balance; balance	平衡		pínghéng	adj/n/v	Lesson six
based on; base . . . on; basis	根据	根據	gēnjù	prep/v/n	Lesson nine
basically, primarily	基本上		jīběn.shàng	adv	Lesson eight
be a guest	做客		zuò//kè	v	Lesson four
be able to	得以		déyǐ	v	Lesson twelve
[of means of public transportation] be behind schedule, be delayed	误点	誤點	wù//diǎn	v	Lesson thirteen
be brimming/permeated with	充满	充滿	chōngmǎn	v	Lesson eleven
be busy with [more formal than 忙着]	忙于	忙於	mángyú	v	Lesson twelve

英文翻译 B	*简体*	*繁體*	*拼音*	*词性*	
be conciliatory, exercise forbearance	忍让	忍讓	rěnràng	v	Lesson six
be difficult to	难以	難以	nányǐ	v	Lesson fourteen
be eager to [more formal than 急着]	急于	急於	jíyú	v	Lesson twelve
be equivalent to	相当于	相當於	xiāngdāngyú	phr	Lesson twelve
be grateful for a kind act and seek ways to repay it [恩 or恩情: favor, kindness] [图: seek] [报 or 报答: repay]	知恩图报	知恩圖報	zhīēn-túbào	idiom	Lesson eleven
be grateful, appreciate	感激		gǎnjī	v	Lesson ten
be in charge of, take responsibility for; [负责人: person in charge]	负责	負責	fùzé	v	Lesson seven
be interrelated	相连	相聯	xiānglián	v	Lesson twelve
be interviewed	受访	受訪	shòufǎng	v	Lesson twelve
be limited to, be constrained by	受限于	受限於	shòuxiànyú	phr	Lesson thirteen
be on an equal footing, be on equal terms	平起平坐		píngqǐ-píngzuò	idiom	Lesson fourteen
be particular about, pay special attention to; exquisite, tasteful	讲究	講究	jiǎng.jiu	v/adj	Lesson four
be popular, be in fashion, spread widely	风行	風行	fēngxíng	v	Lesson twelve
be situated at, be in a position of [所处的时代: the era that people live in]	处	處	chǔ	v	Lesson nine
be stupefied, be distracted	愣		lèng	v	Lesson seven
be surprised, be shocked	吃惊	吃驚	chī//jīng	v	Lesson five
be the same as, be precisely [more formal than 就是]; namely	即		jí	v/adv	Lesson two
be traced back to, date back to	追溯		zhuīsù	v	Lesson four
become sworn brothers/ sisters	结义	結義	jiéyì	v	Lesson fourteen
befriend, make friends with	结交	結交	jiéjiāo	v	Lesson twelve
begin an undertaking, start a venture	创业	創業	chuàngyè	v	Lesson ten

英文翻译 B	*简体*	*繁體*	*拼音*	*词性*	
behavior, conduct, action	行为	行為	xíngwéi	n	Lesson one
belittle, disparage, play down	贬低	貶低	biǎndī	v	Lesson five
belong to, be part of	属于	屬於	shǔyú	v	Lesson thirteen
benefit from, be the beneficial result of	得益于	得益於	déyìyú	phr	Lesson ten
benefit, (someone's) interest	利益		lìyì	n	Lesson one
Benz [brand], gallop	奔驰	奔馳	Bēnchí		Lesson fourteen
blindly, stubbornly	一味		yíwèi	adv	Lesson fourteen
blog post	博文		bówén	n	Lesson five
blood	血液		xuèyè	n	Lesson eight
BMW [brand], precious horse	宝马	寶馬	Bǎomǎ		Lesson fourteen
board a plane	登机	登機	dēng//jī	v	Lesson thirteen
board of directors [董事: board member] [董事长: chairman of board]	董事会	董事會	dǒngshìhuì	n	Lesson ten
both sides, the two parties [对方: other side, opposite side, counterpart]	双方	雙方	shuāngfāng	n	Lesson four
bring about, cause	造成		zàochéng	v	Lesson two
bring benefit to (society, people, things, etc.)	造福		zàofú	v	Lesson six
bringing out implicit or innate qualities; bring into play	发挥	發揮	fāhuī	n/v	Lesson twelve
broadcast, transmit	播放		bōfàng	v	Lesson two
business affairs	商务	商務	shāngwù	n	Lesson ten
business, service	业务	業務	yèwù	n	Lesson ten
by all means	千万	千萬	qiānwàn	adv	Lesson ten
by force	强行	強行	qiángxíng	adv	Lesson thirteen
(praise or criticize sb.) by name; call roll	点名	點名	diǎn//míng	v	Lesson fourteen
by oneself	独自	獨自	dúzì	adv	Lesson one
by, from	由		yóu	prep	Lesson three

英文翻译 C	*简体*	*繁體*	*拼音*	*词性*	
call for help	呼救		hūjiù	v	Lesson thirteen
call into question, question (truth or validity)	质疑	質疑	zhìyí	v	Lesson fourteen
calligraphic style, typeface, font	字体	字體	zìtǐ	n	Lesson six
Camry [Toyota automobile model; 凯: victorious; 瑞: auspicious]	凯美瑞	凱美瑞	Kǎiměiruì		Lesson fourteen
careful and strict calculation, meticulous planning and careful accounting	精打细算	精打細算	jīngdǎ-xìsuàn	idiom	Lesson twelve
carry on one's back or shoulder(s)	背		bēi	v	Lesson one
carry out, execute	进行	進行	jìnxíng	v	Lesson ten
case for study	案例		ànlì	n	Lesson ten
cashier [收: collect, receive; 银 (bf): silver (referring to money here)]	收银员	收銀員	shōuyínyuán	n	Lesson five
cast vote	投票		tóu//piào	v	Lesson eight
cause a great sensation	轰动	轟動	hōngdòng	v	Lesson eight
(intentions, plans, things) cause (a result) [more formal than 让]	使得		shǐ.de	v	Lesson nine
cause, make (something to happen) [more formal than 让 and 使]	令		lìng	v	Lesson six
CCTV [short for 中国中央电视台, China Central Television]	央视	央視	Yāngshì		Lesson nine
century	世纪	世紀	shìjì	n	Lesson eight
chairperson	主席		zhǔxí	n	Lesson ten
character, temperament	性格		xìnggé	n	Lesson nine
characteristic	特点	特點	tèdiǎn	n	Lesson one
chat about domestic trivia	拉家常		lā jiācháng	phr	Lesson one
chicken egg *foo young* [芙蓉: hibiscus]	芙蓉鸡片	芙蓉雞片	fúróng jī piàn		Lesson one
chief, head [校长: headmaster, (university) president; 局长 júzhǎng: bureau chief]	长	長	zhǎng	bf	Lesson three

英文翻译 C	简体	繁體	拼音	词性	
China University Media Union, formed by *China Youth Daily* [《中国青年报》] and 63 leading Chinese universities to share university information resources, communicate between university media, and serve the university students [高校: short for 高等院校 (higher-ed institution); 传媒: short for 传播媒体 (传播chuánbō: disseminate, propagate; 媒体méitǐ: media); 联盟: alliance, coalition]	中国高校传媒联盟	中國高校傳媒聯盟	Zhōngguó Gāoxiào Chuánméi Liánméng		Lesson twelve
Chinese New Year's eve gala [short for 春节联欢晚会]	春晚		chūnwǎn	n	Lesson nine
Chinese translation of Deloitte, a company that provides accounting and consulting services [德: virtue; 勤: diligence]	德勤		Déqín		Lesson seven
choice, option; choose, select	选择	選擇	xuǎnzé	n/v	Lesson one
Chongqing Morning Post, a local newspaper in the city of Chongqing [晨 (bf): morning]	重庆晨报	重慶晨報	Chóngqìng Chén Bào		Lesson twelve
Chongqing or Chungking, a direct-controlled municipality under China's central government	重庆	重慶	Chóngqìng		Lesson two
circle	圈子		quān.zi	n	Lesson three
civilities, polite formula	客套		kètào	n	Lesson four
clan, family	家族		jiāzú	n	Lesson eleven
clash; conflict	冲突	衝突	chōngtū	n/v	Lesson six
classics, canons; classical	经典	經典	jīngdiǎn	n/adj	Lesson eight
clearly demarcated, distinct; evidently	分明		fēnmíng	adj/adv	Lesson fourteen
close friend, buddy	密友		mìyǒu	n	Lesson twelve
cold, indifferent	冷淡		lěngdàn	adj	Lesson five
coldness and indifference; cold and indifferent	冷漠		lěngmò	n/adj	Lesson thirteen

英文翻译 C	*简体*	*繁體*	*拼音*	*词性*	
collaboration; collaborate, cooperate	合作		hézuò	n/v	Lesson three
collect information and report (to an authoritarian figure)	汇报	匯報	huìbào	v	Lesson ten
color, hue	色彩		sècǎi	n	Lesson nine
come into contact with	接触	接觸	jiēchù	v	Lesson fourteen
comment on; comments	评论	評論	pínglùn	v/n	Lesson two
commerce, trade, business	商业	商業	shāngyè	n	Lesson three
commit [犯错误: commit an error, make a mistake, 犯罪 (zuì): commit a crime, 犯法: break the law]	犯		fàn	v	Lesson ten
common saying, popular saying	口头禅	口頭禪	kǒutóuchán	n	Lesson twelve
common saying, proverb	俗话	俗話	súhuà	n	Lesson four
communicate	沟通	溝通	gōutōng	v	Lesson seven
complain, grumble	抱怨		bào.yuàn	v	Lesson two
complete, all present	齐	齊	qí	adj	Lesson one
complicated, complex	复杂	複雜	fùzá	adj	Lesson nine
compromise, come to terms	妥协	妥協	tuǒxié	v	Lesson six
comrade-in-arms	战友	戰友	zhànyǒu	n	Lesson three
concept, notion	概念		gàiniàn	n	Lesson eleven
concept, notion, idea	理念		lǐniàn	n	Lesson eight
concrete, specific	具体	具體	jùtǐ	adj	Lesson seven
conduct oneself	为人	為人	wéirén	v	Lesson thirteen
conduct oneself (according to li), behave with integrity	做人		zuòrén	v	Lesson four
conduct oneself in society	处世	處世	chǔshì	v	Lesson ten
conform to, tally with	符合		fúhé	v	Lesson five
Confucian Philosophical School, initiated by Confucius (551–479 BC) and developed by Mencius (c. 372 – c. 289 BC)	儒家		Rújiā		Lesson four
Confucius, Chinese social philosopher and educator	孔子		Kǒngzǐ		Lesson four
connections, contacts, network	人脉	人脈	rénmài	n	Lesson twelve

英文翻译 C	*简体*	*繁體*	*拼音*	*词性*	
consanguinity, ties of blood	血缘	血緣	xuèyuán	n	Lesson eleven
consciousness [群体意识: group-oriented consciousness]	意识	意識	yì.shí	n	Lesson one
consequence, aftermath	后果	後果	hòuguǒ	n	Lesson ten
conservative	保守		bǎoshǒu	adj	Lesson eleven
consider, give thought (to . . .) [为⋯⋯ 着想: be considerate towards . . .]	着想	著想	zhuóxiǎng	v	Lesson five
constitute, make up, account for	占	佔	zhàn	v	Lesson twelve
consume	消费	消費	xiāofèi	v	Lesson two
contain, include	包含		bāohán	v	Lesson five
contend, vie for, strive for [与⋯⋯ 相争: contend with . . .]	争		zhēng	v	Lesson six
content	内容	內容	nèiróng	n	Lesson four
continue	继续	繼續	jìxù	v	Lesson seven
continue, last	延续	延續	yánxù	v	Lesson twelve
contract, deed	契约	契約	qìyuē	n	Lesson four
contradict oneself; self-contradictory	自相矛盾		zìxiāng-máodùn	idiom	Lesson thirteen
contradiction; contradictory	矛盾		máodùn	n/adj	Lesson six
contrary, opposite	相反		xiāngfǎn	adj	Lesson one
controversy; dispute	争议	爭議	zhēngyì	n/v	Lesson two
converse	交谈	交談	jiāotán	v	Lesson seven
cordial, enthusiastic, passionate; cordialness, enthusiasm, passion	热情	熱情	rèqíng	adj/n	Lesson five
core, the heart of the matter	核心		héxīn	n	Lesson four
corresponding; act in response	相应	相應	xiāngyìng	v	Lesson fourteen
course of events, process, procedure	过程	過程	guòchéng	n	Lesson eleven
(law) court	法院		fǎyuàn	n	Lesson twelve
Courtesy demands reciprocity./ Respond in kind. [This expression has its origin in The Book of Rites.]	来而不往非礼也	來而不往非禮也	lái ér bù wǎng fēi lǐ yě		Lesson eleven

英文翻译 C	*简体*	*繁體*	*拼音*	*词性*	
courtesy, politeness, manners; polite	礼貌	禮貌	lǐmào	n/adj	Lesson one
criticize	批评	批評	pīpíng	v	Lesson two
crosswise, horizontal	横向		héngxiàng	adj	Lesson fourteen
crude in one's manners, boorish	粗鲁	粗魯	cūlǔ	adj	Lesson fourteen
cry out, yell	喊		hǎn	v	Lesson seven
cultivate, foster, breed	培育		péiyù	v	Lesson eleven
customer	顾客	顧客	gùkè	n	Lesson five

英文翻译 D	*简体*	*繁體*	*拼音*	*词性*	
Daoist School of the Warring States Period (475–221 BC) based on the teachings of Laozi or Lao Tze [老子, c. 6th century BC] and Zhuangzi or Chuang Tzu [庄子, 369–286 BC]	道家		Dàojiā		Lesson six
day-to-day, everyday	日常		rìcháng	adj	Lesson four
[of apparel, living, line of work, etc.] decent, honorable; dignity, decency	体面	體面	tǐmiàn	adj/n	Lesson fourteen
declare, aver, state formally	申明		shēnmíng	n	Lesson fourteen
decline (an offer, invitation, etc.)	推辞	推辭	tuīcí	v	Lesson four
decline and yield [辞: decline, resign, dismiss; 让: yield]	辞让	辭讓	círàng	v	Lesson four
deep-rooted, long-established, inveterate	根深蒂固		gēnshēn-dìgù	idiom	Lesson thirteen
deep, deep-seated; deep layer	深层	深層	shēncéng	adj/n	Lesson nine
deepen	加深		jiāshēn	v	Lesson eleven
defend oneself [卫: 保卫, defend]	自卫	自衛	zìwèi	v	Lesson thirteen
deliberately, purposefully	刻意		kèyì	adv	Lesson five
demand, request, requirement	需求		xūqiú	n	Lesson twelve

英文翻译 D	*简体*	*繁體*	*拼音*	*词性*	
describe	描述		miáoshù	v	Lesson two
describe	形容		xíngróng	v	Lesson nine
destroy, wreck, damage	破坏	破壞	pòhuài	v	Lesson twelve
detailed, in detail	详细	詳細	xiángxì	adj	Lesson one
determine the position, characterize (as); positioning	定位		dìng//wèi	v/n	Lesson fourteen
determine, decide firmly; definite	确定	確定	quèdìng	v/adj	Lesson three
develop, exploit (a resource)	开发	開發	kāifā	v	Lesson ten
developed	发达	發達	fādá	adj	Lesson eleven
differentiated mode of association, a term coined by Fei Xiaotong in his 《乡土中国》 [差: 差别, difference; 序: 顺序, order; 格局: pattern, structure]	差序格局		chāxù géjú	phr	Lesson thirteen
dignity and honor	尊荣	尊榮	zūnróng	n	Lesson nine
diplomacy, foreign affairs	外交		wàijiāo	n	Lesson six
direct [间接 (jiànjiē): indirect]	直接		zhíjiē	adj	Lesson nine
disciple	弟子		dìzǐ	n	Lesson six
discover, find; discovery, findings	发现	發現	fāxiàn	v/n	Lesson one
discuss passionately, heatedly debate [热: 热烈(liè), ardent, enthusiastic; 议: 议论, discuss, debate]	热议	熱議	rèyì	v	Lesson thirteen
dislike, antipathy; disgusted with	反感		fǎn'gǎn	n/adj	Lesson six
disperse a meeting	散会	散會	sàn//huì	v	Lesson ten
display, manifestation; show, display	表现	表現	biǎoxiàn	n/v	Lesson three
distinctive feature, trait	特征	特徵	tèzhēng	n	Lesson eleven
distinguish people based on relationships [亲: 亲近, close; 疏: 疏远, distant; 别 (bf): 差别, difference]	亲疏有别	親疏有別	qīnshū yǒu bié	phr	Lesson thirteen
distinguish, differentiate; distinction	区别	區別	qūbié	v/n	Lesson thirteen

英文翻译 D	*简体*	*繁體*	*拼音*	*词性*	
distinguish; draw a clear distinction between	分清		fēn//qīng	v	Lesson seven
do physical exercise, work out	锻炼	鍛鍊	duànliàn	v	Lesson one
do you really mean to say that . . . ; could it be that . . .	难道	難道	nándào	adv	Lesson seven
dominate, control, allocate	支配		zhīpèi	v	Lesson thirteen
draw analogy; metaphor, analogy	比喻		bǐyù	v/n	Lesson six
draw close, draw near	拉近		lājìn	v	Lesson twelve
draw out, pull out [抽时间: find time to]	抽		chōu	v	Lesson twelve
drive away, expel	驱赶	驅趕	qūgǎn	v	Lesson fourteen
due to, thanks to, owing to, as a result of	由于	由於	yóuyú	conj/prep	Lesson three
duty, obligation; mandatory, voluntary	义务	義務	yìwù	n/adj	Lesson fourteen

英文翻译 E	*简体*	*繁體*	*拼音*	*词性*	
Each is in its proper place./ Each has a role to play.	各得其位		gèdé-qíwèi	phr	Lesson eight
each other, one another	彼此		bǐcǐ	pron	Lesson eleven
earthly, secular; the worldly [世俗观念: worldly views, common views]	世俗		shìsú	adj/n	Lesson nine
embarrassed, awkward	尴尬	尷尬	gān'gà	adj	Lesson ten
embody, give expression to	体现	體現	tǐxiàn	v	Lesson six
emerge one after another, spring up in an endless stream	层出不穷	層出不窮	céngchū-bùqióng	idiom	Lesson thirteen
emphasize, lay stress on	注重		zhùzhòng	v	Lesson seven
emphasize, stress	强调	強調	qiángdiào	v	Lesson ten
employee, staff	员工	員工	yuángōng	n	Lesson ten
encase; cover, sheath; set (of . . .)	套		tào	v/n/m	Lesson three
enclosed, confined; seal off, close down	封闭	封閉	fēngbì	adj/v	Lesson eleven

英文翻译 E	*简体*	*繁體*	*拼音*	*词性*	
end, extremity [两端: two ends]	端		duān	bf	Lesson eight
endure hardship, suffer	受罪		shòu//zuì	v	Lesson nine
energy, vigor	精力		jīnglì	n	Lesson twelve
enforce the law	执法	執法	zhífǎ	v	Lesson fourteen
engage in various activities; activity	活动	活動	huódòng	v/n	Lesson one
enjoy	享受		xiǎngshòu	v	Lesson one
enter, penetrate	渗入	滲入	shènrù	v	Lesson eight
enterprise, corporation	企业	企業	qǐyè	n	Lesson seven
entire, complete; entirely, completely [全世界: the whole world]	全		quán	adj/adv	Lesson six
entirety, whole entity, synthesis	整体	整體	zhěngtǐ	n	Lesson three
enumerate, list, cite one by one	列举	列舉	lièjǔ	v	Lesson fourteen
equal to, tantamount to	等于	等於	děngyú	v	Lesson five
equate, be equal	等同	等同	děngtóng	v	Lesson fourteen
escape danger	脱险	脫險	tuō//xiǎn	v	Lesson thirteen
established by popular usage, customary convention	约定俗成	約定俗成	yuēdìng-súchéng	idiom	Lesson four
ethical relations, human relationship according to the Confucian ethics [伦理: ethics]	人伦	人倫	rénlún	n	Lesson eleven
etiquette and custom	礼俗	禮俗	lǐsú	n	Lesson four
Europe	欧洲	歐洲	Ōuzhōu		Lesson eleven
even	甚至		shènzhì	conj	Lesson two
even if, even though [more formal than 即使]	即便		jíbiàn	conj	Lesson fourteen
even-tempered and good-humored	心平气和	心平氣和	xīnpíng-qìhé	idiom	Lesson six
event, incident	事件		shìjiàn	n	Lesson eight
everywhere under heaven, world, China	天下		tiānxià	n	Lesson eight

英文翻译 E	*简体*	*繁體*	*拼音*	*词性*	
evolve, develop	演变	演變	yǎnbiàn	v	Lesson six
example [as in 以…… 为例, 例子, etc.]	例		lì	n	Lesson one
excuse me [used when one tries to pass someone in a crowd]	借过	借過	jièguò	phr	Lesson five
exist, be; existence	存在		cúnzài	v/n	Lesson three
exist; existence	存在		cúnzài	v/n	Lesson two
expand, enlarge, broaden, extend	扩大	擴大	kuòdà	v	Lesson eleven
expect, earnestly hope	期望		qīwàng	v	Lesson ten
expect, look forward to	期待		qīdài	v	Lesson fourteen
expenses, expenditure	花费	花費	huā.fei	n	Lesson twelve
experience; go through (event, era)	经历	經歷	jīnglì	n/v	Lesson nine
explain	解释	解釋	jiěshì	v	Lesson three
extend, stretch	伸		shēn	v	Lesson one
extent, degree, level	程度		chéngdù	n	Lesson thirteen
eyeball, [fig.] attention	眼球		yǎnqiú	n	Lesson nine

英文翻译 F	*简体*	*繁體*	*拼音*	*词性*	
face	面孔		miànkǒng	n	Lesson nine
face-to-face	面对面	面對面	miànduìmiàn	phr	Lesson seven
face, confront	面对	面對	miànduì	v	Lesson nine
fact	事实	事實	shìshí	n	Lesson five
factor, element	因素		yīnsù	n	Lesson nine
fair, just, impartial; fairness	公平		gōngpíng	adj/n	Lesson eleven
fall down	摔倒		shuāidǎo	v	Lesson thirteen
family servant	佣人	傭人	yōngrén	n	Lesson fourteen
family ties	亲缘	親緣	qīnyuán	n	Lesson eleven
farming; practice farming [耕: till (fields)]	农耕	農耕	nónggēng	n/v	Lesson eleven

英文翻译 F	*简体*	*繁體*	*拼音*	*词性*	
feel, sense	感到		gǎndào	v	Lesson five
feeling [same as 感情], emotion	情感		qínggǎn	n	Lesson eleven
feeling [爱情: romantic love; 亲情: family love; 乡情: affection for native place; 战友情: friendship between or among fellow soldiers]	感情		gǎnqíng	n	Lesson eleven
feeling; feel	感觉	感覺	gǎnjué	n/v	Lesson one
Fei Xiaotong or Fei Hsiao-Tung (1910–2005), a renowned scholar and professor of sociology and anthropology. His famous work《乡土中国》, translated as *From the Soil: The Foundations of Chinese Society*, was first published in 1948 and widely referenced by Chinese sociologists and anthropologists.	费孝通	費孝通	Fèi Xiàotōng		Lesson eleven
fight over, snatch, loot	抢	搶	qiǎng	v	Lesson six
Financial Times, a British newspaper	金融时报	金融時報	Jīnróng Shíbào		Lesson seven
first; first of all, in the first place	首先		shǒuxiān	adv/pron	Lesson three
fixed, regular; fasten, set rigidly in place	固定		gùdìng	adj/v	Lesson eleven
flaunt wealth	炫富		xuàn//fù	v	Lesson eight
flow	流动	流動	liúdòng	v	Lesson eleven
focalize, focus	聚焦		jùjiāo	v	Lesson one
follow the crowd, conform	从众	從眾	cóngzhòng	v	Lesson two
follow the trend	跟风	跟風	gēnfēng	v	Lesson two
follow, abide by, comply with	遵循		zūnxún	v	Lesson four
[for facial expressions, pairs/sets of things]	副		fù	m	Lesson thirteen
for the first time	初次		chūcì	adv	Lesson fourteen
Forbearance is the most important principle. [当头: put ahead of everything else]	忍字当头	忍字當頭	rěn zì dāngtóu	phr	Lesson seven
force others aside, squeeze	挤	擠	jǐ	v	Lesson five
foreign teacher [abbr. for 外国教师]	外教		wàijiào	n	Lesson ten

英文翻译 F	*简体*	*繁體*	*拼音*	*词性*	
form, develop into, take shape	形成		xíngchéng	v	Lesson eleven
form, make up, constitute	组成	組成	zǔchéng	v	Lesson three
forward (mail, SMS, etc.), repost (tweet, online post, etc.)	转发	轉發	zhuǎnfā	v	Lesson two
found, establish	建立		jiànlì	v	Lesson eleven
freedom, liberty; free, unrestrained	自由		zìyóu	n/adj	Lesson one
frequently, constantly	时时	時時	shíshí	adv	Lesson nine
friendship	友谊	友誼	yǒuyì	n	Lesson eleven
from beginning to end, all along	始终	始終	shǐzhōng	adv	Lesson thirteen
from start to finish, from beginning to end	自始至终	自始至終	zìshǐ-zhìzhōng	idiom	Lesson fourteen
function, effect	作用		zuòyòng	n	Lesson six
fundamental, basic	根本		gēnběn	adj	Lesson one

英文翻译 G	*简体*	*繁體*	*拼音*	*词性*	
gain, obtain	获取	獲取	huòqǔ	v	Lesson twelve
gather together, pool, collect [凑热闹còu rè.nao: join in the fun]	凑	湊	còu	v	Lesson one
generation, lifetime [同辈: the same generation; 大一辈: one generation older]	辈	輩	bèi	n	Lesson three
generous	慷慨		kāngkǎi	adj	Lesson five
Geniality brings wealth. [和气: geniality; 生: generate; 财 (bf): wealth]	和气生财	和氣生財	hé.qi shēngcái	idiom	Lesson six
get along [共处: co-exist]	相处	相處	xiāngchǔ	v	Lesson six
get in the rear door, secure sth. through pulling relationships/ connections	走后门	走後門	zǒu hòumén	phr	Lesson twelve
get together and have a meal together	聚餐		jù//cān	v	Lesson one
gift, present	礼品	禮品	lǐpǐn	n	Lesson eleven
give an example	举例	舉例	jǔ//lì	v	Lesson five

英文翻译 G	简体	繁體	拼音	词性	
give rise to, lead to	引起		yǐnqǐ	v	Lesson two
glorious, honorable; glory, luster, splendor	光彩		guāngcǎi	adj/n	Lesson nine
go along with (some action)	随	隨	suí	v	Lesson eleven
[of tradition, history, etc.] go back to the distant past, long-standing and well-established	源远流长	源遠流長	yuányuǎn-liúcháng	idiom	Lesson six
going too far	过头	過頭	guò//tóu	adj	Lesson eight
[colloquial] good, fine, strong	棒		bàng	adj	Lesson five
good intention, kind heart [一片好心: the best of intentions]	好心		hǎoxīn	n	Lesson seven
gradually	逐渐	逐漸	zhújiàn	adv	Lesson twelve
grasp firmly, command; assurance, certainty	把握		bǎwò	v/n	Lesson eleven
Greece	希腊	希臘	Xīlà		Lesson three
group	群体	群體	qúntǐ	n	Lesson one
grow, develop	生长	生長	shēngzhǎng	v	Lesson eight

英文翻译 H	简体	繁體	拼音	词性	
hall of one person's speech [堂(bf): hall], what sb. says goes, deciding everything by one man's say	一言堂		yìyántáng	n	Lesson fourteen
handle, deal with, process	处理	處理	chǔlǐ	v	Lesson eleven
Hangzhou, the capital city of the Zhejiang province in southeast China	杭州		Hángzhōu		Lesson fourteen
harm, hurt	伤害	傷害	shānghài	v	Lesson nine
harmonious [often international or societal]; harmony	和谐	和諧	héxié	adj/n	Lesson six
harmonious [often interpersonal or familial]	和睦		hémù	adj	Lesson six
Harmony in the family leads to prosperity in all undertakings. [万事: all things; 兴: prosper]	家和万事兴	家和萬事興	jiā hé wànshì xīng	idiom	Lesson six
harmony without uniformity	和而不同		hé ér bùtóng	idiom	Lesson eight
help sb. up, support with hand	扶		fú	v	Lesson thirteen

英文翻译 H	*简体*	*繁體*	*拼音*	*词性*	
help someone out of embarrassment, lift a siege	解围	解圍	jiě//wéi	v	Lesson ten
hesitant	犹豫	猶豫	yóuyù	adj	Lesson one
high-degree; height	高度		gāodù	adj/n	Lesson six
high-rank managerial personnel, senior executive [short for高级管理人员]	高管		gāoguǎn	n	Lesson seven
hold sth level with palm(s) facing upward	端		duān	v	Lesson five
hold the post of, serve as	担任	擔任	dānrèn	v	Lesson fourteen
hold up (as a model), hold in esteem	崇尚		chóngshàng	v	Lesson three
house maid, nanny	保姆		bǎomǔ	n	Lesson fourteen
how	何等		héděng	adv	Lesson thirteen
how [more formal than 怎样 or 怎么]	如何		rúhé	pron	Lesson thirteen
however [more formal than 但是]	然而		rán'ér	conj	Lesson thirteen
Hsien Chin Hu, a pioneering Chinese anthropologist	胡先缙	胡先縉	Hú Xiānjìn		Lesson nine
Huawei [brand; most famous for mobile phones]	华为	華為	Huáwéi		Lesson fourteen
human feelings, favor	人情		rénqíng	n	Lesson nine
human life, one's lifetime	人生		rénshēng	n	Lesson eight
Humans depend on their face just as trees depend on their bark for life. [皮: (tree) bark, skin]	人活一张脸，树活一张皮	人活一張臉，樹活一張皮	rén huó yì zhāng liǎn, shù huó yì zhāng pí	proverb	Lesson ten
humble language [a rhetoric device, and a type of Chinese honorifics]	谦辞	謙辭	qiāncí	n	Lesson five
humble oneself; self-effacing, self-deprecating	自谦	自謙	zìqiān	v/adj	Lesson five
Hung-ming Ku or Hongming Gu (1857–1928), a Malaysian Chinese man of letters known for his monarchist views and highly regarded for his works in English.	辜鸿铭	辜鴻銘	Gū Hóngmíng		Lesson eight
hurt, do harm to, injure, wound	伤	傷	shāng	v	Lesson seven

英文翻译 I	*简体*	*繁體*	*拼音*	*词性*	
identify oneself with	认同	認同	rèntóng	v	Lesson two
identity, status	身份		shēnfèn	n	Lesson thirteen
if one day (something happens)	一旦		yídàn	adv	Lesson seven
If you do not learn the rules of Propriety, your character cannot be established. [from *The Analects* of Confucius; trans. by James Legge]	不学礼，无以立	不學禮，無以立	bù xué lǐ, wú yǐ lì		Lesson four
ignorance; ignorant	无知	無知	wúzhī	n/adj	Lesson ten
ignore, overlook	不顾	不顧	búgù	v	Lesson twelve
ignore, overlook	忽略		hūlüè	v	Lesson eight
illustrate, show, explain; explanation	说明	說明	shuōmíng	v/n	Lesson one
implement	实施	實施	shíshī	v	Lesson ten
implicit, reserved, veiled	含蓄		hánxù	adj	Lesson seven
improve	改进	改進	gǎijìn	v	Lesson ten
in a word; in short	总之	總之	zǒngzhī	conj	Lesson three
in an awkward situation that is hard to escape from [下台: get off the stage]	下不来台	下不來臺	xià .bu lái tái	phr	Lesson ten
in order, orderly	井然有序		jǐngrán-yǒuxù	idiom	Lesson eleven
In practicing the rules of propriety, a natural ease is to be prized. [from Analects of Confucius; trans. James Legge]	礼之用，和为贵	禮之用，和為貴	lǐ zhī yòng, hé wéi guì		Lesson six
in private, privately	私下		sīxià	adv	Lesson ten
in reality, in fact	事实上	事實上	shìshí.shàng	adv	Lesson nine
in the final analysis, at bottom	说到底	說到底	shuōdàodǐ	phr	Lesson thirteen
inborn, innate; being inborn, innateness	先天		xiāntiān	adj/n	Lesson four
incisive, penetrating, pointed and sharp	尖锐	尖銳	jiānruì	adj	Lesson fourteen
include	包括		bāokuò	v	Lesson six
income	收入		shōurù	n	Lesson fourteen
increasingly, with each passing day	日益		rìyì	adv	Lesson twelve
indeed, truly	确实	確實	quèshí	adv	Lesson twelve
independence; independent	独立	獨立	dúlì	n/adj	Lesson one

英文翻译 I	*简体*	*繁體*	*拼音*	*词性*	
indicate, show, express	表示		biǎoshì	v	Lesson two
indignance; indignant, angry	愤怒	憤怒	fènnù	n/adj	Lesson thirteen
individual (person or entity) [*个体意识*: individual-oriented consciousness]	个体	個體	gètǐ	n	Lesson one
individual [person]	个人	個人	gèrén	n	Lesson one
individually, on one's own	单独	單獨	dāndú	adv	Lesson two
inferior to other people [antonym: *高人一等*]	低人一等		dī rén yì děng	idiom	Lesson fourteen
inform	告知		gàozhī	v	Lesson ten
information, message	信息		xìnxī	n	Lesson nine
Initium Media (https://theinitium.com), Hong Kong-based digital media outlet launched in August, 2015 [*端*: beginning, initium; *传媒*: media]	端传媒	端傳媒	Duān Chuánméi		Lesson ten
innumerable, countless	无数	無數	wúshù	adj	Lesson three
inquire into, discuss	探讨	探討	tàntǎo	v	Lesson thirteen
inseparably close	紧密	緊密	jǐnmì	adj	Lesson twelve
interact with, have dealings with	打交道		dǎ jiāo.dao	phr	Lesson five
interfere	干涉		gānshè	v	Lesson one
interpersonal [*人际关系*: interpersonal relationship]	人际	人際	rénjì	adj	Lesson three
interpretation; interpret, understand	理解		lǐjiě	n/v	Lesson five
intriguing	有趣		yǒuqù	adj	Lesson one
[introduces the object of the main verb, similar to *把*, but more formal than *把*]	将	將	jiāng	prep	Lesson twelve
investigation; investigate [*市场调查*: market research]	调查	調查	diàochá	n/v	Lesson ten
involve, relate to	涉及		shèjí	v	Lesson eight
inwardly, to oneself, secretly	暗暗		àn'àn	adv	Lesson fourteen
-ism [as in 集体主义: collectivism; *个人主义*: individualism; *社会主义*: socialism]	主义	主義	zhǔyì	n	Lesson three

英文翻译 I	简体	繁體	拼音	词性	
[only in object position; formal] it, him, her, this	之		zhī	pron	Lesson one
its, their, his, her [more formal than他的, 她的,它的, 他们的]	其		qí	pron	Lesson four
-ize, -ify [added to a noun or an adjective to form a verb, as in 家庭化: familize, 现代化: modernize, etc.]	化		huà	bf	Lesson three

英文翻译 J	简体	繁體	拼音	词性	
Jackie Chan (1954–), Hong Kong martial artist, actor, film director, producer, stuntman, and singer	成龙	成龍	Chéng Lóng		Lesson three
(traffic) jam, congestion; jam, congest	堵塞		dǔsè	n/v	Lesson two
jeopardize, harm, endanger	危害		wēihài	v	Lesson one
jointly, together; common, mutual	共同		gòngtóng	adv/adj	Lesson eight
joke; laugh at	笑话	笑話	xiàohua	n/v	Lesson one
judge another's feelings by one's own, put oneself in somebody else's shoes	将心比心	將心比心	jiāngxīn-bǐxīn	idiom	Lesson seven
jump a queue, cut in line	插队	插隊	chā//duì	v	Lesson thirteen
just right; precisely	正好		zhènghǎo	adj/adv	Lesson eight

英文翻译 K	简体	繁體	拼音	词性	
keep . . . intact, safeguard	保全		bǎoquán	v	Lesson nine
key [classifier: 把]	钥匙	鑰匙	yào.shi	n	Lesson nine
key, critical; crux	关键	關鍵	guānjiàn	adj/n	Lesson thirteen
know . . . well, familiarize	熟悉		shú.xi	v	Lesson three
Kuang-Kwo Hwang (1945–), professor emeritus, Department of Psychology, National Taiwan University	黄光国	黃光國	Huáng Guāngguó		Lesson twelve

英文翻译 L	*简体*	*繁體*	*拼音*	*词性*	
lack of compassion; compassionless, pitiless, heartless	无情	無情	wúqíng	n/adj	Lesson thirteen
lack, be short of	缺乏		quēfá	v	Lesson fourteen
lack, be short of	缺少		quēshǎo	v	Lesson fourteen
lament; sigh with emotion	感慨		gǎnkǎi	n/v	Lesson thirteen
land, soil, territory	土地		tǔdì	n	Lesson six
law	法律		fǎlǜ	n	Lesson two
law, rule, principle	法则	法則	fǎzé	n	Lesson eight
lawful, legitimate, rightful	合法		héfǎ	adj	Lesson two
leader, leadership; lead	领导	領導	lǐngdǎo	n/v	Lesson ten
lean on one side, turn . . . sideways	侧	側	cè	v	Lesson five
learn of	得知		dézhī	v	Lesson one
learning, knowledge, scholarship [classifier: 门]	学问	學問	xué.wen	n	Lesson ten
lengthen out to, extend as long as [长达两千年: extend as long as 2000 years]	长达	長達	chángdá	phr	Lesson four
lengthwise, vertical, longitudinal	纵向	縱向	zòngxiàng	adj	Lesson fourteen
let out, send out, give out	发出	發出	fāchū	v	Lesson thirteen
Liang Shuming (1893–1988), a scholar and philosopher in the neo-Confucian tradition	梁漱溟		Liáng Shùmíng		Lesson fourteen
lie in, rest with, depend on	在于	在於	zàiyú	v	Lesson six
life	生命		shēngmìng	n	Lesson ten
(one's) life [命: 生命]	命		mìng	n	Lesson thirteen
like, be fond of [好礼: be fond of the rites and etiquettes]	好		hào	v	Lesson four
limited, finite [无(wú)限: unlimited, infinite]	有限		yǒuxiàn	adj	Lesson six
live, survive, subsist	生存		shēngcún	v	Lesson twelve
local government law-enforcement officer, city management [short for 城市管理行政执法局 Urban Administrative and Law Enforcement Bureau]	城管		chéngguǎn	n	Lesson fourteen
lock; lock	锁	鎖	suǒ	n/v	Lesson nine
lose	失去		shīqù	v	Lesson seven

英文翻译 L	简体	繁體	拼音	词性	
loss, damage; lose	损失	損失	sǔnshī	n/v	Lesson eleven
lower, cut down, drop, reduce	降低		jiàngdī	v	Lesson five
lunar New Year gift money given to children for luck and good health	压岁钱	壓歲錢	yāsuìqián	n	Lesson eleven

英文翻译 M	简体	繁體	拼音	词性	
main, principal, chief, major	主要		zhǔyào	adj	Lesson three
maintain, keep, preserve	保持		bǎochí	v	Lesson seven
make a fortune	发财	發財	fā//cái	v	Lesson eight
make an appointment (with someone)	约	約	yuē	v	Lesson one
make better, improve	改善		gǎishàn	v	Lesson ten
make people laugh, entertain; hilarious	搞笑		gǎo//xiào	v/adj	Lesson nine
make, cause . . . to [弄坏: ruin, damage]	弄		nòng	v	Lesson twelve
making the decision, be in charge	做主		zuò//zhǔ	v	Lesson fourteen
manage [管理学: management science]	管理		guǎnlǐ	v	Lesson seven
many, a lot of	许多	許多	xǔduō	adj	Lesson two
master	掌握		zhǎngwò	v	Lesson nine
materialistic; material, matter	物质	物質	wùzhì	adj/n	Lesson nine
meaning, connotation [a.k.a. 涵(hán)义]	含义	含義	hányì	n	Lesson twelve
meaning, significance	意义	意義	yìyì	n	Lesson nine
means (of doing sth.), stratagem	手段		shǒuduàn	n	Lesson twelve
mediate, reconcile	调和	調和	tiáohé	v	Lesson eight
mediator, middleman	中间人	中間人	zhōngjiānrén	n	Lesson eight
member [as in 一员, a member]	员	員	yuán	bf	Lesson one
mentality, psychology	心理		xīnlǐ	n	Lesson two
merit, be worthy of	值得		zhí//.dé	v	Lesson nine
meritorious service, achievement, credit	功劳	功勞	gōngláo	n	Lesson ten

英文翻译 M	*简体*	*繁體*	*拼音*	*词性*	
method, way, means	方法		fāngfǎ	n	Lesson four
micro-blog, micro-blog post [usu. refers to the Sina (新浪: Xīnlàng) micro-blog platform, http://www.weibo.com]	微博		wēibó	n	Lesson two
migrant peasant workers	农民工	農民工	nóngmíngōng	n	Lesson fourteen
military affairs	军事	軍事	jūnshì	n	Lesson six
mistake, error; erroneous, incorrect	错误	錯誤	cuòwù	n/adj	Lesson ten
misunderstanding; misunderstand	误会	誤會	wùhuì	n/v	Lesson seven
misunderstanding; misunderstand	误解	誤解	wùjiě	n/v	Lesson five
mix, blend	混合		hùnhé	v	Lesson twelve
mix, confuse	混		hùn	v	Lesson five
moderate, appropriate	适度	適度	shìdù	adj	Lesson eight
modest; make modest remarks	谦虚	謙虛	qiānxū	adj/v	Lesson five
moment, time	时刻	時刻	shíkè	n	Lesson thirteen
Moments [WeChat's brand name for its social feed of friends' updates]	朋友圈		Péng.yǒuquān		Lesson three
money, wealth	金钱	金錢	jīnqián	n	Lesson eleven
morals, morality	道德		dàodé	n	Lesson four
muddled, confused	糊涂	糊塗	hú.tu	adj	Lesson eleven
mutual; mutually, reciprocally	相互		xiānghù	adj/adv	Lesson three
mutually benefit	互惠		hùhuì	v	Lesson eleven

英文翻译 N	*简体*	*繁體*	*拼音*	*词性*	
narrate, tell about, describe	讲述	講述	jiǎngshù	v	Lesson eleven
nation-state, ethnic group	民族		mínzú	n	Lesson nine
native place, membership [as in 国籍 (nationality, citizenship), 美籍, 外籍]	籍		jí	bf	Lesson five

英文翻译 N	*简体*	*繁體*	*拼音*	*词性*	
natural	天然		tiānrán	adj	Lesson four
nature, natural world; natural	自然		zìrán	n/adj	Lesson six
nature, property, attribute [can be used as a suffix, corresponding to -ness or -ity to form a noun, as in 合法性, 准确性, etc.]	性		xìng	bf	Lesson two
necessary, essential, indispensable	必要		bìyào	adj	Lesson fourteen
negotiation; negotiate	谈判	談判	tánpàn	n/v	Lesson ten
neighbors, neighborhood	邻里	鄰里	línlǐ	n	Lesson eleven
netizen, Internet users [网友: Internet user, cyber acquaintance]	网民	網民	wǎngmín	n	Lesson two
no wonder	难怪	難怪	nánguài	adv	Lesson nine
non- [非物质: non-material, intangible]; have got to, simply must	非		fēi	bf/adv	Lesson eleven
norm; standard; regulate, standardize	规范	規範	guīfàn	n/adj/v	Lesson eleven
normal	正常		zhèngcháng	adj	Lesson nine
not to matter, be indifferent	无所谓	無所謂	wúsuǒwèi	v	Lesson two

英文翻译 O	*简体*	*繁體*	*拼音*	*词性*	
object	物体	物體	wùtǐ	n	Lesson nine
observe, inspect	观察	觀察	guānchá	v	Lesson thirteen
obvious	明显	明顯	míngxiǎn	adj	Lesson fourteen
occasion, circumstance	场合	場合	chǎnghé	n	Lesson thirteen
[an honorific for government officials in traditional China, used sarcastically in the text] literal meaning: official master	官老爷	官老爺	guānlǎo.ye	phr	Lesson fourteen
Olympics [short for 奥林匹克运动会: Àolínpǐkè Yùndònghuì, Olympic Games]	奥运会	奧運會	Àoyùnhuì		Lesson six
(who, when, what, why, how) on earth	到底		dàodǐ	adv	Lesson five
once more	重新		chóngxīn	adv	Lesson ten

英文翻译 O	*简体*	*繁體*	*拼音*	*词性*	
once, ever	曾经	曾經	céngjīng	adv	Lesson two
one step further, further onward	进一步	進一步	jìnyíbù	adv	Lesson nine
One won't be blamed for being extra- polite. [怪: blame]	礼多人不怪	禮多人不怪	lǐ duō rén bú guài	idiom	Lesson four
one's own position (seen as being central) [关系本位: relation-based; 家本位: family-based, family-oriented]	本位		běnwèi	n	Lesson three
opening ceremony [幕: curtain, screen]	开幕式	開幕式	kāimùshì	n	Lesson six
operation [面子运作: face operation, face work]; operate	运作	運作	yùnzuò	n/v	Lesson ten
operation; operate	运营	運營	yùnyíng	n/v	Lesson ten
opinion, suggestion, complaint	意见	意見	yìjiàn	n	Lesson ten
opportune time, advantageous terrain, popular support [origin: *Mencius*]	天时地利人和	天時地利人和	tiānshí dìlì rénhé	idiom	Lesson six
oppose, be antagonistic to; opposition	对立	對立	duìlì	v/n	Lesson eight
oppose, disagree; disagreement	反对	反對	fǎnduì	v/n	Lesson eight
order sb. around	使唤	使喚	shǐ.huan	v	Lesson fourteen
order sb. around	支使		zhīshǐ	v	Lesson fourteen
order, sequence	秩序		zhìxù	n	Lesson eight
organization; organize	组织	組織	zǔzhī	n/v	Lesson fourteen
other people [more formal than 别人]	他人		tārén	pron	Lesson one
(do sth.) out of (politeness, curiosity, compassion, etc.), due to	出于	出於	chūyú	v	Lesson one
outlook [世界观: worldview; 价值观: values]	观	觀	guān	bf	Lesson six
overbearing, aggressive	咄咄逼人	咄咄逼人	duōduō-bīrén	idiom	Lesson thirteen
overpraise [您过奖了: You flattered me.]	过奖	過獎	guòjiǎng	v	Lesson five
overstepping of one's role or authority or ethical relationship with others; overstep one's role or authority or ethical relationship with others	僭越		jiànyuè	n/v	Lesson fourteen
owe, lack [亏(kuī)欠: owe, have a deficit]	欠		qiàn	v	Lesson twelve

英文翻译 P	简体	繁體	拼音	词性	
pass through, get through; by means of, through	通过	通過	tōngguò	v/prep	Lesson two
passenger	乘客		chéngkè	n	Lesson twelve
patriarchal clan system	宗法		zōngfǎ	n	Lesson thirteen
pattern; regular	规律	規律	guīlǜ	n/adj	Lesson eight
pay close attention to, follow with interest	关注	關注	guānzhù	v	Lesson seven
pay, invest (energy or time in . . .)	付出		fùchū	v	Lesson twelve
peace	和平	和平	hépíng	n	Lesson six
pedestrian	行人		xíngrén	n	Lesson two
people directly involved or implicated	当事人	當事人	dāngshìrén	n	Lesson thirteen
people of Chinese descent	华人	華人	huárén	n	Lesson five
period, phase	时期	時期	shíqī	n	Lesson four
perplexity; perplexed, puzzled	困惑		kùnhuò	n/adj	Lesson five
Ph.D.	博士		bóshì	n	Lesson seven
phenomenon	现象	現象	xiànxiàng	n	Lesson two
philosophy	哲学	哲學	zhéxué	n	Lesson six
pickled mustard tuber and shredded pork soup	榨菜肉丝汤	榨菜肉絲湯	zhàcài ròusī tāng		Lesson one
place oneself in another's position, judge others by oneself	以己度人		yǐjǐ-duórén	idiom	Lesson seven
plan, proposal	方案		fāng'àn	n	Lesson ten
platform	平台	平臺	píngtái	n	Lesson thirteen
play Chinese chess	下象棋		xià xiàngqí	phr	Lesson one
play *mahjong*	打麻将	打麻將	dǎ májiàng	phr	Lesson one
play part of	扮演		bànyǎn	v	Lesson six
pleasant, joyful	愉快		yúkuài	adj	Lesson seven
point of view, viewpoint	观点	觀點	guāndiǎn	n	Lesson one
politics, political affairs	政治		zhèngzhì	n	Lesson ten
position, post	职位	職位	zhíwèi	n	Lesson three
positive, proactive	积极	積極	jījí	adj	Lesson nine
possess (characteristics, functionalities, etc.)	具有		jùyǒu	v	Lesson two

英文翻译 P	*简体*	*繁體*	*拼音*	*词性*	
power, authority, right	权力	權力	quánlì	n	Lesson fourteen
power, force, physical strength [人多力量大 (proverb): There is strength in numbers.]	力量		lì.liàng	n	Lesson two
"Practice forbearance for a short while, and the winds and waves will subside."/ Practicing forbearance for a short while will bring about tranquility.	忍一时风平浪静	忍一時風平浪靜	rěn yìshí fēngpíng-làngjìng	proverb	Lesson seven
praise, acclaim, commend, compliment	称赞	稱讚	chēngzàn	v	Lesson ten
praise; compliment	夸奖	誇獎	kuājiǎng	v/n	Lesson four
precisely	正		zhèng	adv	Lesson six
predestined affinity or relationship, fateful coincidence	缘分	緣分	yuán.fèn	n	Lesson one
preference, fondness; love, like, be fond of	喜好		xǐhào	n/v	Lesson eight
present as a gift	赠送	贈送	zèngsòng	v	Lesson four
present time	当今	當今	dāngjīn	n	Lesson nine
principle	原则	原則	yuánzé	n	Lesson six
private room in a restaurant [a.k.a 包间]	包房		bāofáng	n	Lesson twelve
procedure, protocol [走程序: follow the procedure]	程序		chéngxù	n	Lesson twelve
process, course, progress	进程	進程	jìnchéng	n	Lesson fourteen
profession, occupation, vocation	职业	職業	zhíyè	n	Lesson three
profound [深: deep]	高深		gāoshēn	adj	Lesson eight
profound, abstruse	深奥	深奧	shēn'ào	adj	Lesson ten
progressively, step by step	逐步		zhúbù	adv	Lesson fourteen
project, engineering [形象工程: vanity project]	工程		gōngchéng	n	Lesson nine
proposal, suggestion, propose, suggest	提议	提議	tíyì	n/v	Lesson fourteen
protagonist	主人公		zhǔréngōng	n	Lesson nine
prove; proof	证明	證明	zhèngmíng	v/n	Lesson ten
public square, plaza [广场舞: square dancing, plaza dancing]	广场	廣場	guǎngchǎng	n	Lesson two

英文翻译 P	*简体*	*繁體*	*拼音*	*词性*	
publish (article, opinion, viewpoint, etc.)	发表	發表	fābiǎo	v	Lesson two
pull, drag [拖: drag; 拽: pull, tug at (sth.)]	拖拽		tuōzhuài	v	Lesson thirteen
punishment; punish	惩罚	懲罰	chéngfá	n/v	Lesson two
pursue, seek after	追求		zhuīqiú	v	Lesson two
put forward, raise (an issue)	提出		tíchū	v	Lesson five
put in order, arrange	排列		páiliè	v	Lesson fourteen
put on a smiling face in order to please sb.	陪笑脸	陪笑臉	péi xiàoliǎn	phr	Lesson fourteen
put up, construct (platform, shed, rack, etc.)	搭		dā	v	Lesson three
putting it this way, if so	这样说来	這樣說來	zhèyàng shuōlái	phr	Lesson five
puzzled; not understand	不解		bùjiě	adj/v	Lesson five

英文翻译 Q	*简体*	*繁體*	*拼音*	*词性*	
Qingdao, sub-provincial city in Shandong Province [a.k.a. Tsingtao]	青岛	青島	Qīngdǎo		Lesson ten
quarrel, dispute, argue	争吵	爭吵	zhēngchǎo	v	Lesson seven

英文翻译 R	*简体*	*繁體*	*拼音*	*词性*	
race	种族	種族	zhǒngzú	n	Lesson ten
raise, exalt	抬高		tái//gāo	v	Lesson five
rank, social status	地位		dìwèi	n	Lesson nine
reaction; react	反应	反應	fǎnyìng	n/v	Lesson seven
reality; realistic	现实	現實	xiànshí	n/adj	Lesson thirteen
realize, achieve, (dream) come true	实现	實現	shíxiàn	v	Lesson three
realize, understand; clear, obvious	明白		míng.bai	v/adj	Lesson ten
rear (child), bring up	养育	養育	yǎngyù	v	Lesson eleven
reason, rationality [有道理: be reasonable, be convincing]	道理		dào.lǐ	n	Lesson five

英文翻译 R	简体	繁體	拼音	词性	
recognize someone's worth	知遇		zhīyù	v	Lesson eleven
record of actual events; put down in writing	纪实	紀實	jìshí	n/v	Lesson fourteen
redeem, retrieve	挽回		wǎnhuí	v	Lesson ten
refer to, point at; finger	指		zhǐ	v	Lesson two
reflect	反映		fǎnyìng	v	Lesson two
reflection; reflect on, ponder over	思考		sīkǎo	n/v	Lesson one
refuse, decline, reject	拒绝	拒絕	jùjué	v	Lesson thirteen
regard harmony as the most important [和 (n): harmony; 贵 (bf): highly valued]	以和为贵	以和為貴	yǐhé-wéiguì	idiom	Lesson six
regarding, with regards to	对于	對於	duìyú	prep	Lesson four
region, area	地域		dìyù	n	Lesson thirteen
region, district	区	區	qū	n	Lesson seven
regional ties	地缘	地緣	dìyuán	n	Lesson eleven
regretful; regret, pity	遗憾	遺憾	yíhàn	adj/n	Lesson six
related, relevant; be interrelated	相关	相關	xiāngguān	adj/v	Lesson ten
relations with other people, popularity among people	人缘	人緣	rényuán	n	Lesson nine
relative [绝(jué)对: absolute]	相对	相對	xiāngduì	adj	Lesson six
relatives	亲戚		qīn.qi	n	Lesson three
remarks, views, open discussion	言论	言論	yánlùn	n	Lesson thirteen
remind, call attention to	提醒	提醒	tíxǐng	v	Lesson seven
renowned, celebrated	著名		zhùmíng	adj	Lesson eleven
repay, pay back	偿还	償還	chánghuán	v	Lesson twelve
replace, substitute	代替		dàitì	v	Lesson thirteen
report; report [same as 报导 (bàodǎo)]	报道	報道	bàodào	v/n	Lesson thirteen
reporter, journalist	记者	記者	jìzhě	n	Lesson ten
represent; representative, representation	代表		dàibiǎo	v/n	Lesson two
reprimand, rebuke, berate	训斥	訓斥	xùnchì	v	Lesson fourteen
resident, inhabitant	居民		jūmín	n	Lesson two
resign (from a job), quit (a job) [辞去工作 or 辞职 (cí//zhí): resign from a job]	辞	辭	cí	v	Lesson ten

英文翻译 R	*简体*	*繁體*	*拼音*	*词性*	
resign oneself to; feeling wronged	委屈		wěi.qu	v/adj	Lesson nine
resistance; revolt, confront	反抗		fǎnkàng	n/v	Lesson fourteen
resonance, sympathetic response	共鸣	共鳴	gòngmíng	n	Lesson two
resources	资源	資源	zīyuán	n	Lesson six
respect; respect, esteem, honor	尊重		zūnzhòng	v/n	Lesson ten
respect; respect, revere	尊敬		zūnjìng	n/v	Lesson four
respectful language [a rhetoric device, and a type of Chinese honorifics]	敬辞	敬辭	jìngcí	n	Lesson five
restore good relations, become reconciled	和好		héhǎo	v	Lesson six
restore, recover	恢复	恢復	huīfù	v	Lesson four
restriction, fetters; tie up, fetter, restrict	束缚	束縛	shùfù	n/v	Lesson eleven
restriction; restrain, bind	约束	約束	yuēshù	n/v	Lesson eleven
retire	退休		tuìxiū	v	Lesson two
reveal, display, show, exhibit	展示		zhǎnshì	v	Lesson six
rich, plentiful, abundant; enrich	丰富	豐富	fēngfù	adj/v	Lesson five
rite, etiquette and ritual [礼仪之邦: state of ceremonies, state exemplary in observation of etiquette and rituals; 邦bāng (bf): state] [礼节: etiquette]	礼仪	禮儀	lǐyí	n	Lesson four
role, part	角色		juésè	n	Lesson three
rude and brutal	粗暴		cūbào	adj	Lesson fourteen
rule (a country), govern	统治	統治	tǒngzhì	v	Lesson four
rule, govern [礼治: rule of the rites; 法治: rule of law; 治理: govern, administer]	治		zhì	v	Lesson four
rule, regulation	规则	規則	guīzé	n	Lesson two
run amok, cause havoc	闹	鬧	nào	v	Lesson thirteen
rush, dash [闯红灯: run a red light]	闯	闖	chuǎng	v	Lesson two
Russia [short form of 俄罗斯联邦: Éluósī Liánbāng; the Russian Federation]	俄罗斯	俄羅斯	Éluósī		Lesson eight

英文翻译 S	*简体*	*繁體*	*拼音*	*词性*	
safeguard, defend, uphold	维护	維護	wéihù	v	Lesson four
satisfy	满足	滿足	mǎnzú	v	Lesson twelve
say [usu. used with direct quotations in literary or formal narratives, as in问道: asked, 说道: said, 解释道: explained]	道		dào	v	Lesson five
scholar, learned person	学者	學者	xuézhě	n	Lesson three
second	秒		miǎo	n	Lesson two
secondly, next	其次		qícì	conj	Lesson four
secret, secrecy; secret	秘密		mìmì	n/adj	Lesson nine
security guard, security personnel	保安		bǎo'ān	n	Lesson thirteen
seek (opinions, feedback, etc.)	征求	徵求	zhēngqiú	v	Lesson ten
seek profit, gain profit	牟利		móu//lì	v	Lesson twelve
seek the limelight	出风头	出風頭	chū fēng.tou	phr	Lesson eight
seem, look, appear	显得	顯得	xiǎn.de	v	Lesson four
seemingly	似乎		sìhū	adv	Lesson eight
select, employ, adopt	采用	採用	cǎiyòng	v	Lesson eight
self-cultivation	修养	修養	xiūyǎng	n	Lesson four
self-sufficient; maintain self-sufficiency	自给自足	自給自足	zìjǐ-zìzú	idiom	Lesson eleven
senior, elderly, older in age	年长	年長	niánzhǎng	adj	Lesson three
sense, conception, notion, idea	观念	觀念	guānniàn	n	Lesson three
sequence, order	次序		cìxù	n	Lesson fourteen
serious, solemn	严肃	嚴肅	yánsù	adj	Lesson seven
shame-based culture [耻 (bf): shame, disgrace]	耻感文化	恥感文化	chǐ gǎn wénhuà	phr	Lesson ten
share (food, happiness, rights, etc.)	分享		fēnxiǎng	v	Lesson one
share for a joint undertaking [as in buying a gift; a.k.a. 份子]	份子钱	份子錢	fèn.ziqián	n	Lesson eleven
shout and scream, make a big fuss	大呼小叫		dàhū-xiǎojiào	idiom	Lesson fourteen
show, demonstrate, manifest	显示	顯示	xiǎnshì	v	Lesson twelve
showing consideration; be considerate	体贴	體貼	tǐtiē	n/v	Lesson four

英文翻译 S	*简体*	*繁體*	*拼音*	*词性*	
sign up [as in 报名]	报	報	bào	v	Lesson one
since ancient times	自古		zìgǔ	adv	Lesson six
skit, short act	小品		xiǎopǐn	n	Lesson nine
slow, slow-moving	缓慢	緩慢	huǎnmàn	adj	Lesson fourteen
small retailer, peddler	商贩	商販	shāngfàn	n	Lesson fourteen
so as to, so that, with the aim of	以便		yǐbiàn	conj	Lesson twelve
social contact/interaction	社交		shèjiāo	n	Lesson three
social custom	风俗	風俗	fēngsú	n	Lesson thirteen
social status, rank, grade	等级	等級	děngjí	n	Lesson fourteen
social stratum	阶层	階層	jiēcéng	n	Lesson fourteen
society	社会	社會	shèhuì	n	Lesson two
solve, resolve	解决	解決	jiějué	v	Lesson eight
some (kind of)	某		mǒu	pron	Lesson two
space, room	空间	空間	kōngjiān	n	Lesson two
special quality, characteristic	特质	特質	tèzhì	n	Lesson fourteen
special, unusual	特殊		tèshū	adj	Lesson eight
specific to, characteristic of	特有		tèyǒu	adj	Lesson two
spirit, mind, consciousness	精神		jīngshén	n	Lesson fourteen
spoon	勺子		sháozi	n	Lesson one
spread a religion, preach	传教	傳教	chuán//jiào	v	Lesson nine
spread, pass on, circulate	传	傳	chuán	v	Lesson eight
Spring and Autumn Period (771–476 BC)	春秋		Chūnqiū		Lesson four
stable, steady; stabilize	稳定	穩定	wěndìng	adj/v	Lesson eleven
state (of affairs), status, condition	状态	狀態	zhuàngtài	n	Lesson twelve
stem from, has (its) origin in	源于	源於	yuányú	phr	Lesson thirteen
step on	踏		tà	v	Lesson twelve
still, yet	仍然		réngrán	adv	Lesson two
stipulate; provision, regulation	规定	規定	guīdìng	v/n	Lesson fourteen
stop, cease	停止		tíngzhǐ	v	Lesson thirteen
story	故事		gù.shi	n	Lesson one

英文翻译 S	简体	繁體	拼音	词性	
street	街头	街頭	jiētóu	n	Lesson thirteen
stress, pay attention to	讲	講	jiǎng	v	Lesson five
strict, rigorous	严格	嚴格	yán'gé	adj	Lesson fourteen
strong, deep, dense, pronounced	浓厚	濃厚	nónghòu	adj	Lesson eleven
strong, powerful, vigorous	强	強	qiáng	adj	Lesson three
structure, construction	结构	結構	jiégòu	n	Lesson nine
sub-provincial city in Fujian, a.k.a. Amoy	厦门	廈門	Xiàmén		Lesson one
subalternation (in status or quality), differentiated ranking, difference	差等		chāděng	n	Lesson fourteen
subconsciously; subconscious mind	下意识	下意識	xiàyì.shí	adv/n	Lesson thirteen
subordinate	下属	下屬	xiàshǔ	n	Lesson fourteen
sudden, abrupt, unexpected	突然		tūrán	adj	Lesson seven
suffer attack, be assaulted	遇袭	遇襲	yùxí	v	Lesson thirteen
suggest, advise; suggestion, advice	建议	建議	jiànyì	v/n	Lesson one
summarize, sum up; summary	总结	總結	zǒngjié	v/n	Lesson nine
superior, a higher authority, someone higher in the hierarchy	上级	上級	shàngjí	n	Lesson fourteen
superiors and inferiors [尊(bf): respect, respectability; 卑(bf): low, inferior]	尊卑		zūnbēi	n	Lesson thirteen
supply, provide, furnish	提供		tígōng	v	Lesson eleven
supreme, advanced	高级	高級	gāojí	adj	Lesson eight
surface	表面		biǎomiàn	n	Lesson nine
surface area	面积	面積	miànjī	n	Lesson six
surge up; run high	高涨	高漲	gāozhǎng	v	Lesson twelve
surveillance; surveil, monitor	监控	監控	jiānkòng	n/v	Lesson thirteen
symbol, emblem; symbolize	象征	象徵	xiàngzhēng	n/v	Lesson six
synchronize, keep step with	同步		tóngbù	v	Lesson fourteen
system; systematic	系统	系統	xìtǒng	n/adj	Lesson eleven

英文翻译 T	*简体*	*繁體*	*拼音*	*词性*	
tactful, indirect, euphemistic	委婉		wěiwǎn	adj	Lesson ten
take a walk, go for a stroll	散步		sàn//bù	v	Lesson one
take measures to rescue [施 bestow, carry out; 救(bf): help, relieve]	施救		shījiù	v	Lesson thirteen
take no action to fulfill one's duty; negligence of one's duty	不作为	不作為	búzuòwéi	v/n	Lesson thirteen
take over (something handed to oneself)	接		jiē	v	Lesson one
take part in social networking activities; networking activities	应酬	應酬	yìng.chou	v/n	Lesson twelve
take the lead, be the first to do sth.	领头	領頭	lǐng//tóu	v	Lesson fourteen
target, object	对象	對象	duìxiàng	n	Lesson thirteen
team, group [as in报(旅游)团]	团	團	tuán	n	Lesson one
The Analects ["edited conversations" literally], a collection of sayings and ideas attributed to Confucius and his contemporaries, including his disciples.	论语	論語	Lúnyǔ		Lesson six
the beginning of (a period of time)	初		chū	n	Lesson eight
The Beijing News [http://www.bjnews.com.cn/]	新京报	新京報	Xīn Jīng Bào		Lesson eleven
The Doctrine of the Mean, one of the Four Books of the Confucian philosophy. Originally published as a chapter in the *Classic of Rites*, the text is attributed to Zisi or Kong Ji, the grandson of Confucius.	《中庸》		Zhōngyōng		Lesson eight
the former [后者: the latter]	前者		qiánzhě	n	Lesson five
the golden mean (of the Confucian school) [中庸: Mean; 道: the Way]	中庸之道		zhōngyōng zhī dào	idiom	Lesson eight

英文翻译 T	*简体*	*繁體*	*拼音*	*词性*	
The highest excellence is like (that of) water. [from *Tao Te Ching*; trans. by James Legge]	上善若水		shàng shàn ruò shuǐ		Lesson six
The law does not punish numerous offenders./The law fails where violators are legion.	法不责众	法不責眾	fǎbùzézhòng	idiom	Lesson two
the majority	大多数	大多數	dàduōshù	n	Lesson two
the noble and the lowly, high versus low social hierarchy	贵贱	貴賤	guìjiàn	n	Lesson fourteen
the other party (of two)	对方	對方	duìfāng	n	Lesson three
the present day, contemporary	当代	當代	dāngdài	n	Lesson four
the public	公众	公眾	gōngzhòng	n	Lesson one
the rites of Western Zhou Dynasty	周礼	周禮	zhōulǐ	n	Lesson four
the senior and the young, seniority by age [长 (bf): senior, old; 幼 (bf): young, under age]	长幼	長幼	zhǎngyòu	n	Lesson fourteen
The shot hits the bird that pokes its head out./ Nonconformity gets punished.	枪打出头鸟	槍打出頭鳥	qiāng dǎ chūtóuniǎo	idiom	Lesson eight
"The top portion of the character ren is a knife."/ Practice forbearance as if there were a knife hanging above the head.	忍字头上一把刀	忍字頭上一把刀	rěn zì tóu .shang yì bǎ dāo	proverb	Lesson seven
things going as one hopes, satisfactory	顺心	順心	shùn//xīn	adj	Lesson six
things like this, and so on	诸如此类	諸如此類	zhūrú-cǐlèi	idiom	Lesson thirteen
thinking, thought; think	思维	思維	sīwéi	n/v	Lesson seven
thorough; go deep into	深入		shēnrù	adj/v	Lesson ten
thought, thinking, idea, ideology	思想		sīxiǎng	n	Lesson three
times, age, epoch, era	时代	時代	shídài	n	Lesson nine
(book, article) title, (news) headline	标题	標題	biāotí	n	Lesson eight
title, topic	题目	題目	tímù	n	Lesson five
to such an extent as to, so much so that	以至于	以至於	yǐzhìyú	conj	Lesson twelve

英文翻译 T	*简体*	*繁體*	*拼音*	*词性*	
to this day, up until now, as yet	至今		zhìjīn	adv	Lesson six
to, towards	向		xiàng	prep	Lesson one
tolerate, pardon	宽容	寬容	kuānróng	v	Lesson six
tool, instrument	工具		gōngjù	n	Lesson three
traditional; tradition	传统	傳統	chuántǒng	adj/n	Lesson three
traffic	交通		jiāotōng	n	Lesson two
traffic regulations, traffic rules [short for 交通规则]	交规	交規	jiāoguī	n	Lesson fourteen
transformation; transform	转变	轉變	zhuǎnbiàn	n/v	Lesson fourteen
translate; translator, translation	翻译	翻譯	fānyì	v/n	Lesson eight
transmit, pass on	传递	傳遞	chuándì	v	Lesson nine
treat	对待	對待	duìdài	v	Lesson fourteen
treat as, regard as, look upon as	当做	當做	dàngzuò	v	Lesson four
trigger, evoke	引发	引發	yǐnfā	v	Lesson thirteen
troops, armed forces	军	軍	jūn	n	Lesson two
true, real	真实	真實	zhēnshí	adj	Lesson seven
(description or portrayal) true to life; image	形象		xíngxiàng	adj/n	Lesson two
truth	真理		zhēnlǐ	n	Lesson eight
try every means, leave no stone unturned	想方设法	想方設法	xiǎngfāng-shèfǎ	idiom	Lesson nine
try to figure out	揣摩		chuǎimó	v	Lesson fourteen
type case	字盘	字盤	zìpán	n	Lesson six
typical, representative; typical case	典型		diǎnxíng	adj/n	Lesson four

英文翻译 U	*简体*	*繁體*	*拼音*	*词性*	
Ukraine	乌克兰	烏克蘭	Wūkèlán		Lesson eight
unable to, cannot	无法	無法	wúfǎ	v	Lesson three
unceasingly, continuously	不断	不斷	búduàn	adv	Lesson eleven
[slang] uncultured rich people, nouveau riche, local tyrant	土豪		tǔháo	n	Lesson fourteen

英文翻译 U	*简体*	*繁體*	*拼音*	*词性*	
undergraduate	本科		běnkē	n	Lesson twelve
understanding, comprehension; understand	了解		liǎojiě	n/v	Lesson ten
unequivocal, clear-cut; make definite	明确	明確	míngquè	adj/v	Lesson three
unexpectedly, to one's surprise	竟然		jìngrán	adv	Lesson thirteen
unfamiliar [陌生人stranger]	陌生		mòshēng	adj	Lesson thirteen
unified; unify, unite	统一	統一	tǒngyī	adj/v	Lesson thirteen
unique feature, distinguishing quality	特色		tèsè	n	Lesson eleven
unique, distinctive	独特	獨特	dútè	adj	Lesson three
unit (in measurement or organization)	单位	單位	dānwèi	n	Lesson eleven
United Nations	联合国	聯合國	Liánhéguó		Lesson eight
universal, prevalent, common, widespread	普遍		pǔbiàn	adj	Lesson three
unless	除非		chúfēi	conj	Lesson one
UNSC [short form of 联合国安全理事会, United Nations Security Council]	安理会	安理會	Ān Lǐ Huì		Lesson eight
upbringing, culture	教养	教養	jiàoyǎng	n	Lesson fourteen
use (something to serve a purpose)	使用		shǐyòng	v	Lesson three
use in/on [于: more formal than "在…… 上/中"]	用于	用於	yòngyú	v	Lesson eight
use, utilize, take advantage of	利用		lìyòng	v	Lesson twelve
[used with multisyllabic nouns for people, such as 网友, 学生; more formal than 个]	名		míng	m	Lesson two

英文翻译 V	*简体*	*繁體*	*拼音*	*词性*	
value	看重		kànzhòng	v	Lesson eleven
value, worth	价值	價值	jiàzhí	n	Lesson three
vary, alternate	变换	變換	biànhuàn	v	Lesson six
[collective] vehicles, cars	车辆	車輛	chēliàng	n	Lesson two

英文翻译 V	*简体*	*繁體*	*拼音*	*词性*	
venue, place	场所	場所	chǎngsuǒ	n	Lesson six
very, extremely	十分		shífēn	adv	Lesson eleven
vicinity, surroundings	周围	周圍	zhōuwéi	n	Lesson two
video	视频	視頻	shìpín	n	Lesson thirteen
vigorous, full of vitality	蓬勃		péngbó	adj	Lesson eight
violate (law, regulation, principle, etc.)	违反	違反	wéifǎn	v	Lesson eleven
voice (opinion, feelings), express, convey	表达	表達	biǎodá	v	Lesson seven

英文翻译 W	*简体*	*繁體*	*拼音*	*词性*	
Warring States Period (475–221 BC)	战国	戰國	Zhànguó		Lesson four
waver, destabilize, sway	动摇	動搖	dòngyáo	v	Lesson thirteen
way, style, pattern	方式		fāngshì	n	Lesson two
weak (sense of . . .), thin, light	淡薄		dànbó	adj	Lesson two
WeChat, Chinese multi-purpose messaging, social media and mobile payment APP developed and first released in 2011 by Tencent [腾讯: Téngxùn] [http://www.wechat.com] [微信群: WeChat group]	微信		Wēixìn		Lesson three
wedding ceremony	婚礼	婚禮	hūnlǐ	n	Lesson eleven
Western Zhou Dynasty (1046–771 BC)	西周		Xī Zhōu		Lesson four
what one has seen and heard	见闻	見聞	jiànwén	n	Lesson fourteen
What the rules of propriety value is reciprocity. [trans. by James Legge]	礼尚往来	禮尚往來	lǐshàngwǎnglái	idiom	Lesson eleven
whether or not [more formal than 是不是; 能否: 能不能; 可否: 可不可以]	是否		shìfǒu	adv	Lesson seven
whole world [全球化: globalize; 地球: the Earth]	全球		quánqiú	n	Lesson seven
why should, there is no need [何: what; 必: must]	何必		hébì	adv	Lesson one

英文翻译 W	简体	繁體	拼音	词性	
wide-ranging, widespread	广泛	廣泛	guǎngfàn	adj	Lesson four
win	赢得		yíngdé	v	Lesson nine
wisdom	智慧		zhìhuì	n	Lesson eight
with one's own eyes	亲眼	親眼	qīnyǎn	adv	Lesson fourteen
without exception	一律		yílǜ	adv	Lesson eight
without exception, invariably	无不	無不	wúbù	adv	Lesson ten
witness, see at first hand [目 (bf): eye; 睹 (bf): see]	目睹		mùdǔ	v	Lesson fourteen
wood, log, timber	木头	木頭	mù.tou	n	Lesson six
would rather	宁可	寧可	nìngkě	adv	Lesson nine

英文翻译 Y	简体	繁體	拼音	词性	
yield, concession; yield, compromise, concede, give in	让步	讓步	ràng//bù	n/v	Lesson twelve
young of age	年少		niánshào	adj	Lesson three

Speech pattern index by lesson